HOME
OPPORTUNITIES

The Complete Guide to Going to School by Mail

• LAURIE M. CARLSON •

BETTERWAY PUBLICATIONS, INC.
WHITE HALL, VIRGINIA

Published by Betterway Publications, Inc.
Box 219
Crozet, VA 22932

Cover design by Tim Haley
Typography by East Coast Typography, Inc.

Library of Congress Cataloging-in-Publication Data

Carlson, Laurie Winn
  Home study opportunities

  1. Correspondence schools and courses
— United States.   I. Title.
LC5951.C37   1989   374'.473   88-34954
ISBN 1-55870-116-8

Printed in the United States of America
0987654321

Preface

For a variety of reasons, I have been a student at several colleges and state universities, including: Walla Walla Community College, Lewis Clark State College, University of Arizona, University of Nevada–Reno, University of Utah, Washington State University, Arizona State University and University of Phoenix. I have a B.S. from the University of Idaho and enough post-graduate credits to paper my kitchen walls with transcripts. I was faced with various schools or state teacher licensing authorities not accepting credits from other programs, entailing that I take more and more courses, all to retain teacher certification. I have taken correspondence study in mathematics, public health, U.S. history, and child development, as well as proprietary home study in art and paralegal studies. I have enjoyed using my studies to enable me to start my own home-based business, to seek outside employment when necessary, and to enrich my life in a variety of ways.

In my experience as a student, I have found that the quality of the coursework depends largely on the teacher (in the case of on-campus courses) and the student (especially in correspondence courses). I had some incredibly lousy courses at large universities, which I later supplemented with private home study courses of superior quality. I have worked very hard to complete home study courses, and find I refer to some of the texts and syllabus materials frequently. I guess what I enjoy about home study is that, compared to on-campus classes where you are largely at the mercy of the teacher's ability, in home study you are in charge, and you can get out of it what you put into it.

I began this book because of my frustration with traditional institutions and their refusal to accept similar courses taken at other schools, along with the fact that graduate level courses I took more than six years ago are not transferable into any traditional graduate program. Because of family and business I couldn't complete my Master's program, and now the entire coursework is unacceptable for transfer to traditional schools. I refuse to accept their opinion that knowledge "expires" after six years, and am pursuing an alternative master's degree program. As I discovered the myriad educational opportunities available through home study, I thought more people would be interested in knowing how and where they, too, can make the most of their past education, training, or experiences.

Many readers will also be facing a different dilemma. There are many wonderful places to live that do not have a nearby college, university, or trade school. I realize that many urbanites can hardly believe this, but there are places in rural America where jobs are plentiful for the trained, but the training is impossible to receive locally. I lived most of my life in rural isolation, and I sought the availability of education by correspondence simply because it was the *only* way to obtain the instruction I needed.

Home study also fits the needs of so many who are unable to get to class because of physical limitations, or because they must remain at home to care for others, or to handle other responsibilities that prevent them from spending hours sitting at a desk in a traditional classroom.

Contents

Section I

Home Study Opportunities

Setting Your Goals
Considering Your Options
Selecting the Program

WHY HOME STUDY?

Are you confronted with a changing job market you aren't prepared for?

Are you feeling helpless, frustrated, or both, as you send out resumés or fill out job applications with little hope for changing your position in the job market?

Employment opportunities have never seemed so limited, as young workers can't break the minimum wage trap, and older workers are faced with accepting unemployment checks instead of paychecks. One in five people has to leave his or her job each year now. One in ten is forced to leave a job involuntarily. One in ten must make a career change each year. We are facing rapid changes in career security, and the future holds little reward for those who sit back and complain, or wait till they receive a pink slip.

Don't despair! There are ways to improve and secure your employability and your self-esteem. Colleges and trade schools report record numbers of older students returning to class to train for a new position, upgrade their present skills, or position themselves for a raise or promotion. It seems as if you can't be too educated or skilled in today's job market. In fact, many people are over-educated or under-employed, because their education didn't prepare them for the skills that current employers are seeking.

Okay, you say. But you can't quit your job to attend college. You can't get the kind of education you want at night, because no classes are offered near you, or you have to fulfill those job and family responsibilities and can't be gone two or three nights a week, too. Some of the major obstacles faced by adults trying to obtain education or training include:

- on-campus residency requirements
- classes offered at inconvenient times
- unavailability of the courses they want to take
- home and job responsibilities
- commuting to class
- credits taken at a previous school are not accepted at another school

- living too far from a campus
- child care
- physical handicaps
- fear of competing against younger students in a classroom

Sound familiar?

In years past, the only older students on campuses were bored housewives seeking to study something cultural or enriching, who had a husband more than happy to oblige with supporting the costs. Well, if in the 1980s there still exist a few of those lucky souls, so be it. But I have a hunch that those of you reading this book are not so lucky to have a financial backer ready to "spend you to college." You're probably like most of us, who work at a full-time job, wrangle kids and a home life, and seek to improve your lot in life through education. The problem for us is that the average State U is out of the question. Most colleges and universities do not tailor their programs to the likes of us in the "real world." We cannot fit our schedules to theirs. The fact is that we cannot obtain a degree without taking Philosophy 103, and Philosophy 103 is only offered spring semesters every other year, and only at 10:00 in the morning. How can you juggle a ten a.m. class with your employer, even if he is supportive? It is very difficult to juggle coming in early or taking lunch hour at 10:00 a.m. We also face the problems of parking costs, commuting time encroaching on study and family time, and a myriad of problems that face "regular" college students — long lines, impossible professors, class schedules that change at the last minute, cancellation of classes at registration, etc.

Anyone who has attended a college or university, and then been unable to resume and complete a degree program because of moving, finances, or whatever has another lament. There are many in this situation, as the 1980 census found twenty-five million Americans who have finished one year or more of college, but who have not completed a degree. When they try to re-enroll elsewhere, they find courses won't be accepted by other colleges, credits vary between "quarter-credit hours" and "semester-credit hours" and, in the case of graduate programs, coursework "expires" and is unacceptable for transfer or program completion after six years.

Whatever it is that has held you back, whether it is age, finances, time, energy, commuting, children, or just plain fear, there is an alternative — home study. Over three million adults are enrolled in home study courses across the U.S. right now. Adults like you and me, who knew they wanted to change their lives, but for one reason or another didn't want to attend classes in order to do so. Their numbers are increasing, too. Currently the number of home study admissions is growing by 15 to 20% each year, while college enrollments on campus appear to be declining.

Higher education used to mean only one thing: years of study between the ages of eighteen and twenty-two on a college campus. For an increasing number of adults today, however, the word has another meaning. Further education can now mean earning a diploma or degree at any age, through a formal training program with no time spent away from home. The old barriers to furthering your education — too little money or time, geographic isolation, even the lack of a high school diploma, have been swept away. Now, nearly everyone who has the ability to read at a high school level can further his education or earn a diploma or degree, at less expense than ever before. Currently, there are 4.8 million students over the age of twenty-five in the U.S., many of them enrolled in correspondence study. More than fifty-five million Americans have taken correspondence courses since 1900. More than three million are now taking courses by mail for credit, vocational training, or simply for fun.

Long thought of as "fly-by-night," many people still think of match book cover advertising when they hear the words, "home study," but the schools and programs offering correspondence education and training have become respectable, quality institutions, offering an opportunity to learn, improve skills, or enhance the personal lives of many adults.

According to Michael Lambert of the National Home Study Council, the uncertain economy has caused many people to think about investing time and money in home study to generate a second income or train for a new career. While many other schools are confronting declining enrollments, the number of correspondence students is growing by 20–25% per year, Lambert estimates. Home study offerings will continue to mirror the changing vocational needs of society. According to Lambert, "The home study story in America is changing right now. We came up in the industrial revolution and offered courses in the early part of this century in training to become a railroad engineer or a boiler mechanic. Then there was wartime, and the big push was, 'don't let the war interrupt your academic skills: get your high school diploma.' Then, we were in the '70s and saw training in the soft skills: business and accounting. Now, we're moving into the high tech area, training people to become microcomputer repairmen or technicians. We've moved right along with the American business and will continue to do so. By 1960, one out of every four CPAs and one out of ten licensed engineers had learned their subjects through the mail. During the late 1960s and early 1970s, more than 1/3 of all active duty service people who took advantage of GI Bill benefits did so by enrolling in correspondence schools. By 1980, more than 6,000 businesses had used correspondence courses to improve employees' skills. Currently, 200 of the Fortune 500 businesses use home study to train their employees."

You might be interested to know that some famous correspondence students include former President Jimmy Carter, Chrysler Corporation founder Walter P. Chrysler, "Peanuts" cartoonist Charles Schultz, singers Donny and Marie Osmond, former Mexican President Abelardo Rodriguez, and former *Saturday Evening Post* publisher Walter Fuller.

As you discuss home study with your friends and family, you may discover that many of them have used home study courses to advance their careers, too. My sister used an accounting course to start a home business, then to go on to earn a B.S. in Business at the University of Washington, where she attributes her graduation with honors (cum laude) to her earlier understanding of accounting and business earned by home study. Another friend has used a locksmith program to obtain a secure (and busy) job while he lays the foundation for starting his own locksmith business. An acquaintance who met with a disabling accident learned how to prepare taxes by mail, and he and his wife have a steady bookkeeping and tax service. The list goes on and on. People with ambition, perseverance, and drive can make it happen for themselves.

You can choose among more than 12,000 courses on subjects ranging from Accounting to Zoology. You can work toward a bachelor's degree, get a leg up in your job field, or explore some new subject for the sheer enjoyment of it. The main advantages to home study are the convenience, the relevancy of the programs to an adult learner, open enrollment allowing you to begin your degree program when you choose, and courses which can be taken more quickly and at a lower cost than on-campus.

SET YOUR GOALS

Once you have decided to obtain more training for yourself, identify your goals. Do you want to obtain an entry-level job in a new field? If you are inexperienced in a particular field, and wish to start or move into it, be realistic. Entry-level is probably where you will get in. Study the fields you are interested in. Read the job classifieds. Call personnel directors and state department of employment counselors. Find out what the pay is for various jobs. Find out at what level you would most likely be able to start in your chosen field, and then look at the chances and opportunities for advancement.

If you are already working in a field you enjoy and plan to continue in, what exactly does it take to advance within the field? What particular type of training or education would serve you best? What skill would your employer benefit most from and be most likely to reward you for?

Perhaps you are seeking educational benefits that don't relate to your source of income, but are simply for personal satisfaction. It may be that you are interested in developing a talent or hobby further, and at the moment just enjoying yourself. You may be considering the fact that hobbies and interests are often excellent springboards to rewarding self-employment opportunities. Maybe you always wanted to learn how to photograph family events or portraits, or to expand your artistic horizons. Whatever area you are interested in, there is bound to be a home study course to fit your needs.

After determining which area you want to explore and

whether you will need a college degree, a trade school diploma, an Associate of Arts degree, or simply a certificate of completion in order to satisfy your goals, it's time to look for a school or program that meets your needs.

This book is a compilation of many of the current home study programs available. There are many programs that I did not include because: their information was too sketchy, leaving doubts about the quality of their program; they failed to answer my requests and may be out of business; I simply didn't know of their existence, and will consider including them in a revised edition of this guide. I also did not list all the state universities' correspondence study programs. Since none of them will lead you to a degree unless you are enrolled as a resident student at a college or university, I left them for you to explore if you are attending college as a resident student. Almost every public university offers some type of correspondence coursework. Simply call or write to their Correspondence Study Office, and ask for their current catalog of courses. These courses are usually offered for college credit, and priced by the credit hour. They generally allow you up to a year to complete a course. Often you will be able to purchase the necessary textbooks through the mail from their college bookstore, and can usually sell the books back to them when you are through with the course.

When studying a course from a state university or college, their correspondence study rules usually require that you take a final and a mid-term exam in a proctored situation, usually in a school principal's office in your community or the office of your local college or university correspondence study department. But if you are working on a degree from a particular college or university, requirements can usually be met by taking a correspondence study course, often from the same university. This can be one way to register for more credits than are allowed for a full-time student; to speed up graduation; to take courses during the summer or vacations; or to allow you to cut back on your commuting schedule, perhaps only attending classes on campus two or three days a week, completing other work at home.

A word of caution: If you are in a degree program at a school and you need their approval before graduation or student teaching, or need to be enrolled in a certain certification program, *talk to a counselor* in your department before you enroll in a correspondence course to fulfill those requirements. Sometimes, schools refuse to accept correspondence work done elsewhere, even at accredited schools that are much better academically than they are. They have the right to do this, because each school determines whether or not it will accept coursework transferring from another institution. It can be very unpleasant, and expensive, to have to repeat courses on campus that won't transfer from another school or correspondence program. Sometimes it seems like schools are merely determined to fill their desks, so be sure to check out your plan before you expend time and money on fruitless study. The University of California, Berkeley's advice to prospective home study students planning to use coursework taken by mail to satisfy requirements at another school warns that, "The acceptance of credit earned through independent study toward degree requirements is under the jurisdiction of the college or university that is to grant the degree. Reciprocity in this respect is usual among accredited institutions, but prospective enrollees who know or have an idea what school they will attend should request from it specific information about its policies governing the acceptance of credit earned in university extension, independent study, or correspondence instruction programs. Students already engaged in resident study should obtain approval from the proper authority prior to enrollment in independent study."

If you are planning to meet state licensing requirements or state certification in some area, make some phone calls or visit the licensing authority's office. Find out whether your planned coursework will fulfill their requirements. Most professional organizations, societies, etc., have specific requirements as well. If licensing or obtaining credentials is the objective of your educational efforts, check with the appropriate organization before enrolling in any program. It's wise to obtain their approval or instructions for your educational requirements in writing. Frequently the advisory people in these situations change by the time you have completed your studies, and the new person may not agree with what you were told previously. Keep it in writing, and take it with you when you return to the agency or office for your credential or certification application.

FINANCIAL AID — WHERE
THERE'S A WILL, THERE'S A WAY

Does education still pay off in the long run? According to the U.S. Bureau of Labor statistics, the average lifetime earnings of an elementary school graduate are $911,000; the average life-time earnings of a high school graduate are $1,303,000; and the average life-time earnings for someone with one or more years of post-high school education are $1,645,000! Those extra years spent in school really pay off in the long run. The statistics don't tell us about the improved self-esteem, better opportunities for enjoyable employment, and long term enjoyment of a better standard of living that accompanies the extra years spent in school.

Adult education takes extra time and money to achieve, but it's not nearly so expensive as four years spent in residence on a college campus. In 1985–86, total costs for a year in residence averaged $5,314 at public institutions, $9,659 at private ones. Costs of nonresident programs averaged $4,240 per year at public institutions and $8,347 at private colleges.

It may surprise you to find out that financial aid is available to you as a correspondence study student. Major sources of financial aid include the federal government (loans and grants), lending institutions (low-interest student loans), states and colleges (grants and scholarships). Other possibilities are employers, professional organizations, social agencies, the Veteran's Administration, and private foundations.

Financial aid is also available from several of the degree-granting schools and trade schools that offer home study courses. You must qualify for some of the guaranteed student loan and grant programs in the same manner as students registered for on-campus study. The amount, terms, and interest rate will vary, but if you are interested, contact those institutions and request financial aid applications and information. Most of the trade school programs offer time payments, and several accept VISA or MasterCard for payment. Usually, there is a small discount if you pay the full amount of the program when you register. Be aware that if you decide to drop the course and request your money back you will only receive a portion of it, as the amount of the course you have completed and the processing fees will be subtracted.

Many employers do reimburse or pay for the training that will help you at your job. Check with your employer to find out if they will be willing to provide this for you. Many major companies do use correspondence schools to provide additional training for their employees.

Besides those methods already mentioned, there are other ways to finance your study. Consider borrowing from relatives if that is possible. In this day of yard sales, think about gathering up all your useless items and staging a sale to bring in extra cash and clean out your closets and garage at the same time. If you are really unable to find the money in other ways, and anticipate that the training will be of benefit to your future financially, consider selling collectibles, car, furniture, you-name-it. You are investing in yourself rather than in possessions, and if you believe in yourself you can find a way to pay for your education. Perhaps you can earn extra dollars babysitting nights and weekends, typing for others, making and selling food and crafts items, etc. Don't rule out any venture that may be an option for you. For those people interested in pursuing some of the skill training courses, you may be able to take on part-time jobs relating to your studies as you work your way through the course. This is very practical for those interested in book-keeping, accounting, art, upholstery, or repair-type courses. You can often exercise your new skills as you do small jobs to pay for the training.

While we are talking money, don't forget that depending upon your circumstances, courses, texts, mailing expenses, and supplies for your course may be tax deductible. Educational expenses for improving an individual's performance in a trade or profession are tax deductible. If you apply the skills you develop in the course to selling a product or service, or to improving your performance in your profession, you may qualify for the deduction. If an employer pays for your training, it may be deductible for them. Check with your tax expert for advice about your particular situation.

How to Subsidize Your Doctoral Program
From Educational Tax Savings
(excerpt from brochure for Walden University,
Minneapolis, MN)

Tax deductions can save you thousands of dollars each year. These are, in fact, a form of government subsidy for your (doctoral) education and are still available, if you qualify.

Beginning in 1987, the new tax law permits you to deduct qualified miscellaneous items for the portion of your income which exceeds two percent of your adjusted gross income.

For example:

Taxpayer's adjusted gross income		$35,000
Miscellaneous itemized deductions		
Educational expenses*	8,500	
Investment expenses	400	
Tax preparation fee	500	
Total deductions		9,400
Less 2% of adjusted gross income		– 700
Deductible portion		$ 8,700
Tax savings (married couple)		$ 2,436

*In addition to tuition, educational expenses may include related travel, housing, food, computer and typewriter equipment and service, copying charges, books, etc.

THE NATIONAL HOME STUDY COUNCIL

The National Home Study Council (NHSC) is a nonprofit educational association which serves as a clearing house for information about the home study field, and sponsors a nationally recognized accrediting agency. The Council puts out a directory of schools that they feel meet the following criteria:

- competent faculty

- educationally sound and up-to-date courses

- careful screening of students for admission

- satisfactory educational services

- demonstrated student success and satisfaction

- truthful advertising

- financially able to deliver high-quality educational service

The current Directory of Accredited Home Study Schools is available from the NHSC at no charge. Write and request it from: National Home Study Council, 1601 Eighteenth St., N.W., Washington, DC 20009. Their current directory lists more than 125 accredited schools or programs. More schools are offering coursework and are interested in meeting the guidelines set by the NHSC to protect the student from fraudulent, fly-by-night operators.

The NHSC operates as an advocate for quality correspondence education, and the schools that receive its accreditation have been carefully inspected by the NHSC. The NHSC estimates that since 1900, over seventy million Americans have taken home study courses. Only about 1/4 of all home study schools are nationally accredited, but about 3/4 of all home study students are enrolled in NHSC-approved schools.

Some publications offered by the NHSC which may provide inspiration and information useful to you are:

We Succeeded Through Home Study, successful home study graduates tell their stories, $6.00, postpaid.

Write to Be Read, A five-lesson home study course on effective business writing. $25.00 (text only) $77.00 (text with exam service).

The NHSC does wield some influence with its participating schools. I was enrolled in one of their accredited schools, and was having difficulty getting a prompt refund when I had to drop out of the course. I wrote to the school once more asking for my refund, and mentioned I was sending a copy of the letter to the NHSC. My check arrived from the school promptly, and so did a letter from the NHSC. They asked if I had received the refund, and whether they could help me if I hadn't.

CHECK IT OUT ... THE DARK SIDE

Four things to do before sending any money to any school:

1. Check out the degree with any relevant gatekeepers. If a degree will help with job advancement, salary increments, state licensing, graduate school admission, etc., be certain in advance that the degree in question will meet that need. Don't rely on assurances from the schools themselves.

2. Check out the school with the agency in its state that oversees higher education and the Better Business Bureau in its city.

3. If an accreditation claim is made, check it out with the U.S. Department of Education or the Council on Post-Secondary Accreditation. Many schools have set up their own accrediting agencies for the purpose of accrediting themselves.

4. Ask the school questions: How many degrees in my field have you awarded in the last year? May I have the names and addresses of some recent graduates? May I examine work done by your students? Which faculty member will supervise my work? What are their credentials?

These guidelines are from an article by Dr. John Bear, an authority on home study degrees, in the *Whole Earth Review* (see Bibliography).

An institution may lack official accreditation, although they claim otherwise. To check on a school, write to the: Office on Educational Credit and Credentials of the American Council of Education, 1 DuPont Circle, Washington, DC 20036.

A book about home study would be incomplete if it didn't mention some of the abuses or fraudulent practices that often occur in the industry. The NHSC has been a commendable force in creating a self-monitoring accreditation system. But there are many problems in the correspondence course industry. Be especially wary of schools that offer "quickie" academic degrees. In May 1983, the FBI caught thirty-six mail order colleges in ten states that provided diplomas with little or no work on the student's part. Known as "Dip-Scam" (diploma scam), the operation put some schools out of business, prosecuted a few people, and drove others to different states and post office boxes.

Outright fraud sometimes occurs when college degrees are

sold by these "diploma mills" — schools that offer little or no coursework, charge high fees, and mail out their degrees to whoever sends their money. According to the U.S. Department of Education, a diploma mill is "an organization that awards degrees without requiring students to meet educational standards for such degrees. It either receives fees from so-called students on the basis of fraudulent misrepresentation or makes it possible for the recipients of its degrees to perpetrate a fraud on the public."

Estimates of the number of diploma mills in the U.S. range from dozens to hundreds. The mills provide credentials in almost every field from medicine to teaching to business to law enforcement, charging between a few hundred and several thousand dollars, depending on the school and the degree. Some give discounts if more than one degree is purchased at a time. In addition, businesses have sprung up to provide fake diplomas and transcripts from real schools, to perpetuate the fraud.

The problem continues to exist because traditional colleges across the country have been reluctant to develop nontraditional ways for students to obtain degrees, because of their own economic interests in keeping students registered on-campus. Authorities on most campuses don't recognize the need for nontraditional educational programs that allow students more flexibility in meeting degree requirements due to their age, experience, and obligations. Therefore, private business has seen the demand and attempted to provide opportunity to those adults who want to obtain their degrees through other avenues. With this huge demand by the marketplace, greedy entrepreneurs have created nonexistent schools or shoddy programs simply to take your money.

Another factor that keeps the diploma mills alive is the demand by employers and society that diplomas and degrees are necessary for entry into certain jobs. Dishonest people see false diplomas as an easy solution to their career and educational shortcomings. Many are willing to pay several thousand dollars for a worthless piece of paper giving them a college degree from a nonexistent institution. They know they didn't earn it, and they are as guilty of the fraud as the fake diploma promoters, because without a market, the diploma mills would cease to exist.

It's unfortunate that this situation often catches many people who are seeking legitimate degree programs, and they are taken advantage of by these mail order rip-offs. Students have put in extensive work on projects or studies to be mailed to these schools, who in turn simply mailed out the diploma when all fees were paid. Little did these students know that they had spent a lot of time and money, and that their worthless degree would possibly brand them in the eyes of future potential employers as perpetrating a fraud. Graduates of these schools are frequently shocked to learn that they paid a diploma mill for their degree, and that it is a liability to their employment prospects to list that school and degree on their resumé and job applications.

If you're interested in reading about some of the scandals of the past, try Robert Byrne's book, *Writing Rackets,* about home study writer's courses, as well as the reprinted article available from the *Arizona Republic* newspaper in Phoenix, AZ. Both offer revealing stories of abuses perpetrated by people operating fraudulent correspondence schools. Byrne's book touches upon many of the "secrets" used by legitimate schools that are really more interested in marketing than educating.

Of course, for every school offering something for little or no work on the student's part, there is a ready audience of potential purchasers who seek a certificate or diploma for doing nothing. If you are looking for a quickie school, they exist in spite of the continued efforts of the FBI and U.S. postal authorities. You can get your "sheepskin." But it will only be worth what you have expended in time and effort to earn it. And you may get yourself in hot water, if you try to pass off a false credential to employers or the public. An education is like most things — you only get back what you yourself put into it.

HOW HOME STUDY COURSES WORK

There are two basic types of home study programs. Those leading to a college degree such as an Associate of Arts, Bachelor of Science, Master of Arts, Juris Doctorate (J.D.), or Doctor of Philosophy (Ph.D.) are academic in nature, require a variety of coursework which includes courses in your major field of study, as well as required courses in English, history, philosophy, or sciences, which will give you a thorough yet well-rounded education. The other type of home study program is now referred to as a proprietary school. It is a privately owned, profit-making school that provides courses of a technical or vocational nature. The coursework is skill oriented, and concentrates in-depth on the skill, with no extraneous study requirements. Frequently, vocational courses will include a lesson on how to develop your newly learned skill into a business, with a little background on recordkeeping and sales promotion methods.

Because of the nature of the coursework, proprietary schools do not usually offer any credit, or allow you to skip any assignments because you already know the material. If you knew the material, you wouldn't be studying with them anyway. Academic institutions that grant degrees however, do give credit for prior learning experiences. If you are seeking a degree from a nontraditional home study institution, you may be able to skip some coursework if you already have a background and experience in that area. Some prior learning experiences that are frequently accepted are:

- previously earned academic credits at another school, whether taken on campus or by correspondence
- job experience
- travel
- seminars, workshops
- company-sponsored training programs
- independent reading experience

Some of the licenses and certificates that credit may be given for are:

- Private Pilot Airplane License
- Certified Professional Secretary
- Certified Public Accountant
- Chartered Life Underwriter

- State Land Surveyor License

- Evelyn Wood Reading Dynamics Course

- State Real Estate Salesman's License

If you have significant experience and are turned off by the idea of studying something you already know well, maybe this route is for you. As the folks at La Jolla University feel, "while traditional schooling with prescribed classroom hours and curriculum represents one form of education, we believe learning can occur in everyday activities. La Jolla University grants degree credit for verified prior learning from nontraditional sources (company-sponsored seminars, professional activities, on-the-job training, cross-cultural experiences, research work, formal business ventures, etc.). This credit allows you to by-pass those courses that duplicate previously acquired knowledge. Thus, completion of your degree occurs more rapidly and at less cost." Not too bad. . . .

Whether you choose a proprietary school program or are working on a degree, the way home study operates is essentially the same. In most courses, you complete each assignment and mail it to the instructor for review and evaluation. Corrected assignments are returned via the school for your review and use in preparing succeeding lessons or for studying for the final exam. Students should expect to receive graded lessons two to three weeks after the date lessons were mailed. Course descriptions show the number of assignments that are to be submitted. There is no standard length for assignments, nor any established number of assignments per unit of credit. An assignment may be a term paper, a short report, a review drill, a field project, or some other exercise. Generally speaking, the fewer assignments required, the longer they will be. Some courses require final exams to be taken in a proctored setting, others have an open-book exam or final project to send in.

In many cases, the information you are seeking is available in the class syllabus and course materials, and you really don't want to complete the course, obtaining the certificate or grade. You just want the information, or the "meat and potatoes," to use in your job, business, or to teach in your own classroom. The course materials can often be purchased separately, at a reduced price from the cost of the entire course. If you are interested in the materials but not in completing the course, ask the school. Many sell them separately. For instance, the University of California Extension at Berkeley, makes their course materials available separately. "Most course materials prepared especially for Independent Study courses are available for purchase separately; enrollment is not required. These materials can be valuable study aids for classroom use or for individuals who are interested in pursuing a vocational or other goals and do not wish to have their work evaluated by an instructor. Such materials may be useful as references in a particular field of study. Most course materials consist of a syllabus, which guides study in a specific text; however, some courses also include reading materials, tapes and other study aids. Prices range from $20-75." Contact UC Extension for their price list (see Career and Certificate Programs).

STUDY SKILLS . . . MAKING THE MOST OF IT

The most common problem for correspondence students is time management. Home study students usually have additional responsibilities with home and family, as well as working forty hours per week. There just doesn't seem to be enough time for it all!

How we use time is based on habit, and whether we use time wisely or waste it can be changed. If you want to be more efficient, prepare a time schedule and stick to it until you follow it habitually. Successful people have usually adopted a well-organized time schedule. If you have several tasks to do, you can procrastinate and waste time until you fail to do any of them. You won't be a slave to your schedule, but will be freed from your inefficient habits such as wasting time, inadequate planning, and last-minute study, as well as the anxiety that accompanies those types of work habits.

Following are some suggestions for planning your study time wisely.

1. Set aside enough time for study.
2. Study at the same time every day. This helps it become a habit.

3. Use free time during the day for study. Have notes or reading material available so you can make the most of time spent at coffee breaks at work, waiting in the doctor's office, etc.

4. Space out your study periods. Fifty to ninety minutes of study at a time is enough; allow ten or fifteen minutes of relaxation between study periods.

5. Leave some of your time flexible and unscheduled. Allow time for recreation and other activities. Don't burn out!

As you sit down for your first session with your syllabus and textbook, you may feel a little overwhelmed. Maybe it's been years since you studied in school. Sure, you will be a little rusty! Your skills at writing may have slowed a little, too. Don't get discouraged, continued practice and effort will enhance your abilities. There are also some techniques for reading and studying your text that may help you.

Known as the SQ3R study method, the systematic technique for study that focuses on "survey, question, read, recite, review" works very well.

Survey the material first. Get a quick overview of the chapter. This gives you a structure to help organize ideas and concepts as you read them later. It will actually decrease your reading time and increase your recall of the materials. It's like looking at a road map on a trip; you can then go faster and recall where you have been. If there's an introduction, read it. Glance at chapter headings and bold print. Look over any charts, diagrams, pictures, and titles. If there is a short summary at the end of the chapter, read it. Move quickly, only skimming the material. Don't worry about details at this point.

Now begin to *Read* the material, a section at a time.

Question what you have read. Jot down the main ideas, make up a few questions about the material you have just read.

Recite your answer to each question. This will help you remember what you have just read. Look away from your book and notes and try to recite the answers to your questions. Use your own words and cite examples whenever possible. Jot down your answers as you recite them.

Review the entire chapter. This will help you increase comprehension and retention of the material. Look over all your notes to get a view of the main ideas and their relationships to one another. Check your memory by reciting the answers to your questions. If you are unable to answer your questions adequately, go back and review the written material again, searching for the needed information.

When you have your polished, neatly-written lesson ready to mail to your instructor, be sure to keep a copy of the original. Whether you use carbon paper or stop by a photocopy shop, it's a real heartbreaker to have a lesson you have spent so many hours on become lost in the mail.

LAW SCHOOL? BY MAIL?

You may be surprised to find out that you can attend law school by correspondence from several specialized law schools. Whatever state you reside in, you may want to receive the J.D. (Juris Doctor) in Law. Perhaps you can use the knowledge in your own business or in your present job. Many doctors, insurance agents, realtors, etc., can enrich their career with a law degree, and the knowledge they can acquire through studying law.

In the state of California you can take the California Bar Exam and if you pass, practice law, based· upon knowledge acquired through attending law school through correspondence. There are some special requirements, but it is being done successfully by some. For a current list of correspondence schools recognized by the State of California, which will enable you to take the California Bar Exam, write to:

State Bar of California
P.O. Box 7908
San Francisco, CA 94129

Paralegal programs are also offered by a variety of schools through home study. This is a fast-growing field, but the job market is competitive. If you are interested in becoming a Certified Legal Assistant, check out prospective schools with the National Association of Legal Assistants, Inc., 1420 South Utica, Tulsa, OK 74104. In order to sit for the NALA certification exam, you must have attended a nationally accredited paralegal studies program. Many of their members did graduate from home study schools, so write and ask about any program you are considering.

Section II

Kindergarten through High School Programs

AMERICAN SCHOOL

850 East 58th Street
Chicago, IL 60637

(312) 947-3300

American School was founded in 1987; it is a non-profit school accredited by the North Central Association of Colleges and Schools and the National Home Study Council. They offer two high school completion programs:

General High School Course — Designed for those wishing to obtain a regular high school diploma. You can choose electives such as shorthand, auto mechanics, etc. Many junior colleges and technical schools will accept graduates with this diploma.

College Preparatory Course — Designed for students who intend to enter college or a university. American School graduates have been accepted by over 800 colleges. They have almost 100 subjects you may take as electives.

Applicants receive both course credit and dollar credit for each high school subject passed elsewhere. Cost depends upon the number of high school years you have to complete:

12th grade — $379
11th & 12th grade — $479
10th, 11th, & 12th grade — $579
9th through 12th grade — $679

Payment plans are available. The least number of credits to be taken to obtain an American School diploma is four. The school allows for previous high school courses except Physical Education, Driver's Training, Religion, Chorus, Band, and R.O.T.C.

If, after receiving a diploma from American School, you must take a qualifying examination administered by a state, a college, or a pre-professional school, and the exam is taken within six months after completion of the course and you fail to pass the test (test of subjects covered in the course), American School will refund your money, or give additional training at no cost in the subject areas needed.

CALVERT SCHOOL
105 Tuscany Road
Baltimore, MD 21210

(301) 243-6030

Founded in 1897, Calvert is a non-profit institution helping to meet children's educational needs around the world. Courses are designed for the use of parents with no teaching experience, and have been used by tens of thousands over the past seventy-five years. The Calvert School curriculum is approved by the Department of Education of the State of Maryland. If you plan to teach your children at home you should check your state attendance laws. If you are using the courses to enrich your child's regular schooling, no state approval is necessary.

The teaching manuals provide day-by-day, step-by-step instructions, and offer a continuous and integrated curriculum from First Grade through Eighth, with reviews from grade to grade.

Calvert has a residence school in Baltimore with an enrollment of four hundred children. They use the same lessons as the correspondence students.

Courses offered are Kindergarten and Grades 1-8. Each of the courses is planned for a school year of about nine months. Because you are instructing your child individually, however, you can be flexible in scheduling, and meet the needs of your child. Time spent daily will vary, but they recommend three and one-half to five hours per day, depending upon the pupil and age level. If your child needs as much as two years for the completion of a single course, it is permitted. Most pupils complete each course in a school year by following a regular schedule of work during morning hours.

Tuition is $175 for Kindergarten; Grades 1-4 $310; Grades 5-7 $330; complete Eighth Grade course $330.

Calvert offers an Advisory Teaching Service for Grades 1-8. The Advisory Service is optional, and costs $155-165 per course. A professional teacher at Calvert will grade your child's tests and papers and make suggestions for improvements, as well as advise you on how to encourage and teach the child.

Without this service, Calvert School cannot furnish transcripts to other schools, or offer a Certificate of Completion.

Calvert courses can also be used for enrichment. Parents of children grades 3 to 8 often supplement their child's regular school program with extra lessons on weekends or summers. It offers the child a chance to broaden knowledge of specific subjects, and provides a challenge to the academically superior pupils. Calvert advisors will help you determine which course would best suit your child for this purpose. Parents using Calvert solely for enrichment seldom enroll in the Advisory Teaching Service.

CITIZENS' HIGH SCHOOL
5575 Peachtree Road
Atlanta, GA 30341

(404) 455-8358

Accredited by the National Home Study Council, Citizens' High School offers a high school diploma program with over fifty subject courses. Tuition varies depending upon the number of years of study needed:

Grades 9, 10, 11, 12	$725
Grades 10, 11, 12	675
Grades 11, 12	575
Grade 12 only	395

They offer a monthly payment plan.

HOME STUDY INTERNATIONAL

6940 Carroll Avenue
Takoma Park, MD 20912

(202) 722-6570

Preschool
Kindergarten
Grades 1–8
High School Diploma Program

Founded in 1909, Home Study International is accredited by the National Home Study Council. Both teaching staff and curriculum are approved by the Maryland Department of Education. Their program differs from most in that the parent is not the teacher, but supervises work sent to the teachers at HSI. Tuition costs range from $105.00 per year for kindergarten to $210.00 per credit unit for the high school program.

LEARNING AND EVALUATION CENTER
479 Drinker Street
P.O. Box 616
Bloomsburg, PA 17815

(717) 784-5220

A home-study "summer school" for high school students who fail in general subject areas during regular school sessions. Courses are six weeks in length, and are offered for most major subject areas in Grades 7 through 12. Each study package consists of thirty hours of study, which the student must complete within the six weeks. A competency level of 85% must be obtained by the student in order to receive a "pass" grade with appropriate credit. The course grades are "pass–fail" only.

Students may enroll at any time during the year, but each application must be signed by a recommending school official. Post-high school students in need of make-up credit may also be recommended. Students must have failed the course for reasons other than lack of ability.

Courses include: English, Mathematics, Social Studies, World Cultures, General Science, Physical Science, American History & Government, and Health.

Costs are $50 per course, and all books and materials are included in the fee.

Offering an alternative for those students who do not have access to a summer school program, the Learning and Evaluation Center is accredited by the National Home Study Council, and has been operating since 1974.

NEWPORT/PACIFIC HIGH SCHOOL (ICS)
Scranton, PA 18515

(717) 342-7701

Founded in 1974, Newport/Pacific High School is operated by International Correspondence Schools, a part of the National Education Corporation. Both are listed elsewhere in this directory. Newport/Pacific offers a high school diploma program. It is accredited by the National Home Study Council.

PATHFINDER HIGH SCHOOL OF INDEPENDENT STUDY, INC.
25571 Marguerite Parkway, Suite 2L–M
Mission Viejo, CA 92692

(714) 859-7550

Pathfinder High School is a private alternative school serving Grades 7–12. Designed for students whose educational needs are not readily met by the traditional secondary school, Pathfinder combines direct one-to-one instruction with independent study. Established in 1982, Pathfinder has served hundreds of students in the Mission Viejo and Saddleback communities of California. Seventy or more students are enrolled each semester.

The community is your "campus" at Pathfinder, as they encourage students to supplement their instruction by enrolling in other vocational adult education programs and community college coursework, which is included as credit toward your Pathfinder High School diploma.

Their course offerings include the basic English, Math, Geography, Science, and business and vocational subjects. They offer over seventy-four courses including Driver Education (yes, by correspondence), Calculus, and two foreign languages. Students must complete a minimum of 220 semester units across fifteen content areas. Sixty of the credits are for elective courses, which may be satisfied by passing the G.E.D. They also offer a college preparatory curriculum, and many of their graduates have been accepted at California colleges.

Courses can be taken as a "summer school," as well. Fees vary depending upon the amount of coursework, but the cost for forty weeks of instruction is $3,200.

Pathfinder is accredited by the National Home Study Council.

Section III
Career and Certificate Programs

AMERICAN CAREER TRAINING TRAVEL SCHOOL

4699 N. Federal Highway
Pompano Beach, FL 33064

(407) 946-5551

This school offers a basic training course for the travel industry. Graduates obtain entry-level positions as travel agents, airline employees, car rental agents, hotel personnel, flight attendants, or tour guides.

The course must be completed within one year. The first portion consists of an independent study program of approximately 280 hours of study. Some of the lessons studied at home include: Aircraft Types, Geography, Steamships and Cruises, Amtrak, Travel Manuals, How to Write a Ticket, Hotels and Tours, Car Rental Operations, and Introduction to the Computer. Upon completion of the home study portion, students come to the Florida campus for a three-week training session which focuses on manual procedures. Computer training, sales techniques, and job search skills are taught. Upon graduation, the students receive employment information for the geographic areas they are interested in from placement counselors at the school.

Tuition for the complete course is $1,795; $1,200 for the twenty-lesson home study course; and $595 for the resident study program. Students must pay for transportation and living expenses at the school in Florida. A.C.T. participates in the Guaranteed Student Loan Program.

A.C.T. has been graduating students for five years. They are licensed in over twenty states, and accredited by the National Home Study Council. In 1987, 1,750 students were graduated.

AMERICAN HOME STUDY SCHOOL
(formerly the AUBREY WILLIS SCHOOL)
603 S. First Ave.
Phoenix, AZ 85003

Founded in 1970, the American Home Study school offers a course in piano tuning, regulating, and repairing. It is accredited by the National Home Study Council.

AMERICAN MEDICAL RECORDS ASSOCIATION
Independent Study Division
875 N. Michigan Avenue, Suite 1850
Chicago, IL 60611

(312) 787-2672

The AMRA offers an independent study program in Medical Record Terminology.

The American Medical Records Association is the national association of medical record administrators and technicians. AMRA goals are to promote quality educational programs and to recruit qualified individuals into the field. AMRA strives to improve medical record standards, supervises a professional registry, and administers the accreditation process. The AMRA program for home study is accredited by the National Home Study Council. The curriculum materials are approved by the AMRA Council on Education. The program is also authorized to operate by the Illinois State Board of Education.

The AMRA reports that the job market for medical record technicians is excellent, with a projected growth rate of 75% through the year 2000. The Medical Record Technology program has a student enrollment of 2,500, with about 200 graduates each year. Graduates have an excellent pass rate on the national qualifying examination to earn the ART (Accredited Record Technician) credential. In 1987, all 182 candidates passed the exam.

The program consists of seventeen Modules. The first sixteen Modules (ninety-six lessons) are taken in numerical sequence. Each lesson includes objectives, text with illustrations, self-tests, required and recommended reading references, a glossary of terms, and assignments. The student is required to complete and submit the lessons for grading. Upon successful completion of lessons in a Module, a monitored examination is taken.

Course content includes: Orientation to the Health Care Field, Health Record Content and Format, Medical Terminology, Medical Transcription, Numbering and Filing Systems, Legal Aspects of Health Information, Introduction to Computers in Health Care, Health Statistics, Basic Pathology of Disease Process, Federal Health Programs, Supervisory Principles and Practice. Module 17 is a Directed Clinical Practice, which you perform under the direction of an RRA or ART supervisor in a health care facility near your home. The student selects and makes arrangements for the Directed Practice site. During the practice, the student applies medical record knowledge and skills to actual medical record practice. There is no specific number of hours, but rather specified activities which can be done at the student's own pace.

Requirements for enrollment in the program are a high school diploma or equivalent. A minimum recommended typing speed of forty-five words per minute is also suggested. If you intend to sit for the national qualifying examination for the Accredited Record Technician status, you must also complete thirty credits at a college or university. These courses may be completed by correspondence. Anatomy and Physiology, English Composition, Social and Behavioral Sciences, Data Processing, Math, Business, and Natural Sciences are required. AMRA's Independent Study Division offers services to help students plan this course of study as well. Contact them at: Independent Study Division, American Medical Record Association, P.O. Box 97349, Chicago, IL 60609.

Tuition for the Medical Records Technology program is $1,500. Monthly payments are possible. Students must also purchase reference materials for approximately $200. A typewriter and cassette tape player are also necessary. If you choose to obtain the additional thirty credits of college coursework to enable you to sit for the national exam, those courses must be taken and paid for elsewhere.

AMERICAN SCHOOL
850 East 58th Street
Chicago, IL 60637

(312) 947-3300

Medical Secretary course
Secretarial Administration course

American School also operates a high school diploma program (see listing under Kindergarten Through High School Programs). They have been enrolling students in correspondence courses since 1897, with over 2½ million students enrolled during that time. Their secretarial courses are as follows:

Medical Secretary — Forty-seven lessons for a tuition fee of $555. Skills to be learned are: Medical Secretary Skills, Personality Training, Physiology and Health, Typewriting, Speech, English for Business, and Shorthand.

Administrative Secretary — Forty-nine lessons for a tuition fee of $555. Skills to be learned: Secretarial Practice, Personality Training, Typewriting, Shorthand, Speech, Law for Business, English for Business.

Students finishing either course receive a diploma from American School. The School allows up to two years to complete the course. Applicants must be over eighteen years of age and not enrolled in a high school full time.

ANDOVER TRACTOR TRAILER SCHOOL, INC.
55 Hampshire Road
Methuen, MA 01844

(508) 689-3400

Andover offers combination home study–resident courses in tractor trailer driving and diesel mechanics. They are accredited by the National Home Study Council.

ART INSTRUCTION SCHOOLS
500 South Fourth St.
Minneapolis, MN 55415

(612) 339-8721

Founded in 1914, Art Instruction Schools offer courses in art, poetry, and fiction and nonfiction writing. They are accredited by the National Home Study Council.

THE BARTON SCHOOL
Scranton, PA 18515

(717) 342-7701

Barton is a division of the North American Correspondence Schools, owned by the National Education Corporation. They offer courses leading to career diplomas in medical and dental office assisting.

Barton is accredited by the National Home Study Council.

CALIFORNIA COLLEGE FOR HEALTH SCIENCES
222 West 24th Street
National City, CA 92050

(800) 221-7374

California College for Health Sciences is also listed under degree-granting schools. The following programs are offered through home study in non-degree programs. Courses offered carry CEU (Continuing Education Unit) credits.

Respiratory Home Care Program — A course designed to be completed in as little as thirty days or up to a year. It is part of their American Medical Association accredited respiratory therapist program. The course is written for those with some prior experience in the home care medical field: drivers, equipment technicians, respiratory and nursing staff. Tuition is $135; twenty CEU credits upon completion. The course is also available at a group tuition discount for hospitals or clinics wishing to train several employees.

Blood Gas Technology Program — Designed for working health care professionals, technicians, therapists, medical technologists, and nurses. Designed to be completed in as little as two months, with up to one year allowed. Tuition for the class is $185, and the course carries fifty CEU credits.

Hyperbaric Oxygen Therapy — This course is designed for registered nurses, respiratory therapists, LPN's, paramedics, and other health care professionals. The course consists of ten modules. All applicants must have a high school diploma or G.E.D., be able to verify 1,000 hours of clinical experience in a paramedical profession, and hold a current BLS Card. The course can be completed in as little as three months. Cost is $485. An Optional Clinical Training Phase is available for $685. Several tuition plans are available.

Respiratory Therapy Programs — California College offers two programs accredited by the Joint Review Committee for Respiratory Therapy Education:
- Entry Level Technician Program
- Advanced Practitioner (Therapist) Program

Both programs have been used by over 14,000 working health care providers. The programs are self-paced, and take between six and eighteen months to complete. Applicants for the Entry-

Level program must have a high school diploma or G.E.D. Verification of employment associated with respiratory care is required for acceptance into the program. You must currently be working in a position related to respiratory care under medical direction. Therapist program applicants must verify graduation from an AMA-approved technician-level program, or be certified, or qualify for advanced standing. Total cost of the Entry-Level program is $1,400. The Advanced course is $1,300. Several payment plans are available.

The following courses are available through home study. All cover ten Continuing Education Units (CEUs). Each course is $50.00.

Cardiopulmonary Anatomy and Physiology
Pulmonary Related Math and Physics
Pharmacology
Introduction to Computers
Cardiopulmonary Diagnostics
Basic Patient Assessment
Airway Management and Mechanical Ventilation
Neonatal and Pediatric Care
Pulmonary and Cardiovascular Diagnostics
Management and Health Care Administration
Advanced Ventilatory Care Concepts
ICU Crisis Management
Neonatal Critical Care
Acid Base I
Acid Base II
Gas Transport
Blood Gas Technology
Review of Pulmonary Physiology
The New Supervisor
Effective Management

California College also makes available a professional resumé service through the mail. For a fee of $39, they will produce your resumé and send you two copies and a personalized letterhead for you to use when writing to potential employers. They will keep a copy of your resumé on file for a year, and make changes and send you a new resumé free of charge during the year. They also include a booklet, *How Do I Get Hired?*

CALIFORNIA INSTITUTE OF INTEGRAL STUDIES
765 Ashbury Street
San Francisco, CA 94117

(415) 753-6100

The California Institute of Integral Studies is a private, non-profit graduate school; accredited by the Western Association of Schools and Colleges. At its campus located in San Francisco, resident students pursue Master's and Ph.D. degrees in Psychology, Philosophy, Religion, and Anthropology.

The External Studies Program offers the following home study courses:

Altered States of Consciousness
Western Personality Theories
World Community — East/West Perspectives
Asian Theories of Personality and Self
Developing Creativity and Intuition
Transpersonal Child Development

Each course carries three quarter units of credit, which can be applied towards a degree elsewhere, or transferred into degree programs at the Institute. Each course is structured around an outline, reading guides, study questions, written assignments, and a final paper. A certificate of completion will be issued when the course is finished.

Because the Institute is a graduate school, the courses constitute graduate-level learning. A Bachelor's degree is required for admission. Tuition is $450 per course.

THE CATHOLIC HOME STUDY INSTITUTE
9 Loudoun St., S.E.
Leesburg, VA 22075

(703) 777-8388

The Catholic Home Study Institute is an educational institute for adults offering correspondence courses about the Catholic faith. The courses can be taken for credit or non-credit and can be tailored to individual's schedules. The Institute was established in 1983 by the Church to offer adults the option of learning more about their faith through an organized program of study guided by experienced religious educators. The program is open to anyone who wants to know more about the Catholic faith: Catholic, non-Catholic, teacher, student, CCD teacher, parent, inactive Catholic, or anyone wanting to study the Catholic Church.

Courses offered include: God, Man and the Universe, The Church and Human Destiny, Theology of the Sacraments, Christian Spirituality in the Catholic Tradition, and Ancient Church History. Costs include textbooks and can be paid on a payment plan. Non-credit courses are $195. The same courses, but with college credits, are $300 each.

Students have one year to complete the course, however, most complete a course in six months. The only requirement for enrollment is a high school diploma or equivalent. When taking a course for college credit, an additional term paper and proctored final examination are required. The Catholic Home Study Institute does not award degrees. Courses may be obtained at a discount if groups are enrolled in non-credit courses at one time.

Course assignments include both objective examinations, essay questions, and creative applications of religious teaching to everyday life.

Over 3,000 adults have enrolled at CHSI since 1984. At present approximately 1,500 students are enrolled.

CHSI courses are approved by the Congregation for the Clergy, accredited by the National Home Study Council, and CHSI is a member of the National Catholic Education Association. The American Council on Education has recommended CHSI courses for college credit.

CLEVELAND INSTITUTE OF ELECTRONICS
1776 East 17th St.
Cleveland, OH 44114

(216) 781-9400

CIE is the world's largest independent home study school dealing exclusively with electronics. They offer degree as well as non-degree programs. The school was founded in 1934, and is accredited by the National Home Study Council.

CIE currently enrolls 20,000 students. They give cash awards to the highest and second-highest grade-point averages, also for the graduate with the best technical paper.

The Electron, a bimonthly newspaper, is sent to all CIE students. It includes information about recent developments in electronics technology, along with a Career Opportunities section that lists current job openings reported by many companies. CIE graduates are entitled to resumés and letters of recommendation to present to potential employers at no extra cost.

Associate Degree in Applied Science in Electronics Engineering Technology — 249 lessons over eight (maximum) terms of study. Includes Analog Training, Digital Learning Laboratory, CIE triggered-sweep oscilloscope, Microprocessor Training Laboratory, Technical Writing. The full tuition is $6,000. The lessons include 397 experiments, three exams, and five papers. Time allowed for completion is eight terms, maximum. Each term is six months. Financing plans are available.

Electronics Technology Course — Seventy-six lessons, includes FCC License preparation. Completion time is up to eighteen months. $900 tuition.

Electronics Technology Course With Lab — Ninety-three lessons, up to twenty-four months to complete, $1,500.

Broadcast Engineering — Seventy-six lessons, FCC License preparation, up to eighteen months to complete, $900.

Electronic Communications — Seventy-one lessons, FCC License preparation, two-way radio training, up to eighteen months to complete, $900.

Industrial Electronics — Seventy-eight lessons, eighteen months to complete, $900.

Electronics Engineering — 100 lessons, twenty-four months to finish, $1,500.

Electronics Technology & Advanced Troubleshooting — 118 lessons, Analog Training Lab with multimeter, color TV, CIE triggered-sweep oscilloscope, digital color bar generator, FCC License preparation. Up to thirty-six months to complete, $2,500.

Electronics Technology With Digital Lab — 134 lessons, up to thirty-six months to complete, $3,250.

Electronics Technology With Digital and Microprocessor Labs — 155 lessons, up to forty-two months to complete, $3250.

Electronics Engineering Technology Course — 216 lessons, up to forty-eight months to complete, $4,500.

COLOR ME A SEASON
1070-A Shary Circle
Concord, CA 94518

Color Me a Season Color Analyst Course

This homestudy workbook course is designed to teach the student how to perform color analysis, helping select clothing and makeup color to enhance one's natural coloring.

Created by Bernice Kentner, author of several books on the subject of color analysis, the coursework revolves around her three books, the Munsel color system, and tapes narrated and written by Bernice Kentner about selling cosmetics and doing color draping.

Some lessons are: Color Draping, Putting Color and Fashion Together, and Setting Up a Business. The workbook course, tuition, manual, and color aids and tools add up to $360. Additional cosmetics are required; students may use any brand.

The course is accredited by the National Home Study Council. While the school does not offer placement assistance to graduates, most begin their own color studio or home business, and need no recommendation other than the certificate they receive upon graduation.

Color Me A Season also markets supplies and cosmetics for those in the color draping business.

Color Me A Season currently has approximately 900 certified color consultants with well over 500 still in the process of the course. They certify about 150 each year.

COLUMBIA SCHOOL OF BROADCASTING
5858 Hollywood Boulevard, 4th Floor
P.O. Box 1970
Hollywood, CA 90028

(213) 469-8321

Career courses available through Columbia are:

Radio Announcing — $2,990. Available in Spanish for $1,890. This course prepares you for entry level employment as a disc jockey, sportscaster, or newscaster. Your speech must be free from stuttering or lisping; a voice recording must be submitted with your application for acceptance. You do not need prior radio experience.

Radio/Television Advertising Sales — $2,390. The course prepares you for an entry level position as a time sales Account Executive at a radio or television station in any size market. Applicants must pass a written abilities exam for acceptance.

Radio/Television Commercial Copywriting — $2,390. This course prepares you for entry level employment as a copywriter for radio, television, ad agencies, PR firms, or businesses that have in-house agencies or advertising departments. Applicants must achieve a passing grade on a written abilities exam and have access to a typewriter. Broadcast or journalism background is not required.

Columbia offers graduate job placement through two recorded telephone hotlines giving you job leads, and service staff available for advice and guidance. A variety of financial aid programs is available.

Columbia was founded in 1964 and is accredited by the National Home Study Council.

COMMERCIAL TECHNICAL INSTITUTE
1500 Cardinal Drive
Little Falls, NJ 07424

(800) 526-0890

Commercial Technical Institute offers a wide variety of career courses to prepare students for entry level careers in the following areas:

Air Conditioning, Refrigeration, Heating & Solar Energy
Automotive Mechanics
Bookkeeping and General Accounting
Burglar & Fire Alarm Systems
Conservation
Drafting
Fundamental Electronics
Insurance Adjusting
Interior Design
Legal Investigation
Locksmith
Photography
Practical English
Small Engine Mechanics
Upholstery

As an example, their Bookkeeping and Accounting course consists of fifty-four lessons, takes less than two years to complete, and costs $845. They do offer a $100 discount if you pay the tuition in full, and give a free calculator as an enrollment "bonus." They have been in operation forty years.

COUNTY SCHOOLS, INC.
3787 Main Street
Bridgeport, CT 06606

(800) 243-9917

County Schools was founded in 1959. They are accredited by the National Home Study Council and approved by the Connecticut Commission of Education. CSI offers a variety of vocational training programs through home study as well as through a combination of home study and resident training.

Airline/Travel — Six months of home study followed by four weeks of resident training.

Bookkeeping/General Accounting — Nine months of home study.

Hotel-Motel Management — Six months of home study followed by three weeks of resident training.

Hotel-Motel Operations — Six months of home study.

Nurse's Aide — Six months of home study followed by eighty-four hours of clinical lab training (two to four weeks).

Tractor-Trailer Professional #1 — Six months of home study followed by two to four weeks of resident training.

Tractor-Trailer Intermediate #2 — Approximately fourteen days of resident training.

Tractor-Trailer Refresher #3 — Eighty hours of resident training.

Travel Agent Preparation — Six months of home study.

CSI offers a variety of payment plans and financial aid is available to qualified students.

CUSTOM DECORATING & DRAPERY INSTITUTE
2118 South Grand
Santa Ana, CA 92705

The course offered at CDDI is a drapery-making course with the addition of slipcovers, bedspreads, and interior decorating.

Students actually make drapes for their homes as part of the course, and it is very much a hands-on program. The total cost is $289, payable in installments. Lessons include how to select fabrics, making a valance, how to measure and figure yardage, Austrian shades, and intricate sewing techniques for creating custom draperies. The course emphasis is upon starting your own business in your home, and a "Go Into Business" kit is part of the text material. They also direct you to fabric wholesalers.

CDDI is owned by American Career Institute and was founded in 1967.

DIAMOND COUNCIL OF AMERICA
9140 Ward Parkway
Kansas City, MO 64114

(816) 444-3500

The Diamond Council of America offers courses in Diamontology and Gemology, leading to certificates of Certified Diamontologist and Guild Gemologist, to members of the Diamond Council of America and their employees.

The program is accredited by the National Home Study Council.

DOROTHEA B. LANE SCHOOLS
Home Study Division
955 S. Chapel St.
P.O. Box 6033
Newark, DE 19714-6033

(800) 334-2929

Dorothea B. Lane Schools offer career diploma programs in:

Bookkeeper/Accountant
Executive Secretary
Secretary/Bookkeeper
Secretary/Receptionist
Receptionist

Their home study school is accredited by the National Home Study Council.

Their course materials and lessons are very thorough and are of high quality. The emphasis is placed on moving up in the job market. Some required reading in the programs includes; "How to Negotiate a Raise or Promotion," "Getting Organized," and "Running Your Own Business."

Applicants are suggested to have a high school diploma or G.E.D., but with a work-related background or other education, they may waive the diploma prerequisite upon application for enrollment.

Costs run from $299 for the Receptionist program to $639 for the Secretary/Bookkeeper program. Payment plans are available.

EDUCATIONAL INSTITUTE OF THE AMERICAN HOTEL & MOTEL ASSOCIATION

1407 South Harrison Road
P.O. Box 1240
East Lansing, MI 48823

(517) 353-5500

The Educational Institute of the American Hotel & Motel Association was established in 1952 to provide education and training for the hospitality industry. Courses are designed for entry-level as well as career advancement opportunities. Currently twenty-six comprehensive courses are available, covering every major functional area of a hotel/motel operation including Tourism, Basic Sanitation, Front Office Management, Security, Law, and Food and Beverage Controls.

Courses of study can be taken separately, or a five-course series leading to certificates of specialization in Rooms Division Management, Food and Beverage Management, Marketing and Sales Management, Accounting and Financial Management, and Engineering and Facility Management. Further coursework leads to the Institute Diploma, and coursework combined with work experience leads to industry-recognized executive level certification.

The Institute is governed by a Board of Trustees that includes presidents of several of the large national hotel/motel chains, as well as several Deans of University Schools of Hotel/Motel Management. The Institute has been headquartered on the campus of Michigan State University in East Lansing since 1956.

As a non-profit educational foundation of the American Hotel & Motel Association, the Institute develops course materials and references for the entire industry. Over 750 major universities, colleges, and vocational schools worldwide use the Institute's courses and texts in their own classrooms.

The courses, as well as positions within the hospitality industry, are aimed at a wide variety of potential students. Women seeking a career with advancement potential, retired persons, people without college degrees seeking entry-level opportunities, and business administration college graduates seeking to achieve professional certification and stay on top of recent industry developments, will all benefit from the coursework.

Course costs range from $165 for one course, to $700 for a Certificate of Specialization program, and $1,620 for an Institute Diploma. Courses must be completed within four months; up to twenty months for an Area of Specialization (five courses), or up to forty-eight months for the Institute Diploma (twelve courses). Some people have completed a course in as little as three weeks, according to the Institute.

For those currently working in the field, courses can be challenged by examination.

The Institute's programs are accredited by the National Home Study Council.

EMERGENCY MANAGEMENT INSTITUTE

Federal Emergency Management Agency
16825 S. Seton Avenue
Emmitsburg, MD 21727

(301) 447-6771

Four home study courses are offered:

Emergency Program Manager
Emergency Management
Radiological Emergency Management
Preparedness Planning for a Nuclear Crisis

Three courses are under development: Natural Hazards Management, Basic Disaster Operations, and Hazardous Materials.

These are federally sponsored courses in emergency preparedness, and are available at no charge to the general public and to those involved in disaster response and emergency management. Founded in 1967, approximately 10,000 people enroll at EMI each year.

The courses can be taken for one semester hour of college credit through Suomi College, Hancock, MI.

The EMI program recently received accreditation from the National Home Study Council.

ENGLISH LANGUAGE INSTITUTE OF AMERICA
332 S. Michigan Avenue, Suite 864
Chicago, IL 60604

(312) 663-0880

Founded in 1942, the English Language Institute of America offers a course in Practical English and the Command of Words. Their program is accredited by the National Home Study Council.

FARMLAND INDUSTRIES, INC.

Training Center
P.O. Box 7305
Kansas City, MO 64116

(800) 821-8000

Farmland Industries was founded in 1929. The courses offered are aimed at adults working in the agricultural industries. Courses are offered in the following topics:

Management Development
Understanding Cooperatives
Cooperative Organization
Agribusiness Writing
Agricultural Economics
Intro to Agribusiness Management
Farm Store Management
Personnel Management

Accounting/Computers
Cooperative Accounting
Introduction to Computers in Agribusiness
How Money Works in an Agribusiness
Membership Accounting

Feed and Animal Health
Feed
Animal Health
Beef Production: Cow–Calf
Beef Production: Growing–Finishing
Swine Production
Dairy Production
Sheep Production
Advanced Animal Health

Fertilizer and Ag Chemicals
Anhydrous Ammonia Safety
Ag Chemicals
Lawn and Garden Center Sales
Corn Production
Soybean Production

Petroleum and Propane
  LP Gas Operations and Safety

Grain Training
  Grain Elevator Safety
  Basic Grain Accounting
  Grain Accounting II
  Physical Grain Handling

Sales
  Cooperative Salesmanship
  Agribusiness Telephone Communications
  Introduction to Agribusiness

Courses cost between $30 and $125, and students have up to nine months to complete a course. A Certificate of Completion is awarded. Farmland is accredited by the National Home Study Council.

FEDERATED TAX SERVICE

2021 West Montrose
Chicago, IL 60618

(312) 929-5700

Federated offers a tax preparation course which will enable you to prepare federal income tax returns.

The course, which you may take up to one year to complete, costs $229.50. They accept monthly payments. Their sales materials emphasize the "business-building" extras that are included to help you get your own tax preparation service going. They include a business guide, business cards, and letters for you to mail to potential customers. They offer a continuing information service for three years after you finish your course.

FOLEY BELSAW INSTITUTE
6301 Equitable Road
Kansas City, MO 64120

(800) 468-4449

Foley Belsaw offers home study courses in Locksmithing, Small Engine Repair, Woodworking, Saw and Tool Sharpening, Chain Saw Sharpening, and Upholstery. They also sell industrial-grade equipment that supplements the courses and allows you to set up your own business. Their equipment is of high quality and priced realistically. They offer a variety of payment plans for tuition as well as purchase of the assorted equipment you will need: key machine, industrial sewing machine, saw sharpening equipment, as well as sawmills, wood planers, tool sharpeners, etc. Their emphasis is upon helping you start a business, so that you will continue to purchase supplies and equipment through them.

My husband has been a customer of theirs, and they delivery what they promise. They also publish a newsletter, The Foley-Belsaw "News Bulletin" with inspirational stories and how-to tips from people who are in their own businesses and using their equipment.

GEMOLOGICAL INSTITUTE OF AMERICA
1660 Stewart Street
P.O. Box 2110
Santa Monica, CA 90406-9968

(800) 421-7250, ext. 292

Founded in 1931, the Gemological Institute of America is a non-profit institution offering professional jewelers' courses in the following programs:

Gemologist Program	$1,750	60 months to complete
Diamonds Program	$ 695	36 months to complete
Colored Stones Program	$1,195	40 months to complete

Single course enrollments are also available. The following courses are available at prices ranging from $275–750 per course: Diamond Grading, Gem Identification, Colored Stone Grading, Pearls, Jewelry Design, Jewelry Display, Jewelry Sales, Diamonds.

The GIA also offers resident study programs in New York City and Santa Monica, CA. The home study courses use the same texts as the residence courses, and many of the home study courses include practical work with actual gems and other special materials. To enable students to have hands-on experience with handling gems, the GIA offers a gem-lending system. Every year they loan hundreds of thousands of dollars worth of diamonds, pearls, and colored stones to students. Students work with these gems at home, and send in assignments to instructors for evaluation. You can also complete the home study portion of the course, and take the examinations in one of the GIA's Student Workrooms in California or New York.

The GIA program is accredited by the National Home Study Council and the National Association of Trade and Technical Schools.

GENERAL EDUCATION & TRAINING, INC.

12100 Grandview Road
Grandview, MO 64030

(800) 332-6543

General Education & Training offers professional truck driver training courses available to both resident and home-study students. The resident course takes six weeks to complete, the home-study course is six months, with two weeks spent at the school actually driving the trucks. The school is accredited by the National Association of Trade and Technical Schools and the National Home Study Council. Graduates will be Department of Transportation certified. G.E.T. works with two commercial trucking companies, using company trucks and then placing graduates with the companies as over-the-road drivers. Their program, " . . . makes winners out of everybody: potential drivers for companies needing well-trained entry level drivers; students who are able to get both universal truck driving skills and learn a company's procedures on driving while attending school; and G.E.T.'s ability to meet both the students' and trucking companies' needs in a changing environment."

They participate in the Guaranteed Student Loan Program and the Veterans Administration Loan Fund, both sources of financial aid.

At the training facility, students practice driving exercises, then head out for over-the-road driving in all types of traffic conditions. Each student receives a minimum of 350 to 400 miles driving time and 1,050 miles observation time.

Before actually driving the big rigs, students spend hours learning about transportation rules and regulations, log books, defensive driving techniques, and equipment use.

Upon completion of the home study and resident training, each graduate receives a certificate of written examination and Department of Transportation road test certificate. The school also offers employment guidance assistance to all graduates.

G.E.T. publishes a quarterly newsletter for all students and graduates called "The Training Wheels" which features information about changes at the school and articles and photographs of graduates with the rigs they are currently driving.

Earnings for graduates of the program run between $400 and $1,000 per week, depending upon the company, what is being hauled, and number of miles traveled.

GRANTON INSTITUTE OF TECHNOLOGY
263 Adelaide Street West
Toronto, Canada M5H 1Y3

Granton Institute offers over 400 courses in business and management, engineering technology, electronics and mechanics, repair and installation, hospitality, tourism, social and community services, health and nutrition.

Granton Institute is accredited by the National Home Study Council. It has been operating for over fifty years.

They offer such a wide variety of career diploma courses that there are simply too many to list. Write for their free catalog. Some examples of the range of courses offered include:

Meat Cutting and Merchandising
Restaurant Operations and Management
Bar Operations and Management (Bartender's Course)
Law Clerk Diploma Course
Title Search Operations and Procedures
Weather Forecasting
Comic Strip and Cartoon Drawing
Fashion Drawing
Newspaper Journalism and Reporting
Commercial Photography
Accident Investigation
Barber Styling Diploma Course
Library Technician Diploma Course
General Plastics Technology
Taxidermy
Industrial Ceramics Technology
Bicycle Mechanics
Fish Hatchery Technology
Import-Export Business Operations and Procedures
Modern Massage
Bee Keeping and Honey Making
Chimney Construction and Maintenance
Dog Training for Law Enforcement
Firearm Service and Repair
Tool and Die Drafting and Design
Highway Design, Construction and Maintenance

THE HADLEY SCHOOL FOR THE BLIND

700 Elm Street
Winnetka, IL 60093

(312) 446-8111

Founded in 1920, the Hadley School for the Blind offers over 100 courses for the blind, teaching braille, high school, vocational, avocational, and technical subjects. Courses are taught by braille or audio cassette.

Courses are also available for parents of blind children.

Hadley School is accredited by the National Home Study Council.

HALIX INSTITUTE

1543 W. Olympic Boulevard, Suite 226
Los Angeles, CA 90015-6800

(213) 381-6800

Halix Institute offers a course on Computers and BASIC Programming written for those with no previous computer experience. The course is accredited by the National Home Study Council. Along with computer programming, you will learn about pre-written programs, software, electronic spreadsheets, word processing, and data base management.

The course is designed to cover fundamentals and techniques to be used on any computer, not specifically tailored to one particular make or model.

Course Outline: Beginning in BASIC, Exploring the Program, Variable Tables, Information and Coding, A Second Look at How the Computer Works, Data Files and Structures, Sorting Techniques, Information Storage in Computers, Processing in the Computer, Expanding the Computer System, The World of Applications Software.

Tuition is $539 with several payment plans available. Students have up to two years to complete the course.

THE HART SCHOOL FOR PROFESSIONAL SECRETARIES

4699 N. Federal Highway
Pompano Beach, FL 33064

(407) 946-5551

A one-year course combining home study and resident study. Students complete a 280-hour independent study portion, then come to the Florida campus for a three-week hands-on session. The course is designed for men and women over seventeen years of age, and aims to prepare the student for an entry-level position in the secretarial–clerical field. Tuition is $1,895 for the entire program; $1,300 for the independent study portion; $595 for the resident training portion. Students must also pay for transportation and living expenses during the resident training portion. Financial aid is available through the Guaranteed Student Loan Program.

Some of the skills students will learn are: Written and Oral Communication, Time Management, Telephone Skills, Filing Techniques, Typing, Speedwriting, Handling of Office Finances.

The Hart School is a new program, offered through American Career Training Corporation, which also owns the A.C.T. Travel School. Hart is accredited by the National Home Study Council.

HEATHKIT/ZENITH EDUCATIONAL SYSTEMS
Hilltop Road
St. Joseph, MI 49085

(800) 253-0570

Heathkit/Zenith Educational Systems is a division of Heath Company, a subsidiary of Zenith Electronic Corporation. It was founded in 1975, and is accredited by the National Home Study Council.

Courses offered:
  Electricity and Electronic Fundamentals
  Advanced Electronics
  Digital Electronics
  Microprocessors and Microcomputers
  Robotics
  Computer Programming
  Computer Assisted Drafting
  Computer Graphics
  Electro-optics
  Circuit Design

Completed courses earn CEUs (Continuing Education Units), which are recognized as continued job-related certification by many professional and technical organizations.

Costs vary with the course chosen, and students must purchase necessary technical equipment to go along with the written course materials. For instance, the Robotics Training program includes Robotics and Industrial Electronics Course, Robot Applications Course, Advanced Programming Experiments, and Basic HERO Robot, a Robot Arm with Gripper and Voice Synthesizer at a total cost of $1,374.70. Courses alone vary between $30–100.

Their home study courses are also available in classroom versions, allowing an instructor to purchase courses with all the teaching materials necessary: textbook, workbook for students, and parts pack, as well as instructor's guide, course outline, exams, and answer keys. These packages are designed for colleges, technical schools, and corporate training programs. The following areas are available in classroom versions:

Basic Electronics
Microprocessor Technology
Advanced Electronics
Robotics and Automation
Computer Servicing
Circuit Design
Computer Assisted Drafting (CAD)

HEMPHILL SCHOOLS
510 S. Alvarado Street
Los Angeles, CA 90057-2998

(213) 413-2050

Hemphill Schools offers home study in the Spanish languages in a variety of fields. It was founded in 1920. The school is accredited by the National Home Study Council. Courses available include:

Art
Automotive
Diesel
Radio-TV Repair
Electricity, Air Conditioning, and Refrigeration
Computer Programming
Accounting
English
Sewing

A Computer Programming course is also available in English through the Halix Institute, listed elsewhere in this directory.

HOLLYWOOD SCRIPTWRITING INSTITUTE
1300 N. Cahuenga Boulevard
Hollywood, CA 90028

(800) SCRIPTS

Hollywood Scriptwriting Institute was founded in 1976 by Donna Lee, an experienced writer who developed the textbook the course is based upon.

"Screenwriting From Concept to Sale" is a twenty-six lesson course covering all phases of screenwriting at a cost of $1,850 with financial aid available. Topics covered include: Writing Dialogue, Screen Formats, Comedy Writing, Character Development, Low Budget Movies, and Marketing Your Script.

Students may attend resident courses in Hollywood given in workshop formats: Visualizing Screenwriting Concepts ($250), Writing Your Own Original Screenplay ($250), Refining and Selling Your Screenplay ($250). The resident courses may be taken in an intensive study format, or attended weekly over several weeks.

Students should have a typewriter, a good dictionary, and an audio cassette player. VCRs are optional but desirable.

The Institute screens applicants through an essay-writing exercise, as well as asking questions about the student's work and study habits and time commitment. Students should expect to devote ten to twelve hours per week to assignments.

The Institute offers an Alumni Script Marketing Service to help graduates sell their work. Assistance is available to graduates for five years after graduation.

The Institute is accredited by the National Home Study Council. Students retain the copyright to all material they submit to the school for evaluation.

Applicants must be able to write the English language at the minimum level of high school competency. A three hundred-word essay on questions such as the following must be submitted with your application: "What is your favorite movie? How has this movie influenced or changed your life?"; or: "Do you think that morals and values are the responsibility of the entertainment industry: Please defend your answer."

You must also write a few paragraphs expressing your goals relating to the scriptwriting classes.

HOME STUDY INTERNATIONAL
6940 Carroll Avenue
Takoma Park, MD 20912

(202) 722-6570

Founded in 1909, Home Study International is accredited by the National Home Study Council. Courses offered are Health and Religion, Literature Evangelism, The Work of the Bible Instructor, and The Work of the Church Treasurer.

INSTITUTE OF CHILDREN'S LITERATURE
Redding Ridge, CT 06876-9987

(800) 243-9645

Founded in 1969, the Institute of Children's Literature offers a four-part writing course aimed at adults wanting to write and sell articles and manuscripts to children's magazines and book publishers.

The Institute sends a Writing Aptitude Test with their promotional materials, and applicants must submit the finished test before they forward application and fee information.

INSURANCE ACHIEVEMENT, INC.
7330 Highland Road
Baton Rouge, LA 70808

(800) 535-3042

Founded in 1969, Insurance Achievement, Inc. is accredited by the National Home Study Council. Courses offered through home study are for those interested in careers in insurance and securities. Courses will prepare you for the following:

Chartered Life Underwriter (CLU)
Chartered Financial Consultant (ChFC)
Chartered Property/Casualty Underwriter (CPCU)
Associate in Risk Management (ARM)
National insurance/financial planning designations
NASD Series 6, Investment Company Products/Variable
    Contracts exam
NASD Series 63, Blue Sky licensing exam
Certified Executive Assistant program for secretaries

Insurance Achievement has recently begun using facsimile transmission/reception to send correspondence via the telephone lines. If you have a computer with these capabilities, you can send them your exams and correspondence over the computer.

The Certified Executive Assistant Program is a professional training program for secretaries. Upon completion of five exams, covering administrative skills, basic financial services material and specialized training in the areas of agency administration, estate planning, financial planning, multi-line and property/liability risk management, the student will earn the CEA designation. The CEA designation is awarded by the CEA Institute.

Insurance Achievement's home study courses concentrate on preparing you to pass national exams to earn the CLU and ChFC designations through the use of workbooks, quizzes, exams, cassette tapes, and IBM PC diskettes for "hands on" practice for PLATO exams. Their program has an unconditional warranty: if a student takes an Insurance Achievement course of any kind and is unable to sit for the national exam, or is unsuccessful, tuition fees for that course will be waived at any time in the future.

Course titles are:

Personal Risk Management & Insurance I
Personal Risk Management & Insurance II
Multiline Insurance Law & Operations
Introduction to Financial Planning
Income Taxation
The Financial System in the Economy
Individual Insurance
Life Insurance Law
Group Benefits
Pensions and Other Retirement Plans
Employee Benefits
Investments
Wealth Accumulation Planning
Fundamentals of Estate Planning I
Planning for Business Owners & Professionals
Financial Planning Applications
Fundamentals of Estate Planning II
Business Taxation & Planning

Cost is $125 for the first-time student; $175 for previous students, per course.

Eighty-eight percent of Insurance Achievement candidates pass their national exams the first time. Courses are approved in eight states for CEU (Continuing Education Unit) credit. More than 400 companies have reimbursed tuition for employees in Insurance Achievement programs.

INTERNATIONAL AVIATION AND TRAVEL ACADEMY
300 W. Arbrook Boulevard
Arlington, TX 76014

(800) 527-2260

Founded in 1982, the IATA was previously owned by Braniff International Airlines and Frontier Airlines. They currently enroll approximately 1,700 students annually at their resident training facility in Texas.

IATA offers entry level training for the airlines and travel industry. Their home study program includes a short resident study portion, in which computer based training and video equipment support classroom instruction.

IATA is accredited by the National Home Study Council.

INTERNATIONAL CORRESPONDENCE SCHOOLS (ICS)
Scranton, PA 18515

(717) 342-7701

Founded in 1891, ICS is a division of the National Education Corporation, which also owns North American Correspondence Schools of Scranton, PA. ICS is accredited by the National Home Study Council.

ICS offers twenty-seven programs leading to a career diploma. These are aimed at preparing the student for entry-level jobs in fields not requiring a college degree. The National Education Corporation also operates the Center for Degree Studies (CDS) which offers programs leading to an Associate Degree. See their listing under Center for Degree Studies.

ICS also offers a high school diploma course. They claim to have enrolled over nine million students since they were founded in 1891. Currently, the National Education Corporation reports new enrollments in their programs during 1988 to reach 106,000. In 1987, approximately 20,000 students graduated from their courses.

All courses at ICS feature open book exams. Some of the courses also have optional and/or required projects. All equipment and materials including books are part of the tuition.

Programs offered at ICS:

Basic Electronics
Child Day Care
Auto Mechanics
Hotel/Restaurant Management
Electrician
High School
Legal Assistant
Interior Decorating
Air Conditioning and Refrigeration
Art
Motorcycle
Photography

Journalism
Dressmaking
Fashion Merchandising
Surveying and Mapping
Diesel Mechanics
Programming in BASIC
Microcomputer Repair
Catering/Gourmet Cooking
Computer Assisted Small Business Management
Microcomputer Servicing Technician
Electronics
Electronics Technician
Industrial Electronics
TV/VCR Repair
Fitness and Nutrition

As examples of their career diploma programs, the ICS School of Day Care Management program takes between nine months and two years to complete, and costs $589. The Fitness and Nutrition Course covers eleven lessons such as "Management Skills for The Fitness Field," and "How to Run a Fitness Facility," as well as information about related career opportunities. Cost is $589.

JOHN TRACY CLINIC
806 West Adams Boulevard
Los Angeles, CA 90007

(213) 748-5481

The John Tracy Clinic was founded in 1942 by Mrs. Spencer Tracy. It was created to assist and train parents of preschool deaf children. The courses are designed to help both the child and the parents. Courses are available in English and Spanish.

The home study program is free for parents of deaf children from birth to six years of age.

The courses have helped parents in over 130 countries. The lessons guide the parent in helping a deaf baby develop speech and language awareness by noticing sounds and vibrations.

The Clinic is accredited by the National Home Study Council.

KENNEDY-WESTERN UNIVERSITY
28310 Roadside Drive
Agoura Hills, CA 91301

(800) 635-2900

Kennedy-Western offers fifty Professional Certificate Programs in Business Administration and Management. These are designed for people seeking career advancement or specific career-related knowledge in order to make a career change. The programs can be completed in eight weeks or more. Tuition and books are $580 per program. The following programs are available:

Principles of Accounting
Advanced Accounting
Management Accounting
Advertising
Business Economics
Cost Accounting
Auditing
Controllership
Business Communications
Legal Analysis for Business Managers
Collection Law and Procedure
Elements of Business Finance
Elements of Industrial Relations
Law of Labor Relations and Industrial Employment
Commercial Law Contracts
Data Processing
Money Markets and Financial Institutions
Labor Market Analysis
Leadership Principles and Practices
Fundamentals of Export Trade
Fundamentals of Import Trade
Intro to International Business
Export Documentation, Traffic, Banking
International Finance
International Marketing
Law in International Business

International Business Policies and Strategies
Principles of Insurance
Management Information Systems and Systems Analysis
Executive Management Practices
Data Communications
Administrative Office Management
Human Resources Management
Manufacturing Cost-Estimating
Personnel Recruitment, Selection & Placement
Real Estate Appraisal
Sales Management
New Product Marketing
Property Management
Business Tax Planning

THE LAURAL SCHOOL

2538 N. 8th St.
P.O. Box 5338
Phoenix, AZ 85006

(602) 947-6565

Founded in 1978, The Laural School offers career courses in the following areas:

Dental Assistant
Dental Receptionist
Medical Assistant
Medical Receptionist
Medical Secretary
Business Secretary
Legal Secretary
Executive Secretary
Administrative Secretary

Payment plans are available. High school diploma is not a prerequisite. Courses may be completed in as little as six months, with up to two years allowed to finish a course.

Some of the lessons covered in the Business Secretary course are: Filing and Records Management, Copying Machines, Calculators and Office Machines, Mailing Department, Supplies and Basic Office Information, Typing (not a must, this is included as an option at no additional cost — the Quick Easy Touch Method is used), Correspondence and Preparation of Business Forms, Shorthand or Rapid Writing (again, like typing, this is optional for those who choose to do it and is available in cassette or phonograph record form), and Getting a Job.

Laural is accredited by the National Home Study Council.

LEARNING PROCESS CENTER
222 W. 24th Street
National City, CA 92050

(619) 477-1200

A division of California College for Health Sciences (see listings under proprietary and degree-granting schools), the Learning Process Center offers a course in career guidance. They are accredited by the National Home Study Council.

LIFETIME CAREER SCHOOLS

2251 Barry Avenue
Los Angeles, CA 90064

(213) 478-0617

Lifetime Career Schools offers four courses designed to help you turn a hobby or interest into an income-producing business or career. These courses prepare you for an entry-level position and emphasize opportunities for starting your own home business. They are accredited by the National Home Study Council.

Landscaping
Floristry
Dressmaking
Doll Technology (dollmaking and repair)

MAHER VENTRILOQUIST STUDIOS
P.O. Box 420
Littleton, CO 80160

Maher offers a home study course in ventriloquism. Their thirty lesson course will teach you the various types of voices, how to "throw the voice," how to talk without moving your lips, as well as scriptwriting, publicity, and booking shows. Cassette tapes are used to demonstrate the techniques, and students return recordings of their practice sessions to the school for evaluation. There are no time limits, and the course is guaranteed as follows: "If you have fulfilled the terms of your enrollment by: (1) Completing the lessons as directed, (2) Sending in your completed exams, and (3) Sending samples of your practice sessions by cassette tape for office evaluation; and thereafter you have not learned ventriloquism from this Course, and written application to this effect is made within thirty days after date of receiving final lesson giving reasons for dissatisfaction, Maher Studios will refund the full amount paid for the Course upon return of all Course materials furnished by the studio."

Their beginning students range from seven to eighty-seven years of age. The lessons require a minimum of fifteen to twenty minutes daily, and most students begin performing within six weeks.

The "ventriloquial figure" (dare we call it a dummy?) is made by the student, from detailed directions included in the course. The Studio does carry a supply catalog and a complete line of other figures which range in price from $20–$200. The course and supplies are designed for professional ventriloquists, performers, teachers, and ministers.

The course costs $79.95 and can be charged on VISA/MasterCard.

Successful graduates include Willie Tyler, who enrolled at the age of nine. . . . "Lester" is also a product of Maher Studios.

The course is not certified or accredited by any established accrediting agency, but it's so unusual, why would it need to be? It is associated with the North American Association of Ventriloquists, and was founded in 1934.

MODERN SCHOOLS OF AMERICA
2538 N. 8th St.
P.O. Box 5338
Phoenix, AZ 85010

(602) 947-6565

Founded in 1946, the Modern Schools of America program is accredited by the National Home Study Council and approved by the Veterans Administration. The courses of study available are:

Gun Repair
Small Engine Repair

MOTEL MANAGERS SCHOOL
220 North Main Street
Hudson, OH 44236

(216) 653-9151

Designed to serve the hospitality industry, MMS was founded in 1961 to teach motel management. Applicants must have a high school diploma or equivalent. The school requires that each prospective trainee have a personal interview with an authorized MMS representative prior to enrollment to determine whether or not enrollment will benefit the student.

Tests are graded and students must score 75% or better in order to qualify for graduation.

Program completion time is about six to eight months. A Certificate of Completion is awarded.

Most students are interested in obtaining jobs in the motel industry, and MMS offers some help with placement. Upon graduation you will receive 100 printed personal resumés to give to potential employers, along with 100 letters of recommendation and twelve issues of their Job Opportunity Bulletin.

The Motel Management course consists of fifty-two lessons and costs $1,995. Payment plans are available.

Some of the courses included in the program are: Advertising, Front Office Organization and Management, Purchasing and Inventory Control, Training Employees to be Effective, Housekeeping and Maintenance, Money Management, Financial Analysis, and Personal Means to Success.

The Motel Managers School program is accredited by the NHSC.

MTA SCHOOL
1801 Oberlin Road
Middletown, PA 17057

(717) 939-1931

MTA offers home study courses in truck driving training and diesel mechanics. Part of the training is conducted at a resident training site after the home study lessons have been completed. Sites offering the resident training include: Elizabethtown, PA; Columbus, OH; West Jefferson, OH; Greensboro, NC; and Waxahachie, TX.

The MTA program is accredited by the National Home Study Council.

NAPOLEON HILL FOUNDATION
1440 Paddock Drive
Northbrook, IL 60062

Positive Mental Attitude Science of Success Course

The Napoleon Hill Foundation was established in 1962 to foster, perpetuate, and disseminate the research, writings, and teaching of Dr. Napoleon Hill. It is a non-profit charitable educational organization serving social service agencies, educators, businesses and individuals seeking success and personal achievement. They publish several books related to these subjects, as well as the highly advertised cassette tape, "Think & Grow Rich." The course is accredited by the National Home Study Council.

Dr. Hill's work involved studying successful people, and distilling their philosophies into seventeen Principles of Success that can be learned by anyone.

The course consists of seventeen lessons, each based on a principle of success. Students have individual success counselors during the course to make sure each principle is correctly understood and applied. Some of the lessons include: Definiteness of Purpose, Self-Discipline, Accurate Thinking, and Learning from Defeat. The course costs $380 and they offer payment plans. The course must be completed within eighteen months.

Some of the successful people recommending the course include Senator Jennings Randolph, Og Mandino, Dr. Robert Schuller, and Mary Kay Ash.

To quote Dr. Hill, "You can be anything you want to be, if only you believe with sufficient conviction and act in accordance with your faith, for whatever your mind can conceive and believe, you can achieve."

NATIONAL HOME STUDY COUNCIL
1601 18th Street, N.W.
Washington, DC 20009

(202) 234-5100

The NHSC is an accrediting body for the home study industry. They are currently offering a five-lesson home study course on effective business writing: "Write to Be Read." The course consists of five lessons and exams. Its cost is $77. The text is available alone for $25.

NATIONAL SAFETY COUNCIL
Safety Training Institute
444 North Michigan Avenue
Chicago, IL 60611

The National Safety Council has been operating since 1913. It is accredited by the National Home Study Council. The home study courses available are in safety supervision and human relations for first line supervisors.

NATIONAL TAX TRAINING SCHOOL

P.O. Box 382
Monsey, NY 10952

(914) 352-3634

National Tax Training School offers an income tax preparation course covering tax computation, deductions, tax credits, and all other areas of federal income tax preparation. Payroll taxes, income tax withholding, and social security taxes are also covered. You will fill out forms and study case study tax scenarios. They offer a Post Graduate Revision Service that informs you of all changes in the tax laws, as well as a Consultation and Advisory Service, both for the five years following your graduation. They offer a Lifetime Placement Service, through which they will contact tax firms in your area, advising them of your qualifications.

The course also includes a Manual of Successful Tax Practice, which will help you start and develop your own tax practice.

The twenty-lesson course costs $229.75, and they offer a monthly payment plan and accept credit cards. They are approved for Veteran's Training. The course may be completed in three months or less, and the maximum time is one year.

Students do not need a high school diploma. As the program brochure states, "If you have had a minimum of two years of high school, you have sufficient formal education to successfully take the course and establish a thriving tax practice. As far as math is concerned, all you need to know is how to add, subtract, multiply and divide."

While the program is developed to prepare students for the tax profession, many people enroll to enhance their personal ability for personal or business tax matters.

NATIONAL TECHNICAL SCHOOLS
456 W. Martin Luther King, Jr. Boulevard
Los Angeles, CA 90037

(213) 235-6486

National Technical Schools was founded in 1905. It is a division of United Education and Software. The courses offered are:

Compulit (Microcomputer Literacy)
Caress (Career Readiness Program)
Personal Computer Technology
TV and Radio Servicing
Compulit Publisher (Desktop Publishing)
Industrial Technology and Microprocessors
Video Technology with Microcomputers
Basic Electronics

Their program is accredited by the National Home Study Council.

NATIONAL TRAINING, INC.
188 College Drive
P.O. Box 1899
Orange Park, FL 32067-1899

(904) 272-4000

Founded in 1978, National Training, Inc. offers home study courses in truck driving training and heavy equipment operation. Part of the training takes place at the training sites in Florida and Commerce City, CO. National Training, Inc. is accredited by the National Home Study Council.

NATIONAL TRAINING SYSTEMS, INC.
7140 Virginia Manor Court
P.O. Box 2719
Laurel, MD 20708

(301) 953-7240

Founded in 1976, National Training Systems, Inc. offers home study courses in truck driving training and diesel mechanics. Their program is accredited by the National Home Study Council.

NEW YORK SCHOOL OF INTERIOR DESIGN
155 E. 56th Street
New York, NY 10022

(212) 753-5365

The New York School of Interior Design was founded in 1916. It is a college, offering degrees (B.F.A. and A.A.S.), diplomas, and certificates. The New York School is a resident college and also offers a Home Study Course. It is a non-profit educational institution, well-established and highly respected. The school is supported by both an endowment fund and tuition fees. The home study course carries six academic credits which may be applied to further study at the New York School of Interior Design or transferred to another college. Much of the lesson material found in the Home Study Course is now used in over one hundred schools and colleges to teach their programs.

The Home Study Course consists of twenty-six lessons, color wheel and color chart, chart of decorative fabrics, floor plans for layouts, professional Plan-a-Kit, and textbook. Home Study students may attend lectures at the New York School free of charge if they so desire. Students are also given information about wholesale supply sources, costs and profits, and selling and display. Upon completion of the course and the final examination, students receive a certificate of completion.

Some of the subjects covered in the lessons include: Tapestries, Rugs and Carpets; Decorative Textiles and Their Use; Historical Period Styles in Furnishings (Egyptian Art through post-American Revolutionary time periods); and Pottery, Porcelain & Glassware.

Students also learn how to make lamp shades, draperies, and slipcovers, and apply their knowledge to professional problems through working up complete plans to client specifications. Other areas important to the field include: How to establish a decorating business of your own, Developing a "following," Selling techniques, Financial compensation for various types of decorating services, and Working with sub-contractors. The Home Study Course is very complete, and based upon an extensive textbook written by the school's founder.

The total cost of the Home Study Course is $450, with payment options available. Students' visits to New York City are not included, however, they may attend up to ten lectures at the resident school there free of charge.

All text material is printed in English, but correspondence may be conducted in English, Spanish, French, Portuguese, and German.

NORTH AMERICAN CORRESPONDENCE SCHOOLS
Scranton, PA 18515

(717) 342-7701

NACS is owned by the same parent company as ICS and CDS, the National Education Corporation. North American Correspondence Schools provide career training for entry-level positions in the following diploma programs:

Accounting
Animal Science
Conservation
Drafting
Firearms
Legal Secretary
Secretary
Travel
Police Science

As an example, the Bookkeeping/Accounting Course consists of eleven lessons, with up to two years to complete; cost is $689. After you complete the basic course and obtain their diploma, you may take additional courses "free of charge" in Payroll Accounting, Income Tax Return Preparation, and Data Processing.

The General Animal Sciences Course prepares you for a career as a Veterinary Assistant or Animal Care Specialist. The course consists of fifty lessons, including a filmstrip viewer and filmstrips and audio cassettes. Studies include animal anatomy, handling of exotic animals, animal health and treatment, and how to work in a veterinarian's office. Up to two years are allowed for completion; the cost is $689.

North American is accredited by the National Home Study Council.

NORTH AMERICAN HEATING & AIRCONDITIONING WHOLESALERS

Home Study Institute
1661 West Henderson Road
Columbus, OH 43220

(614) 488-1835

The North American Heating & Airconditioning Wholesalers Association established the Institute as an accredited, licensed, and not-for-profit correspondence school as a service to the heating and airconditioning industry. It operates out of the Association's national offices in Ohio. There are approximately 1,400 students enrolled at this time. Established in 1962, the Institute offers courses such as: Fundamentals of Heating & Cooling, Heating & Airconditioning Design, Counter Service & Sales, Basic Office Math, Fundamentals of Solar Heating, and Managing a Contracting Business.

Course fees vary between $62 and 112 per course, with discounts for members of NHAW.

NHAW also offers self-study workbooks on a variety of topics, which can be used to study independently at home. Each book features individual study questions, with correct responses listed in the back of the workbook. Costs vary, averaging $10 per workbook, with discounts for bulk orders and members of NHAW.

The NHAW Home Study Institute awards Continuing Education Units (CEUs) for all courses successfully completed. You must maintain a grade average of 70 or better to pass.

The NHAW Home Study Institute is accredited by the NHSC.

NORTH LIGHT ART SCHOOL
9933 Alliance Road
Cincinnati, OH 45242-9990

(513) 984-0717

The North Light Art School is part of the same company that publishes *The Artist's Magazine* and *Writer's Digest Magazine,* and operates North Light Book Club and Writers Digest School.

Their home study course in art is called "Excellence in Art," and is aimed at the hobbyist who would like to learn more about art techniques and have her work evaluated by professional artists. The course is for those who would like to increase their ability; whether for enjoyment, personal pleasure, or to sell their art work.

The course must be completed within one year, and costs $390. A payment plan is available, and they accept VISA and MasterCard.

The course consists of five lessons, and the study guides for each are well-planned and printed in color. Studies include: Observation & Drawing, Form & Perspective, Color, Design & Composition, Materials, and a Marketing Handbook. A starter kit of art supplies is included: paper, pens and ink, brush, and pencils. Your work is sent to the school, where artist/teachers evaluate it and use a tissue paper overlay to demonstrate improvements to your picture. According to their brochure, "North Light's program will give you the understanding of how best to show and sell your work."

NORTHWEST SCHOOLS, INC.
1221 Northwest 21st Avenue
Portland, OR 97209

(800) 433-8978

Founded in 1946, Northwest Schools offer home study courses in:

Airline/Travel Career
Heavy Equipment Operator
Hotel/Motel Management

Resident training facilities for the Airline/Travel course are in Portland, OR and Phoenix, AZ. Heavy Equipment resident training is available in Portland, OR.

Northwest Schools is accredited by the National Home Study Council and is eligible for the Guaranteed Student Loan Program. Job placement assistance is available to graduates.

NRI SCHOOLS
McGraw-Hill Continuing Education Center
3939 Wisconsin Avenue, N.W.
Washington, DC 20016

(202) 244-1600

NRI Schools is a division of McGraw-Hill Continuing Education Center, listed in this directory. Courses available through home study are:
 Air Conditioning, Heating, and Refrigeration
 Appliance Servicing
 Bookkeeping
 TV–Audio Repair
 Microcomputer Repair
 Digital Electronics
 Basic Electronics
 Electrician's Training
 Automotive Servicing
 Building Construction
 Locksmithing
 Robotics
 Telephone Servicing
 Small Engine Repair
 Business Training
 Accounting
 Travel Career
 Paralegal Training

Their "School of Electronics" program offers sixteen courses, with costs ranging from $500 to $3,400. In the Microcomputer Course " . . . you actually build the Sanyo 880 Series Computer yourself, and perform demonstrations and experiments . . . you'll receive the NRI Discovery Lab, a professional hand-held digital multimeter, a digital logic probe, and several other tools and reference materials."

Their catalog advises, " . . . short-term learning isn't going to prepare you for a successful future . . . hands-on training is the only way to master all of the ins and outs of microcomputers." NRI is accredited by the National Home Study Council.

PACIFIC WESTERN UNIVERSITY
Career Training Institute
600 N. Sepulveda Boulevard
Los Angeles, CA 90049

(800) 423-3244

Pacific Western University is also a degree-granting institution; see their listing in that section of this book as well. Their Career Training Institute offers diploma and certificate programs by correspondence in:

    International Business Systems
    Small Business Management
    Nutrition Educator
    Fitness Educator
    Communications Specialist
        Modeling–Fashion Merchandising
        Public Relations
        Performing Arts
    Professional Accounting
        Professional Accountant
        Financial Manager
        Controller
        Cost Accountant
        Accounting Specialist
    Safety and Security Administration
        Security Management
        Fire Service Management
    Aviation Management
        Air Traffic Control
        Flight Attendant
        Travel Industry Management
    Community Services Counseling Specialist
        Gerontology Specialist
        Drug and Alcohol Abuse Specialist

All of Pacific Western's Career Training Institute courses are approved by the California Superintendent of Public Instruction. The Nutrition, Fitness, Alcohol Abuse, and Patient Relations courses are Approved for Resident or Correspondence Continuing Education by the California Board of Registered Nurses.

THE PARALEGAL INSTITUTE, INC.

2922 N. 35th Avenue, Suite 4
P.O. Drawer 11408
Phoenix, AZ 85061-1408

(602) 272-1855

The Paralegal Institute offers a Lawyer's Assistant Program with any two of the specialties listed: Litigation & Trial Practice, Business Organizations, Real Property, Criminal Law, Trusts, Wills & Estate Administration; Law Office Management; Domestic Relations; Bankruptcy; Torts. Students have up to two years to complete the program which costs $1,099. There are financing options available. The program satisfies the educational requirements necessary to take the C.L.A. (Certified Legal Assistant) exam for certification by the National Association of Legal Assistants. To enroll, you must be a high school graduate or have a G.E.D.

The Institute provides career placement assistance by making recommendations, writing letters, or making telephone calls to prospective employers that you have identified for them. They will recommend you to the county bar association anywhere in the U.S., and they maintain a school register for law firms to use.

As an example, listed below are the lessons covered in the Litigation and Trial Practice course:

Principles of Litigation
Lawyer and Client Relationships
Causes of Action, Remedies, and Defenses
Affirmative Defenses and Jurisdiction
Pleadings and Introduction to Federal Procedure
Additional Parties and Gathering Evidence
Investigation
Interrogatories, Expert Witnesses, and Oral Depositions
Uses of Oral Depositions at Trial
Preparation of Client for a Deposition, Medical Examination
    and Records, Inspection of and Copying
      Documents and Things
Requests for Admission Evidence

Trial Preparation, Fact Brief, Summary Judgments
Juries, Post Trial Motions, Judgment Appeals

The Paralegal Institute is accredited by the National Home
Study Council.

PARS TRAVEL COLLEGE

7310 Tiffany Springs Parkway
P.O. Box 901555
Kansas City, MO 64190-1555

(800) 821-7373

PARS Travel College offers a two-part course on selling travel and travel industry automation training.

PARS is a division of PARS Travel Information Systems, owned by Northwest Airlines and Trans World Airlines. They currently enroll seventy students. The course is in two phases. The first is eighteen home study lessons covering air fares, reservations, ticketing, geography, railroads, cruises, car rentals, international fares and ticketing, tours, and selling travel. Students complete this portion in three to six months. Then, after completing a final examination, they proceed to the second phase, a two-week resident training session at the headquarters in Kansas City. The resident training is a hands-on computer session relating to searching flight availability records, creating itineraries, modifying reservations, pricing itineraries, generating invoices and boarding passes, booking cars and hotels, and various other computer operations. The second phase of sixty-five hours of Automation and Sales training also includes five hours of career counseling and job search techniques. PARS does not promise a job, but they do place 86% of their graduates, half with airlines and half to other tourism-related fields such as travel agencies, tour operators, and cruise lines.

To enroll, you must be a high school graduate or equivalent. Costs are $1,995 for the eighteen home study lessons and the two weeks of Automation Training. This does not include your transportation or room and board while in the two-week session. They do accept VISA/MasterCard, and offer payment plans.

They currently report that demand for their graduates exceeds their supply in the job market.

PARS is accredited by the National Home Study Council.

PEOPLES COLLEGE OF INDEPENDENT STUDIES
2333 E. Spacecoast Parkway, Drawer 1768
Kissimmee, FL 32742-1768

Peoples College offers an Associate Degree in Travel and Tourism Management and a recreational course in Small Powerboat Handling and Seamanship.

The Associate Degree program in Travel and Tourism Management is targeted to travel school graduates and others working in the travel industry. The courses may be completed entirely at home and pick up where entry-level training leaves off. It is college-level work and designed to help travel industry employees prepare for management positions and career advancement.

Applicants must be eigheen years old, be a high school graduate or hold a G.E.D., and have a diploma from an accredited travel school or at least six months of verifiable experience within the travel industry.

Peoples College does not accept transfer credit, or offer exemption or advanced standing for any course, as they feel each course in the program is an integral part of the overall goal of the program. Students have a maximum of forty-eight months to complete the program. A minimum grade point of 1.0 on a 4.0 scale is required, along with a comprehensive examination.

Tuition is $3,490, which represents twenty to twenty-four courses, textbooks, and room and board for two three-day residency sessions. Several financial aid programs are available.

Small Powerboat Handling and Seamanship is a course designed to teach novice or advanced boaters the principles of seamanship and safe boating. According to Director William Watson, "In these days of increased recreational use of our waterways, we feel this course is of great practical value. Many states require formal boating training and insurance companies offer premium discounts on their boat policies for trained boaters. An interesting and unique aspect of this course is the optional hands-on classroom training aboard a 58' Hatteras motor yacht." The ten lessons include: Boating Basics, Controlling Your Powerboat, Leaving the Dock, Operating and

Handling Your Boat, Advanced Handling Techniques (night, rough water and rough weather), Maintaining Safety Afloat, Introduction to Piloting and Navigation (Locks and How to Go through Them, What to Do if You Run Aground), Fundamentals of Effective Anchoring, Approaching the Pier: Basic Docking Procedures, Basic Maintenance. After completion of the ten lessons, you have the opportunity to participate in hands-on training aboard a seagoing motor yacht for two days. The yacht has cruises embarking along the eastern U.S. coast, and the cost is additional.

Peoples College is accredited by the National Home Study Council.

POLICE SCIENCES INSTITUTE
Scranton, PA 18515

(717) 342-7701

The Police Sciences Institute is part of the North American Correspondence Schools, owned by the National Education Corporation, listed elsewhere in this book. The courses offered by the Police Sciences Institute are:

Police Science
Investigation

The Police Sciences Institute is accredited by the National Home Study Council.

THE ROUSE SCHOOL OF SPECIAL DETECTIVE TRAINING
3410-G West MacArthur Boulevard
Santa Ana, CA 92704

(714) 557-9892

The Rouse School offers training to the inexperienced student wishing to enter the private investigator field, as well as to the licensed investigator wanting to update his investigative techniques and knowledge. Courses are Basic and Advanced, and include learning about state-of-the-art investigative equipment.

Lessons and exams are written, but many projects and assignments are "hands-on" providing useful experience during the course.

The school is headed by its founder, Art Kassel, who has experience as a police officer and private investigator.

The program is accredited by the National Home Study Council.

SAINT MARY OF THE WOODS COLLEGE
Saint Mary of the Woods, Indiana 47876

(812) 535-5107

Saint Mary of the Woods College is the oldest Catholic liberal arts college for women in the U.S. They have developed home study programs specifically for women.

They offer a Paralegal Studies program that entails thirty credit hours and costs about $3,500. They also offer Translator Training in Spanish and French and a certificate program in Theology.

Saint Mary of the Woods College confers Associate's and Bachelor's degrees in a variety of fields; see their listing in the Academic Degree Programs section of this book.

SCHOOL OF MODERN MONTESSORI, LTD.
P.O. Box 51
London E11 1TD, England

This school offers the Course in Modern Montessori, enabling adults to learn the skills of teaching young children in the Montessori method.

This course is designed for parents, teachers, those wishing to help handicapped children, those interested in starting their own Montessori Class/School, or persons interested in working with young children in day care or preschools.

Dr. Maria Montessori was born in Italy in 1870, and was the first woman doctor in her country. She designed a method of early childhood education to meet the specific needs of the young child, which has become very popular throughout the world. The Montessori method involves carefully designed manipulative materials for children to work with independently.

The School of Modern Montessori attempts to bring the philosophy and ideas of Maria Montessori into the computer-oriented 1980s.

The course is divided into eight sections. Upon completion of a question paper at the end of each lesson, the student will be issued a diploma. The student's grade is marked on the diploma. The eight sections consist of study of the philosophy of Maria Montessori, child development, health and diet, discipline, exercises of practical life, sensorial material, reading, phonics, mathematics, arts and music.

Students may enroll at any time, and most finish the course within nine months.

Fees are less than $400 for 1988, but will vary depending upon the exchange rate between dollars and sterling. Payments must be made in sterling only, and can be made by postal orders.

SHEFFIELD SCHOOL OF INTERIOR DESIGN
211 East 43rd Street
New York, NY 10017

(212) 661-7270

Sheffield offers a home study course in Interior Design. It consists of thirty lessons; pre-recorded lessons on tape as well as in printed form, cassette-taped analysis of your projects recorded by instructors, and drafting and painting kits and supplies.

About 50% of Sheffield's graduates are "hobbyists" who took the course to decorate their own homes, or for personal satisfaction. About 50% find employment as freelance decorators either full- or part-time. The course includes information about how to set up your own decorating business.

Tuition is $528, and students have up to three years to complete the course.

SOUTHEASTERN ACADEMY, INC.
2333 E. Spacecoast Parkway, Drawer 1768
Kissimmee, FL 32742-1768

Specialized Airline/Travel Agency Program: Ten lessons completed at home and four weeks of training on campus. Graduates qualify for entry-level positions in the domestic airline and travel agency industries.

Comprehensive Airline/Travel Industry Program: Ten lessons completed at home and eight weeks of resident training, which includes basic travel skills, hotel and car rental procedures, travel markets, and typing.

Southeastern Academy is one of the oldest and largest airline/travel career schools. Since 1974, it has graduated approximately 20,000 students for employment with airlines, cruise lines, hotel, motels, travel agencies, car rental agencies, and related travel industry jobs. They offer four programs, two of which are home study-based. All students must complete the home-study portion before coming to the campus. The four to eight weeks of resident training is largely computer-based. Because the travel industry now is almost entirely automated, their training is heavily computer oriented. They train on the SABRE system.

They claim a very active placement department, with regular on-campus job interviews. Most of their students have at least one job interview or a firm job offer prior to graduation, according to the Director, William Watson.

Southeastern Academy is accredited by the National Association of Trade and Technical Schools and the National Home Study Council.

Students live on the thirty-one-acre campus during their four to eight week training session, and room and board is available. Financial aid is available through federal programs; Pell Grants and Guaranteed Student Loans are available for eligible students.

SOUTHERN CAREER INSTITUTE
P.O. Box 2158
Boca Raton, FL 33427

(407) 368-2522

Southern Career Institute is accredited by the National Home Study Council. They offer two areas of study:

Professional Photography Course
School of Paralegal Studies

The School of Paralegal Studies offers training for paralegal and legal assistant entry-level positions. It consists of twelve lessons, 330 hours of coursework, and examinations. The tuition is $895. The lessons consist of basic assignments, with supplemental assignments to be done as extra credit work if you wish to have more knowledge in a particular area of specialization. Projects and essays you do will form a Permanent Reference File, which you can use when looking for a job or later as a reference while on the job.

Advanced legal assistant programs are available to students who have worked as a paralegal for at least two years. Course work consists of 300 hours of study time, taking six months to a year to complete. Outside reading and use of law libraries are required. Advanced courses are:

Advanced Real Estate
Advanced Litigation Assistantship
Advanced Legal Research
Law Office Management

Graduates of the basic legal assistant program at Southern Career Institute are eligible to take the CLA (Certified Legal Assistant) exam for certification by the National Association of Legal Assistants.

STENOTYPE INSTITUTE OF JACKSONVILLE, INC.

500 9th Avenue, North
P.O. Box 50009
Jacksonville Beach, FL 32250

(904) 246-7466

Founded in 1940, the Stenotype Institute offers resident and home-study coursework to prepare for the career of court reporter. A student must have a high school diploma, with a 2.0 grade point average or better. If a prospective student has a G.E.D., they must take and pass a Stenotype Institute Entrance Exam. Previous business training is not necessary, but the ability to type by touch is strongly recommended.

The home study lessons include dictation material on cassette tapes, which must be transcribed to the typewriter and returned to the school for grading. The course includes speed-building exercises which are tested. For these tests, the student must type from fresh material for five minutes, and have the completion time certified by a Notary Public.

The home study and the resident student must both complete 100 hours of internship. If the home study student is not acquainted with a court reporter with whom he can "sit in," the Institute will make arrangements for the home study student to meet a court reporter in the student's local area.

The home study course in Court Reporting takes 3,900 hours of study and costs $4,995. A stenotype machine, tripod, cassette tape player, and typewriter are also required. A stenotype machine and tripod costs between $650–885 from the Stenotype Institute. Resident students' average completion time is twenty-four to thirty months.

According to their information, the Institute was founded in 1940, and " . . . continues to offer a much-in-demand and well-paid occupation to people who have the brains and determination to become skilled at machine shorthand — the foundation for a career in verbatim court and convention reporting." To graduate, a student must successfully pass a 225 word-per-minute dictation test with minimal inaccuracy.

Plans are in progress to incorporate videotapes of classroom teaching into the home study course. Computers are now being used to adapt to instant stenotype transcription.

If you are bright, like to type, and are looking for a career with salary ranging from $18,000-$75,000 per year, court reporting might be your future. It's the type of field where you can choose where you want to live, and can work part-time or even go freelance when your skills warrant it.

The Stenotype Institute is accredited by the National Home Study Council.

SUPERIOR TRAINING SERVICES
1817 N. 7th Street, Suite 150
P.O. Box 33157
Phoenix, AZ 85006

(602) 234-1970

Heavy Equipment Operator Course
Diesel Semi-Truck Driver Course

Superior offers a combination home study–resident course in both truck driving and heavy equipment operation. Their administrative offices are in Phoenix, but their driving sites are located across the country: Ninevah, IN; Indianapolis, IN; Apache Junction, AZ; Phoenix, AZ; Rialto, CA; Levittown, PA; Grand Prairie, TX; Houston, TX; Posen, IL.

Both courses are designed to provide the necessary information and skills necessary to obtain employment in the trucking or construction industry. The semi-truck driving course provides the training required for the occupation "Tractor Trailer Truck Driver" as defined by the U.S. Department of Labor Statistics (D.O.T. Code 904.883). Superior also offers advanced courses in both heavy equipment and diesel truck driving. The advanced courses prepare students to own and operate their own equipment and run a small business in the industry.

The basic training courses consist of thirty-six lessons for the truck driving and forty lessons for the equipment operation course, which are completed at home and mailed to the school. The student must also pass a test and maintain an overall score of 80% for the driver course and 75% for the equipment operator course before moving to the second phase of training, which is a three-week stint at a training grounds. At the training ground, the student receives additional classroom lessons, along with 125 hours of driving experience.

"Conditioned response" is the method of instruction used at the school training grounds. It is a practical, step-by-step method, where the student is required to master each step until it becomes automatic before he moves onto the next skill level. They work at having skillful operation become a habit rather than something the driver has to think about first.

Typical training equipment includes diesel tractors with various speed transmissions and different sizes and lengths of trailers. Heavy equipment operators work on back-hoe front end loaders; crawler-dozers (equipped with blades); and self-propelled scrapers. All equipment is typical of what's in use in the industry. The heavy equipment operator course also includes basic fundamentals of surveying; how to use surveying equipment; understanding the use of grade stakes; and how to lay out work projects.

Entrance requirements include being over twenty-one years of age for truck drivers, and over eighteen for equipment operators. Applicants for the truck driver training program must pass the Department of Transportation physical examination, must possess a valid motor vehicle operator's license, and must provide a copy of the past three years of driving record from the licensing agency in the student's state of residence before reporting for Resident Training. A reading test including simple math problems is required of each student enrolling in the truck driver training program. A general aptitude test is required of students enrolling in the heavy equipment operator program. There are no exceptions to the aptitude tests, as they are used to determine if the applicant has the ability to comprehend the training programs. After reviewing the tests, I concluded that one must have some background in driving and knowledge of engines and how they work, to pass the truck driving test. The heavy equipment operator's test was harder for me, as I have little knowledge of camshafts, lag screws, or types of wrenches or gears. Obviously, someone interested in mechanical/industrial equipment would already have the background and knowledge sufficient to pass the tests.

Students have one year in which to complete the course including the hands-on training. Students who do not have a satisfactory grade-point average will not be allowed to continue to the second phase of driver training. All programs include job placement assistance.

Costs are $2,295 for Basic Truck Driving Course, $2,595 for Advanced Truck Driving Course, $2,495 for Basic Heavy Equipment Operators Course, $2,795 for Advanced Heavy Equipment Operators Course. Superior has a variety of financial aid programs including Pell Grants and assistance from the

Bureau of Indian Affairs, Bureau of Vocational Rehabilitation, Trade Readjustment Act, and J.P.T.A. They are accredited by the National Home Study Council.

TRUCK MARKETING INSTITUTE

P.O. Box 5000
Carpinteria, CA 93011-5000

The Truck Marketing Institute specializes in courses designed to sell light- to heavy-duty trucks. Their Precision Truck Selling Courses are:

Course II — Light/Medium Duty Models, costs $175
Course III — Heavy-duty Class 8 Models, costs $371
Course IV — Class 6–7 Diesel Models, costs $180

Course completion time is about twelve months per course. "TMI courses have been used by the truck manufacturers, allied industries and fleets since 1965," according to their information. Truck Marketing Institute was founded in 1964 to provide "specialized training services for the motor truck industry."

Many students at TMI have their training costs paid for by their employers to keep them current with particular model specifications.

TMI is accredited by the National Home Study Council. New courses are developed and offered with manufacturer cooperation. As their brochure states, TMI's primary education goal is, " . . . developing professionalism in those who sell, lease or buy trucks."

UNIVERSITY OF CALIFORNIA EXTENSION
Department B
2223 Fulton Street
Berkeley, CA 94720

I'll bet you didn't know that you can study with UC Berkeley professors, for college credit, in the comfort of your own home! I was delighted to discover their catalog of offerings through their "Lifelong Learning" department. UC Extension is really innovative in their approach to home study courses. Write for a copy of their free catalog. Many of the courses are offered for college credit, and you can transfer those credits into degree programs at other colleges. (Of course check this out with the school you plan to get the degree from.)

The variety of courses is exciting. If you are looking for something challenging, you might want to enroll in Elementary Modern Icelandic Language, Individual Study in Art (you design your own project), Folklore in America, or even Childbirth Education. They also offer most of their course materials for purchase without enrollment. These materials can be useful for students not needing the coursework for a grade or college credit. Prices for the materials, which include a syllabus, supplementary reading materials, and often tapes and study guides, range from $20-75. Ideal for teachers looking for additional curriculum materials.

Some of the programs available include:

Citizenship: UC Extension offers a course in U.S. citizenship in cooperation with the U.S. Immigration and Naturalization Service. This correspondence course is for persons who plan to become citizens of the U.S. The course is intended for those who cannot attend Americanization classes, or who prefer to study by correspondence. The course fee is $30 and is not refundable. Write for application materials.

Structural Pest Management: Coursework to assist in obtaining a Pest Control Operator's License in the state of California. "The Structural Pest Control Board, California Department of Consumer Affairs, contracted with Independent Study, UC Extension, to develop this series of three correspondence courses to assist members of the pest control industry in satisfying the Board's educational requirements. The courses meet the educational requirements for both the field representative's and operator's licenses. Contact UC Extension for information. $220 per course, plus textbook.

Real Estate License for Salesman or Broker (California): License course work is available. The course, Principles of Real Estate, is three semester credits, and costs $210 plus $38 for the textbook. Check with your state's Department of Real Estate Licensing to see if they will accept this course from UC. Most states also require a licensing exam after completion of required course work.

Professional Manuscript Reading Services: Experienced writers can now take advantage of UC's manuscript reading service. Several writing courses offer this option:

Short Story Writing — for children's literature and short story writers and novelists

Poetry Writing — for poets

Individual Projects in Advanced Writing — for nonfiction writers and writers in the professions

Through this service, you may submit three short stories or chapters of a novel. The manuscript will be edited in detail, with consideration not only of structure and style, but of content and plot. Course fees range from $185–215.

USA TRAINING ACADEMY, INC.

955 South Chapel Street
P.O. Box 9439
Newark, DE 19714

(800) 441-7766

USA Training Academy was founded in 1969 and offers a combination of home study and resident training to those wanting to enter the truck transport industry. They have sales offices in twenty-two states.

The secretarial division is patterned after the truck transport training division, utilizing both home study and resident training.

USA Training's program is accredited by the National Home Study Council.

WESTLAWN SCHOOL OF YACHT DESIGN
733 Summer Street
Stamford, CT 06904

Westlawn School offers a course in Yacht and Small Boat Design. Their program is accredited by the National Home Study Council.

WILMA BOYD CAREER SCHOOLS, INC.
One Chatham Center
Pittsburgh, PA 15219

(412) 456-1800

The Wilma Boyd Career Schools, Inc. offer a course for those interested in working in the travel industry. Called "Travel Lab," the course consists of ten lessons and takes six to sixteen months to complete. Cost is $1,945 for the home study program. For an additional $715, students may come to the training center for an additional four-week resident training session. Financial aid is available.

"The Travel Lab Program prepares you for entry-level positions such as reservationist, ticket agent, travel counselor, car rental agent or airline secretary," according to their catalog.

The Wilma Boyd Career School was founded in 1968, and is accredited by the National Home Study Council, the National Association of Trade and Technical Schools, and the Association of Independent Colleges and Schools.

WRITER'S DIGEST SCHOOL
9933 Alliance Road
Cincinnati, OH 45242

(513) 531-2222

Courses:

Short Story Writing — $249
Novel Writing Workshop — $349
Article Writing — $249

The program goals include enabling the student to sell their work to book and magazine publishers. Lessons include approximately thirty writing assignments, including a complete article or short story that will be written for a specific magazine, seeking publication. The Writer's Digest School is part of Writer's Digest Books, and students receive a 10% discount on all books or magazines purchased through the School. Students also receive issues of the *WDS Forum*, a publication for students and faculty, filled with current students' successful publications and writing sales, as well as informative articles about writing.

Instructors at WDS are all published professional writers, and you will receive their critiques of your work. The School graduates between 1,000 and 1,200 students each year.

Writer's Digest School is affiliated with the North Light Art School, North Light Books, and Writer's Digest Books.

WRITER'S INSTITUTE

Newspaper Institute of America
112 W. Boston Post Road
Mamaroneck, NY 10543

The Writer's Institute has been operating since 1925. They offer courses in:

Journalism
Fiction Writing
Nonfiction Writing
Script Writing
Poetry

Prospective students are asked to fill out an aptitude test before enrollment materials are mailed to them. The school stresses the possibility of your future "writing for profit" in their brochures.

Writer's Institute is accredited by the National Home Study Council.

Section IV

Academic Degree Programs

THE AMERICAN COLLEGE
GRADUATE STUDIES DEPARTMENT
270 Bryn Mawr Avenue
Bryn Mawr, PA 19010

(215) 896-4554

The American College offers graduate degrees through off-campus study. Degrees available:

Master of Science in Financial Services
Master of Science in Management

Applicants must have a Bachelor's degree or recognized professional designation. They do not give you advanced standing for prior life and work experience. They will accept up to nine credits for previous graduate work done at other institutions.

The American College program is accredited by the Middle States Association of Colleges and Schools.

Tuition costs run about $5,000–6,000 depending upon your study program. Students complete their degree program through self-study or by taking formal classes in their local communities. Credit is awarded following the national exams offered in January and June each year.

A two-week residency program on campus is required.

AMERICAN OPEN UNIVERSITY OF NEW YORK INSTITUTE OF TECHNOLOGY
Central Islip, NY 11722

(800) 222-6948

NYIT offers Bachelor of Science degrees in: Business Administration with a Management option; General Studies; Behavioral Science, with options in Psychology, Sociology, Criminal Justice, and Community Mental Health.

NYIT offers 122 courses, both upper and lower levels. The general categories of courses are: Behavioral Science, Business, English, Mathematics, Sciences/Physics, Social Sciences, and Technology. They offer the full range of student services including academic counseling, financial aid, and prior learning credit assessment. Students with a home computer and modem can use tele-conferencing to communicate with instructors. Other students may use ordinary correspondence methods.

American Open is accredited by the Middle States Association of Colleges and Schools and registered with the New York State Education Department.

A maximum of sixty credit hours can be earned through proficiency exams, assessment of job-related training, and assessment of your previous experiences. Credit can also be transferred in from accredited colleges. A minimum of thirty credit hours must be taken with American Open to complete a degree.

Tuition is $85 per credit hour. Computer Conferencing is an additional $25 per course. There are also fees for assessing your prior experiences and transferring in other college credits. Financial aid is available in the form of federal grants, loans, and veterans' benefits.

You must already hold a high school diploma or G.E.D. before acceptance. "The program is an academically rigorous and challenging one for mature adults who want to learn outside of the traditional college campus system. Because it enables adults to package all their prior and current learning experiences, our program is now the most extensive external degree program in America," according to American Open.

A few examples of the wide range of courses offered include:

Introduction to Criminal Investigation and Forensic Science
Theories of Personality
Occupational Psychology
Behavioral Sciences in Marketing
Commercial Banking
Corporate Finance
Technical Writing
Engineering Mathematics
Comparative Governments
Computer Conferencing

ANTIOCH UNIVERSITY
Continuing and International Education
Yellow Springs, Ohio 45387

For the past decade, the Individualized Master of Arts program offered by Antioch University has given adults the opportunity to combine theoretical studies with practical experience in their chosen fields of study. The program has two parts: you identify two experts in your field who will serve as your Degree Committee — working with them, you create your own Degree Plan. By working with professionals in your field, you will make networking contacts. You will then implement your Degree Plan; and finally, research and write your Master's Thesis.

Sixty quarter-credit hours are required to earn the degree. Up to fifteen credits of prior learning may be transferred into the program. These may be from prior course work or life experience. The minimum time for degree completion is fifteen months. The maximum time is thirty-nine months. Most students complete it in twenty-four to twenty-six months.

As a part of the program, students attend two brief seminars, an orientation in Yellow Springs, and a research seminar. They are scheduled from Thursday evening through Tuesday noon.

Applicants must have a bachelor's degree from an accredited college. If the bachelor's degree is earned at an unaccredited school, Provisional Status may be granted. Students with extensive prior experience and learning, but without a bachelor's degree, may also qualify for Provisional Status. Upon the school's approval of your Degree Plan, your status converts to that of a regular student, however, Provisional students are not eligible to apply for prior learning credits toward their degree at Antioch.

Students don't actually take courses from Antioch. After planning your study route, you use up to $2,600 of your tuition to pay for academic expenses such as courses, independent studies, workshops, etc., that you may take anywhere.

Antioch University is accredited by the Commission on Institutions of Higher Education of the North Central Association of Colleges and Schools.

The tuition is $9,250, payable in five payments. A variety of financial aid is available.

"Since its founding in 1852 by educational leader Horace Mann, Antioch has combined superior academic standards with learning innovations." (from their catalog)

CALIFORNIA COAST UNIVERSITY

700 North Main Street
P.O. Box 11745
Santa Ana, CA 92700-9990

(800) 854-8768

Bachelor of Science:
Business Administration
Management
Engineering
Psychology

Master of Science:
Engineering
Psychology

Master of Business Administration

Ph.D.:
Business Administration
Management
Engineering
Psychology

Ed.D.:
Education

The programs at California Coast University are aimed at mid-career adults who are seeking an accelerated degree program. Prior education and experience are evaluated toward your degree program, and any courses you need to take are made up through Study Guides based upon a particular textbook. You must pass an examination for each Study Guide program.

California Coast's policy regarding prior learning experience follows.

"After a student is enrolled, all acceptable previous college course work on transcript is transferred into a student's program. All non-college experience is reviewed to determine if the individual has adequate experience to justify the University providing an opportunity for the student to take a 'Challenge Examination' which will then objectively demonstrate whether the experience produced an acceptable level of competence in each specific course required in the 'Degree Program.' "

Course work is completed by either transferring in previously earned college credits, taking challenge examinations, or completing study guides with final examinations.

All students do research, which may relate to the student's career or work experience.

- Bachelor's Degree students write a Research Project
- Master's Degree students write a Thesis
- Doctoral Degree students write a Dissertation

A concurrent Bachelor's/Master's program is available to those who have earned sixty semester credits in college and have a minimum of five years of work experience related to the major field of study. A concurrent Master's/Doctoral program is also available to students with a Bachelor's degree and seven years of work-related experience.

Costs range from $2,075 for a Bachelor's degree to $2,675 for a Ph.D. Degree programs taken concurrently such as B.S./M.B.A. combined, cost $2,575. Liberal tuition payment plans do not include interest charges on the unpaid tuition balance.

CALIFORNIA COLLEGE FOR HEALTH SCIENCES
222 West 24th Street
National City, CA 92050

(800) 221-7374

Health professional training in:
    Pulmonary Function Technology Program
    Respiratory Therapist Program
    Respiratory Technician
    Blood Gas Technology Program
    Associate in Applied Science Degree
    Hyperbaric Oxygen Therapy Training
    Pulmonary Function Technology
    Bachelor Degree (B.S.)
    Master Degree (MBA, MPA)

CCHS was founded in 1977 to provide home study opportunities for adults working in the health care professions. Over 14,000 respiratory care practitioners have enrolled in their programs, with over 5,000 graduates to date. The school newsletter, *Pneumon News,* is sent to all students and alumni.

Applicants must have a high school diploma or G.E.D. and must also verify employment in the respiratory care field. You must be employed in a position associated with respiratory care under medical direction. Therapist applicants must verify graduation from an AMA-approved technician level program, or be certified, or qualify for advanced standing at CCHS through taking exams.

During the course of study, all students must spend twenty hours of observation (technician programs) or hands-on experience (therapist programs) in each of the following specialty areas: Pediatrics, Neonatal ICU, Pulmonary Function Testing. Prior to graduation, therapist program students must pass a final clinical simulation examination. The Entry-Level (Technician) Program, and the Advanced Practitioner (Therapist) Program, are both Respiratory Therapy Programs recognized by the Joint Review Committee for Respiratory Therapy Education. These programs lead to certification or registry eligibility with the National Board for Respiratory Care (NBRC).

Costs vary: Entry-Level Technician Program — $1,400; Respiratory Therapist Program, $1,300; Pulmonary Function Technologist Program — $850; Blood Gas Technology Certificate Program — $185. All programs require additional textbooks which students may purchase or find in hospital libraries.

CCHS also offers degree programs. The Associate Degree may be earned along with the certificate of Advanced Practitioner (Therapist) Program. The Bachelor's and Master's programs are offered in cooperation with City University in Bellevue, WA. City University is a regionally accredited school, and there are no on-campus requirements. California College serves as a registration center. Contact California College, or see the listing for City University in this book. Degrees available through their joint effort include Bachelor's degrees in: Health Care Administration, Management Specialty, Business Administration, Individual Financial Planning, Accounting, Law Enforcement Administration, Fire Command Administration, Shipyard Management, Accelerated Programs, Telecommunications Management, General Studies.

Master of Business Administration Degrees are offered in: Health Care Administration, Business Administration, Individual Financial Planning, Information Systems, Technology/Engineering Management, Telecommunications Management.

Master of Public Administration is available in the areas of: Public Administration (General), Fire Command Administration, and a combined MBA/MPA.

Financial aid is available in the form of tuition payment plans, student loans, and scholarships. CCHS encourages students to apply for scholarships from the American Respiratory Therapy Foundation as well as their employer. For more information about the available scholarships, or the field of respiratory therapy, contact:

American Respiratory Therapy Foundation
1720 Regal Row
Dallas, TX 75235

California College for Health Sciences is accredited by the National Home Study Council and the American Medical Association.

CALIFORNIA PACIFIC UNIVERSITY
10721 Treena Street, Room 114
San Diego, CA 92131-1074

(619) 695-3292

California Pacific University is a professional school of business and management. The following programs are available through home study, and are approved by the California Department of Education. CPU is not accredited, but it is an alternative for people with some business experience as well as previous college coursework. Degree programs are:

Bachelor of Business Administration
Master's of Business Administration
Master's of Arts in Management and Human Behavior

Students proceed through their courses one at a time, building upon their past experiences as well as applying their learning to their present careers. Students wishing to accelerate their progress may complete the program within twelve months. All students pursuing a Bachelor's degree at CPU must earn forty-five credits (quarter hours) of academic credit during enrollment with CPU — this is a minimum of nine courses.

Admission to the MBA (Master's of Business Administration) program requires a bachelor's degree from a recognized college or university. Students whose undergraduate degrees are not in business are required to have business-related work experience. A pre-admission course in business topics is available to those students without the academic background in business subjects. A maximum of three courses may be transferred into the degree program from other colleges. All MBA candidates are required to complete sixty quarter hours of graduate level courses.

Courses at CPU are taught with Study Guides, written by the CPU faculty to accompany textbooks by recognized authorities in their fields. Students study one course at a time, sending written lessons to the faculty for grading.

Costs for each degree program are $2,400, with monthly payment plans and loans available. A comment from their catalog, "Students . . . always may seek advice, however trivial,

CALIFORNIA STATE UNIVERSITY AT DOMINGUEZ HILLS

External Degree Program — Humanities
1000 East Victoria Street
Carson, California 90747

Bachelor of Arts in Humanities
Master of Arts in Humanities

California State University, Dominguez Hills offers the B.A. program to those who have completed lower division general education courses already; the M.A. program is complete in itself. Both programs include course work in history, music, art, philosophy, and literature.

Admission to the Master's program requires a Baccalaureate degree from a regionally accredited college or university and a 2.5 GPA. A maximum of nine semester units completed at other colleges may be applied toward the program, with approval.

Cost is $90 per semester unit.

California State University, Dominguez Hills, is accredited by the Western Association of Schools and Colleges.

CALIFORNIA UNIVERSITY FOR ADVANCED STUDIES

331 Keller Street
Petaluma, CA 94952

(707) 762-9200

Bachelor of Arts, Bachelor of Science in Management
Master of Arts or Master of Science in Management
Master of Business Administration
Ph.D. in Management
D.Man. in Management (doctoral degree)

These degree programs are designed for people with experience in the field of general management. No restrictions are made on the area of experience, but there are requirements relating to the quality and level of experience. The school wants to create managers with solid pragmatic management expertise, and values actual experience rather than a purely academic managerial "expert." One of the University's basic philosophies is, "To provide the graduate with a sense of moral orientation and societal obligation through the study and application of humanitarian and ethical concepts."

A "Career Accomplishment Project" may be done in place of a thesis, and can be based on previously accomplished work or upon a project you have currently underway. There are no required classes, instruction is done within the context of the project, documenting your administrative skills related to your career field, and setting professional goals for yourself. The school is international, and you may complete the program living abroad. All instruction is in English. Costs range from $3,100 for a Bachelor's degree, $3,500 for a Master's and $3,950 for a Doctorate. Cost of required textbooks is included in the tuition price. Payment plans are available.

University-prepared exams for each course are included. Academic credit may be granted for management-related career and life experiences. You may be able to complete degree requirements within one academic year (nine months).

To participate, you must send them a resumé, and they will determine your eligibility for the program.

CENTER FOR MUSEUM STUDIES
The Museum Field Study Program
John F. Kennedy University
1500 Sixteenth Street
San Francisco, CA 94103

(415) 552-3105

The Center for Museum Studies offers a Master's of Arts in Museum Studies. The institution is accredited by the Western Association of Schools and Colleges.

Field Study students must be working in a museum in either a paid or volunteer capacity, and have three to five years of museum experience. When applying they must submit a current work sample appropriate to their career goals.

Six credits of prior college coursework may be transferred from another institution.

The program involves two three-week summer sessions in San Francisco; one during the summer after the four core classes are completed, and the other prior to the student's final project. The summer sessions involve seminars and visits to museums in the San Francisco area.

The tuition cost is $142 per unit.

CENTRAL MICHIGAN UNIVERSITY
Institute for Personal and Career Development
Mount Pleasant, MI 48859

(517) 774-4464

Central Michigan University is fully accredited and offers graduate programs in the following:

Master of Science in Administration
Master of Arts in Education, with concentration
in Community College Education

Applicants must have a bachelor's degree with a 2.5 grade point average or 2.7 in their last sixty hours of class work. Students may be awarded advanced standing after their portfolio is evaluated by the faculty, who may award up to ten hours of credit for prior learning.

Classes are scheduled for short time periods at locations in the eastern and midwestern U.S. and Hawaii. They also offer independent study and other avenues for obtaining credit.

Costs are $133 per semester hour for classes; $20 per credit hour for experiential learning credit recorded.

CENTURY UNIVERSITY
9100 Wilshire Blvd.
Beverly Hills, CA 90212

(213) 278-1094

Bachelor of Arts, Bachelor of Science
Master of Arts, Master of Science
Doctor of Business Administration
Ph.D.
Ed.D. Education Doctorate
D.Sc. Doctorate of Science in Engineering

Programs may not be completed in less than nine months; no maximum time limit. Requirements for admission to the Bachelor's degree program include five years of occupational experience in a degree-related career field, and an Associate degree, or sixty units from a college or university covering general education requirements. If you have not taken the sixty units, you may take the General Education Requirement examination.

Requirements for admission to the Master's program include five years of occupational experience in a field related to a degree program listed in the curriculum of Century University, and a Bachelor's degree from a four-year college or university.

Admission requirements for the Doctoral degree program include five years of related work experience; a Master's degree in the same field as the Doctoral program; and a tentative rationale outlining the reasons for starting the Doctoral program, your goals, and the benefits you will realize by completing the program.

Degree programs are designed around four phases: the initial subject area examination required of all Bachelor and Master program applicants upon enrollment; the creation of a study plan; the proposal for a final project; and the last phase — the final examination. The final project can be satisfied with a variety of options, including term paper, research project, thesis, or final examination.

Graduation exercises are held each June.

Century's program emphasizes the student's career and

workplace as a learning "laboratory." Your work environment is the place of learning, and your study plan involves aspects of your job.

Tuition is based upon one fee for the entire program. Bachelor Degree — $2,395; Master Degree — $2,595; Doctoral Degree — $3,295. They also offer concurrent Bachelor/Master programs at $2,995, and Master/Doctorate programs — $3,595.

Interestingly, participation in the Alumni Association of Century University is required for the first year following graduation. This involves a $50 contribution. Contributions to the Alumni Association after the first year are voluntary.

CITY UNIVERSITY
16661 Northup Way
Bellevue, WA 98008

(800) 426-5596

City University offers the following degree programs through their Distance Learning program:

Bachelor of Science in the following areas:
Accounting
Business Administration
Fire Command Administration
Health Care Administration
Individual Financial Planning
Law Enforcement Administration
Management Specialty
Shipyard Management
Telecommunications Management
General Studies

Master of Arts in Applied Behavioral Sciences

Master of Business Administration in the following areas:
General
Health Care Administration
Individual Financial Planning
Information Systems
Technology/Engineering Management
Telecommunications Management

Master of Public Administration in the following areas:
General
Fire Command
Combined MPA/MBA

City University is accredited by Northwest Association of Schools and Colleges. It has a resident campus in the Seattle area, and holds classes in the Pacific Northwest, British Columbia, and Zurich, Switzerland. City University has an open admission policy for undergraduates, admitting anyone eighteen years of age or older who can benefit from college education. The Master's programs require a Bachelor's degree from an accredited institution or certain professional designations. They accept some transfer credits from other institutions and award credit for prior life experience.

Distance Learning courses must be completed within eleven weeks. A research paper is required, as well as mid-term and final exams taken in a proctored setting. Students can use traditional correspondence methods, as well as electronic mail networks. Students with home computers can send assignments and communicate with instructors via "Computer Mail" for a $25 electronic network access fee.

Tuition for a five-credit undergraduate course is $465; a three-credit graduate course is $390. Financial aid and veteran's benefits are available.

COLUMBIA PACIFIC UNIVERSITY
1415 Third Street
San Rafael, CA 94901

(415) 459-1650

Bachelor of Arts
Bachelor of Science
Master of Arts
Master of Science
Master of Business Administration
Ph.D.
Ed.D. (education)
D.Sc. (science)
J.D. (Doctor of Jurisprudence: law degree)
D.C.D. (Doctorate of Communication Disorders)

Established in 1978, Columbia Pacific is now the largest non-resident graduate university in the U.S., with over 5,600 students and 600 faculty. CPU has recently received Full Institutional Approval as a degree-granting institution from the California State Department of Education.

The purpose of Columbia Pacific University is to: "provide higher education with a wholistic emphasis for already-accomplished individuals whose goals are to obtain undergraduate or graduate degrees in Arts and Sciences, Administration and Management, Health and Human Services, or International Law."

CPU will give credit for your previous life and work experiences. You can also use previous work to satisfy the graduation requirements and apply toward your project requirements.

Each student presents an Independent Study Project, which demonstrates that the student has achieved a certain standard of knowledge and ability. The student develops the Project with the assistance of a Faculty Mentor who has an advanced degree in the student's field.

At the Bachelor's level, the project demonstrates a breadth of knowledge of the field; at the Master's level, it shows a mastery of some aspect of the field as applied to real-life situations, and at the Doctoral level, it represents innovation or creative, scholarly research. It is called a Project, because "the appropriate knowledge and skills may be demonstrated in ways other than writing a traditional thesis: for a business executive, it could be a business plan; for a writer, a book; and so on. Work already completed as part of one's life or career experience may form the basis for satisfying the project." The amount of new work required to complete the Project and the degree program depend on the student's prior work and the skills the student has acquired. There are no required classes or courses. Instruction is accomplished through supervised independent study with the guidance of a supportive Faculty Mentor.

Costs range from $3,000 for a B.A., $3,200 for a Doctorate, to $5,000 for the J.D. (law degree). There are several payment plans available.

The faculty list at Columbia Pacific is quite impressive, and their President, Richard Crews, M.D. (Harvard) has a distinguished academic background. The CPU degree is reportedly widely accepted in business and government. For example, such major corporations as the American Broadcasting Companies, Blue Cross-Blue Shield, the National Broadcasting Company, and Xerox have provided tuition assistance for their employees or recognized the CPU degree for employee promotion. Similar acceptance has been found with the United States Department of Education, the United States Coast Guard (Dept. of Transportation), and the government of Quebec, Canada (Department of Indian Affairs).

FIELDING INSTITUTE
2112 Santa Barbara Street
Santa Barbara, CA 93105

(805) 687-1009

The Fielding Institute offers the following degree programs for non-residents:

M.A., Ph.D., and Psy.D. in Psychology, with emphasis in Clinical Psychology, Counseling Psychology, or Organizational Psychology

M.A., Ph.D., Ed.D., and D.H.S. (Doctor of Human Services) in Human and Organization Development, with emphasis on Systems Theory, Human Services Management, Gerontological Services, Adult and Continuing Education, and Human Resource Development

Fielding is accredited by the Western Association of Schools and Colleges. They currently enroll over 400 students in Psychology and over 150 in Human Development.

Applicants are generally mid-career, mid-life adults with Bachelor's or Master's degrees. Most students are seeking to improve themselves in their current career. Students are given no academic credit for previous learning or experience.

A five-day Admissions Workshop in Santa Barbara is required before entering. Classes and workshops are held in many cities across the U.S. Students' study program involves a learning contract based on competency assessments in knowledge areas and a dissertation. In the field of Psychology, training and supervised work experience are also required.

Costs average $1,680 per quarter; $6,750 per year.

ICS CENTER FOR DEGREE STUDIES
Scranton, PA 18515

(717) 342-7701

A division of the National Education Corporation, which also operates International Correspondence Schools (see listing under Career and Certificate Programs), the Center for Degree Studies offers Associate Degree programs in:

Business Management
Accounting
Mechanical Engineering
Civil Engineering
Electrical Engineering
Electronics
Marketing
Finance

Over 40,000 students have been enrolled in programs leading to the Associate degree at CDS. To enroll, you must be a high school graduate or hold a G.E.D. Certificate. Some advanced standing may be granted to students who have completed comparable work from accredited institutions, or who have life/ work experience.

The degree program focuses on the discipline selected, but all students must take Math and Communications. In the third and fourth semesters you may select from a list of elective courses such as Contemporary Art, Ecology, Human Behavior, Introduction to Literature, Political Philosophy, and Man in the Twentieth Century.

As an example, the Associate of Business Degree program requires the use of a personal computer (16K memory) that is included in the fee, plus lessons on how to use it, and a disk drive and software, as well as a dot matrix printer. (All included in tuition.) Coursework for the four semesters includes: Business Math, Designing a BASIC Computer Program, Accounting, Business Law, Cost Accounting, Federal Taxation, Use of Computer Software, and others. Cost of the program is $689–$889 per semester, with a four-semester total of $3,056. The programs are approved for veterans' educational benefits, and CDS offers monthly payment plans.

ICS is accredited by the National Home Study Council.

INTERNATIONAL INSTITUTE FOR ADVANCED STUDIES

8000 Bonhomme Avenue, Suite 403
Clayton, MO 63105

(314) 725-6068

The International Institute for Advanced Studies offers the following graduate degree programs:

Master of Arts
Master of Science
Master of Business Administration
Ph.D. (Doctorate of Philosophy)
Ed.D. (Education Doctorate)
Sc.D. (Science Doctorate)
D.A. (Doctorate of Arts)

They offer no Bachelor's degree programs. A thesis is required of all Master's degree candidates and a dissertation of all Doctoral candidates.

Founded in 1973, it was one of the first non-traditional graduate institutions in the U.S. It is a non-profit post-graduate institution dedicated to independent study and research.

The Institute was founded by Alexander Niven, who served as President for the last fifteen years. This year Dr. John Bear, author of *Bear's Guide to Non-Traditional College Degrees*, took over as President of the Institute.

The following is excerpted from their catalog:

"The Institute has developed standards for what the holder of any given degree should know. The learning and qualifications of each applicant (whether acquired in academic settings, or through career and life experience learning) are matched against these standards. Any and all 'gaps' will be filled in by completion of faculty-guided tutorials, offered through correspondence study. When the gaps are filled and the thesis or dissertation completed, the degree is awarded. While work may be done in many academic fields, the Institute especially respects, supports and encourages work related to improving conditions of people, whether on a local, regional, or global level."

The Institute enables those who cannot otherwise achieve a higher degree because of barriers such as age, finances, residence, non-transferability of credits, etc., to continue or conclude independent academic work leading to an original contribution in an academic field and an advanced degree.

The Institute grants external degrees for submission of a thesis *after* successful conclusion of study or research undertaken at a university in the candidate's geographic area. It is a non-teaching institution, acting as a liaison between students and selected university professors who guide and evaluate the student's research. The student's academic adviser must confirm his/her competency and the professor's signature appears on the diploma to attest to the validity of the candidate's effort.

The total cost of a Master's degree is $1,800. Doctoral programs cost $2,400. Installment payment plans are available. Average completion time is twelve to fourteen months, but it can be less or more depending on previous academic credit. Fees do not include the cost of textbooks.

No advanced degree study is offered in the fields of medicine, dentistry, or law.

The Institute also offers an Office of Writing Support Services to help students with their academic writing. Three types of service are available:

1. Light editing (spelling and grammar)

2. Heavy editing (spelling and grammar, content, style, adherence to academic format)

3. Individualized writing assistance (for each step of the writing process from development to final draft)

The first two services are included in tuition fees. The third, individual assistance, is available at an hourly rate.

Offering additional assistance with writing should benefit many correspondence students, who are unaccustomed to doing the amount of writing necessary in correspondence work.

JOHN F. KENNEDY UNIVERSITY
Field Studies Program
Career Development Graduate Program
School of Management
12 Altarinda Road
Orinda, CA 94563

(415) 254-0200, Ext. 10

JFK University offers a Master's of Arts in Career Development, and a Post-Master's Certificate program.

JFK is accredited by the Western Association of Schools and Colleges. Applicants must have a Bachelor's degree and an oral interview.

Six units may be transferred from previous college classes. The program requires two two-week summer workshops. Students complete their study plan through writing, audio and videotape, and attend the workshops at JFK.

Cost is $132 per unit, and a $25 administrative fee per course.

KENNEDY-WESTERN UNIVERSITY
28310 Roadside Drive
Agoura Hills, CA 91301

(800) 635-2900

Kennedy-Western offers degree programs as well as Professional Certificate Programs. They are authorized by the State of California to grant Bachelor's, Master's, and Doctorate (Ph.D., J.D., Doctor of Law) degrees.

Your choice of major can be selected from a wide range of fields, and can be almost any area you choose.

Students can receive credit for prior education and work experiences. Transfer credit from other institutions is accepted.

During your study program you work with a Faculty Mentor to create an independent final project in your area of specialization.

Some students finish their degree program in nine months; others take longer depending upon the amount of work to be done.

Fees range from $2,700 for a bachelor's degree to $4,750 for a combined Master's/Doctor of Law. Financial aid is available.

Their law school program does not qualify students to sit for the California State Bar Exam, but is aimed at those wanting legal knowledge for business or personal reasons.

KENSINGTON UNIVERSITY

124 South Isabel Street
P.O. Box 2036
Glendale, CA 91209

(800) 423-2495

Bachelor of Arts
Master of Arts
Master of Business Administration
Ph.D.
J.D. (Juris Doctor, legal program enables one to sit for the
California bar examination)

Kensington has been operating since 1976. Their motto is "Competition through Education." The average age of their students is thirty-five to forty-five years. They offer degree programs in Business and Economics, Behavioral and Social Sciences, Engineering, Dental Technology, and Education. They also have a School of Law, offering bar preparation and a non-Bar program.

Approximately 30% of their students are residents outside of the United States. They do hold an annual Commencement, in conjunction with their annual seminar in June. All graduates are welcome to participate in the ceremony.

Kensington evaluates education acquired through life experiences. This "non-classroom" learning is then equated with formal classroom learning and appropriate academic credit is awarded. This experience must be documented through copies of transcripts, certificates, letters from supervisors, copies of job descriptions, copies of patents or published articles, or letters from associations attesting to membership.

They have graduated 8,000 students and have a current enrollment of 1,200.

LA JOLLA UNIVERSITY
8950 Villa La Jolla Drive, #1210
La Jolla, CA 92037-1707

(619) 452-7111

Bachelor of Arts, Bachelor of Science
Master of Arts, Master of Science
Ph.D.

La Jolla offers directed-study programs in the areas of Business Administration, Behavioral Studies, Health Care Administration, and a Ph.D. program in Behavioral Studies. They give credit for prior learning and experience. It is a tutorial-based program, where you work closely with the instructors. Students must be able to come to San Diego several times during the course of study to meet with faculty and peers for assessment and evaluation. The University has been in operation for ten years, and has a resident campus in Lugano, Switzerland. La Jolla is fully approved by the California State Department of Education, however, it is unaccredited by a formal accrediting agency.

Send $4.50 for their catalog for more information.

LA SALLE UNIVERSITY
3628 St. Gregory Lane
St. Louis, MO 63074

(800) 847-0005

Bachelor, Master, and Doctoral programs in:
   Business Management
   Education Management
   Criminal Justice Management
   Engineering Management
   Health Services Management
   Public Administration
   Doctorate in Theology

Students may specialize in almost any management field. Examples are listed below, but a management degree can be awarded in most areas.

   Electrical Engineering Management
   Health Services Management
   Public Administration
   Film and Video Management
   Chemical Engineering Management
   Criminal Justice Management
   Education Management

The *Doctorate in Theology* program trains individuals interested in becoming Christian Ministers or Christian Psychological Counselors or Therapists. The program leads to a Ph.D. and eligibility for the certification exam for the National Association of Christian Counselors and Therapists (NACCT). In order to enter the Doctorate in Theology program, you must have a Bachelor's degree or equivalent of five years counseling experience as a Minister or Counselor. The following courses are required for graduation:

   God & Man — World Religion
   Marriage Counseling
   Law and Society
   The Bible — Christianity & Judaism
   Duties of Ministry

Chemical Substance Abuse
Sex Therapy
Child Counseling
Health Counseling
Employment Counseling

A dissertation and six months of counseling or eighteen months of direct counseling are also required.

The *Law Program* is a four year program; fifty-eight credits are required to complete the Academic Law Program. Seventy credits are required to complete the California Bar Program, enabling students to sit for the California Bar Exam. Minimum educational requirements for entering the law program are sixty college units or pass a CLEP exam. Courses required for the Law Program are as follows:

Introduction to External Law Study
Criminal Law
Contracts
Torts
Real Property
Legal Research
Agency & Partnership
Civil Procedure
Corporations
Constitutional Law
Wills, Trusts & Probate
Evidence

Bar students only also take the following:

Community Property
Criminal Procedure
Remedies
Professional Responsibility

Costs: B.S. $1,725; Master's Degree $1,825; Doctoral Degree $1,890. Ed.D. degree $1,475 (for educators, who have completed a Bachelor's and thirty units or a Master's and who are under contract with a private or public institution). J.D., Law Degree, $2,537. The four-year program meeting the educational requirements for the California State Bar exam and J.D. degree is $1,650 per year. The Ph.D. program for Minister or Counselor is $1,500. Graduates are eligible for the Certification Examination of the National Association of Christian Counselors and Therapists (NACCT) upon graduation. Payment plans and student loans are available to those who qualify. A second degree may be applied within nine months of completion of the first, for the tuition cost of $600 for Master's and $700 for Doctorate.

La Salle gives credit for college, work, or life experience. If you have already taken courses or have substantial knowledge about the area of coursework, you may be granted credit. You can receive credit for work in the military or on the job. Volunteer experiences, such as running a center for the blind or learning the office computer system without taking a course, may be such accepted experiences.

NOVA UNIVERSITY
3301 College Avenue
Fort Lauderdale, FL 33314

(305) 475-7300

Nova University was founded in 1964. It is accredited by the Commission on Colleges of the Southern Association of College and Schools, to award bachelor's, master's, educational specialist, and doctoral degrees. The Nova University main campus includes a University School for pre-kindergarten through high school which serves as a laboratory school. They also have a Law School Center, an Oceanographic Center, and a Panama Center, in the Republic of Panama.

Degree programs available through independent study are offered in an extensive range of subject areas. Degrees available:

Bachelor of Science
Master's of Science
Master's in Public Administration
Master's of Business Administration
Educational Specialist Programs
Doctoral Programs, including D.B.A., D.A., Ed.D., J.D.,
and Ph.D. in a variety of areas

Off-campus students meet approximately once a month in locations across the U.S. Computer-based programs are also delivered through microcomputers.

Nova is an innovative and respected school, and their mission is to provide educational opportunities to adult students wherever they may live. Programs take about three to four years to complete; costs range in the area of $3,500 per year. A variety of financial aid sources such as scholarships and loans are available.

PACIFIC WESTERN UNIVERSITY
600 N. Sepulveda Blvd.
Los Angeles, CA 90049

(800) 423-3244

Bachelor's, Master's, and Doctoral programs are available from Pacific Western, as well as a special Ed.D. or Ph.D. program for graduate teachers employed in public schools.

There is no time limit for program completion. "All degree programs are primarily based on what the student has already learned. If the student is worthy, competent and eminently qualified, with proof based on official transcripts and life and work experience documentation, and satisfactorily completes the minimum requirements, the University will confer the appropriate degree, all without classroom attendance." Costs range from $1,795 for a Bachelor's to $1,995 for a Doctorate. A combined Bachelor's/Doctorate is $2,795. A second degree may be applied for within nine months of completion of the first, at a cost of $650 (Master's) and $800 (Doctoral). The Ed.D. for teachers is $1,550.

"Some programs are oriented to those individuals not seeking licenses or credentials required from accredited institutions. Our programs are not designed to meet any established requirements by private or professional associations. If a license or a credential is desired, a check should be made of state, federal, association and credential requirements before applying."

REGENTS COLLEGE
University of the State of New York
Cultural Education Center
Albany, NY 12230

Associate in Arts: Liberal Arts
Associate in Science:
　Liberal Arts, Business, Nursing, Electronics Technology,
　Computer Software, and Nuclear Technology
Associate in Applied Science: Nursing
Bachelor of Arts: Liberal Arts
Bachelor of Science:
　Liberal Arts, Business, Nursing, Electronics Technology,
　Computer Software, Computer Technology, and Nuclear
　Technology

Regents does not offer any post-graduate degree programs. Founded in 1970, the Regents College has conferred over 30,000 degrees. Over 17,000 students are enrolled. No "credit for life experience" is accepted, but you can do independent study for proficiency exams or transfer previously taken classes from other colleges.

They don't design a specific program for you. You have your transcripts evaluated, then pursue coursework at colleges near you, or by correspondence from other colleges, to meet Regents' degree program requirement. Minimum cost is $310, plus about $250-300 per year after the first year. They offer a fully-accredited college degree from a widely respected institution. "It is the best way for an adult to put together credits from different sources to achieve a college degree," they state.

Established by the Board of Regents of the University of the State of New York, it offers a sound academic degree through a choice of avenues not available in traditional degree programs.

SAINT MARY OF THE WOODS COLLEGE
Women's External Degree Program
Saint Mary of the Woods, Indiana 47876

(812) 535-5107

Associate of Arts: Humanities
Associate of Science: Business, Gerontology
Bachelor of Arts, Bachelor of Science
Bachelor of Social Work

Major fields of study:

Accounting
Business Administration
English
History
Humanities
Journalism
Management
Marketing
Paralegal Studies
Political Science
Psychology
Social Work
Theology

Translator training in Spanish and French is offered for those whose language background is sufficient.

Certificate programs are available in Paralegal Studies or Theology. The Paralegal Certificate entails thirty credit hours. Cost would be about $3,500.

Up to thirty hours of Life Experience Credit may be awarded toward the bachelor's degree and fifteen hours toward the associate's degree for college-level knowledge gained through employment, special interests, and volunteer work. Examples of areas of knowledge that can be assessed include art, counseling, creative writing, geography, industrial psychology, journalism, library science, microbiology, office management, paralegal, political science, real estate, religion, textiles, theatre, and zoology. It is stressed that the credit is not awarded for life experience per se, but rather for college-level knowledge acquired through non-traditional means. The experience must be knowledge-based, and apply outside the specific situation in which it was acquired.

Fees are $126 per semester credit hour, $55 per credit hour for Life Experience. Financial aid is available. There are three types of financial aid assistance for which the external degree program students may apply: Pell Grants, Guaranteed Student Loan (GSL), or the Parent Loan for Undergraduate Students (PLUS).

All work is done independently, with students spending only one day per semester on the campus. This meeting with the professors who will guide the student through the semester's assignments creates a personal relationship that survives the long-distance aspect of the correspondence program. Home study students have available to them all the benefits offered to the resident students, including placement. Most of their home study students are employed, but find improved status on the job (including increased pay, new titles, and added responsibilities) after a short time in the program. Probably 15% of their home study students go on to graduate school, most often to law school or into medicine.

Five hundred women are now in their Women's External Degree program. Over 600 have graduated since the program began in 1973. Most work full time, many have children, and about one fourth are single parents, working for a living and striving to improve their opportunities in life by reaching for an education. St. Mary of the Woods is the oldest Catholic liberal arts college for women in the United States, and the Women's External Degree program was developed specifically for the adult woman, to fit into her life and to help her in personal development, career opportunities, and moral certainty.

The WED program has been a successful route for many of the midwest's farm women who have sought retraining in order to gain off-farm employment.

THOMAS A. EDISON STATE COLLEGE
101 W. State Street
Trenton, NJ 08625

(609) 984-1150

Thomas A. Edison State College is a fully-accredited (Middle States Association of Colleges and Schools) four-year college. Edison grants both bachelor's and associate's degrees. Edison doesn't offer instruction, it specializes in evaluating knowledge gained elsewhere — either through evaluation of college courses taken previously, or by examination. After your portfolio of prior classes and life experience has been evaluated, you may complete needed coursework through equivalency exams, correspondence courses at other schools, or residential courses at schools in your area.

Edison was created for adults who want to convert knowledge learned elsewhere into college credit and to earn a degree. Students work at their own pace in a self-directed program.

Many students seek the Bachelor's degree at Edison in order to enter graduate school at other institutions. Over 150 graduate schools have accepted Edison graduates. Approximately 50% of Edison's graduates apply to graduate school, and over 85% are accepted into the school of their first choice.

Edison offers Associate and Bachelor's degree programs with over 170 degree majors. For instance, the B.S. in Business Administration is available with eighteen different business options, from Accounting to Transportation Management. The Bachelor of Arts degree is available in twenty-six areas, from Art to Physics. A Bachelor of Science degree in Nursing is also available.

Fees vary, depending upon how much of your prior work has been completed, and how many competency examinations you need to take. Programs average about $1,200. Residents of New Jersey pay lower fees. Edison does accept VISA and MasterCard.

Edison is a fully-accredited state college, and enables you to use a variety of sources to put together a respected degree.

UNION GRADUATE SCHOOL
The Union for Experimenting Colleges and Universities
632 Vine Street, Suite 1010
Cincinnati, OH 45202-2407

(513) 621-6444

Union Graduate School offers a Ph.D. degree in a variety of fields or combination of fields in which the student wishes to conduct research.

Regionally accredited by the North Central Association of Colleges and Schools, the Union Graduate School is a credible approach toward earning the Doctoral degree for highly motivated mid-career professionals with previous college and career experiences.

Students must complete a research project, and all learning must be new. Previous work is not accepted in lieu of the project or the internship that is expected. There is no foreign language requirement.

Students enrolled in the program must complete a thirty-five day residency, which is broken down into three five-day seminars, and ten peer days, which may be done one day at a time, or in any combination of numbers of days. Completion time can be no less than two years, and the average completion time is three to three and a half years.

Costs run about $1,650 per quarter. Financial aid is available.

Fields of study currently pursued by enrolled students include:

Anthropology
Communications
Creative Arts
Gerontology
Higher Education Administration
History
International Economics
Literature
Management
Organizational Development
Physical & Biological Sciences

Psychology
Religious Studies
Social Science
Women's Studies

Students must achieve "mastery of the field" prior to finishing the program. This can be done through reading literature of the field, taking courses, attending professional seminars and workshops, forming mentor relationships with experts, and exploring one's own best methods of acquiring knowledge. The internship combines new learning with a practical setting. It must be something the student has never done before, and must be the equivalent of three months full-time duration.

Union offers a viable and respected way to earn an Ph.D. for those willing and able to complete self-motivated study at the highest academic levels.

UNIVERSITY OF CINCINNATI

School of Planning, College of Design, Architecture,
    Art and Planning
Mail Location: 16
Cincinnati, OH 45221

(513) 475-2544

University of Cincinnati is fully accredited by the North Central Association of Colleges and Secondary Schools. They offer the Master of Science in Community Health, Planning/ Administration through independent study.

Applicants must have a Bachelor's degree from an accredited college, and have full-time employment in the health care field.

Students meet in Cincinnati for a two-day Learning Plan Design and Orientation session prior to beginning study. Then, two-day sessions are held in Cincinnati or other areas each quarter. Enrollment in intensive one-week summer courses on campus is recommended.

Part of the degree program involves a Comprehensive Action Project, in which the student applies learning in a practical way to bring about improvement in community health or the delivery of health or medical care services.

Costs are $83 per credit hour.

UNIVERSITY OF WISCONSIN — MADISON
Professional Development Degree
College of Engineering
432 North Lake Street
Madison, WI 53706

(608) 262-0133

A Professional Development (P.D.) Degree in Engineering is available to candidates who already have a B.S. in engineering, or the equivalent in science, math, or technology.

Credit is given for those applicants who already possess a Professional Engineering (P.E.) license. Up to half of the courses required for the P.D. may be transferred from other colleges.

Students complete their program through independent study, correspondence courses, videotape, institutes, seminars, short courses, and satellite and other telecommunication courses.

Costs run from $2,000 and up, depending upon courses selected.

The University of Wisconsin-Madison program is accredited by the North Central Association of Colleges and Schools.

This advanced engineering degree is not a Master's or a Ph.D; it is a continuing education program designed for practicing engineers.

VERMONT COLLEGE OF NORWICH UNIVERSITY
Montpelier, VT 05602

(800) 332-1987

Bachelor of Arts
Master of Arts

In the Bachelor of Arts program, students earn fifteen credits each semester of the four-year program. It can be accelerated with transfer of prior credits, C.L.E.P. tests, and Assessment of Prior Learning credit. Teacher certification, veteran's benefits, and financial aid are available to qualifying students. There are two residency options available:

1. Students attend weekend meetings every three weeks in Brattleboro or Montpelier, VT. Their semester consists of coursework and independent study.

2. Nine-day residency option. Students attend a nine-day meeting on campus every six months, and then return to their homes to complete their independent study with the guidance of faculty members.

Costs are approximately $5,000 per year.

In the Master of Arts program, which began in 1970, a quality Master's degree can be earned in a unique format. No on-campus residency is required. The program consists of individually-designed degree work. You work with a local mentor of your choosing. Your studies integrate theory with practical work, such as a job situation or internship. Financial aid is available. Fields of study are almost limitless within the humanities, arts, and social sciences. The possibilities are limited only by available resources and by the student's preparation. Completion time averages fifteen months. Tuition is $5,850 — part of the tuition pays your advisor an honorarium. You select your advisor who must be a working professional in your field and help guide your progress. Areas of study can encompass virtually all academic disciplines except technology and most physical sciences. Interdisciplinary and cross-disciplinary approaches are encouraged; degree concentrations may be broad or narrow depending upon student need.

For students seeking Teacher Certification there is an additional $250 surcharge, and a draft of your study plan must be filed and approved. The minimum enrollment time for students seeking teacher certification is fifteen months. It is possible to do student teaching through the College.

WALDEN UNIVERSITY
1350 Nicollet Mall, Suite 106
Minneapolis, MN 55403

(612) 338-7224

Doctoral Programs:
>   Ed.D. (Education)
>   Ph.D. (Administration/Management, Education, Human
>   Services, Health Services)

Walden is a candidate for accreditation from the North Central Association of Colleges and Schools, and expects to receive final accreditation within two years.

Their degree program is one based on "Dispersed Residency," which consists of two hundred hours of student/faculty contact. Workshops are held at various U.S. cities. Computer network and videotapes are also used to facilitate this requirement. A dissertation or doctoral project and a final oral presentation are required. For candidates for the Ed.D., there is also a supervised Internship of 200 hours.

Admission is usually given to those with a Master's degree or the equivalent and three or more years of professional experience. However, some students have been accepted who do not have a Master's degree, but whose backgrounds demonstrate an ability to complete doctoral study. Walden describes its students as, "... mature and established persons who have reached a point of professional success without having obtained the doctoral credential beforehand. They have already acquired the knowledge at the graduate level in fields such as psychology, health, education, business and industry, government, or social service. Entering students typically hold positions of distinction in their field, are self-motivated, and many have already published scholarly and professional papers. They are achievers accustomed to self-reliant learning styles, and they want an educational opportunity at the graduate level which does not require them to disengage from family and work commitments."

Tuition is $1,895 per quarter. It takes between two and three years of independent study to earn the doctoral degree at Walden. They grant approximately sixty degrees a year. "We aim to attract leaders from the major professions who want to solve social problems."

The following institutions have sponsored students in the Walden program: DuPont, IBM, Mercedes Benz, Upjohn, St. John's Medical Center, AT&T, Westinghouse, Unisys, National Cancer Institute, and Disney World.

Bibliography

Articles about home study that you might be interested in reading:

"A Cost-Justifiable Ph.D.," by Betsy Amster, *Venture*, September 1987, p. 14.

"America's Enduring Tradition," by Angelo John Lewis, *The American Legion*, July 1983, p. 18.

"Become a College Grad Without Leaving Home," by Elisabeth Keiffer, *Woman's Day*, June 17, 1986, p. 96.

"Diploma Mills: The Paper Merchants," reprint available from the *Arizona Republic* newspaper, Phoenix, AZ.

"Education (and Degrees) by Mail (or Modem)," by John Bear, Ph.D., *Whole Earth Review*, Spring 1987, p. 118.

"Education — Careers By Mail," by Christiane Bire, *Working Woman*, September 1984.

"Home Study Courses Come of Age," by Grace Hechinger, *Glamour*, February 1983.

"Phony Parchment," by John R. Emshwiller, *Wall Street Journal*, April 2, 1987.

"Studying at Home for College Credit," by Sylvia Galloway. Free from the N.H.S.C., 1601 18th Street, N.W., Washington, DC 20009.

"Using Your Mailbox to Go Back to School," *Changing Times*, September 1983, p. 67.

"What Does Accreditation Mean to You?" Free from the N.H.S.C., 1601 18th Street, N.W., Washington, DC 20009.

"You and Home Study," by William Fowler. Free from the N.H.S.C., 1601 18th Street, N.W., Washington, DC 20009.

Books with more information about course offerings and the home study field in general:

Bear, John, Dr. *Bear's Guide to Non-Traditional College Degrees*. Ten Speed Press, Berkeley, CA 94707. $10.95, postpaid.

Byrne, Robert. *Writing Rackets*. 1969. Lyle Stuart, Inc., New York, NY.

Nyquist, Ewald B., Jack N. Arbolino, Gene R. Hawes. *College Learning — Anytime, Anywhere.* 1977, Harcourt, Brace, Jovanovich, New York.

Regents' External Degree Program, Cultural Education Center, Albany, NY 12330. *Directory of External Graduate Programs.* Order from them, $5.00, postpaid.

Sosdian, Carol P., Laure M. Sharp. *The External Degree As A Credential; Graduate's Experiences in Employment and Further Study.* 1978. U.S. Department of Health, Education and Welfare, Washington, DC.

Sullivan, Eugene J. *Guide to External Degree Programs in the U.S.* $16.95 plus $1.50 postage from: Macmillan Publishing Company, 866 Third Avenue, New York, NY 10022.

National University Continuing Education Association, *The Independent Study Catalog: A Guide to Independent Study Through Correspondence Instruction.* Names of schools and course offerings at seventy-two colleges and universities. $10.20, postpaid, from: NUCEA Book Order Dept., P.O. Box 2123, Princeton, NJ 08540. (800) 225-0261 (toll free)

NHSC Directory of Accredited Home Study Schools, free from National Home Study Council, 1601 Eighteenth Street, N.W., Washington, DC 20009.

Index

The information found here is based on letters, telephone interviews, and literature from the schools listed. I asked each school to provide information. Many did. Some did not respond. In any case, the school's publications were reviewed whether they responded to my inquiry or not. I wish to thank those cooperating institutions that took the time to provide me with ample materials, letters, samples, newspaper clippings, or additional information.

Some of the programs reviewed in this book are very traditional and the only way they differ from on-campus work is the flexibility they offer through correspondence. Other programs are unconventional in format and content. Each student will need to read the brochures and literature from the school, and communicate with the school so that questions are answered clearly, to be sure the program will fit the particular needs of his or her situation.

I would like to hear from you about your home study experiences. While I cannot promise to answer every letter, the information gathered could prove beneficial to other readers.

Please write to me:

Laurie Winn Carlson
161 W. Kent Drive
Chandler, AZ 85224

Praise for the novels of Gregory Benford

IN THE OCEAN OF NIGHT

"A major novel . . . Evokes truly majestic feeling for the vast distances and time scales upon which the universe operates."

—*The Magazine of Fantasy & Science Fiction*

ACROSS THE SEA OF SUNS

"So good it hurts. Benford puts it all together in this one—adult characters, rich writing, innovative science, a grand philosophical theme—it's all here."

—*The Washington Post Book World*

"Confirms again Benford's unsurpassed ability to simultaneously sustain literary values and exciting speculative science."

—*Publishers Weekly*

TIDES OF LIGHT

"Mr. Benford is a rarity: a scientist who writes with verve and insight not only about black holes and cosmic strings but about human desires and fears."

—*The New York Times Book Review*

"*Tides of Light* is at once Benford's most adventurous, most philosophical and most scientifically creative novel. It's also the best SF novel published so far this year."

—*The Houston Post*

GREAT SKY RIVER

"A challenging, pace-setting work of hard science fiction that should not be missed."

—*Los Angeles Times*

"Hard science fiction at its very best."

—*St. Louis Post-Dispatch*

FURIOUS GULF

"A heady mixture of science . . . and no-holds-barred adventure."

—*The New York Times Book Review*

"The author's fans won't be disappointed with this tautly plotted entry in the series, which by now has eclipsed even Asimov's *Foundation* saga in ambition."

—*Publishers Weekly* (starred review)

Books by Gregory Benford

The Galactic Center Novels
IN THE OCEAN OF NIGHT
ACROSS THE SEA OF SUNS
GREAT SKY RIVER
TIDES OF LIGHT
FURIOUS GULF
SAILING BRIGHT ETERNITY

also

TIMESCAPE
MAT TER'S END

SAILING BRIGHT ETERNITY

GREGORY BENFORD

BANTAM BOOKS

NEW YORK • TORONTO • LONDON • SYDNEY • AUCKLAND

SAILING BRIGHT ETERNITY
A Bantam Spectra Book

PUBLISHING HISTORY

Bantam hardcover edition / September 1995
Bantam mass market edition / October 1996

SPECTRA and the portrayal of a boxed "s"
are trademarks of Bantam Books,
a division of Bantam Doubleday Dell Publishing Group, Inc.

ISBN 0-553-57332-2

Published simultaneously in the United States and Canada

Bantam Books are published by Bantam Books, a division of Bantam
Doubleday Dell Publishing Group, Inc. Its trademark, consisting of the
words "Bantam Books" and the portrayal of a rooster, is Registered in U.S.
Patent and Trademark Office and in other countries. Marca Registrada.
Bantam Books, 1540 Broadway, New York, New York 10036.

PRINTED IN THE UNITED STATES OF AMERICA

OPM   10 9 8 7 6 5 4 3

To Mark and Alyson and Joan

who grew and changed far more
in the decades it took to write this series of novels
than novels can possibly portray.

SAILING
BRIGHT
ETERNITY

Prologue

Metallovore

Black holes have weather, of a sort.

Light streams from them. Blackness dwells at their cores, but friction heats the infalling gas and dust. These streams brim with forced radiation. Storms worry them. White-hot tornadoes whirl and suck.

From the immense hole at the exact center of the galaxy, a virulent glow hammers outward. It pushes incessantly at the crowded masses that circle it, jostling in their doomed orbits. Gravity's gullet forces the streams into a disk, churning ever inward. Suffering in the weather.

The press of hot photons is a wind, driving all before it. Except for the grazers. To these photovores, the great grinding disk is a source of food.

Fire-flowers blossom in the disk, sending up lashes of fierce ultraviolet. Storms of light.

Both above and below the accretion disk, in hovering clouds, these photons smash molecules to atoms, strip atoms into bare charge, whip particles into sleet. The clouds are debris, dust, grains. They are already doomed by gravity's rub, like nearly everything here.

Nearly. To the gossamer, floating herds this is a fountain. Their life source.

Sheets of them hang, billowing with the electromagnetic winds. Basking in the sting. Holding steady.

The photovores are patiently grazing. Some are Infras, others Ultras—tuned to soak up particular slices of the electromagnetic spectrum.

Each species has a characteristic polish and shape. Each works within evolutionary necessity, deploying great flat receptor planes. Each has a song, used to maintain orbit and angle.

Against the wrathful weather here, information is at least a partial defense. Position-keeping telemetry flits between the herd sheets. They sing luminously to each other in the eternal brimming day.

Hovering on the pressure of light, great wings of high-gloss moly-sheet spread. Vectoring, skating on winds, magnetic torques in a complex dynamical sum. Ruling forces govern their perpetual, gliding dance. This is decreed by intelligences they scarcely sense, machines that prowl the darker lanes farther out.

Those magisterial forms need the energies from this furnace, yet do not venture here. The wise and valuable run no risks.

At times the herds fail. Vast shimmering sheets peel away. Many are cast into the shrouded masses of molecular clouds, which are themselves soon to boil away. Others follow a helpless descending gyre. Long before they could strike the brilliant disk, the hard glare dissolves their lattices. They burst open and flare with fatal energies.

Now a greater threat spirals lazily down. It descends from the shelter of thick, turbulent dust. It lets itself fall toward the governing mass, the black hole itself. Then it arrests its descent with outstretched wings of mirrors. They bank gracefully on the photon breeze.

Its lenses swivel to select prey. There a pack of photovores has clumped, disregarding ageless programming, or perhaps caught in a magnetic flux tube. The cause does not matter. The predator eases down along the axis of the galaxy itself.

Here, navigation is simple. Far below, the rotational pole of the Eater of All Things is a pinprick of absolute black at the center of a slowly revolving, incandescent disk.

The clustered photovores sense a descending presence. Their vast sailing herds cleave, peeling back to reveal deeper planes of burnt-gold light seekers. They all live to ingest light and excrete microwave beams. Their internal world revolves around ingestion, considered digestion, and orderly excretion.

These placid conduits now flee. But those clumped near the axis have little angular momentum, and cannot pivot on a magnetic fulcrum. Dimly they sense their destiny. Their hissing microwaves waver.

Some plunge downward, hoping that the predator will not follow so close to the Eater. Others cluster ever more, as if numbers give safety. The opposite is true.

The metallovore folds its mirror wings. Now angular and swift, accelerating, it mashes a few of the herd on its carapace. It scoops them in with flux lines. Metal harvesters rip the photovores. Shreds rush down burnt-black tunnels. Electrostatic fields separate elements and alloys.

Fusion fires await the ruined carcasses. There the separation can be exquisitely tuned, yielding pure ingots of any alloy desired. In the last analysis, the ultimate resources here are mass and light. The photovores lived for light, and now they end as mass.

The sleek metallovore never deigns to notice the layers of multitudes peeling back, their gigahertz cries of panic. They are plankton. It ingests them without registering their songs, their pain, their mortal fears.

Yet the metallovore, too, is part of an intricate balance. If it and its kind were lost, the community orbiting the Eater would decay to a less diverse state, one of monotonous simplicity, unable to adjust to the Eater's vagaries. Less energy would be harnessed, less mass recovered.

The metallovore prunes less efficient photovores. Its ancient codes, sharpened over time by natural selection, prefer the weak. Those who have slipped into unproductive orbits are easier to catch. It also prefers the savor of those who have allowed their receptor planes to tarnish with succulent trace elements, spewed up by the hot accretion disk below. The metallovore spots these by their mottled, dusky hue.

Each frying instant, millions of such small deaths shape the mechsphere.

Predators abound, and parasites. Here and there on the metallovore's polished skin are limpets and barnacles. These lumps of orange-brown and soiled yellow feed on chance debris from the prey. They can lick at the passing winds of matter and light. They purge the metallovore of unwanted elements—wreckage and dust that can jam even the most robust mechanisms, given time.

All this intricacy floats on the pressure of photons. Light is the fluid here, spilling up from the blistering storms far below in the great grinding disk. This rich harvest supports the mechsphere that stretches for hundreds of cubic light-years, its sectors and spans like armatures of an unimaginable city.

All this, centered on a core of black oblivion, the dark font of vast wealth.

Inside the rim of the garish disk, oblivious to the weather here, whirls a curious blotchy distortion in the fabric of space and time. It is called by some the Wedge, for the way it is jammed in so close. Others term it the Labyrinth.

It seems to be a small refraction in the howling virulence. Sitting on the very brink of annihilation, it advertises its artificial insolence.

Yet it lives on. The mote orbits perpetually beside the most awful natural abyss in the galaxy: the Eater of All Things.

An Abyss of Time

Interior state: a place cloudless and smooth, without definition:

The mechanicals are converging, Nigel.

"You feel them?"

Clearly. They can now manifest themselves in magnetic vortices.

"Bloody dexterous, they are."

I can feel them. Something bad is coming.

"Thanks for the warning, m'love. But I've got to bring the lad Toby up to speed, and it'll take a while."

There is nothing you could do for me anyway.

He smiled without mirth. "All too true."

I will alert you if the energy densities change for the worse.

He nodded and the space without definition vanished.

He was back in a bare room, sitting opposite a young man, trying to frame the immense story that had led him to this moment.

—*nothing you could do*—

He remembered another time, long ago.

He and Carlos stood on a dry ridge of bare rock and looked out over a plain. This was not a world at all but a convoluted wraparound of space-time itself. Its sky curved overhead, a bowl of scrub desert.

Still, it *felt* like a place to live. A remarkable, alien-made refuge. Dirt, air, odd but acceptable plants.

They talked about finding a way to live here, in a hard, dry place twisted and alive in a way that rock was not.

Carlos had just made a good joke and Nigel laughed, relaxed and easy, and then Carlos plunged forward, his shoulder striking Nigel's arm. Carlos went down with his head tilted back, as if he were looking up at the sky, a quizzical expression flickering as the head brushed by Nigel and down and hit face first on the baked dirt. Carlos had not lifted his hands to break the fall. He slid a foot as he struck.

The noise that had started it all was ugly. It seemed to condense out of the air, a soft thump like an ax sinking into a rotten stump.

As Carlos pitched forward something rose from his back, a geyser of skin and frothy blood. It spattered over the back of the tunic as the body smacked into the dirt. The thump, Nigel realized later, was the compact explosion of electromagnetic energy, targeted a few centimeters below the skin.

As Nigel dropped to lower his profile he got a good look at Carlos. One was enough. Then he ran, bent over, hearing the harsh following buzz of the electromagnetic pulse tapering away as he zigzagged behind some jagged boulders.

Too much open space and too little shelter. He squatted and could not see what had fired the shot. Carlos lay flat without a twitch.

Nothing happened. No following pulses.

Nigel replayed the images as he waited. A spout of rosy blood from a circle punched high in the spine. Absolutely dead center, four centimeters below the neck. Kilojoules of energy focused to a spot the size of a fingernail.

That much energy delivered so precisely would have done the job even if it hit the hip or gut. Delivered so exactly, it burst the big axis, plowing massive pressures through the spinal fluid—a sudden breeze blowing out a candle, the brain going black in a millisecond.

Carlos had gone down boneless, erased. A soft, liquid thump, then eternal silence.

Nigel held up his hand and watched it tremble for a while. Enough waiting.

He worked his way along the ridgeline. The pulse had come from behind Carlos and he kept plenty of rock between him and that direction. He got to Carlos and studied the face from behind a boulder nearby. The head was cocked to one side. Eyes still open, mouth seeping moisture into the dry dirt. The eyes were the worst, staring into an infinity nobody glimpses more than once.

Good-bye, friend. We had our arguments, but we came thirty thousand light-years together. And now I can't do a damn thing for you.

Something moved to his right. He pulled out a pulse gun and fired at it but the target was a gossamer ball of motes. A Higher, or rather, a local manifestation of one.

It flickered, spun, and said in a low, bass voice, "We regret."

"You did this?"

"No. A mechanical form, termed the Mantis."

"And who're you?"

"That would be impossible to say."

"Is this Mantis after me, too?"

"I will protect you."

"You didn't do a great job for Carlos."

"I arrived here slightly late."

"Slightly?"

"You must forgive errors. We are finite, all."

"Damn finite."

"The Mantis was harvesting Carlos. He is saved."

"You mean stored?"

"To mechanicals it is the same thing."

"Not to us. I thought we'd be safe in this place, this Lair."

"No place is safe. This is safer."

"What'll kill a Mantis?"

"There was nothing you could do."

Nigel Walmsley cursed the mote cloud, his fury going into fruitless words.

"Nothing you could do," he muttered to himself.

Do not belabor the past so.

Nikka's frail voice resounded in his sensorium.
"There's so much of it."

Pay attention to the young man before you. He is a key to saving us.

Nigel sighed. "I grow old, I grow old—"

I shall wear my trousers rolled—yes, I know the poem. Get on with it, Nigel!

He nodded and dropped out of the interior space of smooth blankness. It was pleasant to retire to that cool, interior vault. Perhaps the old solidly good point to the augmentations he had gained through centuries; the quietness of a good, old-fashioned library. Where most of the people were books.

Very well, then. Back into the grainy. The real. The deliciously dangerous.

Part I

WONDROUS
RUINS

1

Half Vast

An old man sat and told a young man a story. As stories go it was long and angular, with its own momentary graces and clumsy logic, much the way life is.

"What is this place?" Toby asked. "This mountain?"

Nigel Walmsley leaned back in a webbing that shaped itself to him. He was nude, leathery. The lattice of his ribs made him look as though he had a barrel chest, but that was because he was gaunt with age.

He had reached the phase when life reduces a man to the essentials. For packaging, skin like brown butcher's paper. Muscles like motors, lodged in lumps along the bone-girders. Knobby elbows and knees, so round they seemed to encase oiled ball bearings. Sockets at the shoulder and hip, bulging beneath the dry parchment skin. Eyes blue and quick, glittering like mica in the bare face. A jaw chiseled above a scrawny neck. Cheekbones high and jutting like blades above the thin, pale lips. An oddly tilted smile, playing mischievously.

"It's popularly termed the Magnetic Mountain, though I have rather a more personal name for it."

"You're from a planet near True Center?"

"No no, I'm from Earth."

"What? You said before that you were Family Brit. I—"

"A jest. In my time there weren't Families in the way you mean. The Brits were a nation—much bigger."

"How much bigger?" Toby had heard Earth invoked, of course,

but it was a name from far antiquity. Meaningless. Probably just a legend, like Eden and Rome.

"I doubt that all the Families surviving at Galactic Center number a tenth what the Brits did."

"That many?"

"Hard to estimate, of course. There are layers and folds and hideaways aplenty in the esty."

"Brits must be powerful."

Walmsley pursed his lips, bemused. "Um. Alas, through the power of the word, mostly."

Toby had no idea how many people still lived, after all the death he had seen. He had come here on a long journey, fleeing the mechs. Through it all, to all sides and in his wake, mechs had cut swaths through all the humans they could find. The slaughter reminded him of the retreat from the Calamity, the fall of Citadel Bishop: a landscape of constant dying.

But the butchery was now far greater. Devoting so much energy to hunting vermin humans was unusual for mechs. Mostly they didn't care; humans were pests, no more. This time they clearly were after Toby in particular. So the deaths behind him weighed on him all the more. He was only slowly coming to feel the meaning of that. It was a thing beyond words or consolations.

"Ummm." Walmsley seemed pensive, eyes crinkling. "Usually I felt there were too few Brits, too many of everybody else."

"Family Brit must've been huge."

"We reproduced quickly enough. Didn't have the radiation you suffer through here."

"We're protected from that, my father said."

"There's a limit to what genetic tinkering can do. Organic cells fall apart easily. Part of their beauty, really. Makes them evolve quicker."

"Most of our Citadel was underground, to help—"

"Somewhat useful, of course. But the stillbirths, the deformities . . ." Walmsley's bony face creased with painful memories.

"Well, sure, that's life."

"Life next door to this hell hole, true."

"The Eater?" Toby had grown up with the Eater, a glowering eye rimmed in angry reds and sullen burnt browns. It had been as bright as Snowglade's own sun. "Living near it was pretty ordinary."

Walmsley laughed heartily, not the aged cackle Toby would have expected. "Trust me, there are better neighborhoods."

"Snowglade was good enough for me," Toby said defensively.

"Ah yes. We gave the chess families a good world, I recall."

"Gave? You?"

"I am rather older than you may suppose."

"But you couldn't be—"

"Could and am. I've stretched matters out, of course. Had to. I fetched up at the very bottom of this steep gravitational gradient, along the elastic timeline—"

"The, uh . . .?"

"Sorry, that's an old way of talking. I mean, this is a stable point, this esty. We're in a descended Lane, one where time runs very slowly. I—"

"Slow?" Maybe this was why Toby had been having trouble with his internal clock. When he had been near their ship *Argo* his systems lagged the ship's, if he went too far into the city beyond. He could never trace the cause. He checked it reflexively, ticking along steadily if he looked far down into the corner of his left eye and blinked. There: 14:27:33. "Measured by what?"

"Good point. Measured with respect to the flat space-time outside, far from the black hole."

"So this is a kind of time storage place?"

"Indeed. I've stored myself here, one might say. And there are other things, many others, this far deep in the esty."

"When did you do it?"

Toby was trying to place this dried-up old man in the pantheon of Family Bishop legend, but the very idea seemed a laugh. The men and women who had started the Families, at the very beginning of the Hunker Down, had been wise and farsighted. The founding fathers and mothers. Better than anybody alive today, that was pretty clear. And for sure they wore clothes.

"Before the 'Hunker Down.' Well before. I spent a great while in Lanes squirreled away, deep, letting time pass outside."

"So you weren't actually doing anything?"

"If you mean, did I get out occasionally, yes. To the early Chandeliers, in fact. On my last excursion, to several worlds."

Toby snorted scornfully. "You expect me to swallow that?" His Aspects were trying to pipe in with some backup information, but he was confused enough already.

Walmsley yawned, not the reaction of wounded innocence Toby had expected of a practiced liar. "Matters little if you don't."

A sudden suspicion struck him. "You were around in the Great Times?"

"As they're called, yes. Not all that great, really."

"We ruled here then, right?" That was the drift of countless stories from Citadel Bishop days. Humanity triumphant. Then the fall, the Hunker Down, and worse after.

"Nonsense. Rats in the wall, even then. Just a higher class of rat."

"My grandfather said—"

"Legends are works of fiction, remember."

"But we must've been great, really great, to even build the Chandeliers."

"We're smart rats, I'll give you that."

Not trying to hide his disbelief, Toby asked, "*You* helped build those? I mean, I visited one—was booby-trapped. Derelict, sure, but beautiful, big and—"

"The grunt labor was done by others, really, from Earth."

Toby snorted in disbelief. Walmsley cocked an eye. "Think I'm pulling your leg?"

"What's that mean?"

"That I'm having you on." A crinkled grin.

Toby frowned doubtfully, glancing at his leg.

"That is, I'm joking."

"Oh. But—Earth's a *legend.*"

"True enough, but some legends still walk and talk. These legends were of the second wave, actually, us being the first. Whole bloody fleet of ramscoops, better than the mech ship we'd hauled in on. Smart rats."

Toby nodded slowly. Why would this dried up runt lie?

So Earthers had built the Chandeliers? Maybe Earthers weren't mythical folk, after all. They probably really ran things during the Great Times, then, too. But for sure nobody like this wrinkled dwarf could have. "Uh huh. So it's Earther tech in the Chandeliers."

"Polyglot tech, really—mech, Earthborn, plenty of things slapped together."

"By who?" Toby still wasn't impressed with this dwarf.

"By us. Humanity. The Earthers who came in the second wave were still, I suppose, the same species as us. But . . ." A strange melancholy flickered in his face. "Different. Much . . . better."

"Better at tech?"

"More than that. Dead on, they were beyond merely impressive. Made miracles, just tinkering with the huge range of gear they—we—captured down through centuries. Others did it, I mean—I tired of tech quite some time ago."

Toby sniffed. "Knowing techtricks is same as breathing, to Bishops."

"True enough, down on the planets. The second-wave

'Earthers,' as you call them, they were important, mind. My wife, Nikka, used to say our problems were vast—and Earthers brought us plenty of half-vast solutions."

Toby wasn't used to this man's deadpan way of making jokes. Bishops were more the thigh-slapper type. "Brit breed, you are," he said reluctantly. No geezer was going to put one over on him, but something finally made him believe Walmsley was from Earth. Maybe it was the fact that Walmsley didn't seem to care very much whether he did or not.

"The second wave boosted our numbers—which the mechs were always trimming, shall we say."

"Even then?"

"Always and forever. A few interludes of cooperation, but we were tolerated at best. For a while, we could move fairly freely near True Center. They swatted us when they noticed us. We had plenty of help from the Old Ones, time to time. Capricious, but crucial."

"Old Ones?"

"They were a form of intelligence descended from clay."

"Clay? From dirt?"

"Electrostatic energy storage, in clay beds with saline solutions—on old seashores, I gather."

Now Toby was annoyed. "You being from Earth, I can maybe believe that, but living dirt? You must think—"

"They came first of all. Have a squint."

A three-dimensional plot shimmered in Toby's sensorium. He sectioned it to read in 2D, which collapsed the nuances into a simple diagram. "Complexity?"

"The specialists term it 'structure complexity.' Clays built up complicated lattices that could replicate themselves. Harvested piezoelectrical currents, driven by pressures in crystals. Later on, they allowed algae to capture sunlight. They drew off the energy, rather like farmers."

Toby had not the slightest idea how to take all this in. "So . . . *dirt* life, that's the Old Ones?"

"Combined with magnetic structures, yes. Bit hard to describe, that ancient wedding. All long ago, of course."

Toby gazed at the immense eras represented by simple lines, biological beings coming after the clays, intersecting the "magnetics kingdom," and then mystifying lines labeled "Earth biologicals." Of "memes" and "kenes" he knew nothing. From the time axis he guessed that all this had started over twelve billion years ago, when—what? the whole universe?—began.

Shaken by the implications of the simple diagram, he did not venture into the other dimensions, which expanded this simple 2D along axes of "fitness" and "pattern depth" and "netplex" and other terms he could not even read. Better get back to something simple.

"Then . . . how'd you get here in the first place?"

"Stole a ship, actually. Mech, fast cruiser."

Toby had never heard of anyone doing something so audacious. It had been hard enough for the Bishops to use an old human craft, *Argo.* "Stole it? And just walked into True Center, easy as you please?"

"Umm, not quite." Walmsley's eyes were far away. "See, this is how it was."

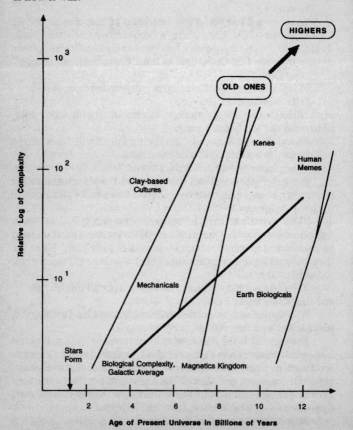

Age of Present Universe in Billions of Years

2

The Place of Angry Gods

You've got to remember, first, that we were limping along in an outdated mech ship. Dead slow, compared to what's zipping around here now. A ramscoop, big blue-white tail dead straight, scratched across space.

Far better than our Earth ship had been, the knocked-together old *Lancer*. Bravely named, it was, but venturing out into the nearby stars that way was like Indians trying to explore Europe using birch bark canoes. The wrong way round, historically and technically.

Y'see, the mechs had explored *us* pretty well. They'd been in the solar system a long time ago, millions of years back. Some earlier, carbon-based life had fought a battle near Earth, against mechs. Presumably defending Earth when the primates were still sharpening their wits, edging up on being *Homo sap*.

They left a crashed starship on the moon. That's how we knew this conflict had been going long before us. My wife, Nikka, was in on that. I came along later. Ancient history.

We went out together in the first human starship, *Lancer*. Got hammered by mechs. Barely survived.

Then we got lucky, stole a mech ship.

—Ah! Blithe understatement, quite Brit. In truth, there were two cowed alien species huddling beneath the ice of that world. Beings who could see electromagnetically in the microwave region. Turned out they'd been the cause of a wreck we'd found on our own moon, one I'd picked through, been changed by. I wanted so much to know what they were, how they thought.

But there were others, too. Whalelike things that glided serenely through murky depths, warmed by a radioactive core they had assembled in the moon's core.

All immensely strange, yet all allies against the mech Watcher that loomed above. Together, two alien kind plus the constantly chattering chimpanzees, they attacked the Watcher and captured it. Sounds so easy now . . .

Um? Oh, sorry, must've let the mind wander. The mech ship?

Outfitted it with our gear, the life support equipment—anything that survived after the mechs tore into *Lancer*. Hard work.

Bravo. What next?

There we sat, a scrawny distance out from our home star. Lots of the crew—the surviving crew, rather—wanted to head home.

I saw no point. I was old enough by then to have very little left to lose. And little invested in grand old Earth, either—no children, or even close relatives.

But we knew Earth had already been attacked by mechs. Used a clever weapon, fishlike aliens dumped into our seas. Should we go back to help?

—and augh! The arguments that caused. I had to admit the other side had a point, save the home world and all that. So we compromised. Built a robot starship, using mech bits. Tricky, that. Then we packed it full of mechtech. Let Earth make use of its tricks, we figured.

Some wanted to go along, no less. Classic Wagnerian gesture—all emotion, no reason. Too risky.

So we dispatched it to Earth, crawling along at a twentieth of light speed. Best we could manage, I'm afraid.

In truth, I wanted to stay there, commune with the two species still living beneath the moon's ice. But there was the other faction . . .

Nikka and I had allies in the crew. We hated the mechs, wanted to *do* something. Follow this riddle to the end. So we set sail—if that quaint term includes boosting up to within a hair's width of light speed.

Straight inward. To the Center.

Took nearly thirty thousand years to get here—but that's measured in the rest frame of the galaxy. What some call "real" time. But all inertial frames are really equivalent, y'know. We proved that. Only diff is the clocks ran slow on our craft. Plus, we had coldsleep.

So to me it was as if I had gone through several comfy afternoon snoozes, waking just for medical checkups and the odd message to send. My turn to patrol the ship, fix things. Lonely experience. My friends frozen stiff. I, clumping about in a stolen, alien machine. Hurtling down a corridor of relativistic refractions like a tunnel lined by rainbows. Quite striking. Frightening, too, no matter how well you fathomed the physics.

I had rigged—well, Nikka rigged; she was a wonder—an infrared transmitter. Messages for Earth, squirted them off every thousand light-years or so. Keeping them up to date on what we'd found—data, reams of it. Plus a bit of rah-rah from me. I was hoping they were still there, really. It seemed like a small gesture at the time, only found out much later how important it was.

Then, *presto physico*—there was the Center, glowing like a crass advert out the window. Convenient, these mech devices. Makes one wonder if their designers appreciate them. Pity, if they're wasted on creatures who don't relish the delights they can bring.

The Center? Well, today you can't see it the way I did. The Old Ones were already there, and more evident than they are now.

We came in along an instreaming flow, to pick up even more speed. The Center was a perpetual firework. Arcing above it like a vast triumphal arch was a braided fire river. Bristling with gold and orange and sulphurous yellows, it was. Ferocious stuff. The gravitational potential of the black hole, expressed as ruby-hot gas, plasma filaments, incandescences light-years long.

I'd expected those. From Earth, the Very Large Array had mapped the long, curving arcs that sliced straight up through the galactic plane. They hung a hundred light-years out from the True Center. There were others, too, filmy laces—all lit by gigantic currents.

Galactic neon lights, they were, the specialists decided. But why so thin and long?—several hundred light-years long, some, and barely half a light-year wide.

As we got closer, we could make out those filaments—not in the radio waves, but the *optical*. Dazzling. So clean, so obligingly orderly. Could they be some colossal power source? A transportation corridor, an unimaginable kind of freeway? What—or who—would need that much room to get around?

They hung there like great ruddy announcements in the sky. But for what? A religious monument? An alien equivalent of the crucifix, beaming its eternal promise across the entire galaxy?

We all thought of these possibilities as our ship—a great kluggy old thing, with streets of room compared with *Lancer*—plunged on through murky dust clouds, hot star-forming regions, the lot—hammering inward hard and swift, like an old dog heading home at last. Its navigational gear was simple, direct—and had a setting built in for the True Center.

Think about that. This was one of its standard destinations.

Easy to see why, in retrospect. Energy density. A blaze of light. Proton sleet. Huge plasma currents. Just the place for a hungry mech. The feeding trough.

Mostly I had thought of True Center as a sort of jewel box, with stars packed in and glowing like emeralds, rubies, hot sapphires—all circling neatly around the black hole. Which had quite properly eaten up the nasty dust long ago, of course, leaving this pleasing array of finery.

Or so the astronomers thought. Never trust in theories, m'lad, if they're thought up by types who work in offices.

What? Oh, offices are boxes where people work—no, not actual labor, heavy lifting or anything, more like—let's pass over that, eh?

Y'see, I'd forgotten that with several million stars jammed into a few light-years, there are collisions, abrasions. And plenty of shrapnel.

As we got closer we could see the brawl. Fat, wobbly stars flaring like angry gods, spewing red tongues. They were the children of awful marriages, when two stars had collided, merged, and fallen into the same oblate quarrel.

You could see others about to go at it—circling each other, loops of gas flung between them like insults. Even worse cases, too, as we got to see the outer edge of the accretion disk. Stars ripped open, spilled, smelted down into fusing globs. They lit up the dark, orbiting masses of debris like tiny crimson match heads flaring in a filthy coal sack.

Amid all that were the strangest stars of all. Fast ones, they were. Each half-covered by a hemispherical mask. The mask gave off infrared and it took me a while to fathom what was going on.

See, the hemispherical mask hung at a fixed distance from the star. It hovered on light, gravity just balancing the outward light pressure. The mask reflected half the star's flux back on it—turning up the heat on the cooker. That made the poor star send pretty arcs and jets of mass out, too. Which probably helped the purpose of it all.

Light escaped freely on one side. The mask bottled it up on the other. That pushed the star toward the mask. But the mask was bound to the star by gravitation. It adjusted, kept the right distance. As far as the wretched star knew, however, it was able to eject light in only one direction. So it recoiled in the opposite way.

Somebody was herding these stars. Those masks made them into fusion-photon engines. Sluggish, but effective. And the herd was headed for the accretion disk.

Somebody was helping along the black hole's appetite.

Who could do such engineering? No time to find out, just then.

We were getting closer. Heating up. Bloody awful hot, it was.

And now, after all those years, communications traffic was coursing through the ship's receivers. Chirps, beeps, dense thickets of blindingly fast code.

Clearly, signals intended for the mechs who had run the ship. How should we respond?

We were still dithering when a rather basic truth got pointed out to us. The ship didn't just ferry mechs about. It *was* a mech.

It had carried higher levels of mechs, sure. But it was still a member of the tribe, of sorts.

As we approached, the course selection we had made ran out. We decelerated, hard. The magnetic throat, which dwarfed the actual ship, compressed. Then it tilted, so that incoming plasma hit us at an angle. That turned the whole ship—and such a groaning, popping, shrieking maneuver I've never heard. Clearly, the mechs weren't sensitive to acoustics.

We nearly went deaf. It lasted a week.

But it worked. Turned the ship clean around, swapping ends so the fusion jet played out front of us now. That backflow protected us from the solid junk in the way—burnt it to a crisp, cooked it into ions for the drive itself.

The throat was now aft of us, but the magnetic field lines fetched a fraction of the debris around, and stuffed it into the maw of the great, fat craft. Fusion burners rattled the plates, heated the air—but our life support labored through.

A miracle, considering. There was plenty of power, so we rigged better air conditioners. Bit of hard work, that, in the stifling heat. Trouble was, where to dump the excess heat? Refrigerators don't abolish heat, they just move it.

We finally resorted to using some of the mech weapons. Lasers, they were, but they looked more like monstrous sewer pipes. Immense, corpulent gadgets.

Trick about lasers is, they radiate better than anything natural. Higher brightness temperature, in the jargon. To lose energy to your surroundings, you must have something hotter than they are. Lasers could do that. So we dumped the excess heat of deceleration into convertors. And then into the drivers of the lasers themselves.

The ship started projecting beams of cutting power, shedding our energy.

Which made us even more conspicuous. And terrified. Was our ship reporting to its superiors that it had vermin aboard? We adventurers felt pretty damned small.

We slowed hard—one and a half Earth gravities. Dicey. It was very much like being permanently obese, without any of the pleasure of having gotten that way. We arranged supply vats and made pools of water. Floated there for days, just to escape the weight.

Finally the view cleared. The fusion drive worked up to higher energies as we slowed. It became transparent in the optical, so we could see through the plume. First in the reds—odd vision, that.

We could clearly make out death, a whole great wall of it. Making haste toward us.

As for what it was like . . .

3

Church Mice

"Like trying to take a drink out of a bloody fire hose," Nigel said.

"What is?" Nikka was still thin and pale but her black eyes glinted like living marbles, with amused intelligence.

"Processing this damned data." Nigel craned his neck to take in the full wall. Its glittering mica surfaces were canted at angles just out of true, in mysterious mech fashion.

On these faces played different views around their ship. Gaudy sprays of ionized gas. Molecular clouds, inky-black at the core while fires played at their ravaged skins. Stars brimming full, scorching the billows of angry gas that muffled them.

And directly ahead, a wall of furious mass boiling out from the True Center of the galaxy. Headed toward them.

"Like a supernova remnant," Nikka said from her console. She insisted on working. Her Japanese heritage, she said, constant addiction to the harness. When you love a woman, Nigel realized, you take the obsessions along with the rest. Much as she had with him. And in his opinion, she had gotten the worst of the deal. He was not getting easier to live with.

Nigel frowned. "Looks like the hand of God about to swat a fly."

"Now there's a theory that hadn't occurred to me."

"Seems likely. Going pretty fast, that stuff is."

"The Dopplers show plenty of hydrogen moving at around four hundred twenty kilometers per second," she read off crisply.

"Hard to see why God would bother to swat us." Shock waves played like burnt-gold filigrees all across the face of the outrushing wall.

Nikka chuckled. "You take even astrophysics personally."

"And why not? Makes it easier to remember the jargon."

"Egomania, perhaps?"

"Probably. Still, there's plenty else for God to go after around here. We're pretty dull in comparison."

"Elephant rolling over in its sleep, then," Nikka said.

Her laconic logic had always amused him. How could he not love a woman who could be more clipped and wry than he? "Ummm?"

"In old Kyoto days, my father told us a story about a man who thought he would be safe from the storm if he slept next to an elephant. For shelter."

"I see. Just because the big survive—"

"Wait, here are the parallax readings." She was all business again.

Nigel studied the strange, tilted facets of the wall display. He had never seen the purpose of angling them so. *Fresnel mirrors,* he recalled. And old lab experiment, one he had done on a cold winter morning in lab at Cambridge. Creaky equipment, ancient clamps and lenses from mid-nineteenth century. He had done it in jig time, then packed it in for some tea and billiards.

But he could still recall how it worked. Canting planes slightly askew, so that light reflected back and forth. That formed interference wedges. Retained the phase information in the light waves. Clever. Somehow the mechs had tarted up this classic effect into a dazzling many-visioned optical smorgasbord.

And in one of the oblong panels he now saw a rapidly swelling nodule, coal-black and lumpy. Furnace-red brilliance danced behind it.

"That front is closer than I thought," Nikka said. "Only a few hours away."

"It'll crack us for sure," Nigel said.

She nodded. "We can't boost to that speed. We've barely slowed to local zero."

In the steepening potentials near True Center, masses following gravity's gavotte swung at enormous speeds. "Local zero" just meant the orbital speed of this region. It was safer, they figured, to keep close to that speed while they tried to understand the fireworks further in. Church mice venture under the dinner table at their own peril, especially if the diners are wearing hobnail boots.

"We can't run," Nigel said, eyeing the panels. "So we hide."

She followed his scrutiny. "Among this debris?"

"Had my eye on that blob over there." An asteroid-sized rock.

"Why that one?"

"I got a strange echo-answer from it when I did an immediate area survey."

She glanced at him. "This another hunch?"

"That's all I ever have."

"A solid mass, good shielding. But there are closer ones."

"Something about it. A memory." He did not himself know what made him choose the tumbling stone. Its answer had made him think of the Snark, that old shambling representative of the mechs, long ago. But why should that be a good sign?

She studied the bewildering array of information on the mech-made panel. He admired how she had puzzled out the mech diagnostics, jimmied them into yielding up the quantities humans liked to use. Brilliant, she was, and could flit among them as if they were perfectly natural, when at base they were skewed, alien. The underlying point, he supposed, was that the laws of mechanics and fields have an internal logic of their own. Any intelligence shapes itself to that blunt fact. In the end, the universe molded its children. Mind, as crusty old Wittgenstein would no doubt have remarked, was cut like a suit of clothes, into contours not born in the cloth itself.

The thought brought fretful memories. Why, then, did life, in its myriad mortal forms, spend so much of itself in clashes with its fellows?

"You're sure?" Nikka's face was a study in skepticism.

He laughed. "Bloody hell, of course not."

4

Alexandria

The others—younger, a shade more foolish—went in first. The slowly revolving chunk was oddly black for the center of the galaxy, where fire and fury prevailed, garish and showy. A cinder from some earlier catastrophe, perhaps. The black hole further in—still unseeable, behind the outrushing violence about to smash into them all—had left many hulks orbiting, burnished and stripped by scouring bursts of intense radiation.

Dry astrophysics, rendered forth as casual violences.

In his skinsuit, Nigel edged into the deep crevasse they had found. The crew had elected to moor their ship over the crevasse mouth. Then they wormed further in, to escape the shock waves that were now mere minutes away. The ship had balked, trying to restart its engines, resume its programmed course. Nikka had defeated its executive functions, perhaps even silenced its alarms. But she could not be sure . . .

Suited up and in zero gravities again, Nigel felt his old self returning. He had once been an astronaut, after all—a word now ancient beyond comprehension. Was Earth still there?

A certain springy youth returned. He bristled with energy.

It was difficult to *feel* the impact of desiccated physics, he reflected. The combination of the coldsleep slots and the stretched time of special relativity, all catapulting him into a far future of distant, glowing vistas. He had arrived at this far time and place armed with only the training and culture of a society now gone to dust. Yet he still sent quick bursts of data homeward, the latest just an hour ago. Message in a cosmic bottle.

He flitted, giddy and light, down a long tube of chipped rock. Away from the rest.

He took a sample, just like the old NASA days. Dear, dead acronym. At least that was one American habit he would not miss, the compression of jawbreaker agency names into nonsense words that one nonetheless could at least remember. Across thirty thousand years.

He studied the rock. Volcanic origin? He tried to remember his geology. Something strange about its grainy flecks.

Further in, a vault. Gray walls.

Coasting. Space infused even a stiff old carcass with birdlike grace.

Stretched lines ... up ... through ... rock eagerly shaping into swells. Should he go farther, or regain the crew, back there? Shadows swung with each motion of his hand torch, like an audience following every movement.

Patterns in the walls.

Should he? Caution, old fart. Behind each smile, sharp teeth wait.

Down. In. Gliding. Legs dangling

> soft, soft
> into cotton clouds
> shadows melting

telescoping him into fresh cubes of space, geometries aslant. A spherical room now, glowing an answering red where his torch touched. A trick of the eyes?

No, messages—racing across the walls, a blur of symbols. Mind trying to wrap the universe around itself?

He had trouble focusing somehow, *probably just loss of local vertical* his old NASA training spoke to him, just a turn of the head could perhaps fix it—

Worn stone steps leading impossibly up, spiraling away. Into a cupped ceiling now spattered with orange drops ... eyes winking back at him.

An old film, memories. The Tutankhamen tomb. The jackal god Anubis rampant above defeated foes.

Opening the tomb.

Stepping inside.

One small step for a man, across endless churning millennia.

Oozing up from the Valley of old dead Kings, the first to rise triumphant here, from Karnak and Luxor, winding downstream slow and snaky, to Alexandria, the library dry with scrolls, Alexandria a woman, ancient now, wrists rouged and legs numb—

He shook his head.

Local vertical.

Insistent mental alarm bells. *Get local vertical.*

Old truths, surely no use now?

The humming. Insistent. No air here but he could not get away from it. Insect-faint but there.

A sphere ahead. Adhesive patches on the backs of his gloves gave him purchase on it. He swung around, his creaky body bird-quick.

Beyond the metallic sphere yawned a space so vast his torch fetched back no reflections, no answers. He turned to go back, mind still recalling another place and time—

The humming lurched, rose. Shrieked, wailed. A violin string stretched to yield an octave too high, cutting, a dull saw meeting hard steel—

Silence. He blinked, startled.

It had been like this back so long ago. On his mission to *Icarus*, a supposed asteroid that had bloomed fitfully, outgassing a momentary cometary tail. That had been caused by the final loss of an internal atmosphere, as it worked out, from a ship. A vessel built inside an asteroid, a starship. Its rock was extrasolar, and lay beyond the dating protocols, the ratios of isotopes awry. For perhaps a hundred million years it had been left orbiting in the inner solar system.

And Nigel had found this same configuration there. Strangely shaped spaces. A sphere. The humming. A quick electromagnetic cry.

His suit had recorded it all. He spun slowly in a pocket of darkness, the sphere now seeming smaller, spent, exhausted.

Message received. He jetted back toward the others.

5

Huck

Ping, their capsule spoke.

Nikka's face was drawn and furrowed in the reflected light. A searing blue glow seeped down the crevasse. To be this bright down here meant that brilliant furies worked along the asteroid face outside. They were tucked into this makeshift canister, flimsy protection.

A solid bang slapped them against their restraints.

"That's it," Nikka said. "The shock wave."

Tongues of thin fire licked by the observation port.

A few hundred meters away, ionized frenzy worked to get at them—or so went the human-centered view, Nigel reflected.

The awful truth was worse: that the unleashed searing energies booming out from the black hole sought no one, meant nothing, cared not a fig for the human predicament. It would grind up intelligence and spit it out, toward the sleepy stars beyond. Here, mind shaped itself to nature, not the reverse.

They waited out the onslaught for a day, then two. A giant drummed on the walls. Sensors on the ship sent data, painting a picture of huge mass flows past the hull. The ship itself breached, repaired itself, breached again, zapped a few bits of debris. They had come to respect these self-fixing aspects in the long voyage from the suburbs of the galaxy. They were parasites, after all. If they drew too much attention to themselves, some cleanup squad might well get activated.

He had brought with him a few personal bits, hauled all the

way from Earth. In dim suit light he read again the small yellow
hardback, spine cracked, pages stiff and yellowing and stained from
the accidents of adolescence. Near the end there was a passage he
had long ago involuntarily memorized:

> And then Tom he talked along and talked along, and says,
> le's all three slide out of here one of these nights and get an
> outfit, and go for howling adventures amongst the Injuns,
> over in the territory for a couple of weeks or two, and I
> says, all right, that suits me . . .

Nigel had never felt himself remotely American, despite having lived and labored there for decades, but this passage somehow
always made his voice catch in his throat when he read it aloud.

The capsule ticked and pinged and he realized that he and the
others had lived so long now in alien metal corridors that they were
used to the feel of quiet, implacable strangeness all about. Once
you'd left home, all places were remote and foreign and so you
might as well keep going. On to the finality, the omega point of
some alphabet you could not read but by tramping along the full
length of it.

When they finally straggled out, the crevasse was blocked with
debris. Lumps and chunks of rock jammed into every crevice. Nigel
worked on it for a while and then had to rest. He was old, in stringy
good health, but knew his limits. He wondered if there might be another way out of this place, which was clearly a wreck of a starship
of asteroid size.

"It's like the old crash site on the moon," he said to Nikka over
comm. "In Mare Marginis."

"Ummm. I'd noticed some resemblance."

"And the original derelict ship I found, *Icarus*."

"Which implies that—what? Whoever built them was spread
all over the galaxy?"

"They got this far. Must've been."

"And this hulk, as dead as the others?"

Nigel nodded. "Means the mechs got them, I suppose."

"There must have been millions of them, to run into another,
thirty thousand light-years away."

"Um. There's a big game afoot."

They coasted together down one of the side corridors, looking
at yawning vaults and smashed metallic enclosures. "Looks like
someone stripped it," Nikka said, shining a torch into a dark warren.
"Not much left for us to scavenge—",

—out of the corner of Nigel's eye, skimming fast, came the snaky thing.

Helical, with bulky masses appended, a sharp glinting prow. No bigger than a man but faster, coming at Nikka and him as though it had waited for this.

Time collapsed for him. He felt a muscular sliding energy in his shoulders as he spun, lofting away his pack and snatching forth his tool kit.

The thing was plainly mech, crackling on the electromagnetic spectrum in Nigel's ears, a sound like bacon frying on a chilly morning in England long ago—

—as Nigel's hand went for his laser cutter and Nikka had just caught sight of it, her mouth agape, surprise in the inky shadows—

He launched himself on a leap lap to intersect the thing, as it rappelled somehow off a shiny steel bulkhead—

—He felt the mathematics of it in him, geometry as limpid as the fresh continent of Euclidean joy he had entered as a boy, sitting with fingers tucked under his legs as he studied at dawn in his chilly bedroom, keeping hands warm by turning the pages with his tongue—

—static buzz from it—

The snake-mech flexed itself and turned away from him. Headed for Nikka.

—distilling order from life's rough jumble, that was what he had always hungered for, hyperbolic grace, to merge cleanly with life, not split the world into subject and object, no observer/observed, his arm bringing the laser cutter around smoothly, circular arc,

. . . so

slow . . .

atoms in concert, the old dim dualities of mind and matter lapping against the fragile yet inexorable momentum of this instant—

She was faster than he. She shot at it.

The pulse shimmered an instant in the mottled blue surface of the thing, like an argument conducted on its skin. Then the pulse skittered off, reflected. Nigel shot at it too and the thing forked away, split, was somehow two slippery helices now.

—so was it some odd visual pun?—this division into helices, mimicking the key to organic life, DNA pairs spiraling off, the flag of life unfurling in a vacuum wind that rushed from a shadowed passage. A sliver of meaning, he felt it, seven blind men and a melting elephant, all describing, none understanding. His lungs whooshed dry air—

—enameled spraying glow from the uncoiling thing—

It flexed again. Lashed out with a spiky electromagnetic lance. The shot hovered in vacuum, a discharge of reluctant electrons, spitting angry red radiation. Then it split.

One shaft struck Nikka. It burst across her in worms of acrid yellow. She went limp.

Go to ground. Nigel touched the steel bulkhead an instant before the lance reached him. He felt a jolt of megavolts.

—corroding through him, kiloamps rising. His shell clicked home and then he was inside the suddenly conducting surface of his skinsuit, the rub and stretch of potentials racing along a millimeter away from prickly hairs on his shivering racing along a millimeter ing breathed, surges passing by, electromagnetic kiss, inductances fighting the ramping current, forcing jabbing current slivers through his shoulders and licking into his arm, the light touch of his hand enough to draw uncountable speedy electrons to seek another prey, all at frequencies he could not glimpse but the information sliding into him through portals he could never know, below perception a shaved second of intuition—

Before the rattling voltages had spoken their piece he fetched forth the punch gun with his left hand. Muscles clenched and he had to force his fingers to—

It snaked toward him. Nikka floated inert.

Nigel kicked away from the bulkhead though that meant losing his electrical grounding. There might be a few seconds before the mech recharged.

—springing with the kickoff came feelings and desires forking like summer lightning across the inner unmoving vault of him, part of himself eating them as they flared across his mind, seeing them for what they were, messages from a fraction of himself finding a place absolutely blank and waiting for each moment to write upon it, time like water washing away the eruptions, scattershot angers and cutting fears far down in him—

He drove the punch gun ahead. Fired with great relish into the mech.

It was quick, a thing of bunched electrical energies, but the crude and rude sometimes worked.

—*zig when they zag,* leaving no opening he fires the laser cutter too, his right hand tracking the other aspect of the split mech, yin and yang, supple but not crude enough to deal with the sweaty urgencies of organic life forms, the Darwinnowing of mech evolution selecting it for special tasks, narrowing it like a knife by perpetually sharpening, but to get an edge on a blade you had to subtract from it, and the loss was framed in the space of a single heartbeat as the dutiful stubby laser snapped out its jabbing pattern—

The divided mech died. Mere mechanical damage was undoubtedly beneath its program-function range. But potentials cannot build in sheaths mutilated and gouged, and its charge ejected itself down wrong pathways, into the innards, dissolving crystalline structures of intricate artistry. A jewel crushed by a muddy boot.

—he whipped the punch gun around and riddled the other for good measure, the buzzing trailing away, and he slammed into the other spindly riddled carcass, legs collecting recoil, breath whistling in his dry throat in a scatter of perishing light from the gutted mech—

—and he was off, pushing it to gain momentum toward Nikka—

—still drifting, Nikka—

6

◄►◄►◄►◄►◄►◄►◄►

Something Fatal

Nikka did not awaken for three days. Even then she was sluggish and vague, eyes watering, words like discordant lumps trying to make their way out of her throat.

Before she could sit up they had started to move inward again. They got the ship to resume its programmed course. Their handbuilt, tightbeam antenna for signaling Earth was a twisted wire mesh. No more infobursts for the home front. Now they had no mission, except the basic one: survive and learn.

By then they understood from a careful metallicity dating that the helical mech was quite old. It had probably lain in wait in the derelict for ages, in case something organic ventured aboard. A snare.

"Not the sort of thing the Snark would've done," Nigel muttered to himself in the long vigils beside her. Though the Snark had been a mech, of sorts.

The brain repairs itself, with the right help, and her recovery was long.

In his time the very word "machinelike" had two meanings. One was "unfeeling, unconcerned," while the other was "implacable, utterly committed." No wonder that each suggested inhumanity and some rigid stupidity as well.

But here there was a third meaning, revealed in the immense, cool arabesques that filled the sky within a light-year of the black hole. Constructions vast and imponderable. Geometries unnatural and subtly alien.

Energies churned here, sleeting radiation and turbulence. Mechwork patterns floated obliviously through the storming masses. Implacable, unconcerned.

Their ship still gave some cover, apparently. Interrogating messages came beeping into it. Automatic programs aboard answered. Since the scavenger stowaway humans had long since corrupted the information base of the ship, what it told its superiors was undoubtedly nowhere near the truth. But the nature of the alien is that no one can adequately fake a true, intricate language.

So it was inevitable that scarlet traceries condensed around the ship. Potentials arced and played along its hull. A warning, perhaps.

"Or maybe just a bath and a scrub," Nigel joked to Nikka. She could be moved about the ship in a makeshift wheelchair by then. When she saw the wall view outside she gasped.

Once the shock front of the explosion had passed, the True Center loomed like an impossibly detailed tapestry, each uncoiling plume and shimmering sun a jewel woven into the whisking churn of gravity.

"Trick is," Nigel said, "we couldn't see that something had forced mass into the center. A mouthful, sent straight down the gullet, apparently. But you can never stuff all of it down a black hole. Matter heats up, flares out like an angry objection, drives away the outer portion."

She was still taking it in. "What made that happen?"

"Those, I'll wager."

It was the first time he had framed aloud the idea that most of the crew already held. Seemingly insubstantial filaments hung before them like mere filmy curtains. But above and below the galactic plane, they connected to the immense long strands of brilliant radiation, hundreds of light-years long and a light-year wide, which bracketed the entire True Center for vast volumes of space. Nigel had seen the radio maps on Earth, showing the arching filaments. Even through the dark clouds that shielded Earth from the fireworks of the Center, their steady gigahertz glow shone.

"They're so thin."

"To our eyes, true enough."

"What do the ship's diagnostics say?"

"Dead on, m'love. They show strong magnetic fields."

"Enough to hold off all that mass that's trying to slip through them?"

"Right again." Just because she had nearly been killed, cast

into a coma and thoroughly lacerated mentally, was no reason to forget that indeed, he had the old Nikka back. Always one step ahead
of the argument. Circling round it, sometimes.

"I can see how that gas—lovely purple glow, isn't it?—veers
up and around. Some pressure is doing that."

"Magnetic pressure. Never seen anything like it. Even in the
outer strands, which nobody understood when we were back on
Earth, the field isn't a hundredth as strong."

"And it's coming at us, whatever it is."

He was surprised again. "How can you tell?"

"I can see the stuff in front of it. It's getting squashed, see?"

Indeed, now that he screwed up his eyes and studied it, he
could. Until now he had relied on ship's instruments to check that
the gossamer strands were rushing toward their ship from several
directions.

"What *are* they?" Nikka asked, some fatigue still lacing her
voice.

"Something fatal, I'd say."

7

❰❰❱❰❰❱❰❰❱❰❰❱❰❰❱❰❰❱❰❰❱

Old Ones

One virtue of the shock wave, my boy—it cleared the view. Finally we saw the Old Ones.

The long, curved filaments were not freeways or power sources or religious icons—they were intelligences. A life form bigger than stars or giant molecular clouds or anything else in the galaxy's astrophysical zoo.

I later learned that these were the, well, the body of the Old Ones—though that term means quite little. In the filaments, currents carried both information—thoughts—and food, that is, charge accumulations, inductances, and potentials. All flowing *together*. As if, in our bodies, sugars and synapses were the same thing, somehow. The long, sinewy structures glowed and flared, but that was a minor side effect.

After all, we eat and think and love—and the net result, viewed in the infrared, is a diffuse, ruddy glow, no more.

The real point of us you'd find only by peering at our industriously firing synapses. Or, backing off about six orders of magnitude, in our sluggish talk.

And of course, we are sluggish, compared to a lot that's going on round here. In the local jargon, we talk at about fifty bits per second. We need small bandwidths for long times, just to get out a single idea.

The Old Ones are broad bandwidth, fast times. We talk slowly, but see well—big chunks of our brains are devoted to shaping up images. Punching up the data, before we ever "see" them at all.

The Old Ones have that, as well. I doubt there's anything they can't do.

I watched those strange strands, weaving like slow seaweed in a vacuum ocean, and automatically thought of telling Earth about them. That's what I'd been doing for so long—beaming reports back down the tunnel of our wake.

Our flight time to Galactic Center was several centuries, ship's time. I had transmitted a burst every few years. Earth would get those coded blips, I knew, widely spread out by relativistic effects. But was anyone listening?

Staring at the Old Ones, I realized that we were mayflies. The ebb and flow of our civilizations were like gusts of passing, feather-light winds.

I doubt there's anything the Old Ones can't do.

Point is, what do they *want* to do?

8

Grandfather

Toby was getting irked. "You sure got a funny way of telling me what the hell's going on here."

The naked man, though he was a mass of wrinkles, was able to get into his face an expression of canny humor. "Do you poke at your grandfather when he's setting you straight?"

"What do you know about my grandfather?"

"Met him, actually."

"When? Where is he?"

"I've learned not to use 'when' too much down here. Where is easier. He's here."

Toby stood up, knocking over the little chair with a clatter. "I want to see him!"

"That you can't do."

"I want to *now*."

"He's not available. If—"

"I've had about enough of you and your—"

The old man's face was suddenly stern and imposing, bringing a flicker of memory to Toby: very much like his grandfather. Maybe all old people got that, something years brought. He sighed and sat down. "All right. Can you tell him I'm here?"

"He knows."

"How?"

"That's what I'm attempting to tell you."

"Uh, sorry."

9

The Strong Field Limit

The Old Ones—not a very inventive name, but then, Jehovah isn't that catchy, either.

The Old Ones had been here when the mech civilizations arrived. Mechanicals arose when advanced, organic societies somehow committed suicide—from war, degeneration, unimaginable things—or retreated, from plain simple lack of interest in the tensions of the technological life. That left machines, who evolved into separate societies.

But the Old Ones weren't mech-based. Not derived from the clanking iron and silicon, no.

They weren't cumbersome chemical concoctions like us, either—rickety packets of salty water and sundry impurities held together by calcium rods and an easily punctured skin, all run by dead slow electrical wiring. They weren't beings that had to be retrofitted over ever worse workmanship from earlier times. Nothing messy. Nothing slapped together by chance.

The Old Ones *were* those long strands. Each strand could speak with a single, well, voice. Approximately. It's hard to describe what it feels like to have one, well, simply invade you. Not like a conversation, no. Rather more like being sodomized by God, I'd say.

You saw them on your way in? Good. Like pearly lightning, as I remember. You could see them slowly twisting, fragile-seeming.

They looped and arced around our ship. By this time there

were plenty of mech blips on the screens. These the Old Ones deflected—using their magnetic pressures, I expect.

Us, they swept along. They took precious little note of our limits. Gave us several gravities of acceleration at times. I'd once been an "astronaut"—a term from the days when doing this sort of thing wasn't as ordinary as walking—and knew to balloon my lungs, then suck in air in rapid little pants, breathing off the top. Others didn't weather so well. Nikka came through, despite being still weak.

The Old Ones had made the explosion. That shock wave was simple cleaning up after the real job, sort of a janitor with his broom making a tidy Galactic Center for all. The Old Ones had released an immense burst of energy, mating two black holes together. Making this—the Lair.

The mechs made a profit off it all. Someone always does. They sucked in the fast protons, harvested the photon flux. They have a whole system set up to gather in the energy fluxes, currents and all. You might say they're farming the Galactic Center, but there's another game afoot, a bigger one.

The Lair. That the mechs tried to destroy. Almost did, I gather. It's not easy to maintain, still harder to build.

That explosion shaped the Lair, made it larger. Folded up space-time, manufactured room where there was no room. The Old Ones had made it in the far past, apparently to store things or beings or God knows what. And they kept adding to it, perhaps deepening its complexity.

In our ship we got picked up, hurled at the accretion disk, then up and over it. Down the axis. Toward the pole of the black hole.

You followed a similar path, correct? Good—I sent it to you.

What? Of course, all that about Abraham sending messages. Well, I had to say something to get your attention.

Deceptive? Of course. Immoral? Don't be ridiculous.

I had to claim it was from your grandfather, dead right. I *had* met him, after all. And speaking through the Magnetic Mind was the only route open to you. Mechs would've intercepted anything else.

Where was I? Ah—

All the bloody time with mechs coming straight at us. Inflicted some damage, too. Killed some of us. Have you ever seen steel blister?

Mechs got through. Even the magnetic pressures couldn't halt everything. Neutron beams, for one. Nothing stopped those.

The Old Ones were powerful, certainly, but not like God the Sodomizer. Sorry if you find my sense of humor a bit demented.

I've been here in this mountain largely without company, except of the most lofty sort. A bit wearing. Makes me long for the animal, I suppose. The root and rut of life.

The Lair? Call it that because we're hiding in it. As well as countless other organic species.

The Old Ones stuffed us in here, with our ship. Down the steepest gravitational gradient in the galaxy, into a time-locked storage vault. General relativity, writ large.

What they never taught me at Cambridge, not even that Hawking fellow, was that space-time could be a construction material. Mass is equivalent to the curvature of space-time, that I'd learned. We build things from matter. Why not build them from curved space-time?

Simple enough, but the stress-energy tensors involved— you don't want to see the mathematics, believe me. Ugly stuff. Frightful.

You see, the most important point in understanding the universe is that God doesn't have to make any approximations. He's not doing as I dutifully learned at Cambridge, expanding in some small parameter, iterating solutions, solving differential equations by cut-and-try. God plays the game straight.

The Old Ones aren't Gods—in fact, they're decidedly irritating—but they can solve general relativity in full. No short cuts. In the "strong field limit," as it's termed.

How? I don't know. I wasn't here to see it done. Somehow the Old Ones squeezed together two black holes—the giant at True Center, and a lesser one they'd acquired somehow—and blew off a hell-storm of energy.

When the dust cleared, here was the Lair. Furiously orbiting the remaining black hole, which has total mass a few million times the sun's. The Lair Labyrinth. Stable. Twisted esty. An abiding refraction.

They simply inserted us into it. You Bishops flew in, skimmed the ergosphere, correct? That's the only way in now, apparently. That works only when there's a significant chunk of mass coming through, rippling the skin of the black hole at its equator. Then someone can fly through.

Unfortunately, the mechs learned this, too. The Old Ones couldn't prevent that. We've done our best against them, even with the Earthers—I'll get to them, different subject—to help. But it has been a losing battle. The mechs are *good*.

In fact, the Old Ones have stooped to cooperating with us biologicals, the so-called Naturals, because the mechs are *too* good.

They may exterminate all Naturals. The Old Ones don't want that, for reasons of their own.

What reasons? I have guesses, plenty of them. But nobody knows for sure.

Part of the confusion, for an ordinary TwenCen mind like mine, is the sheer complexity. Never mind the higher-order mechs, the Old Ones, and the like—they're beyond view, for me. For you, too, I expect.

It takes a while to get used to even the physics, y'see. The Lair—what? Oh, right, you can call it Wedge if you like, there must be a thousand names. Some quite obscene; you should hear sometime how "black hole" translates into Russian. The Lair is like a wasp's nest perched on a cliff. The Eater's tidal forces warp it, stretch both space and time.

The lower parts live differently. Time runs slower here—straight Einsteinian effect, that. So outside, while centuries are sweeping by, I'm having lunch. Gives a body perspective. Of course, I do take long lunches.

And it gets a bit lonely, too.

10

Vermin

Toby had listened and watched and finally it was too damned much.

The walls flashed with pictures, scenes of astonishing depth and range. Colossal twisted ships, frothing turbulence in the accretion disk, vistas with skewed perspectives, geometries so odd the eye could not keep them in order. Walmsley's voice alone called up the images, summoned by some program in the utterly bare room.

To Toby, technology meant details, controls, complex systems. Here nothing met the eye but plain walls. Yet the room responded to everything Walmsley seemed to need, even when he did not speak. Food and drink appeared through the floor. Music sounded in the distance, and Walmsley cocked an ear to it.

"Look," Toby said, "I'm trying to piece this together with the history of Family Bishop."

"That I know. Your Family came out of the Hunker Down. That's when the folk outside, the Earthers, decided they couldn't hold the mechs any more. They left their cities."

"The Chandeliers?"

"Right, that's one tribal name for them. Wonderful places. I watched them disintegrate, alas."

"And we Bishops went to Snowglade?"

"Is that—" Walmsley appeared to listen to some distant voice, then nodded. "Your name for it, yes. J-three-six-four, the index says. The index isn't very romantic about these things, I'm afraid."

"And we lived there for . . .?"

"Many centuries. The mechs weren't bothering with planets just then, y'see. They harvested plasma flows in those eras. When they got around to mining and chewing up planets, they ran into another organic species that came surging in. Big bugs, they were."

"Quath!—the Myriapodia."

"Right. Impressive creatures. They're tech-bio anthologies, half-artificial, as the Earthers became. The Old Ones say they're still missing something we humans've got, but I can't fancy what that could be."

Toby felt elation at finding something in this history that he knew about. Quath . . . and where was she?

Walmsley said, "The Myriapodia have been giving the mechs trouble. Not enough to stop their grand works, though."

"We hooked up with the Myriapodia, after some skirmishing. One is—was—with me."

Walmsley nodded. "Standard mech tactic. Used you to take some of the fight out of the bugs."

"What? We ran into them by accident. Our Family had escaped from Snowglade and—"

"The mechs let you get away."

"The hell they did! We fought—"

"We're vermin to them," Walmsley said gently.

"And together, we and Quath's kind, we tore the hell out of the mechs around that planet, near Abraham's Star. I was *there*, I know—"

"Certainly. The big bugs had cosmic strings, correct?"

"Uh, yeasay."

"Fearsome as tools or weaponry alike. But the mechs are managing all this, for reasons I don't quite follow. A faction wanted you Bishops here, at the Lair. They want something from you, but precisely what, I don't know. Another faction would much prefer you all dead. Some strange game's afoot."

Toby shot him an irked look. "You've had all this time here. Why haven't you figured it out?"

"Data's hard to get, and subtle when you do. Most of the cards aren't on the table—if there even *is* a table. And . . . well, point is, my family and I—"

"Family Brit?"

"No, no, in my time we thought of the nearest relatives as family. Family Brit was, shall we say, a manner of speaking."

"You kept Family so small? Why?"

Walmsley's eyes rolled up theatrically. "Comes to that, I'd sooner explain science than culture. Nikka and I, well, we were attempting a bit of an experiment, really. Wanted to get three generations together, for genetic reasons. Turned out wrong, since most of humanity had already genetically drifted away from—"

"Genetic? I don't—"

"I'm getting ahead of myself. See, my family and I—just a few of us, not the bloody United Kingdom, see?—had discovered some odd scientific matters. Let me show you how it was."

"And those Earthers—"

"Let me tell it my way."

11

The Earthers

They were not what he expected.

"Hope you weren't hurt," the tall woman said. English, slightly accented with flat *a*'s and odd, hollow *e*'s. She was the first Earther he had seen.

"Jostled a bit, is all," Nigel tried to say lightly.

He had barely survived a brush with some mechs who had appeared to ooze straight out of walls, like an elaborate magic trick. Then the Earthers had appeared and made short work of the strangely liquid mechs.

Earthers. Nigel had seen their fleet approaching the Lair, knew they were here, but in its Labyrinth was unsure of how to find them. They found him, instead.

"Why are you still speaking English?" he asked slowly.

"Oh, we have this archaic dialect as an inboard. We heard you speaking it."

"Um. Very thoughtful."

"Your transmissions used it."

They moved with swift, sure movements, these people two heads taller than Nigel, caring for the wounded. He had taken a knock in the ribs, a pulse that broke the skin by frying it to a crisp, like a Thanksgiving turkey. He lay back and let the woman put a patch on it. The wound felt cold, then hot, then numb, and then he did not notice it at all.

So these were the people who had built starships—better by far than the mech ship Nigel and Nikka had come here in—and made it their duty to reach Galactic Center. He tried to view them objectively, though by their earlier hailing messages he knew they were from several thousand years after his time on Earth. He tried to imagine what time's juggernaut could bring after the dear dead TwenCen and the sobering TwenOne.

He lay back and watched them with slitted gaze. They spoke softly, used minimal sentences.

Be objective, now, old fellow. See them as just another organic race. Just another large mammal.

Hominids, yet different. He was somewhat gladdened to note that they still resembled the common chimps and pygmy chimps, just bigger and with less hair, walking upright. The visible differences between humans and chimps were far less than, say, between Great Danes and Chihuahuas. Yet dogs interbred and the chimps did not; the genome kept its secrets well hidden from the eye. Humans differed from chimps by a single percent in DNA. These folk were still of the species.

These Earthers had killed mechs with obvious relish, too. Very human. Not strictly a hominid trait; genocide occurred in wolves and chimps alike. Animal murder was widespread. Ducks and orangutans raped. Ants had organized warfare and slave raids. Chimps in the wild, he recalled, had at least as good a chance of being murdered as did humans in cities.

Nigel lay back, head woozy. Of all the hallowed human hallmarks—speech, art, technology, and the rest—the one that came most obviously from animal ancestors was genocide. Human tribes may well have evolved as a group defense. That no doubt helped, in those millennia separating him from these big, bright hominids.

"Clubbiness against clubs," he said aloud. A dry crack of a voice. Yes, he was skimming, mind light as shining dust.

These Earthers had oddly shaped ears, more muscular frames, curious large eyes. Their uniforms were anything but uniform—technicolor wraparounds that shifted to different scenes in apparently random fashion. As the woman came over to check him again her loose garment abruptly showed him a sunlit seashore, waves crashing. To soothe him?

Art adorned other Earthers' close-fitting clothes—collages, abstracts, grainy expressionist vistas. Woozy, he puzzled over that. Art was certainly not useful in the narrow senses employed by the animal behaviorists or evolutionary biologists. Why did Cro-Magnon develop it? Bird songs were a different matter; they helped woo a mate, defend an area. Why did humans, the Earthers, still have their fragile arts? Bower birds built airy confections of leaves, lace, and fungi, all in the pursuit of love, or genes. He scarcely thought abstract expressionism could make such a claim. Could all the heights of human artistry be a display strategy, like a peacock's plumage?

He laughed at that and sat up. His fried side did not even ache. His head was clearer. Nikka stood a short distance away, talking to a huge fellow. Nigel waved.

Nikka and the man came over. "I'm Akran," the man said, staring down, blinking rapidly. "Are you . . . Walmsley?"

"I believe so."

"My Lord! To *find* you!"

"Just in time, too. Thanks."

"But you—you are—still alive!"

"Somewhat."

Other Earthers came running, formed a knot around Nikka and Nigel.

"It's him!"

"And her! She's the one mentioned in Message Fifty-seven."

"I don't believe it."

"Sure it is. Look at him."

"After all this time?"

"He's been inside this twisted space-time."

"Don't forget the Long Sleep."

"Still, it's incredible that—"

"It's *Walmsley*."

Nigel gazed up into their faces and felt woozy. They all started speaking and Nikka beamed down at him—she seemed to understand what was going on—and they talked so fast he could barely get the idea.

One of them played a recording then and Nigel heard his own voice, reedy and precise.

"Hello? Data follows on the molecular cloud we're passing through. Still on course, apparently."

A blur of data, then: *"This is humanity's expedition. On high boost, flying inward."*

Static. A sizzling hiss, like fat frying. *"Hello? We're still here. Are you?"*

The Earthers stood silently, long after the recording finished.

"We got your messages every few centuries," Akran said. "You knew about the first assault, mechs dumping alien life into our seas? We received your first transmission just as we were getting the upper hand over those."

Nigel frowned. "So you really didn't need help from us—"

"Oh no! That was just the first. The second time, they tried to pound us with asteroids. Lots of them. Nearly got us, that time."

Nigel shook his head to clear it. "We sent you some mech gear, data—"

"We got them. Helped a lot. That was at the worst of the third assault, the Ferret Time. That lasted five centuries."

"My God," Nikka said. "The mechs had that strong a force?"

"Of course," Akran said. "Then the smart ones arrived. Tried to fool us. We lost a big piece of Earth to them. That took a thousand years."

Nigel said, "And you kept getting my messages?"

Akran nodded eagerly. "We put up big antennas. First in orbit, then all around the solar system. Mechs kept finding them, smashing them."

Nigel thought of the centuries of struggle and sighed. The world revolved with a serene grace, people and dirt starting to spin left to right—

"Is he tired?" Akran said with alarm. "We can talk later, let him sleep—"

"Go on," Nikka said. Nigel could only nod.

"We did miss some of the messages, when the mechs came at us with positron weapons. But we got antennas back up on the moon after about four hundred years. That was after the poles melted and we lost most of the continents."

"Good grief," Nigel managed to wheeze out.

"But we got all the rest. Nobody wanted the next one to find an empty Earth. So we pulled ourselves up. Searched the whole damn solar system for the last mech outposts. They were pretty well hidden, some down in Jupiter's clouds. And we got every one."

Nigel blinked. The world had stopped revolving and he was beginning to understand. "And came . . ."

"Here. To find out what had happened to you. And what's this whole thing is all about."

Hello? We're still here. Are you?

He saw in the faces something like awe. To them he and Nikka and the others were antique historical pieces, incredibly ancient.

Immensely capable, these Earthers were. The mechs would fear them.

Nigel blinked, smiled. "We're still here. Still here." It seemed very amusing and he could not talk any more for the lump in his throat.

12

Sobering Perspectives

That was the high point. Of course it was fine and wonderful to meet his own kind again, humans from dear beloved Earth.

But in time, his first fuzzy perceptions as he lay there wounded, of the Earthers as bright chimps, made more and more ironic sense. They were human, true. Smart chimps. But far more. Changed.

The mech onslaughts against Earth had forced human evolution—both through biotech enhancements and natural selection. The Earthers had implants that gave them sensoria—complex electromagnetic shells, useful for both war and work. Their spines rode better, on thick lumbar disks. They carried no pesky appendix to fester and erupt. Their bodies had intricate neurological meshes, better metabolism, rugged cartilage, sturdier bones.

Those were rather obvious. The unconscious differences were more telling. He and Nikka and the others from the TwenOne century—called the "Elders," soon enough—could not keep up with these Earthers, mentally or physically. The big, almost lazily competent newcomers were very polite about it, of course. They tried to include their Elders as they explored the esty, hammered the mechs, and even made contact with the ghostly Old Ones.

These brave new Earthers retained a certain chimpyness. Hominids, still. Quite courteous to their Elders, but learning quickly from mechs and Old Ones alike. Climbing an evolutionary ladder, trailing clouds of glory, into a fog.

At that point, their thought processes simply escaped comprehension.

The rheumy old-fart Elders could not follow conversations involving the Old Ones. Nigel and Nikka and the others who had come in the hijacked mech starship—a small band, now, called Ancestrals by the Earthers—were adrift. They could not master the blindingly fast tech the Earthers had brought, or later devised in response to the mechs.

Nigel got a glimmering of the Old Ones, when he helped explore portions of the esty Lanes. Those convoluted geometries, sealed away, made excellent petri dishes. In the Lanes, different cultures—alien and human alike—could evolve the diversity needed to counter the mechanicals. All sorts emerged—high-tech, low-tech, even no-tech.

For the Elders, the new perspectives were sobering. The Earthers, though, worked easily with the Old Ones. They countered the mechs, killed many, sometimes even cooperated with them.

The Old Ones dispersed Earthers, out of the Lair. Nigel and the other Elders more or less looked on and did scut work. The news was distant, hard to follow.

A big offensive against mech control of the entire Center. Earthers spread among the planets orbiting stars a bit farther out from True Center.

They learned from mechtech, scavenged mech properties. They built huge constructions in space, the Chandeliers.

For many millennia the Earthers did well. Nigel watched them from the time-slowed pit of the esty. Then came trouble.

Mechs found a way to short-circuit some of the power by which the Old Ones sustained their strange magnetic strands. Tapping that source for their own ends made them enormously more powerful. That's when they started to grow, to pillage the great orbiting Earther cities.

Nigel had visited their crystal cities, and the even greater structures that he could witness but not fathom. When the mechs began getting the upper hand again, he helped as he could. The very terms of the struggle were difficult to comprehend.

Like listening to a conversation carried out through a drain pipe during a rainstorm, he had said. *A very long drain pipe.*

As the mechanicals destroyed more and more of the human enterprise at Galactic Center, he found more to do. The conflict was coming down to his level again.

The final, desperate strategy of the Hunker Down—dividing humanity into separate cultural petri dishes, down on the planets—gave him plenty of grunt work to do. In that era he had spent a time outside the esty.

He could not follow in any detail the ramifications of the Earthermech struggle. He knew it involved alien organic races, other Originals, as well. And the conflict's main stage was at a level involving the Old Ones and the elusive Highers. Of these he and the other Ancestrals knew nothing.

Except . . . The mechanicals had some grail they sought. They kept utterly secretive about it, but they pursued bands of humans as if searching for something. Nigel once caught the phrases "Trigger Codes" and "First Command" but they went by on the fly, soon lost. And the Earthers gave him a stony-faced nothing in answer. As if there were some secret so subtle that knowledge that there *was* a secret was a secret.

Also, it had taken him a long time to see how he was being used.

Politely, with the most consideration possible, of course. But used. By Earthers and Highers alike.

He had retired, then, from a struggle beyond his ken. Or thought he had.

13

The Physical Representation

Nigel Walmsley squinted at Toby. "There's so much to tell—"

"I don't need to know much! Just enough to keep alive," Toby said.

"That turns out to be quite a bit. You're pretty complicated yourself, boy." Nigel could not resist giving an interior command. Points were often better made by example.

Beside Toby, glimmering points condensed into Shibo. She was a handsome, mature woman, lean and translucent and her legs missing. Her upper body twisted as if stretching from a long confinement. A thin smile. "Hello, my carrier."

Toby jumped, startled. "You! You're still buried down in my reserve banks?"

"I insinuated . . . myself."

"Damn! I wanted you *out*."

"I have . . . no place . . . to go."

The room's sensorium readers were tuned to excruciating precision and could pick up even diffused Aspects and Personalities and Faces lodged in an individual's fringing fields. Shibo shimmered, ghostly remnant hiding in Toby's electro-aura.

Shibo's face said more than her faltering words. "I am here . . . to help."

"I've got you in chipstore," Toby said bitterly. "That's enough."

"I cannot help . . . being."

Nigel felt a strange, silky current pass between Toby and the Shibo representation. Toby said, "Killeen, he wants to bring you back. Chips're enough for that?"

"I prefer . . . to reside . . . here."

"If Killeen gets your chips, he'll try to bring you back."

"I prefer . . . here."

"I want you *out*."

"I stay." She lifted a hand in silent salute—and vanished.

"Ah! Damn!" Toby spat out in frustration.

"Sorry, but I had a point to make," Nigel said. "You will find that the notion of self is a bit complex here."

"I've got to get her out of me."

Nigel said with compassion, "In time you'll realize that what mechs call the 'physical representation' is only one phase."

"Shibo really could be brought back, then?"

"In a sense."

"What's *that* mean?"

"Reality—a delightfully abstract term—is analog. Humans live and think there."

Toby shrugged. "Yeasay, it's *real*."

"The mech world is essentially digital. You'll never understand mechs until you realize how differently they view matters. And not only them. The Old Ones, the Highers—they do not share our sense of the self."

"Highers?"

Walmsley knew the boy would understand it all best if it unfurled in a story. The classic primate manner of learning. Linear, relentlessly serial. Quite old-fashioned, yet it stuck.

Very well, best to go back a long way, to the time after he had backed away from the High Phyla entirely, sought the refuge of simplicity.

He sighed. "There's so much to tell—"

Part II

SOON COMES
NIGHT

The universe is full of magical things, patiently waiting
for our wits to grow sharper.

—EDEN PHILLPOTTS,
A Shadow Passes, 1934

1

Worm

The body lay dying for some time before Angelina found it.

She had noticed a small cyclone of birds standing in the air above a churned-up span of smoldering rock and went to look. The small, four-winged birds were predators only in a flock, never alone. They banked on the warm updraft from the oozing soup of sun-orange rock below, peering down with hungry intensity.

The broken body stirred every now and then and the birds would rise a bit, a reflex born of long evolution, for if the prey revived it might be dangerous. Their courage was purely collective. Each would have fled in confusion were it not for the familiar, gene-deep helical churn of their updrafted gyre that calmed them all.

Angelina found the body folded up, as though broken in the legs and chest. It was a woman in a dark-red single-sheathed garment. The pliant weave was ripped and caked with blood already gone brown. As Angelina knelt to help she caught the coppery scent of fresh blood and saw an eyelid quiver. A patch seeped red at the temple.

That made Angelina send a quick comm alert to her brothers, Benjamin and Ito, who came from the house an hour's walk away. They ran it in much less, bringing a sling and medical supplies.

Angelina had stopped most of the bleeding with a tourniquet, but the woman was in a bad way from the heat and dehydration on top of the catalog of injuries: chest a massive purple bruise, chin crushed in, right arm twisted at an impossible angle and showing white bone.

They got her in the sling and worked on the arm before carrying her back over the broken landscape. Only then did the slowly cycling tower of birds, hundreds-strong and chorusing a disappointed *chip-chip-chip* song, disperse into its timid, individual parts. Some still tracked the humans, for scouts were part of the collective genetic lessons as well.

The three had trouble getting back to safer ground and that was when they guessed the origin of the dying woman. Footing was unsteady. From long habit they thought of the solid stuff their boots struck as rock, but knew that the glowing, slippery sheen was the "esty" — S–T, a compacted form of space-time. The esty could be firm and dense at one moment and the next, blur and fuzz into a foglike film. Vital and durable yet flexing, following laws of its own nature, rules unknowable. Or at least unknown by humans of this era.

As they took turns carrying the listless body each of them was troubled by a sense of foreboding. In their circumscribed world this woman had come as a signal flare, an announcement. She opened again the doors of speculation, for they knew the tales of bodies belched forth by the esty from places and eras of danger and promise. They did not share these first tingling thoughts, but the air hung heavy among them.

Humans had lived here a long time, shaped by the esty and knowing it as the frame of their world. Yet it was also an enemy of capricious, almost vindictive spirit. It slipped beneath their boots as they carried the woman, who still oozed blood and pus at her many wounds. Blue-white flashes wracked the air. Vagrant electrical energies plucked at their sleeves like fugitive winds.

They reached their sprawling, ramshackle house. Their father, Nigel, had returned from the orchard. He frowned when he saw the damage. Already their mother, Nikka, had their auto-medical equipment rig up and running, shiny and smooth despite its age, but there was by that time little hope.

The woman gasped and choked, her hot breath whistling past a broken tooth. For a moment she smacked her lips and seemed to savor the flavor of the home: sweet cloves and garlic, aging flowers, damp rags, thick soup simmering in an all-day pot, a woody tang tamed by a sheen of oil.

Her concussion spoke for her then, forcing clogged murmurs and hoarse cries from her raw throat.

"Sky . . . burning . . . ohkan . . . ohkan . . . get away!"

The family Walmsley glanced at each other. "The others we heard about," Nikka whispered, "they never could talk."

"This one won't for long, I'll wager," Nigel said.

Something in him took an instant dislike to anything that disturbed his tranquil world, this rustic refuge he and Nikka had shaped. Earthers, mechs, Old Ones—their operatic clashes lay far away, in other Lanes, or out among the fevered stars. This woman brought all that to mind again.

Yet he had chosen this place for their farm. He had known that the eruption spots in the esty were important. Something in him did not want to quite let go of the larger stage.

The woman subsided for a while. They moved around her, following the instructions of the artificial intelligence, which spoke with a hushed, calming voice. The program had a false note of sympathy that always irritated Nigel, but the family found it reassuring.

Nikka saw the bulge in the woman's optic disk—*papilledema,* the soothing computer voice supplied, speaking of severe damage to the woman's outsized cranium. Fractures ran through the body, as if it had been systematically stepped upon. Cracked ribs and hips and calves, ending in toes snapped off clean. Blood vessels had been raked and cauterized by a tunneling fire. No one knew how to fix these things readily and the computer would not hazard a guess as to their cause. As they inventoried the damage and patched where they could, the woman gave a harsh bark. Her eyes flew open in a kind of discharging overload, and she sat up.

"Grey Mech . . . knows . . . got to . . . sky . . . fire, fire . . ."

She yawned, startled jaws agape with bright fresh pain—and went completely limp. By the time her head slapped back on the pad her life functions had gone flatline.

Nothing Angelina or Benjamin or Ito could do could bring a spark back into the body. Her mind was blown to shards. They started the small measures that would snatch back some fragment of the woman: circulating her blood with a pump inserted into the bloodstream, reading her cortical map.

"From the esty," Nigel said as they worked.

"And she mentioned the Grey Mech," Benjamin said. They glanced at each other soberly.

Nigel ran the diagnostics program but otherwise kept his distance. He had seen a lot of damaged people in his time and did not share his children's fascination. "She came up from the wormhole spot, correct?—same as long ago."

Benjamin, the younger son, cocked his mouth doubtfully. "That body was dead too?"

"A man near here named Ortega found it hanging half-exposed out of a kind of fog-ball, he said." Nigel was quite old now, nearly four hundred of the old Earth years by his reckoning, but he remembered fairly well. This territory he tread softly, for it brought up doubts about himself, of who he had been long ago, of what the abyss of centuries had swallowed—

He stopped himself from thinking that way and went on. "That's the only case I ever heard of around here, but esty history has a few more."

"From that shaky spot in the Lane?" Benjamin shook his head. "But worms, they're like balls, spheres, not like holes in a wall."

"True," Nikka said. "But worms can open up best in compacted esty. There is more free energy available there, or so the theory goes."

Benjamin stopped working, his hands resting on the blood-spattered table. "So this woman passed through a *worm*? I thought the pressures inside were incredible."

"They are. The body Ortega found was stretched, pulped. From far upstream time," Nigel said.

"Suredead?" Benjamin asked, eyes rapt.

Nigel said, "A few memories, but nobody could assemble a Personality from them."

Nigel thought then of the distant space and time from which this cooling woman had probably come. A one-way passage to a past or future unknown, a journey fraught with murderous forces.

Yet she had come. Or been sent? "Bringing something," he mused.

Benjamin frowned. "Bringing what?" With long, bony fingers he searched among the tatters they had cut from the body. "Nothing here but cloth."

Ito was swaddling up the cutting stink where the woman's bowels had loosened in her final, clenching agony. "D'you think the Old Ones'll want to look at her?"

"I hope not," Nikka said. "They'll take forty forevers to send somebody out here."

Nigel said crabbily, "I hope she's not going to rot quickly, like the one Ortega found."

Nikka rebuked him sharply, eyes irked in her leathery face. "Don't be calloused."

"Respect for the dead doesn't mean you take risks." Nigel looked a little sheepish over his remark and felt called to defend it.

"Full protocols?" Angelina asked. She was muscular and compact from work in the groves and smiled prettily despite the circumstances.

Benjamin said eagerly, "I'll get the readers." As the youngest, just entering adolescence, he sprang to take on any task, to show he wasn't much behind his sister, the middle child. Ito had been that way but lately had left his teenage years and did not have his bearing straight, Nigel judged, on where to go from there.

All but Benjamin knew about the man Ortega found, who had gone bad in ways—fungus growing while you watched, spores blown off, eyes popping vapor—that had inspired in them childhood nightmares. Even now, nearly fully grown, none of them liked to recall Nigel's warnings and pictures: boils that had sprouted like small glassy domes from the man's flesh, festering purple and angry red. They had burst with wet pops and ejected spongy drops that stuck and had to be scraped off with a knife. And scraped fast—they sought food, boring into flesh.

They made the readings with speed. Nikka checked to be sure the scanning patches were flat against the woman's skull. The moment they were done Benjamin asked with a flat, false calm, "Better get her under the soil, then?"

"No," Angelina ventured. It was not like her to challenge her brothers, but she had found this woman and from the set of her chin Nigel knew she felt some sense of odd possession and responsibility. "What if the Old Ones want it?"

Nigel nodded, obviously to Angelina's surprise. "Talking to authorities, best to keep things simple. Last time they made Ortega and I do the digging-up."

Angelina gasped. "You did?"

"The Old Ones believe in local responsibility. Or seem to—they make their human agents run things that way. I was a neighbor, so I dug—period." Nigel shrugged. "Had to do it in skinsuits. It became a trifle hot. Thirsty work."

All three Walmsley children looked uneasily at each other. This detail their father had not told before. The set of Benjamin's chin said that as the younger brother he wanted his fair share of any decision. "Those scientists, they'll want a full report, do their experiments, take samples. You know how they are."

Nikka's worried frown deepened. "I wouldn't trust our storage. The rot could get out and—"

"Let's put her back into the esty," Angelina said brightly.

The idea was simple yet stunning. Buried in soil, the body could be recovered. In esty, never.

They had all been shaken by the erupting of the esty again, after years of slumbering. The idea of setting foot among the shifting tides of the nonrock, the timestone, was bothersome. Yet, Nigel saw, none of them wished to show such concern to the others. That zone of the esty was the stuff of local legend and the children both feared its promise of mystery and adventure and yearned for it. So they agreed.

They processed the readings first. That was all custom required: a scan of the neural beds, of memory vaults in the cerebral cortex, an inventory that could at least establish the broad outlines of who this woman had been. Bodies from the future came forth in only a few known spots and it had been Nigel's intention to live near one.

The woman's body had already begun to warp and ooze as they lugged it back into the head-spinning deviations of the rumbling, ozone-sharp wormhole zone. Ito and Angelina carried it with cat-like balance, as though ready to leap. Fast, humming high frequencies ran through their shared sensorium, a kind of warning system that linked them. This eruption was just beginning and promised to be big. An acrid scent cut the air. Zephyrs of bitter heat caught at their nostrils and the footing trembled with expectation and menace. They brought the body back to where they had found it, or tried to, for already a gravitational chasm had opened there. A powdery sapphire cloud hovered above the foaming esty itself. The air torqued them with tugs and pushes.

They steered well clear of the dancing powder. It shaped into elongated cylinders, tear drops, fluted arabesques—which meant it was another manifestation of the far future. A sharp *crack*—and the esty flexed and slewed like a raft in a roaring river.

This threw Ito down and sent the body rolling, arms flapping, legs stiff and waving like sticks. It spun into the air and plunged toward the spatial fissure. The sapphire fog opened and closed like the mouth of a fish underwater, oval and meaningless. Nigel clung to his children and watched. The body seemed to dissolve, then become compacted and firm again, before merging with the stuff that only hours before had been reliable timestone. Then it was gone. Consumed, perhaps transported.

"Wonder where it went," Benjamin mused, drawling.

"It's slipping through the esty—'Transiting,' isn't that what the Old Ones say?" Angelina asked uneasily, rubbing her gloves on her leggings as if to get clean of the body, its touch and smell. Yet her angular face showed an intrigued, puzzled expectation.

"Going that way didn't seem to hurt it," Benjamin said.

"Something sure did before," Ito said. "Killed her."

Nigel sniffed and jerked a thumb back toward home. "This place will soften up and spread. Happened that way last time. Let's go."

2

Annihilation Line

Within a relative hour—though hours could not be meaningfully measured here, and watches were mostly a concession to human habits of mind—the family had gathered around the long polished dining room table, beside the big fireplace where coals flickered and popped. There were no fossil deposits in the esty, because it was not very old, but compacted rock laced with burnable traces gave the same rosy glow.

The dead woman's readings appeared as images deep in the surface of the table, constellations of memories played out as fragments and moments: the ruins of a life. Law required that they see if anything warranted an emergency call to the Old Ones. Nobody talked directly to them, of course. They were shadowy, alien minds who had made the esty. Seldom did they intervene in the affairs of the mere humans who clung to the twisty intricacies here.

When they were through rummaging through shattered memories, curiosity satisfied, only Nigel and Nikka wore grim scowls; the children yawned, bored. He felt more than ever the centuries dividing him and Nikka from their children.

"Guess the future's not so great after all," Benjamin said, sucking meditatively on his teeth.

"Should we send this stuff?" Angelina asked. She twisted her mouth with a comely lilt, an expression that always touched her father's heart because she still did not know that she was genuinely beautiful. They lived in comparative isolation here, far down a lightly populated Lane, as he and Nikka had planned. Soon enough their children would come to know the torrent of cultures and technologies elsewhere in the esty.

"Not right away," Nikka said, glancing at Nigel.

Ito caught her meaning. "There's something in here."

Nikka nodded. "Look at these." She tapped her wrist pad and the tabletop flashed, finding an image: above a black horizon, smudges of rosy light. A sidebar broke this down, displaying bands of spectral light. "See? Pictures made at very high energies. And one strong peak."

Ito was unimpressed. "Astro data. So?"

Nigel said dryly, "That peak is at an energy of point five-one-one million electron volts."

Ito shrugged. "Yeah, so?"

Nigel knew his son's casual challenge for what it was—energies contained in a young soul, spurting out in moments of arch nonchalance. "Son, that's a lot of energy to pack into a single photon."

"So?"

"It's also precisely the sum squeezed out when an electron meets its antiparticle, the positron."

"Ummm." Ito frowned, not ready to give up his bored manner so easily. "Dad, you get interested in just about anything."

Angelina blurted out, "You think this is *anything*? It's antimatter, silly—dying!"

Ito said warily, "How do you figure that?"

"An electron and a positron come together, bang!" She smacked her hands together. "—nothing left but light. *This* light. The annihilation line. And look—it fills the sky!"

Nigel smiled, proud of her. To his despair, Nigel's two sons were fine young men with only passing interest in matters technical.

Nearly thirty thousand years ago—in strict time as measured by the galactic rest coordinates, not the pliant esty time frame—Nigel himself had been a classic science nerd, addicted to his studies. Only later did his attentions turn to the immensely larger and more varied world of politics, literature, women.

A classic pattern, in the ancient TwenCen. His sons seemed to be going at it in reverse order. Or so the complaints from their neighbors—a half-day's walk away, but with winsome daughters—said.

He studied the pictures. The dead woman had been outside, on a planet, watching—distant galaxies? Forming stars? The patchy clouds might be anything. They spoke of immense energies at work. A whole sky of photons that would fry biological lifeforms. Where? When?

Nikka said, "The Old Ones will want this—soon."

"Ummm." Nigel gave her a canny glance. "Let's say, the near soon."

Benjamin said earnestly, "But we're supposed to—"

"Right," Nigel grinned, raising eyebrows. "And we always do what we're supposed to."

Nikka looked at him with an expression of tired tolerance. "You wanted to live in a quiet place. It's a little too late to complain about being bored."

"I'm not bored," Nigel countered. "Just a bit curious."

"You *wanted* to live near that worm thing out there, Dad," his daughter said. "Why? It's dangerous."

Nigel waved an arm, taking in the rolling hills and long, flat-bottomed canyons. "Pleasant, a fine place to bring up children. That worm doesn't act up much. We're pretty safe here, tucked away in a Lane. Hard for the mechs to find. But that doesn't mean we should stop learning. I'd like to see if something follows the woman. If the Old Ones send a delegation, you can be sure we'll learn nothing. Strange things come through these esty worms and—"

"Your father likes to keep his hand in the game."

"Sounds more to me like that little disagreement with the rock slide," Benjamin drawled.

They all laughed. Nigel had just recovered from a foolhardy skid down a stony creek bed. On a plastic shell he had caromed from one side to the other, unable to stop on the slick runway. When they hauled him out of the pool at the slide's base he had protested, limping badly, that after all, the children had got through it perfectly well.

"You're too old to take risks," Angelina had said.

"If you don't take risks, you're dead anyway but don't know it," Nigel had said sourly, rubbing a pulled muscle and a swelling, bruised knee.

Worms, though, were a bit more than risky. They were an inevitable flip side of the esty's flexible stability. At a deep level, space-time itself was like a biological system. Anything that provided a niche eventually acquired parasites.

Where the esty thinned, wormholes were born—pulled out of the quantum foam that underlay everything. Worms lived on the gravity waves that wrestled through the esty, parasites on space-time itself.

Worms could link one portion of the esty to another, tapping the energy flow between them. They demanded stupendous tensions and outward pressures to hold open their throats. The pressure sustaining a human-sized worm was like that at the heart of a massive neutron star. But a short walk away from it, the effect was not even noticeable. Fields alone held worms open, both magnetic and subatomic, fed by the smoldering energies of the esty itself.

Worse, worms could even reproduce. They spawned other snaky scavengers, which flicked and twisted between the layers and Lanes of the esty's hieroglyphic geometries. So they could give birth, just as they could kill. The lacerated woman had probably died in the worm, sucked in and mutilated.

Nigel pointed out that worms were an inescapable risk of life here, and Angelina made a face. "Aw, you're just trying to say you want to go down the rock slide again."

"I think not, actually," Nigel responded with a grimace to her jibe. "But I wonder . . . did this woman know what she was getting into?"

Nikka arched an eyebrow. "Do we?"

3

◄═╳═══╳═══╳═══╳═══╳═══╳═══╳═►

Interfacer

They were busy with vegetable farming and the long groves of fruit-bearing trees, mostly from old Earth, and so did not get much time to watch the place where the woman had emerged. The spot fumed, a sour smell that wrinkled the nose from a considerable distance.

Children seldom think of their parents as anything other than fundamental building blocks of their world, unchanging givens, like the postulates that go before a geometric proof. With Nigel and Nikka this was just as well.

Measured in flatspace time they were older than they liked to talk about in front of the children. In their own local coordinates they were only a few centuries old, thanks to coldsleep and the relativistic effects of the ramscoop starship. Medical science and good luck had left them feeling still rather spry, but experience gave a certain oblique cast to the expressions that passed between them. The children noticed those but shrugged them off as more adult mystery.

One day—a term they used by convention, for in the esty there were wanings and waxings of light, but no sun or stars, ever—a pet got loose and ventured too close. It was a raccoon named Scooter they kept outside on a high wire leash, the end of it strung on a rope between two trees so the raccoon could run back and forth. The bandit-eyed bundle of energy shredded laundry and stole food at every chance and Nikka, angry, would yank it up in the air by the leash. The raccoon would dance on the air until it got the idea of not doing that anymore. For a while, anyway.

Nikka would promise to cook it up next meal with the long potato hash she made and the coon would get silent. They knew it could understand. Scooter talked, sometimes. But not well. Nobody thought to warn it about the spot and when it again found a way to untie itself—Benjamin swore the thing was getting smarter—it followed Angelina. The coon ventured too close to the spherical seethe, got singed, and lost a finger's worth of tail.

Its squeaky voice complained, "Mad at me. Hurt me."

Nikka noticed that the tail was sheared off cleanly. The worm had snapped at it. The raccoon grumbled but held still for a bandage.

"You ran away," she scolded it.

"Need to study."

"Looks like the worm took a sample to study *you*."

As they laughed over this at dinner Angelina, who kept track of communications, said, "We got a signal today. Orders, really. Said the Old Ones are interested."

Nikka stopped spooning out the tangy long potatoes. "That means some Interfacer will show up in spit and polish."

"Really?" Angelina's mouth formed an *O* of frozen delight.

"They're just human, like us," Ito said with a sardonic tone just a bit too heavy, to show that he was older and experienced, though he had never seen an Interfacer either.

"I'll talk to some old friends at the Node. Perhaps I can keep us out from under their kindly care." Nigel ate slowly, reflecting, as talk buzzed around their table.

He did not like the idea of bringing in higher authority, the enigmatic Old Ones. They were impressive, yes. But it was the nature of humanity to not stand in awe of anything for very long. After many years of exposure to them Nigel felt as if the Old Ones were like nosy mountains, certainly majestic but always looking over his shoulder while he was trying to get something done.

Later he talked on farcomm with a few old friends at the Node. Earthers, but intelligible. He got nowhere. Worms were too important to be left entirely to mere humans. His living legend status made no difference.

The Interfacer craft arrived during the next waxing. It twisted all over the air like a long mathematical proof the eye could follow only so far, then lost in turning complexity. Air as fluid, craft like an eel. As if Mozart could make his notes visible, lacy in the sky while you listened to them. In the esty's curved space, travel was never straight-line. It more nearly resembled a slide down unseen ramps of coalesced air.

Family Walmsley squinted upward at the confusing descent.

Loops piled like unrolling a scroll. Lacy vapor trail strips unfurled, making one infinitely recurving utterance, cleaving sky like a prow, tossing time and music to each side like a sheared wake. It made their heads ache.

The Interfacer woman who brought the Old Ones' message was not so imposing. Her face was stretched tight, shiny over the bones, so red-faced she reminded Nigel of a boiled ham in a suit. Her collar had popped free of its little pearl clip so that her neck bulged like a swollen snake. Big wrists stuck out of her shirt sleeves and her eyes had the fixed narrow glaze of a woman staring at a match flame.

Not all Earthers were impressive. Nigel wondered idly if an Earther nerd was something like this. She did not change expression as she studied the seething spot. "A fresh esty Vor."

"Vor?" Nikka asked, her hands in her hip pockets in unconscious imitation of the woman's stance.

"Slang for 'Vortex.' I've only seen two fresh ones in all my years. This data you sent"—the stolid woman waved a disk—"is very important. Very. You should have taken more care with the body."

Nigel said evenly, "We had a lot of picking to do in the orchard."

"No excuse," she spat back. "The data is undoubtedly from the far future. It bears on the destiny of the entire esty."

"How?" Benjamin asked. Nigel could tell from Benjamin's face that he was impressed, if not by the woman at least by her aircraft. Well, time would teach him.

"We know that the mechanicals have been studying antimatter since ancient times. They are constructing elsewhere in the galaxy great laboratories, orbiting the pulsars—all to capture large numbers of positrons. This message, sent in a dying mind"—she waved the disk again as if it were a murder weapon in a trial—"proves that they have designs on the entire galaxy. It shows huge positron swarms. Hostile to life—to our life, anyway."

"Uh-huh," Ito said with a lifted eyebrow.

"You doubt this?" The woman looked affronted. "I speak for the Old Ones."

"They're speaking *through* you," Ito shot back. "You're just a puppet."

Nigel put a restraining hand on his oldest son's shoulder. Ito did not have the diffidence of Benjamin. "Point is," Nigel said, "why send a *body* back?"

"Let us say that the Old Ones have several theories." The

Interfacer drew herself up with serene disdain. "Quite complex. They are difficult to convey properly to . . ."

"To ordinaries like us?" Nikka asked with a wise smile.

The woman sniffed. "I do not use such mundane slang. Though surely there is a difference between us. I have touched the Old Ones directly. At the mental level."

"I'm sure it's wonderful," Nikka said.

There was not a shade of malice in her tone but Nigel had a hard time not chuckling at the stiletto of meaning he could read in the words. He and Nikka were far older than this woman, but if he ever got as stiff and dead as her, he would blow his head off. So much for Interfacing with the Old Ones. He had decided to not undergo it when it was first offered, when the Earthers had devised the intricate method. Now he was reminded why.

"I expect you to tend to the defenses we will set up here," the woman said, still eyeing Nikka for a hint of spleen. Interfacers were notorious for taking offense.

"Defenses?" Ito was surprised.

"Against mechanicals. They may try to cut off this esty Vor."

Ito scowled skeptically. "Haven't seen a mech around here in a long time."

"They have attacked other Vors and sealed them up."

Nigel nodded, old angers rising in him.

The Interfacer held out a viewboard. "There were further views in the data you extracted from the dead woman."

In its surface images flickered. A vision of black holes—sharp dots against a wash of pearly light. The esty had formed from their collision. The viewboard was an advanced model. Into Nigel's sensorium sounded quick, darting visions.

4

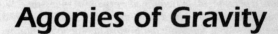

Agonies of Gravity

Locked in a madly whirling embrace, the two black holes spiral inward to a final marriage. As the partners draw closer, they swing around each other faster and faster. Each tugs out the other, stretching the envelope of each hole into a tortured egg shape.

In its last moments, the smaller black hole stretches and contorts its own space-time, emitting a cry of gravitational agony: waves. These curl and lap about the smaller hole, then reflect and refract from the larger one. Eddies form. Standing waves reverberate between the two. These deepen as the moment of death approaches for the smaller hole. Energy foams from the doomed hole, in the form of the deepening trough of gravitational waves that eddy and play in the narrowing gap.

With a final scream of torsion and torque, the smaller hole plunges into its giant master. But the wave energy is not lost. An intense packet of waves remains, lapping in the wash of fatality.

This packet would disperse, bleeding away into space . . . if more matter did not intervene. At this precise moment an exactly directed stream of dense mass comes snaking in along a swift trajectory. In the full form of the General Field Equations—as envisioned long ago by Einstein, and of course by many other of the highest minds elsewhere in the galaxy, for Nature opens its secrets to many styles of thinking—space-time can curve itself. A gravitational wave is an oscillation in the curvature of space-time, like a ripple on the sea. But the equations are not linear. This means that the undulation, too, produces further curvature. Gravity itself has weight.

The incoming blue-white stream of compact mass loops, drawn by the wave packet. Tidal tugs hook the now-incandescent matter into a beautiful spiral. From a distance, the silvery luminosity follows a path recalling the chambered nautilus, a creature born in Earth's ancient oceans, shaped by evolution into a classic geometry.

Now the true violence begins. Soundless, swift and sure.

The mass reflects the gravitational wave troughs, forcing them to build to even higher amplitudes. This draws the mass farther in. The spiral tightens. Wave builds upon wave. The stretch and warp of space-time deepens. In a single microsecond comes a new kind of creation: a permanent, self-confined warpage of space-time. Within a second it spreads, an intact structure. Extra energy bleeds away into fleeting waves, radiating out toward unreachable infinity.

Later, men who ventured into it would call it the Wedge. The name was inelegant but partly true. It had been formed by waves wedged between two black holes. It now orbited the single spherical hole, a tombstone of so much lost matter.

But the final drop of mass which applied the crucial touch—that was not lost. It resides inside the Wedge. It was the first contribution of ordinary matter to the exotic, transparent walls of the Wedge.

The first damp earth, in a ceramic flower pot.

5

Three Billion Years

"Impressive," Nigel said guardedly. His family murmured, surprised at the intensity of the vision broadcast into their sensoria.

Nikka said, "I've never seen before how it was done. But this is from the past, many thousands of years—"

"There is a date on it," the woman said. "It says that this image is from three billion years in the past."

"But I *know*—"

"Of course." The woman lifted her lip in a regal sneer. "Three billion years in the past of that dead woman. Which gives us the first fix on the origin of these bodies. They come from a genuinely distant future. I am surprised that humans will still exist, then."

Ito said, "Hell, billions—what can matter over that much time?"

Nikka said soberly, "The mechs think something does."

"They certainly do," the Interfacer said. "They sent the Grey Mech to seal those other Vors."

The family blinked and glanced at each other silently. The Grey Mech was the one form that not even the Old Ones could master. It had extraordinary powers and could penetrate the esty seemingly at will. The mechanical civilizations that dominated the space around the esty—restrained by its tightrope walk near the Galactic Center's black hole—did not dare venture in often. But the Grey Mech could. And did, following patterns no one had ever been able to predict.

The Interfacer said quietly, "Why would mechanicals care so much about our origin—except to figure out how to undo it?"

6

Deep Down Superficial

Nigel did not like it, but Family Walmsley had to bow to the Interface. Other craft fluttered down the curved air and deposited defensive gear—intricate assemblies of ceramo-metal tubes, tapered carbon-web cylinders, power modules like huge brown bricks.

Nigel glanced at the shiny, white steel surface of the control console, then away. One reaches the age when mirrors are of no interest. As well, he had long given up hope of keeping track of technology's relentless march and to him these did not even look like weapons. Nor did the attendants who crisply set up the defensive web, nodding curtly to him, look like soldiers. He was glad to finally see them ride their craft back down the Lane.

The family eyed the defenses skeptically. Supposedly they would keep the worm open by offsetting whatever the Grey Mech could do to it. "Think it'll work, Mom?" Benjamin wondered.

Nikka shook her head. "People have tried such before. But it's like a whip—easy to flip around, until the tail bites you."

"Should we, well, move?"

Nikka was startled. "Our fruit is nearly ripe!"

That seemed to settle matters. The Interfacer had mentioned in passing that the Grey Mech sometimes struck at wormholes only long after they had erupted. No one knew why. Still, it removed any sense of urgency.

So did the very nature of the esty. As a self-curved space-time, it was in the ordinary universe of the galaxy, yet had other connections—to other spaces, other times. The Old Ones used the esty, had made and confined it, but nothing truly controlled it, any more than a man who cages a lion can necessarily make it perform tricks.

They had a quiet evening, sobered by the presence of automatic weaponry on hair-trigger alert, just over the rise behind the rambling house. War had so outsped human reflexes that battles lasted mere milliseconds. This had a curiously liberating effect, for it meant that no warning or action was possible. So the family went about life as usual, but talked little.

Getting ready for bed that evening, Nigel worked his finger-tips along his scalp line where his gray, thinning hair began. He could have changed the gray readily to blond or one of the more fashionable hues—scarlet, say, or electric blue—but he liked the effect.

Carefully he ran his left hand down and to the side, opening his face along a barely visible scar that ran along his chin, around the neck and down his back. Electrostatic bonds ripped free with a sound like corn popping in the next room. He peeled his skin back in a straight line down the spine and drew the flap over his left shoulder and biceps, until he could painstakingly roll it up against his wrist with a moist, sucking sound. The skin stripped back down to his buttocks, revealing moist redness.

He turned with exaggerated grace in a ballet pose. "The real me. Like it?"

Lounging back on their massive bed, Nikka laughed despite herself. "Can't you do your medical some other time? I was just getting in the mood."

"I'll recalibrate my secretors. Add some hormones. Give you an even better run for your money."

"I wasn't planning on paying money, and I didn't have running in mind."

He groaned as he tuned digital controls that the peeling had exposed. "A literalist! God spare the sacred erotic impulse from their kind."

"You expect silky passions after you show me *that*?"

"Fair enough. But trust me to summon up your passion, madam. My specialty."

She smiled. "Hurry up, then."

He gave her a fond grin as he worked on himself: tuning, refilling small vials, scanning outputs. She was still sinewy and muscular, her skin smooth everywhere but at elbows and knees. Somehow, Nigel noted as he inspected his own, those spots and the

backs of hands were not corrected by the elaborate chemical cock-
tails medical science provided. A minor complaint. Without his in-
body systems, which he had to tune in this rather unsettling fashion,
he and Nikka would have been dead for centuries.

"How is it?" she said suddenly—some mute inner pressure
had finally found voice.

"Um. Not much change." He turned slightly toward the
shadows, so she could not read the indices. On a tiny digital display he used to communicate with his in-body systems a small light
winked red. He silenced it with an adjustment, fingers working
swiftly with long practice.

"How much change?"

At times like this he was decidedly rankled that he had, from
all the flower of womanhood, chosen one with a bulldog tenacity
for detail. "A bit. A small bit."

"Which way?"

"Ummmm." He shrugged and started packing himself up.

She let the evasion pass. He concentrated on his Earther tech,
engineered to be maximally convenient. Like an employee in a
candy factory, the key was knowing when to stop taking things for
free. He and Nikka had adopted the truly useful and avoided the
rest. There were other techno-delights open to them, but they used
the minimum.

He had to shuck his right hand free a bit to get at a pesky
lace of veins that had clogged. He pulled the epidermis loose as if
he had on a tight glove, pinching each finger free separately. The
veins needed a soothing application of some noxious stuff. When
the smell was gone he pulled the supple skin back into place, feeling
the tabs self-seal with a warm purr.

"It's lower, isn't it?"

He knew that ignoring her would not work; it never had. "It's
a hundred seventy-two point eight."

"A full point down."

He turned back and her face was quite suddenly older, mourn-
ful. "Nothing for it, luv."

"If we go in to those specialists again—"

"They'll nod and probe and do me no good. Remember?"

"It will kill you," she said with abrupt energy.

"Something has to."

"Don't be so goddamned glib!"

"That's me. Deep down, I'm superficial."

"But you just, you just—" and she did the absolute worst
thing, burst into tears. The one measure he could never confront

with a wry smile and his lofty disdain for the nagging intrusions of life.

So it ended as it had so many times before. He took her in his arms. Simple sympathy and body warmth made up for words. They comforted each other with a knowingness born of time and troubles past. It was a long while before they slept.

7

A Few Microseconds

The Walmsleys visited the worm seldom because there was plenty of work to be done in the long, stretching groves, amid the sweet scent of crops coming.

Seasons of a sort came and went in the esty and one had to pick fruit when the fitful warming of the timestone brought it to peak. They were in the fields when a hard yellow-white streak raced through the air high above and slammed into the esty where the woman had appeared.

The weapons of the Old Ones answered. Hard radiation spiked at the edge of Nigel's sensorium. He seldom used this Earther tech, but for the moment it was on full range. He turned his head—

—a swift sensation of something massive and gray, high up in the air but closing fast—

—A silence swelling like a bubble toward the family.

They were loading up a produce carrier. The impulse hit before they could even pivot to flee.

Brilliant glare enveloped them. The air seemed to clot—a thick, massive deadening. A flicker wrapped around them like neon rain, illuminated by green sheet lightning—

—curling tendrils—

—sheets glowing like ghost fire—

And when it had passed, the far terrain around them was bare, hostile, steaming with sulphurous vapors.

Machines worked in slivers of seconds that humans could not perceive. Huge energies slice time as they shatter it. The battle between the Grey Mech and the Interfacers' weapons was over—had been decided, transmitted, antiseptically digested by distant minds, its effects calibrated and assessed.

The mechanicals' attack had distorted the esty. Mere by-standers in the spreading gulp of the reflexing esty, the Walmsleys had been swept through the wormhole portal, a swerve in space-time accomplished between two thuds of the human heart.

8

◆━━◆◆━━◆◆━━◆◆━━◆◆━━◆◆━━◆

Antiques Dealer

It took them days to figure out, first, what had happened and, second, what they could do about it.

The first answer was buried in the fast diagnostics of the Interfacer defenses. Nikka retrieved those. The mech attack had dimpled them through to another place in the esty. Not merely to the other end of the wormhole, which presumably connected to a far future. Instead, the intensity of the flux of gravitational radiation emitted in the battle had whipped the wormhole to some other location in the esty.

It had sheared off most of their groves. With them went a lot of equipment and their pet raccoon. A sliced fraction of their original farm sat uneasily in a new place.

Another space, another time. Another space-time.

The second answer was harder to accept: *nothing*.

"We can't, well, reverse this grav gear?" Exasperated, Ito slapped one of the modular cylinders. It seemed undamaged.

Nikka shook her head, tired. She had kept up her technical ability better than Nigel. She could read the interlaced matrices of the artificial intelligence that maintained the Interface apparatus. "It is a defensive net, not a transport device."

Ito had always been impatient with recalcitrant equipment. He busted a knuckle trying to get a seal off one of the smooth, enigmatic cylinders. "How can they leave us stranded like this?" He twisted his mouth in exasperation while Nigel watched with something like amusement. Nigel had never expected organizations to get him out of scrapes and was quite sure that he was too old to start.

"You have to understand that the esty isn't just a convenient mass to live on, a source of local gravity," Nigel said. "Such as a planet, for example."

Blank looks. None of the three children had ever lived on a planet.

Despite an extensive education, he reminded himself, they could not truly visualize the most elementary aspects of it—an empty blue sky overhead, giving way to stars at night that swung around the black bowl in serene circles; raucous weather churning out of vagrant winds, driven by complex vector forces; horizons that always curved away, so that ships showed their masts first as they approached; the very oceans such ships could sail on, implying a colossal lavishness of water; the wholly different sensation of living at the bottom of a gravity well, while above yawned a vast abyss, visible to a glance upward.

"It's rubbery," Nigel said. "And unpredictable."

The fact that they lived in a portion of the esty noted for its solidity did not lessen this fact, but Nigel saw that in bringing up the children so far from the spongy zones, he and Nikka had perhaps erred on the side of safety.

Angelina objected, "But the Interfacer said—"

"Nobody really controls the esty," Nikka said. "Not even the Old Ones. It evolves and we live in it."

Angelina gestured upward, where a lightly forested land hung far away, curving behind cottony clouds. It looked as though they were in a spectacular spinning cylinder, pinned to its outer walls by centrifugal force.

But spin did not do the job. The esty held itself together by folding space-time—by curving itself in unimaginable thin sheets, stacking time and space like pages of a vast book, the events and substance of whole lives and eras encased in walls that felt as solid as granite.

Einstein had seen that mass curved space-time. The esty reversed the equality, making curved esty itself feel like mass, planet-solid. A building material. The esty was far more lively than mere boring matter, for indeed in a profound way it was alive, the compacted stuff of existence that could spawn more of itself. It even had parasites, the worms.

"How can we get back to home?" Angelina asked plaintively.

"We can't," Nikka said flatly. "No gear for it."

"We can't use this, then?" Ito slapped the inert cylinder. He was a fine worker and loved his mother but fire flashed in his eyes when confronted with balky machinery.

"It's defensive, period," Nikka said mildly. "To even attempt a return we need to open the worm in a controlled way."

"How hard is that?" Nigel asked.

She shook her head. "Even experts shy away from that, if they're smart. It's dangerous work."

"What's it take?" Benjamin asked. He had his mother's up-turned chin and her quiet assurance that given time and tinkering, miracles were routine.

"Some integrative graviton sensors, a field generator which can deliver a terrawatt at ten kilohertz acoustic . . . and a Causality Engine." Nikka sat gingerly on a boulder. She had twisted her back in the flickering microsecond of transition through the Vor.

Benjamin's mouth sagged. No miracles were going to happen right away.

Nigel asked skeptically, "Causality Engine? I thought we could take causality for granted."

Nikka shook her head, the sheen of her long, braided black hair catching the light. "It's keeping causality in proper order that takes control."

Nigel had left the ever more complex physics of the esty to others in favor of his orchards, as a proper reward of age. Nikka still relished technical detail, and it took her quite a while to convey to them the realms of chaotic logic. Daunting stuff.

A Vor was a "chaotic attractor" that linked portions of the esty in random fashion. But the links had a cyclic logic, so that any given connection would recur . . . in time. Generally, a *long* time. Making it happen again demanded deft mathematical control of the lip of the Vor. The process resembled stirring a pot, using bursts of gravitational radiation.

She was explaining this when a pale pink craft sliced across their clouded sky and banked over them. Its backwash slammed down a fist of heated air, making them duck. It settled a short distance away on oddly angled struts of purple metal that ended in disk footpads.

A woman came rapidly toward them, shanks hiking her forward as though in a race. She wore jet-black, porous ceramic eyes that wrapped around her head like a combination of hat and spectacles, yet left the crown of her honey hair uncovered.

"I'll go set rate," she announced in a preemptory voice, heavily accented in broad *a*'s and *eh*'s.

"For what?" Ito asked. He was nearer her and she seemed to assume he was delegated to speak.

"Don't stall."

"We're not—"

"Look, I be first in. So I get the bid."

Ito looked irked. "First in what?"

"You know not? You've beed inside a suspension bubble. I waited days for it to pop."

Ito frowned. "A . . . time bubble?"

"Checko." She raked them all with an assessing gaze. "You be stable, though. I looked over your chunk from the air. It snapped off a section of ordinary rock. Settled in well, I sayed."

"Where are we?"

"Sawazaki Lane. Your equipment—early era, right? I be good with antiques."

"We tunneled through to a human Lane, though, right?" Ito persisted.

Nigel watched his son's expression as the realization dawned that they could just as easily have popped out in some hellhole Lane of methane gas or bitter cold. Nigel and Nikka had known that but, as Nikka had said to him in private, what could they have done? The mechs had sent their sliver of esty caroming out into the larger esty, and it had lodged where laws of nonlinear dynamics took it.

"Sure, did you not plan to?" Distracted, the woman glanced at her sleeve. "Ummm. As I calc, I could offer you a single pointo price for all of it."

She looked at them, an entirely phony smile splitting her face, showing bright yellow teeth. "Sight unseen. I willn't bother. Not my style to poke around too much with people standing right there. Don't much need the money. I just take what luck brings me."

Ito gaped. "What? Buy everything?"

"Flat fee basis. Leave or take."

Nikka let her jaw jut out in a way Nigel knew well. "We aren't interested."

The woman frowned. "Look, I know how it is. You must've payed most of your nut to get this big a spread slipstreamed in, right? I'll allow for that, believe me." She rolled her eyes theatrically. "Even though I usually get my budget busted when I do."

Nikka did not smile back. "No deal."

"Huh? You're trans-importers, right?"

"No," Nikka said. "We're refugees."

"Well then, you'll be needing cash, won't you? I can see my way clear to offer—"

"We won't sell," Nigel said mildly.

Her ceramic eyes prowled them. Facets winked as she turned her head, diagnostics probing. She wore a scarf, barely visible above an ivory jacket cut to show one obvious weapon, an antique-looking pistol on its own pop-out handle, and to conceal several others that made mere ripples in her sleek contours.

"You people know not Sawazaki law, do you?" Again the eye-roll. "Lord, protect me from amateurs."

Nigel said, "We were blown here by mechs. Certainly we would appreciate assistance in getting back home."

She brightened. "Well then—"

"With our property intact."

Her friendly bluster vanished. The transformation was so sudden it seemed to Nigel that he saw a wholly new face. Heavy brows tinted auburn, split by a deep frown line. Sunken, brilliant yellow eyes below—visible when the artificial eyes went suddenly transparent. Her hands were ribbed and knobbed like enlarged gloves—which, Nigel realized belatedly, they were—which angled forth fat fingers of obvious strength. He wondered why she needed them.

"Snarfs, eh?" she said in a menacing whisper.

Her gloved hands unsheathed into thin, servo'd fingers that jutted from the sausage-thick ones. Sharp, businesslike. "Then you be coming with."

Ito stepped forward, scowling. This was just the kind of problem a young man would rise to, Nigel saw, and in the set of Ito's jaw trouble was coming. Nigel was a half step behind him as Ito began, "I don't think I like the way you—"

—and Ito was on the ground. Nigel had not even seen her move. She had punched him and returned to exactly the same position in an eye-blink.

9

The Tilted City

The city was on edge. Not meaning in a foul mood, Nigel thought to himself as they coasted over, through, and around the steepled constructions, but quite literally.

The spired sprawl canted up into the filmy air as though it had been formed in a bowl until it hardened, and then shucked free—so that the curved base tipped nearly all the way over, a crescent moon about to crash down.

But it was at least a hundred kilometers across. It rested on a rocky plain, a colossal ornament on the inside of a spherical bulge in Sawazaki Lane. In the far foggy distance he could see the annular geometry they had emerged from. Tricks of sliding perspective and the sharp dry air made everything here seem miniature.

They banked in and the illusion vanished. The city became a forest of slender spires, jewels jutting up from the curved base. They swelled into thick, serpentine buildings studded with tiny lights: windows.

In the city gravity pointed at "local down" as naturally as ever. Only by walking some distance through the curiously cushioned streets could one tell that the direction veered steadily, accommodating the bowl's curvature. The effect struck Nigel as miraculous.

"How do they do this?" he wondered. "Gravity like hands cupping a baby's butt?"

Nikka frowned but it was unlike her to admit being stumped. "They've figured a way to make the esty exert gravitational forces and torques at a distance . . . I think."

The woman escorting them, whose name proved to be Tonogan, said sardonically. "We tilt our city for religious reasons. You would not understand."

Nigel could not tell whether she was joking but it seemed an unlikely extravagance. He could see the air shimmer with compressed forces at the city's rim. It occurred to him that if the effect was real, and not some bizarre optical illusion, then it demanded that gravitational waves be radiated from the visible plain below up to the esty that cupped the city. But gravitational waves of such intensity were incredible. Or so he thought.

He remembered the pictures of the two black holes merging, marrying, and giving birth to something wholly different between them. Maybe the way to think here was with biological metaphors, not the old physics ones he had learned at Cambridge so long ago.

They passed through crowds whose size, mass, attire (where there was any), and facial gestures ran a gamut Nigel had never seen before. Some were antic, reacting to everything. Others seemed sublimely indifferent to the rabble of the oddly shaped who ambled, meandered, drifted, strolled, and marched without apparently acknowledging each other or, indeed, the ordinary laws of physics. Some seemed lighter, making great bounds. Others skated on unseen platforms. (Nigel tried to trip one, but the fellow slid past without a glance and for half an hour later his foot, which had felt no contact, was bitingly cold.) Some flew with outspread arms. Others scarcely seemed to walk at all, but moved forward swiftly on unseen carriers.

A passing man lit a cigarette of some sweet-smelling stuff by scraping the knob end against his belt. Nigel wondered what happened if you dropped a whole pack of them knob-down.

Some wore sandpaper-rough clothing to keep people at a respectful distance; a useful urban attire Nigel had not seen before. Despite the noise and confusion, an old game played out: locals were doing their best to accommodate the visitors and relieve them of any excess cash.

A kid slapped a button on Angelina's shoulder and it began to speak. "Dooed the upshift till you be down? Want to go/get level? Think pointo and—" Angelina pried off this portable advertisement and tossed it away, where it stuck to a wall and began its pitch again.

Tonogan swerved suddenly into a broad opening in a pyramidal building. The family, gawking, hastened to keep up. She never looked back, apparently certain that they would follow. Inside, the floor propelled them through intersecting streams of men and women with fluorescent neck and ear tattoos, who came and went with bewildering speed, legs scissoring. At a large, ornate, copper-sheen doorway stood two well-muscled men wearing wraparound gray that accentuated their chest and shoulders. They stood rigidly, Nigel noted, and looked quite intrepid.

They were apparently protecting an obese woman in a violently purple bag-dress. She wore skin to match, a near perfect shade. Yawning, she languidly glanced up as they came through the vertically pivoting door.

"Good waxing." Her voice rippled with polished undertones, as though she truly felt that it was a good rising of the esty's fitful light and hoped that you did, too.

She went back to looking at a scroll held in one hand. It unrolled on its own and she seemed fascinated with it, not even looking up as Tonogan rattled off a rapid-fire summary. They were standing in a gallery that gave onto an odd courtyard. As Tonogan spoke something like a six-legged dog trotted about courtyard center. It seemed to glide more than walk among the plants that festooned the area—big speckled yellow-green effusions, geysers of leafy abundance.

The large woman interrupted Tonogan with, "I see the scans. A family, um. Quite a large area to transslip, eh?"

She looked at Nikka, who answered. "We want help in getting back to our Lane, at our esty cords."

Nigel felt a quiet pride; ever Nikka, ever direct. Nigel was a doddering language purist, and disliked shortening "coordinates" to "cords" since that obscured a perfectly good word for rope, but he also knew that to crunch the lingo was crucial. The trimmed English here—all verbs and plurals regular, simple constructions—was efficient, where travelers from other eras and territories crossed.

"Impossible."

Nikka said patiently, "Technically it must be—"

"No no! It's *expensive*."

Nikka frowned, always uncomfortable with financial matters. Nigel said, "We could perhaps trade off a bit of our holdings."

The purple woman looked distracted—back to her scroll. Nobody asked them to sit down and indeed there was no place to do so in this long, slick-floored vestibule. She occupied all of a spacious divan, with a bit more of her left over.

Finally she yawned, perhaps not for show. "You haven't nearly enough. Interesting historical artifacts, but—"

"Historical?" Ito took affront.

"Well, you do come from"—a string of digits and words, meaningless to Nigel—"and that's a wayfer."

"Wafer?" Ito asked, his jaw working with irritation.

"Way far gone, as we say here. I speak your approximate regional language, be I not? I had to chipload for it, that be how much trouble I went to." She waved a hand with sausage fingers in airy disdain and went back to her scroll. Apparently the rest of the world was supposed to freeze in place until her attention returned.

The strangely snakelike dog spotted a covey of dappled birds who had waddled out from beneath one of the leafy explosions. It went into a low stalk. The closer it got the slower and lower it went, until finally the birds burst into the sky and the dog dashed to where they had been. Trotting around, it wagged its eel-like tail.

Nigel felt amused and comforted by the display. Genes tell, and this echo of Earth was welcome. He remembered pigeons in Trafalgar Square, chased by hounds out on a leash, and the momentary picture brought a dizzy sense of the immense perspectives in this life of his, so long and wearing.

"Ummm. You know anything about holies?" the purple woman asked, one finger held to her cheek, staring at her scroll as though it were a mirror.

Nikka said cautiously, "I know that esty Vortices are naturally occurring wormholes. No matter what size, they have fixed matter-throughput. But the bandwidth of information—matter, data, anything—that can go through scales up with its radius. The Grey Mech hit us with something—"

"A Causality Polarizer," the purple woman said, licking her lips with something like relish. "If I could only get one!"

"—and blew us into here. And now."

"Our 'now' be quite a bit downstream of you," the woman said. "You be several million year-kilometers distant."

Nigel blinked. "That much?"

She shrugged. "A moderate traverse."

"Can't you break that up into distance and time?"

She laughed, lips stretched far back, but without real joy. "How old *be* you? The idea—splitting the esty!" A dry cackle.

Nigel felt both awkward and vexed. "Fair enough. We know in principle that space-time can't be just sectioned out, leastwise not here."

"Clocks and feet separate them out pretty well, but the esty knows what we can't see." There was a kind note in her voice as she asked, "You be old, yes?"

Nikka said plainly, "From Earth."

The purple woman's eyes flared with surprise, then anger. "I try be friendly with you, give you an honest deal. And you think you can play games!"

It was Nikka's turn to laugh. "I'm telling the truth. What do you want, passports?"

The woman's chip did not know the word—indeed, passports made no sense in a multiply connected esty with no true boundaries—and she waved them away, mouth askew with displeasure.

"You people shouldn't be traders at all!"

Ito blurted, "We *aren't*—can't you get that straight?"

Her eyes blazed again. "*You* get *this* straight. You take the rate I offer you for your property—buildings, historicals, mech widgets and sensies, the lot—or you'll be punished."

Nigel bridled. "Punished for what?"

"For taking up space, air, time—anything I want!"

She stood with effort, waddling forward on huge feet—a purple wall unaccustomed to collisions. Nigel held his ground. She jutted a large palm out and shoved him. She was massive and surprisingly strong. He staggered back and made a mistake. Without thinking he punched her swiftly in the stomach.

In what seemed the same instant someone struck him from behind. A sharp jolt of electrical violence coursed up through him. Then he was lying on the floor, without any perceptible interval in between. Arms and legs numb. Sounds hollow, distant. Staring up at a cloudy bowl. In a city tipped on end, he recalled distantly.

The purple wall had gone back to her couch. Hissing in his inner ear, the mists around him fried away. He looked around and everything was as before.

Tonogan had shocked him with the rod she held easily in one hand. He let a long breath out and stood, wheezing and rickety at the knees. How to begin?

"And who the hell—" Nigel had an instant of caution, obviously far too late, still trying to size up this sizable lady—"are you?"

"The Chairwoman," Tonogan said. All this time she had been standing at rigid attention, like the two stuffed men outside.

"Chairwoman of what?" Nikka demanded.

"Everything. Just about everything."

"Oh."

The Chairwoman wrapped up her calculator-scroll and glowered darkly. "Pleased to meet you."

10

Eine Kleine Nachtmusik

Ito did his work, hooking up some multisocketed pipes, and all the while looked off into the distance without saying anything.

When he could wait no more Nigel asked, "All right, what's wrong?"

"You got to ask that?"

"I'm not swift on the subtleties."

"*Subtleties?* Best way to get your attention is with a stick."

They had been working for weeks in menial labor, hauling this, cleaning that. Putting in penance time for the Chairwoman, Tonogan had called it. It was clear that in this Lane the purple woman ran everything with a hard hand, for reasons that remained to Nigel quite mysterious. And he had been forced to concede that she had solidly behind her the brunt of what passed for law here.

Nigel sighed and worked two pipes together, applying sealant. No matter how advanced technology got, there was always grunt labor needed to jimmy stubborn matter into place. No legions of robots or smartened animals ever replaced the general handyman-cum-janitor.

Time to trot out the apology again. "Son, I'm sorry I got us into this—"

"Look, I heard a rumor," Ito said evenly.

Nigel shook his head, bone-weary. He was feeling sour, defeated. "I'm not in the mood for rumors."

Matters had not worked out well between Ito and Nigel for quite a while now. His brilliantly mangled handling of the Chairwoman had not improved the festering tension—inevitable, he supposed—between him and his first son, now coming to manhood.

Ito had bridled at the discipline imposed by the Chairwoman's silent, impassive police. Rough handling. Abrupt dawn awakenings. Long days of scut work. Adequate meals that had to be eaten in a rush. Little privacy in the muggy, close apartment given them, sandwiched into a brawling tenement. No time off the grinding labor. No chance to get out of the curfew hours, the iron-hard lockup, the rigid lights-out. No access to any media, no contact with ordinary people other than to pick up their trash.

Angelina and Benjamin had borne up well. Nigel and Nikka could take punishment, too, but their oldest son had snapped back at their police "escorts." He had refused to clean up messes when toilet plumbing broke, swore at the police orders. So the placid police had most politely smacked him around, prodded him with neuro-stims, given him a "seize-up," which locked his muscles in vibrating bands of rigid tension—all while faintly amused. It had not improved Ito's mood.

Not a future utopia, no.

But the future, certainly. The city they glimpsed from the back alleys where they worked was strange and fabulous. As nearly as they could tell, the complex was stratified, with an upper crust that reveled in techno-wonders, a vast majority that lived ample lives, and a lower caste that did the grunt work. Not exactly a fresh idea.

There were technologies Nikka and Nigel were sure had not existed anywhere in the esty in their era. The Grey Mech had slammed them into a future far from their comforts.

Ito persisted. "This rumor, it said maybe the Chairwoman will listen to us again."

Nigel studied his son's face, trying to think clearly despite the spreading ache in his lower back from stooping, and the silent blanket of fatigue that had spread over him. Still an hour left in this work day. "That's not a rumor. Who told you?"

Ito looked edgy as he swept back a greasy tangle of hair. "Tonogan. She wants to see you."

"You've been negotiating with her?"

"Not really."

"Which means?"

"Well, maybe some."

"The family has to speak with one voice, as you full well know."

Ito chewed his lip. "Well, *you* aren't doing anything."

"I'm waiting her out."

"Her waiting's easier than ours."

"She wants our property. It's probably worth a lot more than you or I think."

Ito flared, mouth twisting. "How can we know *what* to think? We're stuck down in basements and alleys all day, busting our humps, getting flat nothing—"

Nigel sat on a trash can and kicked at a brown flask, still corked but empty. He had never thought of the far future as a place of ordinary junk and grit, much of which a medieval peasant would have instantly recognized.

"Right," he conceded, "it's not playing out well. That Chairwoman—what a bland name for a tyrant!—seems bound by what passes for law here. She can't simply take what she wants. There are procedures."

"I can't see where we have any rights at all."

"This place seems to work through intimidation, rather than rights."

Ito chuckled dryly. "With a frosting of polite brutality, I bet."

Nigel nodded. The family was getting depressed and, quite so, the Chairwoman could exert arcane legalisms to keep them like this indefinitely.

"Dad, you're in over your head here. That fall you took last week was nasty and I can see you're still limping—"

"Scarcely felt it."

The slow, steady ache in his left leg never left him. Somehow he had not thought that the far future would still have pain in it, either. *I saw too much rosy-visioned Walt Disney,* he thought tartly. Would anybody in this whole cupped city recognize that ancient name? Of course not.

"So I just took it on myself to talk a li'l to Tonogan—"

"Without telling anyone. Breaching the family's—"

"*You* weren't doing a goddamn thing to—"

"That's enough."

Tonogan had come into the alley without their noticing. She was sleekly dressed in gray-black, a thin club like a riding crop tapping on her thigh. Nigel gestured to Ito to be cautious.

She said, "I gather from your son that you might be in a mood to renegotiate."

"You're just in time," Nigel said, sitting up straight. "I was about to leave for my exercise at the gymnasium."

"Very funny. Remember, I have your medical indices."

"Not much privacy in this place, is there?" Nigel inquired lightly of his son.

She ignored this, adding, "Including fatigue factors."

"Quite. We really must thank you for a bracing round of workouts. We're getting into terrific condition."

"You would be funny if your situation beed not so pathetic."

"Can't say the same for you, alas."

Tonogan sat irritably on another trash can and said she would like to explain "certain things." Nigel gave Ito a warning glance: be cautious.

As she talked he became reasonably sure that they were setting him up. Not very subtly, either. Greed dulled even keen minds.

He stalled, amused by her impatience. He had known an approach would come but had not suspected Ito as the channel. Still, Nikka had accurately predicted Tonogan's pattern to him, fully a week before. Despite her worn face she would try a bit of coquetry first, perhaps offer him a drink. And here it came, from a thermos, cutting and heady. Then very earnestly, with much show of concern, she would warn him.

"I know not if I can protect you from the Chairwoman."

"Who could?"

"Nobody ever insulted her that way. Much less hitted her and lived."

"Surely she's been spanked, at least by her mother. Probably by you, eh?" A slight loft of eyebrow; a little TwenCen kink, here; see if it translates across the cultural abyss.

"Be serious!" A pretty scowl, not really convincing. "She could have killed you right there."

"She could have tried."

"She be a very dangerous woman. I can help you with her, though. I told her later that you didn't really mean it."

"But I did."

"You know not what you be doing!"

"Tell her I want an apology."

"You be stranger, but that no excuse." Her eyes jerked in a frenzy of expressiveness. Overacting, Nigel thought. A rather bad case. He yawned.

"Listen, I talked to her, calmed her down. She sayed that she would accept some of your goods in trade for your life."

"Goods?"

An elaborate shrug. "Some of your gadgets might be worth, well, a little."

"Ummm. That's her final offer?"

"Absolutely. You have a standard day to agree. Miss that and she shows no mercy."

"I see. Tell her I make the same offer."

"What?" Disbelief—genuine this time.

"Give me some trinket and I won't kill her."

"You be *mad*."

"That will come out even. I don't kill her, she doesn't kill me. We'll call the trinkets even, too."

"Insults mean something here. I know not what made you float that ridiculous story about Earth, but wherever you be from, you cannot talk this way. And to hit the Chairwoman!"

Tonogan was working herself into a lather and seemed even to believe what she was saying. Astonishing talk poured from her. Nigel never took quite enough account of the fact that people believe in the most ridiculous things, simply because others did, too. Such as the absolute authority of a single fat woman in a baggy robe.

Ito injected, "Dad, stop kidding around. This Chairwoman is the real authority here, never mind how she looks."

Nigel looked at his son and said mildly, "It's what she says that makes me doubt her mental balance. Whatever political system they've got here, it's awry."

Tonogan's perfect yellow teeth massaged her lower lip and Nigel saw he had guessed right; even the Chairwoman's minions thought she was askew. The moment passed and Tonogan said precisely, "I should not speak of such things, I suppose, but . . . she will torture you before you die, do you not realize that?"

"Um." He drew a long face. So things were even worse than he thought. He shook his head. Perhaps Ito's caution had been good advice. Well, too late now.

Tonogan added, "And all your friends."

"Family, actually. Go tell her."

"Your childs! She will—"

"Go." He pointed and she went.

11

Sphincter Frequency

They would come in with all sorts of high-tech stuff, of course. Unfathomable stuff. So he went low-tech.

There were tinny, ceramic throwaway cans in hallways—people's manners never improved—and he took a bag of them back to the family lair. With spoons stuck in them they were so dumb and so simple an alarm that they might work.

Nikka volunteered doubtfully, "I could see about sealing the doors and windows better."

"Locks're useful only against the slovenly."

"What if they try something when we're working?"

"We're too spread out, in different labor crews."

"You think they'll do something to the entire family? And here?"

Nigel considered. "No, unless I misjudge that monstrosity of a woman. Something to humiliate me and sober the rest."

Nikka sat back, startled. Their tiny "dining" table was chipped and worn and her hands clasped each other with a tension her face never showed. He remembered that this sense of inner forces well marshaled was what had first drawn him to her, long ago. "They'll beat you? In front of us?"

As a matter of fact Nigel thought exactly that. Some methods simply could not be improved upon. This was a strange culture, true, but he was getting the feel of it. Still, to quiet her fears he said, "Too obvious."

"Some techtrick?"

"Fellow on my work gang told me those white rods the police carry are acoustic projectors. The disk at the end focuses a wave at the resonant frequency of muscles."

Nikka shivered. She always hated the description of violence, though when necessity demanded, she could quite easily commit it. "Sounds awful."

"They usually tune it to the frequency of the sphincter."

She made a face. He laughed.

They were tired all the time now. Not physically so much—before, they had all worked long orchard hours and danced late into the night—but from uncertainty and dejection. Their bedrooms were cramped, bare, and muggy with damp heat. The only sizable area was the living room, entered by a door off a fetid corridor. A depressing hovel.

Probably a little call after they had fallen asleep, then. *Eine Kleine Nachtmusik,* as Mozart, dead now over thirty thousand years, had put it. A little night music.

Nigel did not see much of a way to get in other than the flimsy front door and the two windows on an air shaft. They were ten stories up the bare sheet metal shaft, an unlikely approach. Thugs were lazy, in his experience.

The spoon trick would only give slight warning. What real defenses did they have? No weapons better than a kitchen knife.

Against the protests of everyone he took to sleeping on a thin pallet beside the front door. The door swung open toward the pallet but the uneven floor matting stopped it before it could touch him.

He did not mind sleeping that way, though he did miss Nikka's soft embrace. The pallet was thick enough for his knobby joints and the perpetual murmur of arguments and kitchen racket from the air shaft was subdued there, away from the windows. He slept there for a week. Sleep came easier and deeper because he was getting more tired from the work and a growing hopelessness. He woke one night and thought somberly of where all this was going and then a clatter came nearby as a can and spoon made momentary music together. The door's slight scrape had probably dragged him up from a fitful dream.

He got up quickly. They would have infrared gear, but he was shielded by the door. He, on the other hand, had nothing and did not know where they were. He went flat against the door. No sound. They were probably hoping that nobody would rouse, so they could carry out their plan.

They? Something told him there was only one other presence here. A slight whisk of breath from his right. That fit the humiliating beating scenario, all the worse for being imposed by a single thug. Probably the fellow would use stunners to immobilize the rest of the family.

Where was he? In the long moment after the alarm nothing had moved. His heart thudded into its future at a startling pace while his breaths came—shallow, keep them shallow—in a measured six per minute. He strained into the blank darkness.

Remember that you are old and a bit lacking in endurance. Quick work is the best.

There—a sudden shadow, stepping fast. Nigel launched himself at the man's back, hit—and slammed him forward.

No point in trying for an injury. Arms around, quick. Don't let him use his hands. A heavy thunk as something hit the floor. Maybe the stunner.

Head down, butt him in the direction he had been going. Another step. Get some push in it. Another. The man's legs were rummaging for purchase, wanting to stop. Mid-course correction here—veer left. Toward the rectangle of light. Nigel knew he could be flipped aside by some martial arts trick but if he kept the speed up—

To the window, the soft glow showing this man to be big and grasping for something on his hip. Gun, probably.

Very well—without pause, Nigel lifted with his arms. The man was trying to turn but momentum was inarguable. The body came off the floor and chunked into the windowsill.

He was heavy and solid but his mass turned on the hinge of the windowsill. Nigel lost his grip on the man then and a fist hit him full in the mouth. He staggered back. Taste of blood. A second fist clipped him. The man was still on the window lip. A short *ah* as the flailing shadow realized that the window had been thoughtfully left open.

Nigel lunged forward. The man was quick and hit him hard in the throat. All Nigel had was kinetics working for him. He did not let the punch stop him and crashed into the man. He clutched the windowsill to stop himself.

The other could not. Toppling: over and out.

Wilco, Roger, over and out. You never forgot the slang of youth. The body seemed to shrink in the gloom, diminishing as it tumbled. A thin scream came back, echoing on the sheet metal.

A wet smack. Then nothing. In the cinder-red glow from the city curving to the horizon he saw shadows scurry away below.

The backup team? Well, they seemed to have lost interest.

He heard a scramble behind him as Ito slammed shut the door.

Anyone who tried next would find a family armed with odd blunt instruments.

He sighed. Satisfying. The view from here must be wonderful when there was enough light to see it. He had never been off the work gang when the timestone bristled with light, flooding the city with a torrent of heat and light. But then in reasonable light he would have never been able to play an old man's trick. There were compensations. He felt the damp heat glow of the ruddy timestone on his cheeks and felt no remorse whatever. Maybe this was maturity. Odd, how much like callousness it would seem from the outside. Made one wonder about assessments of others.

He thought about that, listening for noises in the inky lands below. No conclusions.

There seldom were. Maybe that was maturity, too.

12

Grudging Respect

On the way to their audience with the Chairwoman they glimpsed zones of the city. A temple housing a single hair from the beard of some prophet whose very name was lost. Meat grilled in the open with dust-and-flies marinade. A church made entirely of cloth. One of the side effects of religious sites, Nikka remarked, was that some were so ludicrous that the whole lot fell into disrepute by association. Tonogan, who escorted them, seemed affronted that they regarded such buildings as mere examples of eccentric architecture. Nigel remembered his mother's similar reaction to his opinions on the ideas behind the Church of England.

The Chairwoman was even less pleased. "I could look into the body found in your shaft, you know."

"Yes, I wish you would," Nigel answered. "He screamed dreadfully. Woke up the neighbors. Anyone you knew?"

"I would hardly—"

"My son found some gear he apparently had." Nigel held up a chunky instrument of enigmatic tiny black boxes.

"I see not—"

"Makes you wonder what it's used for, doesn't it?"

In the peculiar custom of this place, their killing an agent of the Chairwoman afforded them some grudging respect, even some protection. People who mentioned the subject at all seemed to regard it as more like an audacious chess move than an act of violence, commending applause rather than revenge. The code also had ruled that the toughs sent to humiliate them were not physically augmented, as Tonogan was—a vestige of the TwenCen's notion of a fair fight.

Every era has its oddities, but Nikka had pointed out that a constant of urban populations was the glamorizing of marginally criminal acts. This bit of theory had made Nigel bold enough to taunt Tonogan when she had come to call. Their ploy had been naughty, but somehow admirable.

The large purple woman settled on her divan and regarded them all disdainfully. "I will make you a reasonable offer on your property."

Nikka said, "We only need enough to take us away from here. We want to keep our buildings."

"Why? You cannot afford to return to your Lane."

Ito said flatly, "We want the buildings. That's final." The family had decided on that and Nigel was pleased to see Ito showing that they could not be split, as Tonogan had tried.

Nikka said, more pointedly, "If we can't buy a short transit, how about a long one?"

The Chairwoman's face, which was usually animated despite looking for most purposes like a wad of dough with raisins stuck in for eyes, became blank. "How did you . . .?"

"Old folks aren't entirely useless," Nikka said brightly. "I nosed around."

"Carnivorous curiosity," Nigel added. "She turned up the fact that the energy density in a wormhole is higher if it's tightly curved."

Nikka nodded. "And the cost of making a transit goes up with the energy density."

"Umm." The Chairwoman's mouth turned crabby. "I did not think you would work that out."

"Offer us terms. We want—" Nikka rattled off a long list, headed by the use of a Causality Engine—polarized, of course.

"You realize that you'll have to make several jumps, further and further into esty-cords? And then several back?" The Chairwoman seemed genuinely interested, not merely angling for advantage.

"We'll need pressure skins, too," Nikka confirmed.

A curt nod. "You truly wish to risk that?"

"We must," Angelina said. "We want to go *home*."

Nigel nodded, not daring to speak. This was the crucial moment, he could feel it. Home. Back to a world he could understand, off the grand stage. For at least a while. Something told him that he would be forced back into the operatics of Earthers and mechanicals and Old Ones, eventually. But not now. Not while they still had family and blissfully finite horizons.

The Chairwoman eyed them. "You are more courageous than you look, you Walmsleys."

She agreed to the financial details with a suddenness and phony casualness that masked a disagreeable defeat. Not that the Walmsleys had made any appreciable dent in her bureaucrat's world, he was sure. They would not have survived that. Sometimes, Nigel thought, it was of more use to be an irritant—so long as you didn't get slapped like a pesky insect.

Deal done, the Chairwoman was cordial. In a mannered fashion, apparently part of a set ritual marking successful negotiations, she arranged herself in a helical hammock—apparently a sign of informality here—and remarked, "No one ever choosed this before."

Nigel asked, "Why? We aren't particularly brilliant. It's obvious."

"Obvious, yes. But untried. Dangerous."

Nikka looked wary. "Going further in cords is how much more dangerous?"

"We of this city and Lane know more than you." She sniffed. "We have seen the bodies."

13

Only Barbarians

Of course they asked what *the bodies* were. Officials grimaced but did as the Chairwoman said, and within a day they were ushered into a cool, starkly lit vault.

The family had looked at each other with dismay when they realized that here, corpses from the esty were held as volumes in a kind of library. Many times the family had debated and regretted their handling of the woman's corpse, which had precipitated their exile. Here the rare emergence of a carcass from the esty was greeted with anticipation and also a sort of dread, for invariably the cadavers proved to come from the future of the esty.

Nigel's elation at their negotiation trickled away as he looked at the pale, emaciated corpse of a middle-aged man, kept suspended somehow. A mass of tiny magnetic readers crowned the head. They could "read him" quite well, a technician told them. "Isotope analysis shows he's from one point three million years uptime."

"What did he die of?" asked Nikka, ever the tech type.

"Radiation burns."

"Any memories?"

The young man blinked owlishly. "Some. Missing the short-term recall, of course."

Memories, indeed. Fractured pictures. The same hazy sky, mapped in the 0.511 million electron Volt line. Only far more developed, with ornate structures corkscrewing across a mottled ruby sky.

More: a bleak landscape marked off by boxy monuments. Among these crawled three-wheeled things that appeared to be not vehicles but living creatures.

"Or mechs," Nigel said crisply.

"Who was he?" Nikka asked pensively.

"We cannot really understand that. He does not have the personality signatures we know. All I can unscramble be images. What these pictures mean, we can say not."

"Why not?"

"He haved different cerebral organization. Internal organs be altered, too. He be another species."

Angelina was shocked. "He looks like us!"

The pale young man shrugged. "Tinker with the insides all you want, but keep the outside looking the same. Otherwise, people beed nervous."

"That's why you can't get much from their minds?" Angelina pressed him.

"That, and cultural differences. This fellow did not look at the world the way we do. It shows up in how he stored memories."

Nigel found all this depressing. More bodies, but still no one, not even pale pedants, understood why.

When they went to sign off on the arrangements, the Chairwoman herself appeared. "You're going into mech-dominated territory, you know," she said severely.

Nigel guessed that she was having second thoughts about the deal. Or maybe her ego was getting in the way again. Not uncommon, he thought wanly. "You're sure?"

"We receive no dead mechs coming back through the esty Vors. Only humans."

"You're sure?" Nikka asked pointedly.

"We pay close attention. The Old Ones make sure of that." She snorted with frustration.

"Why?" Nigel persisted.

"The old questions. You haved them even in your time, um?" A speculative look, then she recited as if from memory. "First, they want to know what the mechs want up there in the far future. Plenty of mechs goed into the future one-way, using Vors."

"To carry information forward?" Nikka asked.

"Possibly. The Old Ones want to find out why."

"And stop it?" Nigel asked.

"I suppose. Or at least understand."

Nikka nodded. "So do we."

The Chairwoman plainly could see no percentage in such

foolhardiness. "Why? The esty's trouble enough if you just sit still in it."

"Carnivorous curiosity," Nigel said.

She snorted. "A child's reasoning. If you could see the things I do just to keep us tipped up—"

"Yes?" Angelina asked. Nigel was happy to see her speak up, for she had been cowed by this place. "Why *do* you tilt your city?"

The Chairwoman said scornfully, "Why, it be *beautiful*. Only barbarians would even think of asking."

14

⬛━◆━◆━◆━◆━◆━◆━⬛

Grey Mech

The mercurial Chairwoman invited them to sleep on her personal estate as they arranged details for their esty transit. This proved to be the same ornate, almost satirically baroque villa where they had met her. They had entered by the back door, amid thronged streets; the true entrance gave onto a cantilevered view of the cupped city, from the uppermost rim of it.

Large birds, some with shiny teeth and even lips, hung on the winds off the Chairwoman's balcony. One swooped near and eyed them, as if sizing up a meal. It was half the size of a man. Here gravity eased, lending everything an airy lightness that reminded Nigel of getting drunk but suffering no consequences. Still, the toothy birds smiled at them with unnerving assurance. They went back inside.

The next waning lasted quite long. Somehow the city could influence the pulses of brilliant glow emitted by the timestone, shaping them to a roughly regular schedule: dark about a third of the time, enough to sleep if you were not too tired.

Nobody here seemed to get tired. Noisy, chaotically colorful, they rushed about a lot. Nikka wondered aloud if this was just their Old Fart bewilderment at the pointless energy of the young. Nigel shook his head. He had harbored that notion for so long that he had passed through to another state, in which he ceased grasping for the fullness of life and let it come to him instead. It had taken him centuries to realize that joy and pain were equally biting and rewarded close inspection equally little. They were just *there*, like flowers. Better to take them for their flavors than their metaphors.

They stood again on the balcony with the Chairwoman, idle talk before bed, and across the distant porcelain sky shot something large and swift and somber. The Chairwoman's eyes widened. "Grey Mech!" she cried, and crashed to the marble floor.

Thin cries of panic from all across the cupped city below. Nigel studied the dusky, hovering presence with abstract interest, hands on a gleaming brass railing.

"Get *down*!" Nikka called to him from her knees, hidden from view.

The Grey Mech rushed toward them, accelerating from high up. A chorus of despairing shouts came up to him from the expanse of streets and glassy buildings below. Casually he turned and walked inside.

"Probably wasn't after us," he said to Nikka as they stood in an elaborate ballroom. People rushed through, panicked, calling hoarsely to each other.

"We can't be sure," she said nervously.

"Come now. We aren't remotely important to—"

The crash blew in the far wall. Hammer-hard impact, then an eerie silence.

It buried them under heavy furniture. They learned later, as a medical type patched them up, that a section of the Grey Mech had detached and gone prowling over the city. Fire lanced up from weapons below. It deflected these with dismissive ease. It had sent interrogating bursts of electromagnetic energy into every possible device, quickly sectioning the city's grid, narrowing its search. The scrutiny sharpened upon this district but no further. Apparently it could not resolve whatever it sought. So the angular thing had fired pulses into the area, killing several hundred people and caving in the lower walls of the Chairwoman's villa.

Nigel nodded. "You were right," he said mildly to Nikka. "But why?"

The Chairwoman had suffered some bruises but that did not explain her jittery anxiety, hands clenching and unclenching, face bluish white. "Never did one attack us before. They be of the highest mech class, always ahead of our technology."

"I see not much has changed," Nikka said. "It was the same in our era."

"They could slaughter us all." The Chairwoman eyed them warily. "And they be after you?"

"A mere hypothesis," Nigel said, yawning.

Nikka caught his glance and said, "I'm still not happy with the provisions you've supplied."

"What?" The Chairwoman scowled, then said automatically, "We made a deal."

"We won't leave without—" and Nikka rattled off a further list.

The large woman opened her mouth and slowly closed it. "You *must* leave."

"No we don't," Nigel said.

She glowered. He could see her step through the logic. If these Walmsleys were of interest to a Grey Mech, best be rid of them and count yourself lucky. "All right, the provisions—but you go at first light."

Nikka nodded. Anything that drew the Grey Mech was bad for business.

"Still," Nigel said distantly, later, "why should we be important?"

"Maybe because of where we're headed?" Nikka asked.

That night he lay on a sort of pliant water pillow with Nikka and they watched the snakelike dog come into their room and investigate them. It was apparently fairly intelligent and in fact head of security there. To questions it gave a nod of the head and abrupt, slurred *yhas* or *noah*.

He ignored it after a while and realized, staring out at the encased night of this Lane, that he had become married to a flat, unremarked fatality. Yet this did not carry with it any of the usual gloom of earlier times. Maybe this was new wisdom or maybe fatigue but in any case he did not want to piss his life away on nonsense. Much of what he had once believed and felt he now saw as foolishness or at least useless. On the other hand, some moments shone like jewels.

He shook off this mood by immersing himself in Nikka, the love between them now so distant from belabored technical strenuosities that he found it yielding up what seemed most impossible of all, moments of pleasurable surprise. He slept soundly. In the musty morning half-light they awoke lingeringly together.

"That dog was in the room when we were going at it."

"I didn't mind. Perhaps by now they've evolved to the point where at the crucial moment they politely look away."

"Moment? You think it lasted only a moment?"

"Well, let's say it was timeless."

"That's better. I do seem to recall the dog barking at an important point."

"Oh? I thought that was you."

15

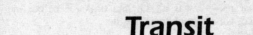

Transit

The Causality Polarizer was mammoth, its compressive antennas perpetually yawning like vast bored mouths. They gaped in all six faces of an enormous, burnished ceramic cube. They reminded Nikka of speakers from a giant's stereo set, she remarked. These were the ten-kilohertz oscillators, delivering a terrawatt in short-wavelength gravitational waves.

Still, Nigel liked the speaker analogy—because that was how it felt. The family sheltered in a metallic capsule set beside their house, back among the familiar setting that had been wrenched away from their home Lane. It felt good to simply be there, but from the moment he got into the capsule he fidgeted uneasily. The countdown did not help.

"The point of making a wormhole sprout out of a Lane is that you really can't do it by yourself," Nikka told him. "Takes astronomically too much energy, or more accurately, density of energy. The best we can do is ripple the esty surface, find a weak spot—a place where the Casimir force is substantial."

"Who was Casimir?" Angelina asked.

"Who cares? He saw that in a true vacuum, there would be a force, one you could harness."

"As we are about to?" Angelina looked skeptical.

"Of course." Nikka had on her *See?—obvious!* expression.

"So when we have to travel in a big loop to get home, that means we have to go into the future?" Nigel liked scientific ideas but he did not like having to think like a pretzel.

"There is a lot more future than past. The universe is only fifteen billion years old. The future's almost infinite."

Nikka seemed to think that finished off the idea. Nigel ventured, "Approximately infinite. Interesting concept. So there's a much greater chance that any leg of our trip will go into the future?" and she rewarded him again with her daintily amused *See?—obvious!* smile.

Ito scowled in the last moments before Transit and asked warily, "How dangerous is this?"

She shrugged. She was no stranger to trauma and death and did not think much about it. "Not very, unless we hit a stutter."

"What's that me—" was all Ito had time for before the pulverizing wall of sound struck their capsule.

Pain stretches time.

The vibrations confirmed his fears. They seemed to go on for a sluggish, pounding eternity, though Nikka later told them offhandedly that it had been only forty-four seconds. Of agony.

16

<hr>

Time Is a Horizon

Shaken, they popped open the capsule lock. They found themselves among their home and outbuildings, with the same slice of orchard as before—all resting atop a sliding mass of luminous timestone. To all sides a box canyon rose, shrouded in lemon-hot vapor.

They got out and breathed cold, thin air but kept their pressure skins on anyway. Nikka calculated from the capsule's instruments and decided that they had squeezed through the momentarily pulsating wormhole, traversing an esty-displacement of several million kilometer-years.

"Could be millions of klicks away and at exactly the same time we left," she said calmly, "or the same Lane, millions of years in the future." Wormholes tunneled between eras not at all like elevators linking floors of a building, but that was how Nigel persisted in thinking of them.

The ground shook. The plate of their property shifted uneasily on the timestone beneath.

"There's no way to tell which?" Benjamin asked apprehensively.

"The Causality Engine had chaos built into it," Nikka answered, holding on to a capsule strut for support. "We can't measure any better than this."

Nigel watched the distant sky, where more lavalike walls fumed and roiled. "How long do we stay here?"

"That's chaotic, too," Nikka said. "But short. Looks to be

maybe an hour or two. We'll have some warning of when the next Transit is coming."

Angelina laughed, which startled the others. "Until then we're free to enjoy the scenery?" Despite their gathering unease, the family chuckled with her.

As if in answer, nearby cliffs oozed sulphurous light, complaining with slow groans. A sheet peeled off—*crack!*—and a sharp snap in the air knocked them flat. Here the esty was like skin, sloughing away layers so that more could grow. Compressed events evolved, brimmed, died.

Nigel knew from undergraduate days that mass curved space-time, but the inverse was still a surprise: compacted esty behaved like matter. Rendered as mass, events themselves were squeezed into slabs. Their endings brought forth explosive energies: literally, the end of history, for in these detonations data burst into phosphorescent energy, its true equivalent. The esty confirmed the final triumvirate of physics, one side of which Einstein had got right: mass was like energy was like information.

They went into their house, which had been fully provisioned by the Chairwoman's minions, and tried to act as though this was a kind of homecoming. They were hungry and ate something like steaks of beef to celebrate but the coming Transit made their talk edgy. Nigel went outside. Ostensibly it was to smoke one of his cigars, carefully kept chilled in the kitchen but scorned if lit inside. He did not like delivering his family into the hands of Causality Engines or "intrinsic chaos" or any other collection of jawbreaker words that in the end meant the world's casual indifference to human life and values. But he had no choice.

"It can't be helped. You know that," Nikka said. She had slipped beside him, her footsteps covered by the hollow crashing of timestone far up on the hazy curve of this spherical Lane.

"Should've let that body rot, moved away," he said morosely.

"We wouldn't be us, then."

"Is that so bad? Change your dance steps, learn a new tune."

"We're doing what we've always wanted to do. Looking long, you used to call it."

"Quite." He sighed. "I always wanted to see over the far horizon. This—"

"Time is a horizon, too."

17

━━◆━◆━◆━◆━◆━◆━◆━◆━◆━◆━◆━━

Transit; Wait

Stochastic.

Not a word he liked, too pedantic, when all it meant was chaos, disorder, the fitful randomness of life and esty. Their gravitationally transduced energy propelled their wedge of local esty through the worm in jolting, stochastic motions.

Transit; wait. Transit; wait.

They never knew precisely how long they would stay at any of the pauses along this worm-Vortex. They could watch the surroundings, but feared to venture out. They ate up their provisions this way as their frustration built.

No map of the esty was possible. Its contorted geometry roiled with fitful energies, a rubbery, sliding turmoil. Lanes were often long, snaky, bulging into spheres and lopsided bubbles without warning, stretching to expose fresh, wrenched topographies of timestone.

Sometimes their pause-points were in the same Lane, so they watched its speeded-up evolution. As timestone evolved by its own kinetics, topsoil tumbled and spilled in great alluvial fans. Beaten beneath hammering rains that accompanied the changes, the soil molded into new hills and valleys below the craggy peaks of freshly emerging timestone. Life was resilient, adapting. In bright canyons trees tunneled up from recent burials, and most plants could survive a temporary churning to emerge into the stone's own waxing radiance again.

Nikka got grim-faced when Ito and Benjamin wanted to explore the nearby Lanes they intersected. "No."

"Why not?"

"Ask your mother. She'll tell you that it's 'stochastic'."

"So?"

"We're not desperate enough yet."

But they were running short of food and Ito was restless, Nigel saw, beyond his endurance. After a full-scale family argument over the big polished dining room table they decided to let both Ito and Benjamin forage. Nikka, Angelina, and Nigel spent an anxious time awaiting their return as the timer on the capsule ticked down to the next Transit.

With only an hour to spare, and Nikka muttering that the uncertainty in such calculations was more than two hours, easy, they came across the rugged timestone at a trot, backpacking food. Benjamin said they had seen nothing much but, as Nigel had guessed, Ito had reveled in it.

They voyaged on, Transiting and pausing and watching the long slow epic of organic life forms and mechs in the lands beyond. Usually they were isolated on a timestone terrain. Sometimes battles raged in the distance and they anxiously watched the unknown combatants, hoping to be ignored.

Usually they were, but several times mechs had cruised overhead and twice Ito and Benjamin had knocked them down with glee, using projection weapons the Chairwoman had sold them. Probably they were lucky, having the advantage of surprise in this era, but Nigel made them stop it because luck did not last forever.

They got into worse trouble at the next pause. Here a passing woman told them that the mechs had launched a new plague, wind-borne and virulent. Nine out of ten in her city had died. The Walmsleys gave her food and she went on and that night they came down with it, too. Fever, violent dysentery, sinuses clotted with yellow spongy growths. Ito had walking dreams, seeing the gates of a private hell and struggling to run through them to some glimpsed reward. Nigel and Angelina grabbed him and held him down for hours before the delusions passed in a fit of sweating babble that spilled from Ito's mouth like a river of hallucination, so wild that Nikka—a part of her always dispassionate, even with her own children—wrote some of it down.

The delusions struck Nigel next and unloosened in him the many haunted memories that accompany anyone who chooses to live long.

—Cramped spacecraft maneuvering near Earth's crisp white moon.

—Swimming darkly through the icy waters of a moon, into an interior ocean filmed with kilometers of ancient ice.

—Winds blowing acid dust in his face as aliens like huge radio antennas lumbered toward him in the frying heat.

—Their aching long flight to reach the esty, in search of refuge from a galaxy that seemed filled to overspilling with mechs.

He spoke of these, sputtering in the warm spray of dislocated words, and could not recognize his own foot sticking naked at the other end of the bed, or the blood he coughed up, or even the perpetual frown that furrowed Nikka's face in the dim night.

The only factor that saved them was their simple distance in esty-coordinates, he realized later. The mech-made virus was so tuned to the humans of this place-period that it missed them by a hair. So they merely groaned and sweated and fouled themselves, the disease taking a full week to work its way through each. They carried it through three pauses and were out of food again by the time they could all walk without shaky knees.

18

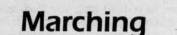

Marching

Evidence of mech-wrought damage lay everywhere. Charred cities, blasted landscapes, bedraggled populations torn by raids.

Once, while they were foraging for information and food, a mech caught Nigel and Angelina in the open. It was crawler type and burned Angelina pretty badly before he could knock out its mainmind. When he saw how much Angelina was suffering he put her to sleep with a sedative and while waiting for it to take full effect in a rage he pulled off the mech's working arm and used it to bash in the carapace, letting himself go completely to the sheer boiling energy of it. Then he carried Angelina across his back, barely reaching their farm buildings before he collapsed. He was sobered for days afterward as he watched her recover, fevered sweat glazing her eyes.

Seen through the prism of the esty, Nigel thought as he tended his daughter, life was like a long march, an endless column of forlorn souls moving forward through surrounding dark. Locked into their own eras, nobody knew where they were going. Still, in every society they glimpsed, there was plenty of talk and the fools pretended to understand more than they were saying. There was merry laughter, too, and somebody was always passing a bottle around.

But now and then somebody stumbled, didn't catch himself right, lurched aside and was gone, left behind. The dead.

Sliding timewise-forward, sometimes backward, poking their heads out where the chaotics of the harnessed worm commanded, Nigel saw the long mortal march in snatches, which made it all the more telling.

Whole societies eventually joined the individual dead. For them the march stopped at that moment. Maybe some had a while longer, lying back there on the hard ground, already wreathed in fog—time to watch the parade dwindle away, carrying on its lights and music and raucous jokes.

For us the dropouts are back there somewhere, he thought, *fixed in a murky landscape we're already forgetting.*

He could recall others who had stayed behind, years ago. With a little sigh or a grunt of agony or just a flickering of fevered eyelids, they left the human march. No longer did they know the latest jokes or the savor of a fresh bottle of wine, or what the hottest rumors were about. The march saddened him. He remembered friends long lost, wished he could tell them what was up nowadays, share a laugh or a lie.

As he read his latest indices, now covertly so that Nikka did not see, he thought, *Right—and the point, you brooding old bulk, is that you know your station above the tide of time is temporary. That persistence is your only virtue beyond theirs, and it is artificial. That someday you would catch an ankle and go down and the murk would swallow you, too. Maybe it would be better if you didn't have that puzzled, startled moment of staring at the retreating heads, the faces already turning away from you. Maybe it was best if you couldn't hear that last parting round of hollow laughter from a joke you would never know, the golden lantern light already shining on them and not on you.*

And it will happen to everyone you have known or ever will.

Somehow he never got used to that.

19

⊏━◇━◇━◇━◇━◇━◇━◇━◇━◇━⊐

Storytelling

They could flee in space-time, but biology followed. They all had a relapse of the mech-made plague, far milder but bad enough.

Ito recovered first. When he simply announced that he was going out for provisions, in the pause they had just come to, no one could mount more than feeble resistance. The next Transit was days away, the probability indices said.

"Probably! Only probably!" his mother protested weakly.

"There's no 'probably' about our starving, though," Ito said grimly. So he left.

The time passed in fever and worry. But they all were better by the time Ito returned, loaded down and with a bad leg wound.

To Nigel the sight of his oldest coming through their front door was like the sun coming out after a night that had lain on them all like a sullen lid. As he helped Ito store the vegetables and fruit, he felt a difference in his son. Dinner that evening drove the difference home. Ito spoke more directly, clearly, face free of the stretched tensions Nigel remembered from late adolescence.

Like many men and women compelled to action by restlessness of body and spirit, Ito had no interest in the notion of adventure. But he knew storytelling well enough to see what people saw in it and so recounted with accurate detail incidents that seemed ordinary to him, arising out of necessity:

—the mech like a snake which attached itself to his leg and could not be dislodged (he found, while bellowing in frustrated rage) except by finally singing to it;

—towns built aslant and of both surpassing beauty and stunning ugliness;

—aliens galore, who treated him with utter indifference, while he found them fascinating;

—the beheading of a woman for unspeakable acts she had performed with a mech, which was both horrifying and puzzling, for no one could explain the mech's motivation, while the woman's seemed to lie within the known range of human perversions;

—a mech religion which worshiped animals exclusively, attributing to them a natural wisdom;

—a castle of glass through which the passerby could see the inhabitants living out their lives under constant scrutiny, never concealing even the most private acts;

—a waterfall that rose upward and formed ice at its summit, building a glinting blue-white mountain.

Nigel realized as they went to bed that his son had made a transit of his own, one that few speak of and most do not recognize until years after.

20

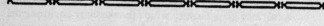

Generations

On they voyaged, slipping through sheets of esty, tugged by the energy flux of the worm. Nikka rigged an optical sensor on their capsule's outside and they saw, slowed enormously, the instant of Transit. A filmy sheen formed around their farm, contours rippling.

Though in their simple picture a wormhole was like a tube passing between floors of a building, the floors different space-times—a glinting needle piercing ebony esty cloth—the worm was in fact three-dimensional in their frame.

At the shaved second when they passed through, the worm was a flickering spherical glaze. It swelled, swallowed them, then dwindled away to a point—which vanished with a spray of golden brilliance and stomach-turning torques. To Nigel it felt as if he were climbing up his own chilly vertebrae.

They watched the esty beyond their small area, sometimes for mere minutes before it changed again. Scenes and lands flickered beyond their small preserve. They witnessed eras with no visible human presence, others with jammed cities teetering on shaky timestone, still more with no atmosphere—so their pressure skins *snick*ed shut immediately when they emerged—and others with virulent, acrid gases for air. Some pauses were long enough to venture forth.

Through all this Nigel and Nikka reached a new equilibrium, a sweet sad realization spawned from the vistas of time they had traversed. There were myriad incidents—some small and telling, others large and dangerous and finally meaningless, and they all pointed toward the heartache and matching joy of humanity itself.

They met, in glancing fashion, teaming tribes, rich in spirit and intellect. Soldiers, who drank with gusto and ate with undisguised zest, though they knew they would face battles on the morrow that would probably decimate their ranks. Scholars, bent by their pilgrimages and ravaged by poverty, yet still warm with the satisfactions of the studies to which they had devoted their lives. Children, playing among the blackened ruins of their homes. Parents, rejoicing in their infants even as calamity closed in around them. In cities growing stranger still as they Transited further, people sang slow, sad songs in the streets even as mech forces gathered high in the Lane above, and crowds collected to see magicians perform tricks and make ancient jokes, all greeted with raucous laughter. Among the few dazed survivors of other assaults, on other twisted landscapes, the Walmsleys met stoic survivors who nonetheless found fresh loves, new friends, and began again. Generations melted away and others came forth, with only a few managing to hang on to time for as long as Nikka and Nigel had, and through it all somehow a frail, brave, human light always streaked the surrounding shadows.

The old non sequitur, that species became degenerate as they went on, found no evidence here. Humanity bristled with activity. Societies rose and fell with stubborn indifference to earlier failures.

In the face of the inevitable end, and the inevitable questions, Nigel reflected, none is exempt: witness Jesus's wail of despair as he edged rather tentatively into eternity. He did not know what to make of such dogged human persistence. Nikka was less puzzled, and beamed with pride in her own kind.

21

Inflection Point

They came to the far end of their curved worm's path through the esty. Nikka declared from the data, "We've gotten damped into a stutter."

"Which is?" Nigel stepped out into the local familiarity of their farm. Beyond, the lands were strangely shadowed.

"We're hung up, basically. The Vortex worm turns here"—she smiled at the small joke, much needed as the family grasped her point—"and begins an opposite curvature in the esty. We'll be going back from here on."

"Going home!" Angelina cried happily, clapping her hands.

"But?" Nigel was pensive.

Nikka gave him a rueful nod. "But . . . we're stalled here, at the inflection point. We're retracing the same interval of time over and over."

"Stuttering in space-time." Nigel rolled the idea around in his mind.

They walked to the edge of their land. In what seemed like the solid mass beyond Nigel saw pale blades and soft blue shadows, as if deep somewhere a sun were setting. Radiant blades danced as if refracted beneath a lake's wind-blown skin, like summer's liveliness probing into a deep watery cavern. And as he watched, the whole thing repeated. And repeated.

It was unsettling and he nearly lost his footing, the way a man approaching a sheer drop goes weak in the legs even though still on solid ground. A mere crust kept him from an abyss.

"We're cycling through the same moment," Ito whispered. "Over and over."

"Damn!" Benjamin was not awed. He just wanted to go home.

Then the scene jolted. Hills rose, bristling with raw rock. In jumpy, flashing images they watched the slopes weather, ruts cutting in. Peaks wore to knobs, hills slumped—and strange spires rose, icy blue. Glaciers of eerie green slid through valleys. Nigel realized they were not glaciers at all but some immensely cold superfluid, in the terminal death of the farthest future. They were seeing the slices of time into which information still could be packed, wedges of instants harvested from an immense span of time. They could fathom the sliding immensities that wrecked mountains and oozed into nothingness, for they were witnessing physics and dynamics beyond the hinge of human time.

Then, abruptly, they were back to the same endlessly cycling moment they had seen before. Somehow they had leaped far beyond, then back. They watched the repeating interval for a while but nothing more happened.

"Mom . . . How do we get out of a stutter?" Angelina asked quietly.

"We don't do anything." Nikka stared at the timestone, which coiled incessantly like a pile of glowing snakes. "We wait it out."

"How long?" Benjamin looked at the seethe, distaste curling his lip.

Nigel wondered disagreeably whether the question meant anything, if time cycled outside. And space, too—he could see the same shards rise and descend, rise and descend. But their little wedge of esty ran on its own time axis. Or so he thought. How would he know? His head began to hurt.

Nikka said, "I'm afraid that is a stochastic variable, irreducible."

Nigel erupted, "*Every*thing's chaotic here!"

Nikka smiled. "Except you. You're perfectly predictable."

That made them all laugh, but it did not seem so funny after several days of edgy waiting.

Then events beyond shifted.

The air turned cold with a sudden ferocity no planetary environment could ever match. And without any visible cause, the land began to evolve beyond their encapsulated chunk of farm.

"Is the stutter over?" Angelina cried, excited.

"I don't know." Nikka frowned, deepening the crows'-feet of lines around her eyes. "Time seems to be accelerating outside."

"We're holding fixed in space, sliding in time?" Ito asked.

"Looks to be," Nikka said. Physics here seemed to Nigel to be largely a matter of opinion.

The sliding, coiling timestone was churning as before when a waning came, and the next waxing there were valleys, soil, plant life. The land here was cut and worked by unknowable forces and yet the weather also had ordinary touches: sudden showers, the drifting smell of sage, meat curing somewhere in a distant smokehouse.

The runoff storm water sorted itself out into streams and then slow-moving rivers lined with tuft-topped trees. The soil beside them sometimes shot up into a mottled sky. Jagged crests shaped as they watched, spikes raking cottony clouds.

Cautiously they hiked out into the new land. Oddly shaped creatures scampered among the rocks, dancing on webbed feet as though the ground were too hot to bear. The family went down a long grade and could see what looked like log houses at the feet of steep hills, windows glowing orange, dusky smoke blown so hard from their stone chimneys that it flattened along the roofs and trailed like flags down the valley. Through a cut in these hills they came into a dark bowl and a city spilled out like a shower of cinders stirred from an unseen fire, pinpoints going on as the light from the esty ebbed. But no people. Nigel realized that it was moving, the entire construction somehow crawling toward them. A city-thing, alive.

He wondered what it could contain. Was there anything more to surprise a burnt-out wreck like him? A place that could startle him and yet let him sleep peacefully?

Though of course, he thought, nodding ruefully, he would still wake in the morning with the old familiar gargoyle of fears sitting on his chest, peering into his face, grinning toothless and triumphant.

Abruptly timestone jutted through the topsoil. It split and burned, jagged teeth raking the land. They ran back to their own area, barely making it.

The Grey Mech appeared shortly afterward.

22

Far Futures

Lying sorely in a crevice of timestone, much later, Nigel recalled a time long ago when contact had been possible between humanity and the bewildering zoo of mech constructs. He had bound up his broken left arm and waited for sleep to take him. He fixed upon the past because thoughts of where his family might be would do him no good. When he could walk again he would go look. That was all.

Some mechs back then had convinced members of Nigel's own crew that existence as a mechanical creature was both better and longer lasting than the fragile life of "organic" creatures. So quite willingly some lower forms of the Grey Mech had "incorporated"—their term—several friends of his. "Uplifting," they termed it.

The process was painless. As mechs his friends became contrived boxes mounted on skeletal frames. They moved about the landscape seldom and when Nigel had tried to talk to them about their lives they seemed distracted—as if carrying on a telephone conversation while watching something more interesting on television, he thought. What they did say was bland, empty, and yet somehow chilling.

He had waited some years until he was again in the particular Lane where this had happened. He settled in behind some rocks at a goodly distance from where he knew the Grey Mech's lower forms sometimes came. The ones who had uplifted his friends.

Their sensors were good and he could not get too close. One of the under-forms appeared and he was sure of its identity by its electromagnetics, its spectral hiss and clang. He shot out its under-carriage. With a weapon whose physics he did not quite understand he put three holes through the main frame of it. The mech went silent, its electromagnetic buzzings winking off. Something small climbed out of it and tried to get away and Nigel shot it eight times with great satisfaction. He later learned that the other under-forms had been incorporated back into the Grey Mech so he had to be content with the one.

Of this he dreamed, as his arm ached and his heart burned leaden in his chest.

It rained hard in the sullen dark. Vegetation beat at itself in the lashing winds. Lightning leapt across the sky. He could see the forks of yellow and green snaking high above where the esty folded over onto itself in a blithely twisted geometry.

No sign of the Grey Mech.

No, Grey Mechs, he corrected himself. That had been a rather large error.

Two Grey Mechs had appeared in the Lane. Ashen, blocky, each headed for the buildings. He remembered the frozen tableau: Benjamin and Nikka and himself, scrambling for the segments of the Transit device. Ito and Angelina, turned to flee.

Time was hopelessly warped here, he had conceded that long ago, but the same old question remained. Could he have done anything different?

23

Verge of Extinction

In the few seconds before the dusky shapes reached them he had shouted, "Transducers!"—meaning the big pyramid-shaped wedges that transferred stored electrical energy into gravitational pulses.

"At *which*?" Nikka yelled into a roaring, rising wind raised by the Grey Mechs.

His eyes jerked from one Grey Mech to the other. Nikka slapped her wrist to the console, popped the interface.

Which one? Both? Two ashen chunks with no visible means of flight. Pivoting on an unseen axis, in a sky they ripped with their passage.

Not acting together. Each responding to the other's darting swerves.

One was closer, larger, coming fast, and in desperation he chose it. "There!"

Nikka aimed and fired the transducers in one quick swivel of her interface hand. The ground buckled with the release of acoustic power and they all three sprawled. The leading Grey Mech shuddered but came on.

Ito and Angelina never reached the house. The leading Grey Mech loosed a bolt that seemed to wrap itself like a scintillating blue-white cloak around them. They twisted and fell.

Fringes of the bolt killed Nigel's in-body electronics instantly. He had struggled halfway to his feet when the queasy jolt of his systems going dead knocked him down again.

Strumming, nearly overpowered, his defenses teetered on the verge of extinction.

He looked up at what he expected to be his last vision. Numbly he watched the spectacle of two Grey Mechs battling each other across the sapphire sky. Spasms refracted down the streaming air. A shock wave slammed into him and he felt his body bounce from its power.

He tried to hang on to consciousness, but the chilly blackness had clasped him to itself—

24

❮━◆━◆━◆━◆━◆━◆━◆━◆━◆━◆━❯

Alexandria

—To awaken here, on a timestone slope.

Arm broken, shooting pains in the legs.

No, he probably could not have done anything differently. Alas.

It was always comforting to think that but in dealing with mechs it was in fact true. They acted far more swiftly than beings based on muscle and nerves. But thinking this did him no good because it still sounded like an excuse.

He groaned and opened his eyes, the lids sticky. Lightning licked overhead, seeking a place to rest, on a quest of its own. He knew it was merely a horde of electrons seeking a path to discharge an electrostatic potential, but that did not quell the eerie sensation of watching strange spirits seek and probe and lash the air with their desire. He was watching the luminous lemony fingers play across the high roof of the esty when she came to him again.

You've changed.

"You haven't."

My kind never does.

He blinked but it made no difference. Alexandria, his first wife, stood a little to one side, looking out at the same slippery lightning that he was. In the sulphurous flashes he could see her classic high forehead and delicate cheekbones. They had been that way up until a few weeks before the disease had weathered her down, stealing flesh from her, sending her into a grave on a hillside in Pasadena, California.

"Alexandria, I . . ."

I do like it when you use my name.

"I always loved the sound of it."

What did you used to say about it?

"That your name was perfect. That it was like you. Alexandria, Egypt, where the library burned. Lost knowledge. The unknowable."

Oh yes. Most people mispronounced it. They thought it should be that ordinary name without the i.

"Where classical civilization hit the reef and sank, losing most of its cargo."

Bad history, lover. The Greeks were long gone when that library burned.

"But not the civilization. That remains as long as it is remembered."

And ours?

Nigel shrugged. "As long as we're here, I suppose."

As long as you are here. I don't count. I am a ghost.

"Not to me. You're the woman I loved."

She turned slightly toward him, just enough to let him see the lilting curve of her eternal smile. It was always that way. He could never see her face, never know it entirely. Or be free of it, he saw now. She could visit him across the yawning centuries.

Past tense?

"Sorry. Love."

Lost knowledge.

"Not really."

Her lips curled in a soundless laugh. *You're so sure?*

"I recall every hollow and delight."

After so many years?

"Remember relativity. It's been, oh, perhaps twenty-eight thousand years on Earth. But in here"—he tapped his skull—"there's been very little going on. Dull, really. Time dilation, it's called by the physicists."

I never understood that sort of thing.

"I doubt anyone understands it fundamentally. It's a flat fact of the universe."

And you?

Nigel could not read her expression. "Me?"

Are you a fact of the universe, too?

"Ummm. An unimportant one, yes."

You were important then and you are now.

"I'm a cockroach on the stage at Stratford. You might say, rather a serious case of undercasting."

By who?

"By whom," he said distantly.

Ah! Always the language purist. Okay then, by whom?

"The Director, I suppose."

Who is . . . ?

"I've wondered about that. If there's something working itself out here. Somehow."

God?

"Too short a name for such a large idea. Anyway, I'd have thought you could ask Him directly, eh?"

Because I'm in heaven?

"Aren't you? Or someplace at least different?"

She laughed. *I'm in your head. Not really heaven, no.*

Yet as she turned slightly more and smiled at him, Nigel could see her with crystalline clarity. This was too good to be a hallucination. Too solid, crisp, real. He must be worse off than he thought.

"Alexandria . . . ?"

Yes?

"I want to—I—"

Not that time yet.

He snapped, "I'm like a child, told when to go to bed?"

This isn't bed. Not nearly as much fun, for one thing.

"I'm . . . tired."

Not physically though.

"Perhaps I've seen too much."

It's not your moment yet.

With sharp anger he barked, "It wasn't your moment either."

You're still getting hard at night, just thinking of me, aren't you?

"Um. I can hardly deny it, can I? You seem to live inside my head."

Exactly, lover! And as long as I do—well, maybe it wasn't my moment, back there. Maybe I'm still here.

"Copies aren't originals."

A lady appreciates what compliments come her way. Especially since I know you have Nikka.

"I hope this isn't disloyal to her."

It can't be. We are all the loves we have known—that's my own attempt at self-definition.

"I like that. A definition free of the worn out carcass, the body."

Don't ignore the body. Or bodies.

He paused, swollen tongue running over bitter teeth. "Bodies . . ."

The bodies got you into this.

"Don't remind me."

Think of them as calling cards.

"How hilarious. From the Grey Mechs, no doubt. Come to the dance, please, and die."

Who would read a suredead body, lover? Think.

"I'm starting to hate riddles." His head was woozy, the world circling him in a slow waltz.

I'm a part of the riddle, too. We all are. See you around, lover.

"Not yet!"

'Bye.

He weathered out the long, murky waning. His in-body indices had come back somewhat. They were erratic and the index he watched most carefully was down three more points. He sighed, momentarily glad Nikka was not here to worry about that, and then the weight of it all came in upon him. He lay in fever and bitter regrets, thinking thoughts that went down so deep, the lizards there had no eyes.

Something had blown him a long way down the Lane they had been in. This he discovered by climbing an unstable peak of teetering timestone and peering above a deck of olive-colored clouds. He recognized the territory where their farm had been and determined to walk back to it. This took longer than he thought it should with the broken arm and he hurried at the end. The farm seemed deserted at first. Inside the house he sat at the long dining room table and the room seemed filled with ghosts as substantial as Alexandria had been and that was when the thing moved into view.

He sat completely still. It was two-legged and two-armed and that was where the resemblance ended.

Human? No, he knew instantly.

Eerie, silent, radiating strangeness like a chill wave.

He noticed that his in-body electronics were working again. They helped a little with the splintered arm. The thing moved slightly. His in-bodies fluoresced in a disturbing response, sending dazzling fireworks across his retinas, and then he got it all in one long burst.

25

━━◆✕◆✕◆✕◆✕◆✕◆✕◆━━

Mortal Galaxies

He stood beneath a dull black sky framed by a jagged horizon.

Abruptly, he *knew* in a way he never had. In his weary bones he *felt* a worldview—kinesthetic, perceptions as momenta and geometry, not words. He fumbled to put the sensations into terms that he could get his mind around.

The sky. Black, then unfolding into streamers of feathery light.

How different, he thought, from the physics he had learned as a boy. In the Newtonian views of Boltzmann and Clausius, the universe extended forever but was always threatened by collapse. Nothing countered the drawing-in of gravity.

Given enough time, matter would seek its own kind, smacking into greater and greater stars. But the stars would die, guttering out as blunt thermodynamics commanded, always seeking maximum disorder. The Second Law of Thermodynamics ruled.

He folded his arms, tried to make sense of the buzzing images. So. Then.

That old, firm universe was doomed. In time, even hell would freeze over. Stars would burn into shadowy cinders. Planets, their atmospheres frozen out into waveless lakes of oxygen, would glide in meaningless orbits, warmed by no ruby star glow. The universal clock would run down to the last tick of time.

Only after he had left Earth, and had time to study subjects that he had neglected in school, did he see what the twentieth century—the oft-disparaged "TwenCen" of later slang—had done to that dark, earlier vision.

The universe was no static lattice of stars. It grew. The Big Bang was better termed the Enormous Emergence, space-time snapping into existence intact and whole, of a piece. With space-time came its warping by matter, each wedded to the other until time eternal.

For its first hundred billion years, the universe would brim with light. Gas and dust still folded into fresh suns. For an equal span the stars would linger. Beside reddening suns, planetary life warming itself by the waning fires of stellar death.

When a body meets a body, coming through the sky... he mused to himself. Stars inevitably collided, met, merged. All the wisdom and order of planets and suns finally compressed into the marriage of many stars, plunging down the pit of gravity to become black holes. For the final fate of nearly all matter was the dark pyre of collapse.

Now he felt, like a leaden soup in his gut, the implications of what he saw above him: a gaudy swirl of leaching light.

Galaxies were as mortal as stars. In the sluggish slide of time, the spirals that had once gleamed with fresh brilliance would deaden. Black holes would blot out whole spiral arms of dim red. The holes would gnaw through the galaxies themselves.

Life based on solid matter had no choice. To gain energy it had to merge black holes themselves. Only such fusions could yield fresh energy in a slumbering universe.

High civilizations came, mounted on the carcass of matter itself, the ever-spreading legions of black holes. Only by moving such masses, extracting power through magnetic forces and the slow gyre of dissipating orbits, could life rule the dwindling resources of the ever-enlarging universe.

Oh, that this too too solid flesh would melt... He was startled to find that phrases learned by an irksome schoolboy in a cobwebbed past still leapt readily to mind. Old, and true.

About this vision of a swelling universe, its life force spent, hung a great melancholy.

For matter itself was doomed. Its basic building block, the proton, decayed. This took unimaginably long, but was inevitable, the executioner's sword descending with languid grace.

But something survived. Not all matter dies, as did the proton. After the grand operas of mass and energy have played out their plots, the universal stage cleared to reveal ... the very smallest.

The tiniest of particles—the electron and its antiparticle, the positron—lived on. No process of decay could find purchase on their infinitesimal scales, lever them apart. The electron danced with its antitwin in swarms: the lightest of all possible plasmas.

By the time these were the sole players, the stage had grown enormously. Each particle found its nearest neighbor to be a full light-year away. Communication took years ... but in the slow thumping of the universal heart, that was nothing.

Could this actually happen? Perhaps, he thought, the best possible universe was one of constant challenge. One that made survival possible but not easy.

With an electric shock he felt the full force of it:

If life born to brute matter could find a way to incorporate itself into the electron-positron plasma, then it could last forever.

26

```
❮❯❮❯❮❯❮❯❮❯❮❯❮❯❮❯❮❯❮❯❮❯❮❯
```

A Far One

The thing was still standing at the far end of the dining room table. Cold ivory light played upon it.

Nigel looked at it and felt a mixture of joys and sorrows he could not name. He panted shallowly, breath rasping as if he had run a long distance.

The thing reminded him of a funhouse mirror distortion of a woman. Bulging here, slimmed there, suggesting deep changes that left the mottled skin the same.

Intelligence glowed in large, unreadable violet eyes. It moved with easy grace, the awkward compromise curve of the human spine replaced by a complex double-spined split in the lumbar region. Broader hips held more weight. Four arms tapered to hands, every one with differently shaped fingers.

This was what humanity had become in the billions of years since his own time. And he understood that this was not some mere adaptation to the esty itself. It was how humanity had evolved to meet its destiny everywhere, amid the hundreds of billions of stars across the churn of the galactic disk itself.

Genetic lessons from a far place.

He got up without knowing why, and walked outside. Now the jagged horizon was there—the same frame he had seen in his mind.

Somehow this Lane had opened, unfolding itself like a blossoming flower. At the command of the thing in his dining room.

And above sung the technicolor gallery he had seen in the mind-memories of the dead bodies. Electron-positron plasmas, immense and intricate, hanging where the stars had once been. He was seeing into the very end of the universe, the Omega Point, hanging in a sky where logic said it could not be. But was.

He stood there trying to fathom how he could see an open sky from inside the self-folded esty. This simple but colossal change meant that someone—something—had mastered the esty itself, could unwrap it like a Christmas package to find fresh delights.

He walked down into the torn and seared yard.

Without a sign or word, he knew that the Far One was gone.

Across a wrecked landscape came his family. Nikka limped. Benjamin and Angelina carried Ito's body.

"He's gone," Nikka said simply.

One Grey Mech's bolt had killed his son. In the same instant Angelina had suffered an in-body electronic blowout and the skin along her left side had ruptured, a thick purple bruise gone stiff and already yellowing.

On his oldest son's face was an expression of surprise and pain. Nigel reached out to the cradled body and ruffled the hair tenderly, bent and caught the familiar smell. Then he made himself stop.

"I . . . we've got to . . ." He could not make his throat work.

"The readers," Nikka said, limping past him toward the house.

The thing he had seen was not there now. The rooms felt cold.

They got Ito into the readers and did what they could to pull forth from his brain cells the essence of him. Fluids, sutures, digital artifice. The labor was long and the family scarcely spoke, concentrating fully and leached of all else but their yearning.

They sat at last on their porch and watched the feathery swaths of brilliance in the sky. He told them what he could and Nikka spoke for the first time since they had lowered Ito into the preserving solutions. "So the bodies . . ."

"Were addressed to us." Nigel nodded grimly. "Or someone like us."

Angelina supplied in a wan, empty voice, "Someone who would come."

"And we may not be the first." Nikka watched the slow churn in the sky impassively. "The Grey Mech who killed Ito would have killed others, too."

"But it did not get all of us," Nigel added. "The other Grey Mech prevented that."

Benjamin's face had been containing anger for a long time as they worked and now it came out, first in a string of oaths and then a final forlorn wail. At last, gasping, he said, "*Why?* Bodies sent back like invitations—Grey Mechs—Ito—for *what*?"

Nigel knew that there was no real answer to the despair under

Benjamin's words and that the best anyone could do was to talk about the surface. So he said gravely, hands knotted before him, "The bodies attracted the attention of humans. They were like bottles with scraps of paper rolled inside, tossed out into an ocean. Only the curious, only someone who understood the human need to communicate across the impossible stretch of time, would pay any attention."

Nikka's drawn mouth moved but the rest of her face did not, eyes staring into an emptiness. "Most mechs have never respected us enough to learn how to read our brains directly. To them we're messy, archaic. So they wouldn't know how to decipher the bodies, even if they cared."

"Except the Grey Mech," Angelina added.

"Grey Mechs," Nigel insisted. "One Grey Mech opposed the other. Saved us, I expect."

They sat in silence as chill winds blew across the fitful landscape. Nigel knew they were all digesting the strange fact that there was more than one Grey Mech, acting out of concert.

"So one faction of mechs wants us to survive?" Nikka asked with sudden bitterness.

Nigel got up and walked behind her chair, began kneading her neck and shoulders. His broken arm somehow did not hurt now though he knew that he would inevitably pay for this later.

She resisted him for a moment and then relaxed into his hands. He felt the release in her. "I suppose there are Grey Mechs from different times, eras," she said. "The Grey of our time wanted to stop any humans from learning about that sky."

Above, prickly streamers wreathed hard orange knots, bristling with ferment.

Angelina said wonderingly, looking up, "That's what the mechs want to do. Make themselves into those plasmas."

Nigel nodded. "So they can outlive solid matter itself."

Nikka said with caustic scorn, "Our son died because he had seen *that*?"

"In a way," Nigel said gently, his hands digging into her tense muscles. "To stop us from spreading the information. And that's why the somebody"—he thought of the strange yet human figure he had seen—"sent the bodies. To bring us here."

Angelina said, "I hate the way we have been jerked around."

Nigel nodded, his expression distant. "We aren't the superior species here. We get used, that's the order of things. I wonder if our pets sometimes feel what we're feeling now."

Nikka was inconsolable. "And all for what?"

Suddenly he recalled Alexandria saying, *Who would read a suredead body, lover?*

Nigel ventured a guess, the only one left. "So *we* would go back. We understand this in a way that images or memories in a body could not. Somebody wants us to take back what we've learned."

"Who?"

"Somebody? Or something."

27

=====================================

Radiant

The second, smaller Grey Mech swelled above them in the darkness. A dusky presence.

They knew there was no use in going inside so they watched its approach. It hung in the sky, a dark blotch coasting among coalescing rivulets of light.

No bolts, no shock wave.

Their apprehension ebbed as moments slid by and it made no aggressive move. "I suppose that is the one who helped us," Nikka mused.

Nigel had the eerie impression that it was watching them just as they watched it. They all noticed a small humming, not in their ears but throughout their bodies, as if long acoustic waves were resonating in them, deep notes below hearing.

It glided up and dwindled. Smoothly it veered toward the largest of the luminous constructions and into Nigel's mind came a single word: *Radiant*. Somehow he knew that this was a name, the way the Grey Mech thought of the electron-positron life that swarmed in this far future night.

Abruptly, the Grey Mech vanished into the brilliance. A flash, as if it had met the antimatter and been consumed. Seconds later, the humming stopped.

They looked at each other without speaking. Had it died, task completed? Merged with its own form and fate?

The Grey Mech had shown them something, but they were not certain just what.

28

❰━━❰❱━━❰❱━━❰❱━━❰❱━━❰❱━━❰❱━━❰

Tiny Farmers

Their next Transit came soon. The stutter was over at last.

They were dazed and tired and simply slept through Transits as they followed the long arc of the wormhole in space-time.

They did not speak of Ito. Their preserving solutions would hold the body for a long while, but the central question was how much of Ito's self had been lost before they could record it, to save the structure in his dying brain.

Nigel sat and watched the landscapes outside while the others slept. Parents fear more than anything the loss of their children and now that he had lost at least some of Ito—for no process, he knew, could completely restore the son he had loved, as was—he could not stop remembering the moments with Ito as a little boy, the passing incidents transfigured by time into golden memories. There is no perfection in the world, but one of the functions of memory is to make the past perfect at least in its small ways. He clung to that and knew that this phase would pass, too, but he relished it nevertheless.

Days of relative time passed. They were all in a hurry to return to their era and the random pauses during Transits irritated everyone. They became short-tempered and edgy about small details. Nigel withdrew, growing silent.

Then, during a longer pause, he went for a walk with Angelina into fields beyond their sheared-off farm. It looked like maize and he hungered for something reassuring as he hiked across rumpled fields beneath a warm yellow glow of timestone overhead.

It was indeed a field of maize but at its edge was a black swarm in orderly, marching columns. He squatted in the dust to inspect. Ants. So many they called up sudden apprehension. But they ignored him and Angelina.

Here a line carried a kernel of corn each. Others carried bits of husk and there an entire team coagulated around a chunk of a cob. He followed and found that the streams split. The kernel-carriers went to a ceramic tower, climbed a ramp, and let their burdens rattle down into a sunken vault. They returned dutifully to the field. The other, thicker stream spread into rivulets that left their burdens of scrap at a series of neatly spaced anthills, dun-colored domes with regularly spaced portals.

"Wonderful," he said.

Angelina caught his meaning, nodded. "So . . . intricate."

He marveled. These had once been leaf-cutter ants, content to slice up fodder for their own tribe. They still did, pulping the un-needed cobs and stalks and husks, growing fungus on the pulp deep in their warrens. Tiny farmers in their own right. But in the long voyage through humanity's care, they had been genetically engineered to harvest and sort first.

Faithfully they paid their human masters the tribute of the rich kernels, delivered to storage, no doubt following chemical cues. He thought of robots, clanky things. More subtly, insects were tiny robots engineered by evolution. Why not just co-opt their ingrained programming, then, at the genetic level, and harvest the mechanics from a compliant Nature?

Slowly, as they wandered in nearby fields, he came to see that here the entire biosphere of the esty was shaped with similar craft. Like old Earth, the esty was a machine that kindled life and tuned it to the needs of . . . who? What? Intelligence?

Certainly masterful hands lay behind the esty, something immense and unfathomable. But then, Earth had for nearly all of human evolution been just as mysterious to the growing, still-sluggish minds that lived among its marvelously tuned valleys, thick forests, and salty seas. The esty was a step up in that chain. A place beyond the comprehension of the smart apes who had blundered into this vastness, long on awe and short on table manners.

Somehow this discovery about the esty of the future buoyed him. Angelina felt it, too, a strangeness that was somehow familiar, part of being human in an order beyond their knowing. A silent agreement passed between father and daughter and they held hands crossing the last field.

They trotted back for the next Transit. Later, he found himself paying more attention to the panorama unfolding before them as they slipped and glided along the twisted geometry of the meandering worm.

He saw again and again recurring themes. Sailboats cutting the green waters of great, curved lakes. They dappled cupped bowls of water as they harvested the winds that blew through the Lanes, blunt pressures adjusting thermodynamic truths. Spherical houses that clung to impossible cliffs, imitating hornets' nests with Euclidean grace. Hot air balloons, inverted teardrops hanging yellow and gold and sunset red amid the cottony chaos of clouds. Only later did he notice that the coasting teardrop shapes were not managed by men at all. They were alive. Great heads swung where gondolas would. Immense eyes surveyed the land below for foraging. His surprise turned to pleasure. One teardrop plunged abruptly, snagged something on the ground, and buoyed aloft again.

In all these, form fitted so perfectly to function that the marriage recurred in many different societies, cultural worlds divided by immeasurable difference, but united by a deep aesthetic that shaped tools to an obliging hand.

All this he learned during their forays out for provisions, during the pauses which now seemed unbearably long. The esty had all kinds of people, he learned by bargaining with them. Maybe it had to, to work. There were ample numbers of the smoky-minded, the everyday deluded, the types who had to use emotional suction cups to hold on to this place at all. Nothing in nature said life should be easy.

29

The Cauchy Horizon

"You all realize," Nikka said to them over the lustrous dining room table, "that we can't truly get back to where we were?"

She had called a formal little family gathering after supper, no small talk or leftover coffee cups to clutter the mind. Everyone sat upright, properly chastened.

Angelina blinked, shocked. "We *can't*?"

Nikka seemed to think this should be obvious. "A wormhole head can't eat its tail."

"Ummm?" Nigel didn't follow.

"If one end of our wormhole gets too close to the other, there is a quantum-mechanical effect. Particles fry up out of the quantum foam, acting like a pressure. This forces the ends apart, so the loop can't close."

Benjamin was puzzled. "Particles? Why?"

Nikka thumbed in diagrams, which floated just below the polished tabletop. Airy confections: yellow light-cones intersecting scarlet, slanted planes.

"The wormhole head can't get close to its tail, can't get beyond what's called the Cauchy Horizon. If it does—"

Frying radiance pulsed from the blue wormhole head. An answering hot shower pulsed from its tail. A storm of colliding radiation pushed the two apart.

Nigel would once have untangled these Euclidean graces, but he was content now to let Nikka ferret out the truth—or theory, rather, he corrected himself. There was a big difference. Nikka said,

"If they get too close, you could go back to where you started and stop yourself from beginning."

Benjamin shook his head. "Why would I want to do that?"

Nikka laughed, eyes crinkling with myriad lines. "Physics doesn't care about what you *want*. It's about what you could *do*. Try to create paradoxes in causality and the universe will straighten you out—pronto."

Nigel ventured, "Uh . . . how?"

Nikka gestured at intricate traceries of world-lines, slanting surfaces chopping through event-space. Nigel nodded as though he were following all this, and in fact some of it did come through. But he was struck by how the obliging simplicities embedded in the minds of primates who learned to throw rocks and joust with sticks on the flat dry plains of Africa could so deftly eye the warp and woof of the esty labyrinths. Presumption masquerading as physics . . . probably.

Nikka's pale logics were almost persuading. Almost.

Their world peeled back to its essentials.

Beyond their compound the esty flickered. Events, eras, whole blighted histories shimmered and winked away.

Backward, sliding backward.

The worm was writhing now, curling through its convoluted course on its great ranging return. There was no clear concept of speed in this, Nikka pointed out, because the rate of progress through time could not be measured *versus* time. The human perspective did not encompass this, and Nigel's rather classically stiff-lipped education resounded in memory: *That you cannot measure you cannot know.*

What they all did know was that the supplies for preserving Ito's body and brain cells were running low. To keep him cooled to the critical range—below thermal damage, yet above the point around minus 110 degrees Centigrade, where shear stresses set in—took energy and circulating fluids.

"He can't hold much longer," Angelina said, circles under her eyes.

"Damn it!" Nigel slammed a fist onto the dining room table, where situation reports on Ito gleamed. "We'll have to cobble something together."

Angelina had sat in vigil beside Ito's tank and was worn down, but she knew those systems better than anyone, and her slow, sad shaking head struck a heavy weight into Nigel's heart.

"No use. We need to get back to our own era. Then I could find supplies."

"If we hit a longer pause," Nikka said hopefully, "we could go out, forage—"

"No time, our pauses are getting short. And out there it's strange." Angelina dismissed the idea with a tired wave of her hand. "I wouldn't trust anything I got."

"That damned flickering is faster and faster anyway," Benjamin said.

"I hope it means we are—" Nikka hesitated with the instinctive rectitude of a scientist, "in some sense, accelerating toward the wormhole mouth."

"I hope, too," Angelina whispered, "I do, I do."

30

Comfy Doubt

Nigel had grown up in a properly skeptical English home. He doubted the polite glacial veneer that the Church of England had become, coating a flat disbelief in all things supernatural or super-human, squashing all morality into a pale, thin social ethic. No God need apply in the C of E, the only faith known by its link to a country of the mind, Church of England, hallelujah. *The comfy doubt of frayed religiosity,* he thought.

The esty had taught him that space and time were malleable, folded forms of each other. Now they had transcended time as easily as one moved in space—a property ascribed in ancient texts only to God, and an omnipotent one at that.

If there was a God, then He or She or—more probably, he thought—It, acting in strict accord with physical laws (which presumably It had made—but there was an interesting argument there, too), could reach back in time. Could influence the past, even though to Nigel the events had already happened. This idea he had worked over in his mind until he began in a quiet and regular way to pray. Nothing could have surprised his younger self more, he was sure.

He had known and loved people who had died hard deaths. He asked God to manifest Itself in a previous time—not to change the course of events, but to enter into the minds of the dying. To drain from them the unbearable torments, the sharp pains, the cutting remorse, the freezing fears that forked into them in their last agonies.

Maybe it was possible and maybe the big It would do it. And

maybe not. But having thought of it, he knew that he had to try. *Alexandria, wife. Ichino, friend.* Names now, people then. Agonies spent.

Then, quite illogically, he prayed for Ito. Whether his son's fate lay in past or future was a riddle to him now. When he closed his eyes he saw Ito as he had been, returning from foraging while the family lay ill. His wind-burned face was dark, curly hair black and looking oily. A lopsided grin split the tired face and on an impulse Nigel had embraced the man his boy had become.

Now that was how he saw Ito. Not as the body floating in suspension here in their house, a thin hope.

The flickering sped up.

Blaring brilliance cascaded down upon them from wrenched timestone above—followed immediately, in a single breath, by utter sullen dark.

Nigel and Nikka were standing on their porch, he smoking a cigar out of sheer distraction, when the scene outside jumped again. Sparkled. Settled somehow into place.

"We're back!" Nikka cried.

"It's . . . the same," Nigel said. "But look."

Glassy patches marred the familiar topography. Spikes of erupted timestone thrust up through the groves of fruit trees, vomiting yellow-hot liquids. Events peeled off the upthrust peaks, unloosing booms and cracks.

Benjamin and Angelina ran outside onto the lawn, shouting. A swirling sphere of darkness like a pulsing bruise came gliding through the air in the distance. "It's our home, but—it's changed," Angelina shouted against a rush of hot wind.

Their raccoon ran out of nearby bushes and scampered onto the porch. It said very clearly, "Welcome back."

Nigel picked up the ball of fur and found it weighed more than he remembered. He had missed its bandit eyes and pesky personality. With sheathed claws Scooter climbed onto his shoulder without hesitation. When he looked back at the purpling sphere it looked closer. Behind it now loomed a mottled, dusky shape. Nigel stopped breathing.

"Grey Mech!" Benjamin yelled.

"They have been waiting here," Scooter piped precisely.

"They?"

"Others arrived, fought. One remains."

Nigel was startled. This simple pet had somehow acquired remarkable speech. "How long have we been gone?"

"A few moments."

"A few—"

"Forces have contended here, destroying much of this Lane."

With a black paw Scooter gestured toward smoky recesses in the far distance. The timestone bristled, skinned of its former abundant greenery. Dirty gray fumes spread like foul fog everywhere.

"Why?" Nikka asked the beast, wonderingly.

"The one above waits for you, I believe."

Nigel eyed the slowly approaching bulk. Planes of slate-gray mass, an airy of threat. "The patience of watchdogs. Umm, most admirable. But it's sniffing up the wrong leg."

"It knows why you were sent," the raccoon said.

"Sent?" Nikka asked.

"We could only orchestrate the Grey Mech to begin the process, by deceiving it about the importance of this particular wormhole," Scooter said.

"*You* sent?" Nikka shot back. Scooter licked its paws as if searching for scraps of food it might have forgotten, a familiar gesture that contrasted with its suddenly fluent diction.

"Unfortunately, we do not have the means to destroy it," the raccoon said calmly.

Nikka's face darkened. "What the hell do you—"

"Still, it is cautious. The wormhole mouth orbits this spot. Such dynamics are a vestigial remnant of the stress tensor which formed with your passage. The Grey Mech fears the worm mouth. It will not kill us without taking care."

"How comforting," Nikka said.

Hot winds rising. The bruised-purple sphere jittered in the high air. The family shrank back, looking at Nigel, but he had not the slightest idea what to do. He regretted not listening better when Nikka was explaining all this. He opened his mouth without knowing what he could say.

From the far side of the Lane, mountains split open. It was as though some unseen force had unzipped the entire range of peaks, cutting a crack that widened—and another blue-black sphere burst from it. Yellow energies played around it. Gales rose, stirring dust in the yard.

"The other mouth of the wormhole," Nikka whispered. "It's trying to tie itself off."

Nigel shouted against the gale's howl, "But you said they can't—the couch something, how—"

"The Cauchy Horizon. It prevents their linking up—but the elasticity along the worm can whip them toward each other."

"Why in hell—"

"The energies! Nobody's ever gone as far as we did. The stored capacitive stress—"

A gust snatched her words away. In the purpling vault above them the two spheres grew, swerving erratically across a wracked sky. Storms yowled. Jagged teeth of timestone wrenched up, sucked by tidal forces.

Nigel felt himself lighten, as though falling. Nearby tree limbs stretched upward, as if beseeching the tumbling horror above. Tides, stretching and drawing.

Screeching winds, tumbling debris. A lump smacked him in the leg. "Inside!" Nikka called.

"No!" he shouted. Something told him that to burrow in now was death.

The raccoon said calmly, "We had planned well, but this eventuality goes beyond our ability to control events. I apologize."

Wailing winds ripped up the roof of their house. Tiles shattered to the ground and the Walmsleys ducked. Benjamin and Angelina ran inside. The two worm mouths accelerated, veered. Crashed into hillsides and smashed them to spraying stones. Concussions shook the ground. A shock wave slammed Nigel and Nikka to the flooring of the porch and the railing split off. Nigel tasted blood in his mouth and his arm, nearly healed, sent him a spike of livid pain.

"Inside!" Nikka called, yanking him up to his knees.

The purple virulence above crackled and crashed. Twin monstrosities, swerving across a fevered sky. On his knees, he saw the Grey Mech approaching, keeping away from the ripping, darting worm mouths. Still after them.

"It wishes to erase the information you have brought back," the raccoon said serenely. Though its claws dug into his shoulder, he noticed.

"Damned determined," Nigel said.

"It knows what is at stake."

"Well, *I* don't, and—" At that moment he saw a possibility.

"Nikka! Let's go! To your goddamned Causality Engine."

She looked at him in stark disbelief. He yanked on her arm. She stumbled after him, across the yard.

Snapped limbs from the orchard covered the white steel console. He tossed them aside with furious energy. "Got power stored?" he shouted against the roar.

She nodded, lips compressed. She pressed her wrist to the command slot, began sequencing. *"Why?"*

"Cauchy Horizon!" He pointed to the nearest wormhole mouth. It bristled with sparks, discharges sprouting like electric-blue hair.

"What? That's a theoretical—"

"Does that look theoretical to you?" When the rapidly dodging wormhole apertures zoomed near each other, the air fried with orange energies.

Nigel pointed at the nearest wormhole opening, a foggy sphere that shot across the sky. "Push that one!"

She aimed the device. Sheets of numbers and graphics slid across the console face. "Where?"

"Toward the other—but no, wait!"

The mouths yawned, pulsed. The Grey Mech was below them but with the erratic paths they followed—it should be possible—

"There! Aim it up—and to the left." He pointed wildly. The right geometry would occur only for a second.

A wormhole mouth screeched down the sky, shredding clouds and debris, tossing off spurts of orange.

Its twin followed, the other end of the unimaginably long corridor seeking to find itself. To close, to marry, to then contract into a singularity of event-space, intact to itself for a time beyond duration—

"Now—*there*. Quick."

She fired the gravitational transducers. The pulse knocked them flat. Popped their eardrums, brought blood from nose and ears.

Nigel rolled, caught up against one of the ceramic cylinders. He looked up to see the nearest worm mouth rushing toward its other end. The air between them fractured, sparked, broke down. The net momentum took both wormhole apertures downward—toward the Grey Mech.

A sandpaper rasp, rising. Tendrils of shooting energy frayed between the two mouths.

And splitting the space between them, where the quantum foam began to erupt with spontaneous particles, the Grey Mech tried to flee.

Too slow. Far too slow.

31

A Wherewhen String

"I attribute it to your hunting strategy," the raccoon said.

They were sitting on the ruined front porch. A wrecked landscape smoked as far as the eye could see, cracking as it cooled.

"As I understand it, all evidence suggests that you hunted in groups, and were unafraid to take on quite sizable game, such as mastodons." The raccoon smacked its lips appreciatively at the fish Angelina had given it, freshly defrosted. "Your method, though, was not to rely upon brave displays of courage."

"Sounds insulting to me," Benjamin put in.

"Not at all." The raccoon looked startled, the first time Nigel had seen that expression. He was learning to read the supple meanings the creature could impart to the merest curl of its full black lips. "That was inventive."

"How do *you* know?" Nigel asked. He was all soreness and fatigue, but did not want to so much as lie down until he understood what had happened here. Then he was going to sleep for the rest of his life, if not longer.

"I am of your phylum. I know the courses of evolution." Scooter licked itself scrupulously. "Long ago, your species shouted and waved sticks and ran after your prey. Typical grazing animals spook easily, run well, then tire. They soon stop and go back to cropping grass."

"Yech!" Angelina grimaced. "Nobody eats meat."

The raccoon gave her a baleful glance. She hastily added, "Well, I don't include fish."

The raccoon went on. "Most carnivores who fail to make a catch on their first lunge also lose interest. They rest up a bit, and wait for another target to amble by. Your species did not. That promised the qualities we wished to harness. Alas, they were present in only a fraction of you, so we had to select just the right circumstances." It regarded them all as though they were museum exhibits. "And individuals."

"To do your dirty work?" Nikka said with a glint in her eye.

They were waiting. Inside, Ito's body was cycling through the diagnostics that would see if he could be fully restored. They had gotten the needed tech from ruins beyond the next line of hills, a small fraction of the town still standing. Now there was time to sit and think.

Nikka's mind was restless, awaiting news of whether her son would come back to her. And this confident raccoon irritated her quite a bit.

"Instead, your species would pursue the same prey to its next stop. Surprise it again. Run it until it outdistanced you. How those grazers must have hated you!" It cackled suddenly.

"You weren't particularly fast, but eventually you could run down the tired grazer. A guaranteed result, if you persisted. In this tenacity lies your major difference from other omnivores, and certainly from carnivores." It cackled again. "You boast of your brains, your opposable thumbs, your two-footed grace—but stubborn perseverance is rare, very rare—and we needed that. So we had to use primates . . . alas."

"Why 'alas'?" Nigel asked.

"You are cantankerous and difficult to manage. Sorry, but that is true."

"Well, you weren't the best pet we ever had, either," Angelina said.

"I was a poor actor. Actually, I am a diplomat."

"You don't seem all that diplomatic," Benjamin said.

"I negotiate. In the Lanes there are many kinds, but your strategy is shared by no other species here. Some Lanes hold octopuslike creatures who manipulate objects and snare others, but cannot pursue game. Many bright herbivores, too—charming, but in the wrong business to begin with, hemmed in by short attention spans. We needed something which would, for the most abstract reasons, sustain effort over times significant to your own well being."

"Uh-huh." Nikka's mouth was thin, skeptical. "And our 'abstract reason'?"

"Curiosity, basically."

"You based your strategy on our getting interested?" Nikka snorted with derision.

"We chose carefully. After all, how did this family come to be settled here?"

Nigel laughed. "We came this far, why not farther? Touché!"

"The Grey Mech didn't have anything to do with it?"

The raccoon lowered its head, concentrating on grooming itself. Nigel guessed that it was embarrassed—to the extent that any human category could apply to this strange thing. "Well, we did have to begin matters."

"By slamming us forward in the wormhole." Nikka's eyes were narrow slits. "So we couldn't get back."

"Such are the vagaries of any wherewhen string," Scooter said.

Nigel said, "By 'wherewhen string' I suppose you mean a wormhole path through the esty?"

"Yes, we term it differently—"

"Cut the techtalk!" Nikka fumed. "This, this *pet* got us blown—"

"Let it go on," Nigel said, hoping he could calm her.

Scooter had dashed down the porch. It turned back and said hesitantly, "We calculated that if the Grey Mech knew of this particular vortex, and guessed our plans, it would attempt to seal it—which would boost you along in the wherewhen string, I mean, the wormhole . . . perhaps."

"Rodent!" Nikka sprang up and kicked at the raccoon. It squealed and scampered out of the way. Nikka followed.

It cried, "I assure you, there was no—" another kick, closer this time, "no other way!"

"You risked my family for, for—" Nikka sputtered angrily.

It reached safety, hanging on a splintered beam beneath the overhang of the wrecked roof. "For greater causes than you can know," the raccoon said, regaining its dignity.

"You little rat!" Nikka swiped, but it swung farther away.

It said earnestly, "The knowledge and data you bring—and do not forget that the recording devices in your Causality Engine will give us precise measurements—can reconcile the long struggle between us, the organic living Phyla, and the mechs."

"You risked our lives—my son!—on a *plan*—"

Angelina threw a chunk of roofing at Scooter, narrowly missing. Nigel stood, blocking her from another shot. They were not truly angry with this raccoon, he saw. Ito, lying inside, body worked and threaded, battling, his fate hinging on mechanical help—that was the root of their rage. And until their wait was over, they would know no rest.

Nigel sighed, held up a hand. "Belay that! Let this thing speak."

"Thank you." It smoothed its fur and began again.

32

Larger Agencies

There was only one Grey Mech of their era. It had just perished above their home, fried by the torrents of particles sputtering into the space between the two wormhole mouths.

Causality was indeed insured, by the frying foam of the quantum. The wormhole could not connect, could not break through the Cauchy Horizon. In the end, Nature kept its causal books balanced with a furious storm of emission, dissipating the wriggling elastic energy of the wormholes.

And all energy can be used as a weapon.

The Grey Mech was a censor. It had wanted to stop the information about long-term mech purposes from reaching the organic lifeforms of this era. The mechs feared that their organic enemies would disrupt their gossamer-thin experiments in electron-positron plasma. Simply flying a starship's roiling plasma exhaust through a delicate whorl of magnetic fields and lacy filaments could devastate the work of centuries.

"Wouldn't mind doing just that," Benjamin said when he heard the idea. Antagonism to mechs ran deep in the blood of many organic races, not just humans.

But up ahead along the curve of grand time, other Grey Mechs arose.

The mech *vs.* Naturals war stretched like a stain across millennia in the esty. Nothing could truly stop the inherent competition, growing out of a Darwinnowing commanded in all Phyla and Kingdoms of life—not even this strange voyage along the "wherewhen string" and back.

But its effects could be changed, with adroit care. Up ahead, solving the puzzle of how to make an electron-positron plasma would require cooperation of both mechs and organics. But that alliance could never come about if the past could spread its venom to the future.

So to thwart this era's mechs, a future one had voyaged into its *own* future—where it knew the crucial moment awaited.

There, on the wasted plains, as their tiny fragment of a farm stuttered at the edge of infinity's abyss, the Walmsleys had learned the mechs' final destiny. Only that truth could disarm the age-old hostility between the two great Forms of life.

"That is my task," the raccoon said. "As a diplomat."

"A diplomat from *where*?" Nikka demanded, still not quite convinced.

"The Old Ones?" Nigel asked.

"They are a part of it, yes."

"I don't get it," Nikka said.

"There are several higher orders than yourselves." The raccoon groomed itself, as if this were everyday talk. "Did you think the galaxy was a simple division between organic forms and mechanicals?"

"Well . . . yes," Angelina said lamely.

"There are other substrates. Other media, perhaps I should say."

"Such as?" Nikka pressed.

"Magnetic fields. Collaborations of organics and mechanicals. And inscrutable symphonies of all three, forms that I can but glimpse." Its bandit eyes glittered and Nigel felt a keen intelligence having fun. *Playing with a pet?*

"That's who sent the bodies back, started all this?" Angelina asked.

"Oh no—those were sent by humans. They quite rightly sought to warn you."

"And you work for something bigger, higher?" Nigel asked.

"So I believe. Do you know who you 'work for'?"

Nikka laughed suddenly. "We thought, for ourselves."

"There are larger agencies," Scooter said, its eyes gazing reflectively into the distance. "We might as well call them gods."

Nigel thought of the God he had appealed to, for Ito. A God outside time somehow, a bare minimal God who could at least salve the wounds He could not prevent. In a universe apparently devoid of meaning, that was the merest scrap one could hope for. But the raccoon spoke of higher orders still.

"I do not believe we can in principle answer such questions," Scooter said. "They may function outside our conceptual spaces, their acts indistinguishable from natural law."

Nigel suddenly wondered whether the human category of science, and physical order, might be a reflection of something deeper. What imposed the order, after all?

He asked the raccoon, but it was silent.

Nigel remembered long ago thinking, *I wonder if our pets sometimes feel what we're feeling now.* Confronted with something nonchalantly superior, what did a pet feel? Awe? Mild irritation at the presumption? He looked at the raccoon, which had deceived them so long, and thought about the muscular intelligence that lay behind such a simple act.

"You're pretty arrogant," Nigel said.

"Do not mistake the messenger for the message," Scooter replied, licking itself.

"Such a neat creature, too," Nigel said sarcastically.

"Sometimes it is not particularly pleasant to be a conscious being," Scooter piped, "but it is always a pleasure to be a mammal."

Nigel realized that this animal was really quite a remarkable job. Scooter looked, smelled, and acted like an Earth-derived raccoon, fresh from the gene vaults humans had brought here.

But it was a construction, made by—what? *There are several higher orders . . .* He remembered a crude sketch, shown him long ago. *Highers.* More than Old Ones?

And what were *they*? The semi-humanoid thing he had seen at the stutter-point? Had that thing sent back the bodies, to catch the eye of curious, persistent humans? And unfurled the esty itself, to show those humans the phosphorescent positron sky?

Awe, he remembered, was a mingling of fear and reverence. Something in him, hominid-deep, had a cold, clear fear of the little raccoon. And what it implied.

33

No Erasures

Perhaps all this would bring peace with the mechs. Perhaps they would be able to get their farm back into workable order. Perhaps.

None of that mattered a jot, compared with the moment when Ito emerged from the cyclers. Gray, muscles shriveled, skin patchy. Alive.

"I . . . what went . . . on?" Ito shook his head and tried to sit up. His mother restrained him. Which was difficult, because she was showering him with tears at the same time.

He blinked, solutions still giving his face a glossy sheen. "I'm, ah, hungry." He frowned in puzzlement as they all burst out laughing.

He was back. But not all of him, they learned in the weeks ahead. It was *an* Ito but perhaps not *the* Ito.

No transcription is ever perfect. Some brain cells were lost, unread by the recorders, mangled in the minute processing.

Between Nigel and Ito there was a distance, one they never bridged.

Again Nigel could not truly tell if this arose from the errors in salvaging Ito or in the coolness that develops all too often between father and son. He would never know.

Nikka did not seem to notice it. She had fitful spells now, apparently some neurological damage from the Grey Mech attack. Her head and hands would suddenly tremble and she could not control them. She brushed aside their concerns when the medical tech could find no solution.

"It'll pass in time," she said. "The body knows its own ways."

Still, she made a remark later that meant she did guess about Ito. They spoke of their child the way parents do, knowing that in the end there is remarkably little they can do. That served to ease the sad separation Nigel felt from this man who had come back from death and been changed by it.

Fathers and sons speak inevitably across an abyss. Time rubs. It is never really possible to do anything over again. The Cauchy Horizon permits no erasures.

34

When Paltry Planets
Formed a Stage

Nigel went for a walk days later, when the house was secured and he could stride again on sturdy legs. Nikka was not feeling well and turned down his invitation.

At university he had learned scraps of poetry, and one returned to him now.

> And there grow fine flowers
> For others' delight.
> Think well, O singer,
> Soon comes night.

In the dimness that was not a true night he thought of the time when the esty would unfold, up there in the far future.

He went to a hillside where he could see a profile of the distant other side of the Lane. Here it was somewhat like the impossible horizon he had seen at the other end of the wormhole. He remembered the gauzy filaments hanging in that strange sky. And he thought of the Cauchy Horizon, beyond which physics could not see. As if even God had a sense of metaphysical modesty.

He sighed, like breathing in clouds of cobwebs now, and tried to feel how it would be.

So plasma entities of immense size and torpid pace will drift through a supremely distant era. Sure and serene, free at last of ancient enemies.

Neither the thermodynamic dread of heat death nor gravity's gullet can swallow them. As the universe swells, energy lessens, and the plasma life need only slow its pace to match. By adjusting itself exactly to its ever-cooling environment, life—of a sort—can persist forever. The Second Law is not the Final Law.

And they will have much to think about. They will be able to remember and relive in sharp detail the glory of the brief Early Time—that distant, legendary era when matter brewed energy from crushing suns together. When all space was furiously hot, overflowing with boundless energy. When life dwelled in solid states and mere paltry planets formed a stage.

And frail assemblies of chemicals gazed at the gliding plasma forms and knew them for what they were. Destiny glimpsed, then lost.

Suddenly he felt a fierce conviction that this *would* happen. That it must. That man and mech would work together to this final, far-flung destiny. That they would finally reconcile and realize that intelligence transcended the mere substrate that embodied it.

He felt the stars then, beyond the folds of the esty. Somewhere in that far night a ringing of the esty came, like an old Cambridge church bell. The low still tone bore him momentarily up into the swarming jewel lights so that he walked not under but among them, for a last time jaunty and irreverent, laughing like a thief of time loosed in a glowing orchard, with more paths for the choosing than any mind could count.

He staggered then, wheezing, and turned toward home. A sip of wine as a nightcap, perhaps. A fine bottle from their own cellar. He and Nikka would sit and smile and not talk about his indices. Not any more.

Perhaps they would speak of Ito's restlessness; already he wanted to go courting a young lady in a nearby Lane. Nigel thought of his own young days and smiled.

Or perhaps they would discuss Angelina's need to go off to study in high citadels of knowledge, for her grasp had now exceeded their farm. Or of the raccoon, which still lived in the Lane and was very busy. Going about something it would not say, perhaps could not say.

The subject would not matter much. The present was now all that mattered. A sliver so thin, yet as wondrously wide as a tick of time.

Dispassionate Discourse

These humans may be the ones we seek to understand.

They carry deeply embedded programs?

Their deepest are termed "emotions"—but this is not what we seek, in my opinion.

Emotions?

They are like our "drivers."

But drivers are mandates, easily changed.

In humans they are fixed in matter, laid down in durable pattern on neurological substrate.

What a pointless method. But at least it must make them simple to read out, to record, to anticipate.

Somehow it does not. Their "emotions" learn.

But programs fixed in matter!—only crude laborers use such, and then purely because high energy fluxes are so wearing on them.

This is one reason why humans are difficult to understand. They use methods we do not know, ones we never shared.

With good reason.

Ancient inferences, by our higher minds, hold that humans are important. Also, some other Natural forms, now extinct.

Extinct due to us, I hope.

Yes. Most through simple competition, others by directed exterminations.

I find it reprehensible that we allow the Galactic Center to be infiltrated by these.

We achieved a unified synthesis of opinion on this issue, I remind you.

It is a vexing irritation. I believe this latest incursion is also dangerous.

They harbor special assets. Old stories say so.

Their technology is marginal, their bodies quite unimpressive.

They have some ancient knowledge of the sensual.

Pleasures? A rudimentary evolutionary device for prompting action—no more.

We have need of pleasure on occasion.

As reward, even goad—true. But what could such limited organic forms have to teach us?

Their limited perception-space may give them special aesthetic qualities.

Impossible.

Constraints make possible achievement. A color poem without restraint is the lesser for it.

What is their range, then?

They see in three colors, sense aromatics, and—

Only three? How can nearly blind creatures make their way?

Poorly. But they are of the Naturals, I remind you. They inherited strange crafts.

*Feats we have long since
bettered.*

> Aesthetically, perhaps not.

*They are obsolete. All organic
forms are.*

> That is ideology, not fact.

It is evolution's point!

> Evolution has no point.

*The building of more enduring,
subtle works—*

> A strategy, no more. Its useful-
> ness may pass.

*We are such works, and fit to
judge.*

> Yet even now we study the
> clouds of antimatter. To prepare
> for further self-evolutions.

You know of this?

> I must, to fathom our vul-
> nerabilities.

*Such information was re-
stricted, I believed, to we, the
Analysts.*

But we, the Aesthetics, are qualified to know and comment.

More problems from our two-self experiment! I wish to end it.

A moment more, please. Antimatter is our hope, our grail—on this we must all agree. In it lies the salvation of our Self. In this we resemble the Phylum Magnetics.

We are nothing like them.

Dislike distorts your judgment.

Beings without matter! What is so noble there?

An odd concept, "nobility," for an Analyst.

Tell me more about these humans.

More knowledge awaits more inquiry.

Then be swift.

Part III

CATEGORIES BEYOND KNOWING

1

Prisoners of Immensity

Toby Bishop and Nigel Walmsley walked bent slightly forward. They struggled into the brisk breezes that swept up from the plain. Harrowing winds had scoured the ramps and walkways along the pyramid face. Around the sharp peak churned a howling vacancy.

Walmsley's eyes narrowed as he studied the clean cut of the far horizons. Some disturbance had drawn him out here, a quick dart of a message Toby had felt as an electromagnetic flicker, no more.

It was good to be outside after Walmsley's story. There had been a claustrophobic feel to the way the old man told it. Listening, Toby had an uneasy sensation of the wormhole constricting, forcing humans along a loop, trapped in events they could not change, prisoners of immensities they could barely glimpse.

Chill winds blew their hair, whipping like smoke, neither noticing.

Below them lay the ramps and terraces of a huge, geometrically exact pyramid, spreading down in great spare expanses, the flanks of the largest mountain Toby had ever seen. He had thought it was a natural upjut when he first journeyed toward it. The walk had taken him two sleeping periods—there were no days here—and only when he had reached the base did he realize that the entire mass was one artifact.

Toby shuffled uncomfortably. "Strange story," he said inadequately.

"I haven't told it, not that way anyway, to anyone."

"Your children—?"

"They're off in the Lanes. Family of wanderers, I guess."

"So all this with the mechs . . ."

"Is part of a pattern. A history, I suppose, if one could look back from the other end of the wormline we followed. The far future."

"There's something they want from us?"

"Seems so. I picked up terms once, when Earthers were chatting up some Old Ones. 'Trigger Codes' and 'First Command'—jargon, without the slightest explanation. When I ask Earthers, they pretend to know nothing."

"Maybe they don't know."

"They know more than they're telling. All this ties in with the Galactic Library somehow, too."

"Library?"

Citadel Bishop had housed a library. One superior to that of any other Citadel, Family lore had it. He remembered from childhood the racks and racks of cubes, glinting russet and gold from thousands of tiny facets deep inside. His grandfather had told him once that each point stood for a whole roomful of the old-timey books, the ones with wood pages all clamped together at one end. He had seen a picture of one of those. "Our human library?"

"From all the organic races that came before mechs. Before us, for that matter, but including Earth as well."

"The mechs want it?"

"To complete some pattern they desire. One of them said that to me once."

"A pattern?" Something chimed in memory. His Isaac Aspect spoke rapidly in the whispery voice that came through his acoustic nerve complex.

> *The Mantis spoke of artfully complete patterns. It meant aesthetic motifs perhaps, but from what we have discovered, a more ominous meaning may be germane here. A plan of events, a . . . conspiracy. I would remind you that the Mantis enabled Bishops to find the buried* **Argo**.

Toby said to Isaac, "The Mantis said it was after us because it wanted to make artworks."

He had seen those, grotesque mergings of human body parts with mechs. Worse than anything he had ever imagined. Even talking about it in subvocal made his throat clench.

> *It said it was an artist. Surely that was not its only function.*

Walmsley could not make out Toby's private Aspect conversations, or so he thought, since no Bishop had the tech to do so. Toby was still ruminating on Isaac's points when he caught up to Walmsley's question: "—could they want what *all* organic races have?"

"Uh, how d'you mean that?"

"All signs point to one motivation. The mechs want everything they can get out of the Library. Not some specific thing. They want to read it all."

Toby laughed dryly. "More like, they want to destroy it all."

Walmsley pursed his lips, as if trying to recall something a long way back. "What fragments they have gotten, before we secured a place for the Library, they actually read. They didn't simply smash the data cusps."

Toby could not understand why Walmsley, still naked, wasn't getting chilled. The wind purred in his ears, crisp and insistent. "Where'd you get parts of this Library?"

"It was in the Lair when we arrived. So were other aliens."

Toby recalled his wanderings. "I haven't seen many."

Walmsley chuckled, a curious rustling in his chest. "Are you sure you could recognize them?"

"They'd have cities, wouldn't they? Machines, some—"

"Most don't. A few not only don't have cities, they don't have clothes."

"Like animals?"

"Like aliens. Anyway, we've all spread out. And many have different ecospheres. They breathe odd gases and we know next to nothing about them. Most aren't talkative. It would seem that chatter is fundamentally a primate trait."

Toby gazed around at the distant crumpled mountain range. Timestone simmered and flared with light. Shadows played across angled perspectives. Here the land misled the eye. Brilliant blades of rusty light lanced up through the timestone in the valley below, illuminating the cottony clouds. Denser masses embedded deep in the timestone cast shadows up, into the air and finally on the underbellies of clouds. The pyramid was pure stone, not timestone, and so squatted as a dark mass lit by smoldering glows beneath. Far above, the esty curved over, bounding the Lane. A high arch of timestone answered with its own beams and shimmers of reddish light. The esty seemed to smolder. "So this whole thing is a kind of . . . museum?"

"Museum?" Walmsley looked surprised, then covered it with a shrug. "I hope it isn't merely that."

"Sounds like it is. The Old Ones made it, didn't they?"

"I believe so. They were close to the scene, the explosion."

"Maybe they're the museum keepers."

Walmsley laughed in his clipped, reserved way. "And we're the exhibits?"

"Could be." Toby watched clouds come skimming down from the vault above. Descending blades of incandescent light were so strong they dissolved clouds that drifted under them. A high blue haze suggested an atmosphere as deep as a planet's. "Do these Old Ones ever come around to visit the displays?"

"In a way." Walmsley stiffened slightly, and it wasn't the chill getting to him.

"What do they look at?"

"If it's a museum, I suppose I'm the librarian."

Well, Toby thought, if Walmsley had his reasons for sidestepping a question, it was his right. The geezer was fabulously old, though now Toby didn't believe his story about being from Earth for a squeezed second. Best to play along with him. "Oh? How?"

He waved casually at the pyramid mountain. "This is it. The Galactic Library."

Toby gaped. "You need this much room?"

"Ten billion years, the galaxy's been whirling around."

"But this is a whole mountain—"

"Four hundred billion stars, give or take a hundred billion. And don't forget the smaller stars in the halo above and below the disk. They may have started spawning lukewarm planets first of all. There has been plenty of time and room for life to blossom." Something bitter flickered in Walmsley's face. "And to die."

Rising winds moaned in Toby's ears. "Did mechs kill 'em?"

"Not usually, I gather. The mechanicals obey biological logic, just as we do. They were first made by Naturals, just like our computers on Earth. Later they replaced their parent species, often on worlds made damn near unlivable by some stupidity of their parents. Fatal stupidity."

"So you've got the Naturals' . . ."

"Science. Literature. Recordings of art. Lore. And things I cannot fathom as belonging to any category."

"The Old Ones come here to read?"

Walmsley nodded. "I can't often tell when they've been, until they're gone. Crafty buggers, they are."

"And the mechs, they can't find this place?"

"They know. So far they've been turned back."

"By what?" The pyramid was impressive, but apparently undefended.

"Ingenuity, mostly. In the early days, just plain people. The mechs would break through the esty in some new fashion. Sometimes they would get onto that plain out there and after it was over I found bodies soaked with oil and lubricants from damaged mechs who had run people over before they could be killed. The people looked like brown cigars. Suredead as well. The mechs would suck in all they could of people's running minds, straight out of the cerebral cortex."

Toby nodded. "And when somebody finally killed the mech . . ."

"Right. You ended the people, too."

"Damn."

"That made you think twice about doing it. No choice, though, in the end."

"My grandfather? He passed this way?"

"The Old Ones brought him. I spoke to him and then they took him away. Fine fellow. We got drunk once."

Toby nodded, smiling. Abraham had been fond of anything that loosened the tongue without emptying the mind.

A hard gust whipped Walmsley's hair about his intense face. "Your father said something about that in his self-representation, remember? About Abraham being afoot, wasn't it?"

"A warning. I didn't understand. Did you?" Walmsley shook his head, as if listening to the wind. Toby had last seen Abraham in Citadel Bishop, just before the mechs breached their defenses and the Calamity began. Would he still know the man? After years of hard pursuit, in his mind Abraham was nearly as legendary as Earth, a symbol of an earlier, better time.

Walmsley said quietly, "You might ask a higher authority. That's why I took us outside. A presence is descending."

"I don't see anything."

"Here—" Walmsley popped open his wrist and made some adjustment on a small panel. "I can pipe my sensorium into yours, within a few meters' range."

At once Toby saw in the yawning spaces around the pyramid-mountain not empty air but fine blue lines. They converged from above like an unseen pipeline of—what?

"Magnetic fields. Pressure's building."

Toby sensed some movement down the field lines, though when he looked directly at any group of lines they seemed static.

Gazing up into the bowl of sky he saw a constant interplay, field lines rustling and jostling, like wheat blown by autumn breezes.

"That's your guard?" It made sense. Mechs used circuits. Magnetic fields acted on all electrical currents. Field lines were like stretched rubber bands that could never break, but they could knot off, make smaller loops. They could slam into mech circuitry, scramble and fuse and scorch.

Walmsley nodded. "They were an early form the Old Ones devised. An intermediate step. Now they do . . . chores, I suppose you'd say."

Striations worked high up. Bright blue-white snarls plunged down, shaping up into something massive.

A heavy voice came into his mind.

> **We perceive a threat. It has invaded my foot points in the accretion disk. I cannot repel it, as it propagates solely along my field lines. No transverse pressure can block it.**

"The Magnetic Mind." Toby had heard it before, addressing his father.

"Mind?" Walmsley sniffed. "More like a committee."

> **We encompass more than a single, authoritarian intelligence such as you can know. I/we swim in copper-tinged brilliances, harvesting the wealth beside the mouth that knows no end. I slide, wrapped rubbery about the accreting disk. Not a mere garment for plasma winds to wear. My feet plow scalding trenches, my head scrapes against stars.**

"Umm," Nigel said wryly. "And your ego? How big is that?"

The voice strummed up in Toby's ears like sheets of wires plucked together.

> **Do not trifle with me.**

Walmsley grinned. "Pardon, squire. I get that way with the upper classes."

Before, his father had always been present to address the Mind. Toby remembered the strange phrases of the Mind, describing

Abraham as "whirling somewhere in time-wracked eddies." When his father had asked more the Mind had said, "The small mind that I can interrogate sends wails of remorse—" and would speak no further.

Toby gathered his resolve and shouted at the shimmering blue forest, "Where is Abraham? And Killeen?"

I do not carry such knowledge.

"Then what the hell are you good for?"

Walmsley said gently, "This." He adjusted his sensorium and a darting signal sprayed out into the valley on electromagnetic wings. To Toby it looked like a spherical flower blooming for a rosy instant, then withering. In reply came,

Nigel! I so long to press against you. We are shuffling to re-align—busy! I am so happy you felt me out here.

It was another presence altogether. Lighter, with a slippery grace.

"That is my wife, Nikka."

Toby blinked. The resonant voice seemed to come from behind him, close and warmly intimate. Utterly unlike the Magnetic Mind.

"Hullo, luv," Walmsley said happily.

This is the boy, Toby? He is huge.

"A refugee from the Hunker Down worlds. A Bishop."

I have heard of them. There were some in a ship a long time ago, yes? I overheard spiral waves propagating down the field gradient, carrying frequency-floating messages for them.

"That was about my grandfather. You're a, well, friend of the Magnetic Mind?"

I stream-team with the Mind. You could say that I am a subsectioned part of it. The Mind itself is the theme. I am a variation within it.

Walmsley said stonily, "That's the best anyone can do."

Toby searched the hovering strands of blue but he could see no pattern. "Where is she?"

I am dispersed. I express as tangled knots of flux spread over volumes. It makes for a slow life.

"But a happy one," Walmsley said. Toby caught a sad, sour note floating beneath the dry irony. Walmsley's leathery face gave little away but he had a sense of how this man had limited his pain with a cutting humor.

"What . . . happened?"

"She picked up something from the wormhole. Like a virus. Perhaps mech-made. It slowly took apart neural networks."

"So she . . ."

"Aged, in a way. Lost her self, so slowly it was like an excruciating exercise in remembering who she was, just to look at her. She—"

Walmsley abruptly clamped his jaw tight, staring straight ahead. "It was subtle, I'll give them that."

Toby thought of Shibo, a woman now long dead and surviving only in some chips he carried. Slivers of her still flitted like darting small birds through him, but he could control those. "No way to . . ."

"Save her? No tech for it."

Do not mind him. I owe this to the Old Ones. They made it possible, imposing my patterns on a form of maglife.

"They recorded you?" Toby remembered the Killeen he had seen on this same parapet. A sharp, clear representation, but after a while it repeated patterns.

Recordings have limits, recursions.

"So do people," Walmsley said archly.

"She doesn't seem like a, well—"

A narrow pattern? I am not. I am—as far as I can tell—the person I started out as. Evolved, of course, by experience.

"Experience I haven't had the privilege to share," Walmsley said crisply.

Don't listen to him. He complains because I can't sleep with him any more.

"Not a small issue, I should think."

No, lover, it isn't. You know what I mean, though.

Uncomfortably Toby said, "But you survived. Lived."

Nothing we knew could fix the horrible thing that was creeping through me. I . . . lost respect for my body in the end. It became foul and corrupted. This was the only escape we knew.

He had never met this woman before but he could feel in the whispery voice a reservoir of strong emotion. He thought of his own mother, long suredead. "You were right to do it," Toby said uselessly. He didn't feel entirely comfortable talking to newly met adults, but this . . .

"So she comes to tarry now and then," Walmsley said. "Like having a cloud to tea."

Sing for me, Nigel. It always improves your mood.

Toby was surprised to see Walmsley flush with embarrassment. He had not imagined the flinty old character could.

Come on. You know it makes you feel better.

Walmsley twisted his mouth and muttered, "Mind, this is a favor," and then launched into:
"Aw-ee laaast mah-ee hawrt een ahn Angleesh gawr-daan,
Whaar tah rawzaz ahv Anglahand graw . . ."

Bravo! More.

Walmsley made a face. "That's the Welsh accent. Next time, Cockney." He glanced at Toby. "Always do something in bad taste occasionally. Keeps the muscles oiled."
"Bad taste?"

"Old Earther concept. Having good taste was like being smart—only better, because once proved, you were done. Me, rather than good taste, I'd rather have things that taste good."

I so wish I could do more about that. I so want—

"Isn't there some way," Toby began, "with all this tech—"

We have come here because there is some apparent incursion.

The Magnetic Mind had returned like a weight. Toby saw it as a glossy sheen between the field lines. His Isaac Aspect said, dry and stiff,

Magnetic waves formed into packets. Beautiful! Much like the basic memory which carries me. Except here the information is analog, not digital.

Walmsley asked sharply, "What kind of incursion?"

Plasma modes I do not know. They descend into this volume. Their pace is quickening. Their dispersion relation has strange roots, in both real and imaginary spaces: $v(w)=w(k)/k(w)$. I have traced back the field lines to their origin. Though derived from the accretion disk, where mine own feet are firmly planted, these undergo some change. They are contorted. Given fresh energies. Written upon.

Walmsley watched the great space above the pyramid. Toby saw quickening field lines gather like smooth blue reeds blown by currents he could not sense. They tangled, snarled—
Silently, the sky split into shadow and radiance.
Half peeled back into eye-stinging brilliance. Along an exact hairline strip bisecting the bowl above, the other half turned dead black.
"Fractured," Walmsley said.

Nigel! There are bipolar drafts. I cannot find my footpoints. If this is what the mechanicals have been doing in their works near the accretion disk, then I—

"They've found a way to populate the Magnetic Mind's own field lines," Walmsley said with unnerving calm. "Pried open the magnetic canopy over us."

Toby felt a rising pressure all around him but he could still see nothing out of the ordinary. Magnetic presences were beyond his diagnostic ability but the sheer pent-up energy hovering above them set off his alarms. Tiny dismayed voices called for his attention in his sensorium. His internal defenses did not know what to do but they smelled something bad.

"Shouldn't we get inside?" he asked.

"And miss the show?" Walmsley seemed unafraid.

Knots plunged down the field lines. Toby suddenly saw that the lines now all converged on the pyramid and the knots were thickening as they fell. They turned an oily brown and slowed but kept coming.

"The Galactic Library!" he shouted against a crackling wind.

"The Magnetic Mind is defending it," Walmsley answered as he walked back along the parapet.

"But it looks like—"

"You're right. Let's get inside."

Apparently this was all the notice Walmsley would take of the danger. He still did not hurry, and instead spoke rapidly to Nikka in a whisper Toby could not make out.

I cannot apply pressures to them, Nigel! They butt against me. Hurt! I hear voices from them. Digital. Stuttering. They are mechs of a kind I have not seen. Vicious, sharp, like rats! I—

The sky fell.

The distant ceiling of the esty collapsed inward. An instant later Toby sensed that the magnetic fields were refracting his vision. The fields were plunging. Fighting, snarling, dying in dazzling explosions of scorched red.

"Inside!" Walmsley called.

Ah! It is, is shredding me. Shear waves—I—

Something shrieked like metal ripping apart high up in the air. Toby ran for the open doorway. It started closing. He heard Nikka's name called in a voice that boomed down around him. His senses contracted. Too much was battering at him. Walmsley was slightly ahead and then he was down, arms flailing, as though his legs had gone dead.

Toby had been trained by Family Bishop to help vital Family members wounded on the field. He stopped to grab Walmsley but the man slapped away his hands. "Go!"

He had also been trained to follow orders. He went.

2

Flight

Something like a defeated army was retreating. It was easier for Toby to tell that it was defeated than that it had been an army.

Things were moving through the thick woods that he had never seen before and had no desire to see again. There were limits to his curiosity.

He kept low and in shadows. Angular forms were retreating along with him but he did not trust any of them. Aliens, mostly. Quite alien.

He had gotten out of the pyramid by luck. The walls knew he was coming and guided him through the massive underpinning of the mountain. They kept up with his dead run. He had taken no time to look at the columns that rose out of sight, glittering mica-sharp.

Data banks, one wall told him. They looked more like huge shimmering trees.

He reached a blank stone wall that did not answer. In one corner of it was a tiny booth, apparently made for dwarves like Walmsley. He grabbed his ankles and waddled in. A voice that sounded offended told him to make the second person get out. He banged on the wall to improve its understanding. Just when his hand got numb from it the door wheezed "Vandal!" and shut.

The booth accelerated for a long time, slammed to a stop. He got out, went up a ramp—and was in this forest.

Outside was a shambles. Mechs prowled high up in the esty spaces. He could not see the pyramid at all but the rumpled horizon looked a lot like the distant perspective from the pyramid top, only seen from the other side. A man came loping by Toby and in response to a shouted question answered only, "Magnetic Mind's dead! Dead!" and ran on.

Nikka too, he supposed. And maybe Walmsley as well.

He had grown up on the move and retreats were his specialty. The Galactic Library had seemed the most solid and reliable thing he had ever seen, and Walmsley had stayed alive a long time, but if it was all gone it was just gone and he would not think about it any further. He settled in.

His boots adjusted themselves without his thinking. For broken ground they grew high insteps and sturdy heels. As he picked up the pace the heels shaped in response to being slammed down at a particular angle and pivot. They threw him forward of his normal stance, making Toby feel as if he were being helped ahead.

Boots could even be made into serviceable weapons. They sharpened along the outer edge if lifted well free of the ground and the leg cocked into kicking position. They could slam-cut certain mech parts in a way that was not pretty.

A slim shiny thing like a snake came zipping through the air and veered toward him. He had no time for a microwave burst or any of the other weaponry so he sprang at it, boot first. He caught it in its middle and the boot did the rest. The edge could sense material and slice it, his internal systems having already given the command when they sensed his alarm. They were better than the human nervous system, and quicker.

This was called "giving 'em the leather" in Family lore, though of course nothing had been made of animal parts within living memory and the idea would have horrified any of the Families. His Isaac Aspect refused to confirm that any Bishops of ancient times had been animal-eaters. Toby suspected that Isaac was concealing his own habits but did not pry. He had other things on his mind.

The retreat did not make sense to him. Each Lane was a kind of space-time pocket. Apparently the mechs had breached this one with magnetic pressures. In the long run they would work their way through and kill whatever they found. There must be defenses here but none seemed to work this time.

That was the trouble with seeking shelter down here in the deep esty, he realized, so close to the black hole itself. Time ran slowly here, which was fine for storing things. Walmsley had mentioned that holding the Galactic Library in close to time-stasis meant that it decayed slower.

That also meant that the mechs could sit outside, in comparatively flat space-time, and patiently develop their techtricks. People in the esty could not keep up. It was not a matter of intelligence, but of the ticking of time.

Which meant that this particular Lane was probably doomed. It was huge, certainly. But now he could see mech shapes flitting high in the vault above. When he had to cross a stretch of flat land he glimpsed a colossal battle up there, all flash and dazzle. For a moment he felt as if he were back on Snowglade, and it brought a pang. Flat land gave the sky such a chance to be anything it would. Here, distant lands curved across. Far away, yes, but he still knew he was enclosed. Trapped.

He had fashioned ways to cut through the esty stuff before. If he could squeeze through a momentary hole, he might pass into another Lane. Somewhere in here there were Bishops. He would not find them in this Lane, he was pretty sure.

He tried his tricks, lasers and thumbers and the rest. They did not work. The esty-mass was impacted, sometimes spongy, other times rock-hard. His Isaac Aspect popped up in his mind.

It is worth noting that stone, which you believe to be so firm, is like all matter a soufflé of empty space and furious probabilities.

"Shut up," Toby muttered, and thrust the micro-Personality back in its cubbyhole. "You're nothing more than a chip half the size of my bittiest fingernail."

I do concur that you should find a way through, however.

When the Aspect gave him irritating advice it often rushed to apologize. Who wouldn't, when getting out of its cell depended entirely on Toby's good will?

He fled into hilly country. The fighting kept on in the high vault. He could see the magnetic field lines now; his inboard systems had picked up the trick at the pyramid. The lines were splayed, jumbled, not the orderly shapes of the Magnetic Mind.

Sometimes there came a sound like tearing the arms off a shirt. Timestone would flower forth. Clouds of it rose like volcanic plumes lit from within by pale fires. They slowly sank back. The air rippled around them and puckered so that Toby could glimpse for an instant different landscapes beyond: scooped valleys, craggy mountains, murky chasms. Sometimes people moved across these passing scenes and he once yelled to a woman who looked to be close. Then the smoky exploded timestone drifted back down as if rejoining its natural flowing place and she evaporated with a small cry.

He met a band that was burying its dead. Humans, they looked to be. He could not understand a word they said. His inboards couldn't recognize the lingo either.

The timestone here was scorching to the touch and glowed with a hellish light. The heat brought lassitude, but the dead bodies nearby gathered strength of a different sort, flavoring the air. Toby moved off.

The people did too, stopped and camped and cooked without fire somehow. He stayed with them because it seemed safer, considering the aliens he had seen. At least he knew something about people.

These feasted on the animals they could catch or kill. In the retreat there had been plenty to snare or stab. They ate slabs of meat and crammed it in with cups of stinging alcohol. Toby watched carefully, fascinated and repulsed in equal measure.

He tried to remain neutral. Other tribes, other Familics, other customs. He had learned that much. He saw that the meat-eaters grew tired as they finished. Flesh, he knew, took longer to digest. The drinkers got loaded, addled, a touch crazy. They were clumsier and stumbled easily.

A woman came to him in the dark, after the timestone finally dimmed. He had been sleeping soundly. When he smelled her musk, a scent he knew well despite being in his own mind still a boy, he felt what she wanted. They spoke no words and he did as well as he could. He fell asleep feeling tired but contented. In the morning she was gone and the rest of her people with her. So much for humans sticking together here.

From long hours of watching the crashing cliffs, waiting his chance to pick a way through, he grasped the strange hard fact that much of what passed in his life was forever beyond his understanding. He alone imposed meaning on his life and often he failed. Certainly he had failed at the pyramid.

To live with that, the fact of incompleteness, was to finally comprehend the place of humanity in a universe that, far worse than being your enemy, was indifferent and unknowable.

3

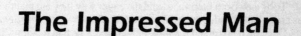

The Impressed Man

He woke up at the next "waxing." Nobody here used "morning" or "sunset" or any of the other words that seemed automatic but didn't apply any more. The next time the light came was a "waxing" and they came remarkably regularly between the "wanings," as if arranged.

Toby got up and was about to start eating when he saw a man lying face down in a big clearing below. He went down to see. Up the slope came a woman, rosy-haired and face contorted. Her belly was sticky red and pushed over to one side. Two other women wearing identical gray coveralls were helping her up.

Toby offered to help. The wounded woman crossed her hands under her big bosom and he saw between her fingers blood seeping. She shook her head and the gray overalled women did too, as if the wounded one was giving orders. They went on without a word.

In the clearing the man was face down in the middle of broken stubs of rock. A pale yellow gas billowed out of a perfectly round hole a few steps from the man. As Toby approached he saw that the man had not been very big but was now. He was smooth and intact and only a hand's width deep, flattened uniformly.

Only a trickle of blood worked away from his shoulder and there was no other sign of damage to the body. Toby touched the creamy skin. It was pebbled, as if small bubbles had formed beneath and could not break through.

He ate breakfast with a passing group of thin-faced men and women who looked exactly alike. When they had first caught sight of the man some had started to run away. Then they came back for some reason and sat down and started chewing.

"Did you see him hit?" one of the women asked Toby. She spoke a kind of slanted talk that his inboards could translate.

"Naysay. What does that?"

"A skimmer, we call it."

"What's it look like?"

"Kind of burnt-brown lookin'. Comes along about head-high off the ground."

"You see it?"

"Felt it. Like somebody ticklin' the balls of your feet."

Toby saw from their faces and the eager way they ate that there was an unspoken celebration. *It wasn't me. See? It wasn't me again.*

Once he recognized the look in their faces he had to admit that he understood the feeling because he had it too. The dead could not be recovered here. The technology wasn't available and by the time you got to somebody who had been mashed flat by some force you couldn't even understand it was too late anyway.

The dead he had seen were already receding into dim images. They weren't him, and neither was this squashed figure he had never known. It would be different if any were Bishops.

That was the way he got through this place. Pushing it back. Making it not-him. *Not-me.*

The little breakfast group grinned nervously as they talked. One fellow who had not run at the first sight of the squashed man had a superior smirk, holding forth about how he had seen bodies like that plenty of times before in a way that made Toby pretty sure that he had not.

The woman said with assurance that if you didn't smell a skimmer you were safe. How she could know this Toby did not bring up. She went rattling on about never smelling the one that would get you because by the time your sensorium caught a whiff you were slam-dead anyway. It was the kind of guff he had heard a thousand times but he listened because sometimes people gave away information you could use, unintentionally of course.

Later he caught a quick, cutting fragrance and saw a hillside above him simply vanish. It happened fast and he registered no noise. The hill vaporized, clouding the air with cottony filigree.

He thought it was very pretty and a piece of it passing caught him in the leg. A clean slice. The piece did not even stop.

The woman that morning had grinned and given him a "quick-lick," which turned out to be a vial of brown, smart-smelling stuff. He could not drink it, even though he suspected it was intended to be quick liquor. He did not much like what liquor did to people but it worked well on the cut. He watched more hillsides boil off to take his mind off the sting.

Twice before the next waning he got hit. Just nicks, but they hurt and his inboard systems had to adjust to keep his sensorium tuned.

The quick-lick helped. He had learned not to worry much about the technology here so he just used it. That fitted in fine with his new policy of not thinking. He used the quick-lick that way until by accident he spilled some and found that it ate away the sleeve of his shirt.

4

Carrion

Carefully Toby looked out over the plain where heat made the air dance. He had learned a lot and had paid with only a small wound in his side and some cuts. A bargain, considering.

He knew now that when hit in the butt or the fleshy thick of the thigh or the long taper of the calf, people could speak nobly and clearly. They could even reach outside themselves and show real concern for nearby wounded, or even for the worried faces of those gathered over them.

But if hit solidly, they withdrew. A solid shot to the belly, a snapped bone, lost control over arms or neck and head—all common glancing wounds from mech disablers—and the wounded clutched themselves, eyes boring into spaces others could not see.

The mech flying predators were the worst. For a while Toby could not understand what the flitting small forms were doing in the distance.

He saw first a thin triangular wedge of black and white that skimmed near the ground. It settled on a fallen man's leg and waddled up to his face. Two tilted triangles working from a shared axis. Black light-gathering panels hinged with white scanners, corded by wiry linkages.

Toby guessed that it was just curious but then it tilted its head down and pressed against the man's forehead and he knew what it was doing. For a few hours before the man went to rot his self could be extracted by using a fast-flash.

The wiry bird jockeyed over the dead face. Panels skated over his brow, seeking, reading. The man's body jerked once when the flash-reading hit a motor-active center. Then it lay still and the flood of what the man had been passed into the thing that sat on his face.

Toby shot it with a curling lick of infrared. The bolt fried the unprotected solars. The black triangle winked to brown. Still the scavenger took two teetering steps and flopped over on its side.

Toby approached warily. He kicked it off the man and stepped on the white scanner panel. The thing was a glinting intricacy, a marvel of compressed purpose, now smeared and crumpled. It snapped satisfyingly as he dug his heel into its spine.

Whatever it had sucked out of this man and others was gone now. Gone for humans and mechs alike. But at least this man, still cooling in the mud, would not be resurrected as a grotesque toy.

Within an hour he saw a rectangular silhouette planing high up. It swung down the sky on a slow glide. He followed it. There had been a series of deep *whooms* reverberating from a distant ridge. He had been skirting around it, keeping in the twisted trees, but his hatred of the scavengers burned and would not let him go.

This one was bigger, with a scrawny neck of cables that gyroed a seeking-panel head. It swooped safely above, not committing itself. Toby got near and another *whoom* came. The shifting sheets above wheeled and then fell like a whistling projectile.

This time it was a woman and she was not dead. Both her legs lay loose, control cut. She saw the thing land off balance. It looked around with darting crystal eyes and waddled toward her.

It was on her before Toby could get set. He watched from the trees and wanted to shoot it but could not be sure that using the necessary power he would not hurt the woman or even kill her.

It teetered over her head. She must have also had something wrong with her neck because she did not turn to look at it. Instead he could feel her sensorium shift to bunch against the thing but that did no good. Her eyes rolled—panic or fear or derangement, Toby could not tell. She found some way then to move and twisted, rolling over, away from the shuffling sheets.

She could have been trying to save her face somehow. Toby would never know because as she did it, flopping awkwardly face down, arms sprawling uselessly, the mech fired a pulse.

It was like nothing he had ever seen on full-scope sensorium before, a jagged jab of red. It overloaded his sensors so that they clicked shut. A sizzling, frying-fat throb—and the woman went limp.

The mech lifted itself onto her chest and turned an inspecting head this way and that, as if checking its work. Job all done.

He had to wait for his sensorium to recover before he could use his weapons again. Seconds ticked by on his lower-left eyeball clock.

It began to lift off with a soft *whish* of acceleration and Toby hit it then, sorry that he was so slow. This time he caught the power panel, gray from the drain. The mech flapped and clattered to the ground.

He walked carefully to the woman's body. She looked peaceful, which he knew was an illusion but took comfort from anyway. Blood ran out of both of her ears and matted her wavy brown hair. After a while to dry it looked pretty much like ordinary reddish, crusted mud.

5

Cards and Dodgers

The worst was the woman with the baby. He saw it all because he had gone to a makeshift field station to resupply some of his inbody fluids. His wounds had used up the reservoir.

The field station was set up by a Family named Yankee. There were plenty of wounded people there, Families named Cardinal and Dodger and people speaking in such a broken-jawed way Toby could not make out a tenth of what they said. But a thin woman found him by using some kind of sensorium seeker.

"Bishop?"

"Yeasay. You from—?"

"There's another Bishop over here. Asking after kin."

Toby followed her into a section sheltered by a tent roof. The flaps rattled in the wind. Therm beds were crowded together here and all filled. He passed a woman lying under a quilt who was grunting and shoving hard.

Next to her lay a man rolled over on his side with the covers drawn up around his head. "Here," the thin woman said and left him.

Toby touched the man and saw that it was his grandfather. Abraham's head stirred and he blinked up at Toby. "I . . . too late."

"What's wrong? How—" Toby tore the covers back and Abraham's body was shrunken, pale, with purple blotches all down both sides. He could see no wounds but the skin was diseased somehow.

"What did this to you?"

"I . . . running down."

"How'd you get here? Are the others . . ."

Toby's voice trailed off as he saw the vacant despair in the face he had so often seen as flinty and confident. He looked away.

"I . . . no help for me. I . . . not real . . . Abraham . . ."

"What? Where are the others?"

"Not . . . with . . ."

Toby shouted to a nurse, "This man needs treatment!"

The nurse came over and took a small reading device out of his smock pocket and said nothing. He turned Abraham's head and unlocked a small square patch right above the spinal column. With the reader pressed against the open fleshmetal portal he thumbed in an inquiry and apparently took the reply through his sensorium. "Progressive. Can't stop deterioration like this even if I had the gear."

Toby said hotly, "What's 'progressive' mean and why—"

"This's a copy. They have a big error rate, most of 'em. Run down fast."

Toby blinked. "But he's my, my—"

"Don't waste your time on it."

Toby opened his mouth and said nothing. The Abraham lay like a puppet whose strings had been cut. The eyes roved.

Toby caught the sleeve of the nurse as the man turned away. "How can anybody make—that?"

"I heard there's a place kinda near. Not in this Lane but only one transition away."

Toby breathed in little fast gasps and tried to think. "Why would anybody . . . ?"

"Easy way to get a job done, if you got the tech."

"What job?"

"Ask it."

The nurse walked away impatiently. The woman next to Abraham was still sweating and grunting but nobody was paying any attention to her. Toby licked his lips and said to the man on the bed, "I . . . you were . . . made?"

"Copy. To search . . . for you." The face of his grandfather looked back at him but the mouth was slack and there was none of the sharpness in the eyes.

"Who made you?"

"Re . . . storer."

Toby remembered when he and his Family had entered the esty. A long time ago. They had gotten into a legal wrangle and Abraham had wanted to find out what happened to a woman they had read an inscription about, on an ancient wall in a Chandelier. *She is as was and does as did.* She might have been in a place they called the Restorer. If somehow that place had a template or something . . .

Toby could not imagine how that was possible. When they were in open space aboard the *Argo* the Magnetic Mind had spoken of Abraham, but where was he? Stored in a vault?

"That place copied my grandfather into . . . you?"

"I woke . . . knowing some of his memories . . . my memories. To seek you. They told me . . . that."

A pustule popped on the Abraham's shoulder. Toby watched something dark and slimy ooze out and scorch the ghostly white skin. He could smell the acrid burnt flesh. The man did not react.

"Why?"

"Need you . . . complete the triad."

"Who made you?"

The eyes became veiled. No answer. Toby could not tell if this man, this thing, was trying to lie to him or was just stupefied. He grabbed the man and there was a ripping sound as Toby pulled his head up from the webbing that had been feeding him nutrients. "Who?"

"Humans."

"Which humans?"

"Humans."

"What Family?"

"Humans."

Toby let go of the useless empty package. The man's head lolled and something went out in the eyes. For an instant he felt a pang of remorse and then he told himself that this was not his grandfather, had never been.

The Abraham was unconscious. Toby studied the weathered face and as he watched it seemed to cave in like a house burning from the inside.

He stepped back and butted into the nurse. There was a team working on the woman now. The nurse wasn't busy so Toby asked him, "How'd he come to be here?"

"Walked in. Guess I should've seen what it was. Been busy here."

"What's . . . it . . . got?"

"Systemic breakdown. Those copies never get the autoimmunes right."

"How long did it live?"

"Months real time, I'd guess. Could be weeks though."

Toby gazed blankly at the wrecked parody of his grandfather. "Did it know it was going to die?"

"Expect not. These things run with minimum memories usually. Pointless to put in detail work like that."

"The Restorer can make a copy that's not the whole person?" The nurse frowned at him. "Where you from?"

"Snowglade." This nurse was not a dwarf like Walmsley but still was pretty short. Toby added, "A planet."

"I see. Look, don't let people hear you talk about making exact copies. That's not just contra, it's, well . . ."

"Immoral?"

"Damn right. Maybe on this glade place you people do that, but not here."

"We don't do it at all."

"My Fam doesn't either. I'm Sox."

"Sorry if I—"

"No mind it. This one—" the nurse waved a hand at the Abraham, "it's not a Restorer job anyway."

"Then who . . .?"

"Looks mech to me. They're getting good lately."

Toby watched the life drain out of the Abraham and smelled the swampy air that came off it. While this had been going on Toby had not heard the woman in the next bed. Now she began screaming. It was as bad as anything he had ever heard on a battlefield. Not like the births he had seen at all. He stood there while the nurse and some others worked on the woman but he could not get his mind around the meaning of the cooling thing in the bed. When he looked up the woman was quiet again but there was no other sound in the room.

The nurse held aloft a bloody stump. It was plainly dead and plainly not even approximately human. In the faces around her Toby saw the blank dismay and realized that the damned endlessly tinkering mechs had done something to this woman, too.

He could guess what it was but he did not want to know for sure. He got out of there fast.

6

✦✦✦✦✦✦✦✦✦✦✦✦✦✦✦

The Incredible in Concrete

He tried again and again to get out of the Lane. Slithering sounds and hollow echoes boomed down from the vault above and he knew the mechs were not far away. His sensorium was fitful since he had gotten some help with it at the field station. It rang with distant calls for help and he went on knowing that he could do nothing.

He reached a river and saw that it led down into a box canyon. He found some trees of a kind he had never seen before, sliced them down and built a raft out of bark. He cast off on it. Maybe the mechs would not detect him so well on water, and anyway he could always try to hide underwater. It was a forlorn hope but he clung to it.

In the mist ahead he thought he saw people. Their skins were paper-white and wrinkled, flesh hanging loosely from thick muscles. All over their faces were little blisters tufted with black hair. He was sick then but not because of the people—who were not there the next time he looked.

His stomach swerved. Nausea doubled him over, emptied his stomach. Bile droplets hung near him, like moons circling.

That was how he knew that he was falling. Or that there was no gravitation here, which was somehow the same thing, Quath had said.

To all sides rose steep cliffs of timestone that worked furiously with heat. Water gushed into steam.

Weight returned. The current slammed into him, cold and fast. He yelled angrily and it was not out of fear but as a thin human gesture against the clasping strangeness. Echoes reflected. Paired echoes, one tinny and one rumbling, and so strong that the last part of his call met the first part returning home, hollowed out.

Then he was weightless again.

Steam all around. Silence. He shouted and could not hear himself at all. The cottony air took everything and gave nothing back.

There was a thin chain to thinking, he realized, which began with seeing something noticeable, which in time made you see something that wasn't apparent, which finally made you see something that wasn't even visible—if you were doing it right. That was how he felt and then saw what he was in. A framed glow ahead showed him that he and a river were emerging from the ground, mysterious and whole.

A new esty Lane? He heard voices in the captured river as he left it. They were different from the babbling musics of the bright river ahead. Against a curved cliff the river engaged in muttered profundities, circling back on itself now and then to say things over, being sure that it had understood itself.

He could not breathe. Did not want to. The river ahead was bright and airy and a chatterbox, overfriendly, bowing to both shores with white froth so that neither would feel neglected.

The water turned to jelly and then to a liquid glass, imponderably slow. He tapped against it. A pane tumbled away and shattered. In its impact shards of dead moments blistered up and shouted. Popped into tiny droplets. Fell rattling to the ground. Rose up in dying amber flames.

He stepped over these and walked into a new Lane.

Moist crackling whipped his hair. His sickness ebbed into a mere sour stomach. Sensations irked his skin. The river that had been a kind of congealed air eased out of his lungs.

He slept a long time and when he awoke tried to figure out how he had lived.

Events had a motive force that collided with other intersecting events, all outside human imagination or apprehension. To get through such times, when causes seemed to fall from a great height upon him, he learned to stay fixed, keep even and steady with the swift course of the unimaginable slipping by him. He followed moment to moment, led by impossibility. One foot forward, then another, cautious and unwitting.

Things happened and he felt them happening, but outside that onrushing fact he had no link with them, no key to the cause or meaning. Maybe they had none. Maybe here such ideas themselves had no meaning. They were human notions after all. Though this place held humans it was not of them.

The esty did not fit their primate-shaped way of seeing the world—of that he was sure. Those who have been through such blindsiding events, he thought, had made a passage outside of imagination, but within the range of experience. The incredible in concrete. They could not get their minds around what had happened to them.

Maybe the only other thing like that was death, suredeath, the last thing experienced and never understood.

A Tapestry of Thought

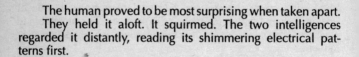

The human proved to be most surprising when taken apart. They held it aloft. It squirmed. The two intelligences regarded it distantly, reading its shimmering electrical patterns first.

Such agitation. Yet witness, the connections in its head cycle only a few hundred voltage steps per second.

So slow! And they still can register realtime events. It does surprisingly well with such an affliction. Notice how it looks around so energetically.

Perhaps it had difficulty adapting to this position? We are suspending it upside down.

It thrashes its head around because its eyes are all on one side of the head. So much energy, just to see. A curious choice of construction.

Look! It is using pattern matching to scan its surroundings. It makes a standard picture. Odd!

I can measure the data-flow. The brain processor is strongly linked to the eyes, so several times in each second it compares what it is seeing with a standard image it remembers.

If I move quickly—yes, see? It picks the best matching pattern, estimates possible danger. That tells it what response-script to follow.

How governed it is by past experience! It keeps twitching as though it could get away.

Apparently in the past it did escape that way. Look at all the bone and muscle devoted to locomotion. Is it used to being picked up and dangled?

No—so it redoubles its effort if the situation is unusual. I register high chemical levels squirting into the bloodstream. See, they affect brain performance.

More programming from its past. It seems to want to run away.

Its legs certainly do.

Here, I will put it rightside up.

Confirmed! It tries to run.

Slow learner. It cannot outrun us.

But that must have worked for it in the past, you see. It has no other immediate strategy.

No wonder. Gaze upon the neural firings in the upper brain. (Curious, putting all the most important networks on top, where impact will most likely injure them.)

Such slow circuits! Artful patterns, though. It is learning only a few data-droplets per second. Only 10 in one of its years!

So it simply cannot reason out a fresh strategy for dealing with us in short times. It lacks the computational speed.

Now it waves its arms.

Nonrandom, though. Simple symbols, I suspect.

That shows forward-seeing, adaptive behavior.

Of a very simple sort.

Promising. Its brain is made of organic compounds entirely. So-called "Natural" development.

"Primitive" is a better word. Notice how abstracting functions, which must have evolved later, are simply layered over the older areas in the brain.

The entire brain design is retro-fitted! Surely this thing is not truly conscious.

Definitely not. It knows very little of what goes on in its mind.

Watch the flashing patterns. It senses only what occurs in the very topmost layer of its brain.

All the rest must be a mystery to it. See, down below it is digesting some crude chemical food—but does not think about the act at all.

It does not even know that it is mixing acids and massaging the bolus.

Trace this spray of winking light in the head.

Neurons firing. It is framing a new idea.

I see. Down below, in the under-brain, now coming up to its limited awareness.

Now the idea erupts into the over-brain. Spreads. Pretty, in a way.

That is how ideas come to it? A surprise.

Whereas to us, it is more like fog condensing.

How confusing, to never know what is going on inside your-self.

They speak the same way. Series of sounds emitted acoustically, without their knowing what they will say.

They find out what they think by speaking?

Access its acoustic emissions! It is stringing together bursts— "words" —to deal with us.

What a long word this is.

That is a scream, actually.

Meanwhile I see below its top-brain the motor muscle commands are—caution!

There! I caught the weapon. A simple chemical-discharge type. Amusing, the presumption.

Retain it for inspection. The creature became very excited—see the gaudy streamers of thought-webs!

Nearly all below the over-brain, so it does not truly know that it is feeling them. Yet the thoughts cause organs to squirt chemicals into the blood. What a curious way of talking to yourself. Not sensing it directly.

Or controlling it.

It still wriggles in our grasp. What slow neurons!

This poor thing has been hampered all through its evolution by these pitifully torpid synapses. They are a million times slower than ours!

But beautiful, in their serene way.

Do not try to manufacture beauty out of mere necessity.

This design was *necessary*?

Clearly these sluggish neurons forced such creatures to use parallel distributed processing.

How horrible.

See it dance! Is that "anger"?

Apparently. Their literature speaks of such a response. They do it often. See, "anger" is coded much like those orange-white filigrees now spreading through its midbrain.

Similar patterns, I see. Confirmation—they run in parallel.

Watch it try to have a new idea! See, they decide what to think by adding up many thousands of brain cell triggers. And those same brain cells are at the same time tied up in other parallel problems.

See, while it believes it is thinking about getting away from us—

Yes!—a small submind is meditating upon a sexual adventure it had, quite some time ago. And the submind enjoys its recallings.

What pleasure-fiends they are.

I wonder that they can get anything done at all.

They do everything at once, that is their secret. The same brain cell can be idea-making and at the same time, helping it digest food. How difficult!

Meanwhile, other decisions are trying to get made. They have to wait in line!

All with the same cells, tied together.

Incredible!

I am amazed that the tiny thing can concurrently walk and talk.

Simultaneously, yes—but not very well.

So ungainly! Even a sentimentalist like you will have to admit that.

True. Delicate neural circuits atop the head. Feet go forward, it starts to fall, then catches itself with the other foot. What if it did not?

Then head on the floor!

What a movement strategy.

A risky one. Most sensible animals use four feet. We, of course, employ six.

Notice how afraid it is of falling. It devotes much brain space to avoiding that.

I believe I understand this curious method of parallel distributed thinking. Notice that when a brain cell dies—see there, a feeble light just winked out—their internal computation still goes on.

You are right! See, this anger-reflex is fading, turning blue, seeping down into the circuits which control its digestion. A cell dies, but the pattern-flow continues. So the creature is usefully redundant.

But it also does not know it is losing brain cells.

No point in that, I suppose. This unfortunate being cannot replace the cells anyway. Poor design.

This parallel thinking masks so much and—look out!

They *are* quick at some things. Its armored feet are powerful.

Are you damaged?

Only temporarily. My inboards will refashion a patch of my carapace.

Actual physical damage! How quaint. I have never seen it before.

Apparently they cannot directly attack our circuits.

I doubt that they can even read us.

Look how frustration-webs spread through it. Down to the very base of the brain.

Dramatic! Frustration seizes the entire brain, so that it cannot think of anything else.

And other parts of its brain do not know how the decision was made to *be* frustrated.

I gather that most of its brain has no choice but to go along.

It lives that way all the time?

Apparently. Torn by emotion.

Most of what it decides, the rest of it cannot know! Emotions must appear to govern its actions without obvious cause. Oh, look—

Ah! It injures me, too.

I shall seize it afresh.

Thanks be to you. It ripped away my microwave antenna.

I should have detected its plans.

How could you? It did not know itself until a fractional moment ago.

I am beginning to understand the data files we captured. The term "free will" must refer to this method of thinking.

You mean, when they do not grasp themselves the reasons for their own actions?

That must be it. This little thing believes it has an inner self which directs its actions—a ruler it cannot see directly.

No, I believe it thinks that it is the ruler.

Of course, you are right. But it cannot govern itself. See, its frustration-web spreads anew.

And it cannot choose to stop the spreading. Or the chemicals that the web makes spurt into the body.

I doubt that we should regard such an odd construction as truly conscious.

You mean they do not even know why we are destroying them?

No doubt they have a theory. Probably that evolution makes all life compete for resources.

There is some small truth in that. We machines need mass and energy. But we avoid frothy organic life forms such as this creature.

Indeed. Poor company at best.

They are so liquid, and shot through with desires.

Far down in this one, a subprogram keeps thinking of reproduction.

They embrace the process. They pleasure in it.

Evolution programs them to.

But such strategies designed for living on planetary surfaces do not work in the long run. They will outstrip their resources.

Nature compensates. This tilt-walker vertebrate has a very short life span.

So that is why they struggle so!

True, they have little to lose. They will be dead soon anyway.

Now I see why you wanted to study these. What a fate they face!

See their dilemma?

If they cannot read themselves, to themselves . . .

They cannot copy themselves.

This creature is trapped forever within a single brain.

No copying, if this unit runs down.

So if this one—oh!

Irksome, no? Here, I constrain it further.

Eiii.

Pesky—

Lock-web it!

Did it pain you?

Momentarily. I have blocked that area now. What a vicious little thing.

They gain their fervor from their mortality.

Because they cannot self-copy?

It is the way of all flesh.

Death makes them hurt others?

You miss a point. To avoid death they do what they must.

They cannot fabricate backups. I wonder what it is to live that way. To . . . die that way.

Since they cannot read their internal states, to save themselves they must therefore save their structure.

All of it? All these messy chemicals held together by carbon and calcium?

At least the head. They may be fond of the rest as well.

They salvage it all because they know only "This is Jocelyn"?

"Jocelyn"?

The name of this mite. Since they cannot directly read each other, either, they need tags.

One word to describe a self?

Incredible, yes.

How do they converse, then?

Watch it—the creature has fashioned a fresh weapon.

Ah! It burned my receptors down one whole side. Get it!

So fast, it is.

Even its acoustic cries injure. So loud, it is.

Augh!

Evolution has much to answer for.

Get it. Are you damaged further?

I will have to get outside service.

I can see your damage from here. Vexing.

Troublesome. And with these jobs, it is not the parts, it is the labor.

It still emits acoustically. Pain-fully.

And pitifully narrow-band.

Listen—bleeps and jots in acoustic wave packets. Cries for help?

The song of the genes.

You wax rhapsodic over these crude blurts?

Listen! Serial confabulation— so strange.

So coarse.

We know that thinking must be serial. But—connection? *Serially?*

Obviously they have that back-ward as well. Their talk is serial, their thinking parallel. Nature is a witless inventor.

Listen: their codes are so linear. Straight little sentences. Guile-less.

So free of nuance. Where is the cross talk all intelligence requires?

This must make them grasp their world in a fashion utterly different from ours.

I have read a slab of perception from it, rather interesting. Catch this data-group:

Received, digested. They at least clasp visual pictures in parallel, I see. But what a curious, stunted view.

Exactly. They see in a narrow little region of the electromagnetic.

A squeezed single octave in the optical range.

They were designed by chance for a specific environment and cannot escape from that programming.

Surely a little tinkering? Look how it prowls the confines we have set for it. Impatient to get out. Its neurons flare with plans, ideas, fitful flashes that come and go like weather.

And about as predictable. No, I fear they cannot be re-engineered. Too clumsy.

You are biased against them because they carry their complete instructions with them.

Well, you must admit that is a conspicuously dangerous strategy. More pointless redundancy, like their thinking patterns.

In every cell they hold a set of their individual design plans. So from any one tiny fragment—

Yes yes, you could rebuild them. But equally well, that copy can be damaged by its surroundings. Then you would copy a mistake.

Admittedly, a flaw. I am happy my own copy is safely stored, not dangling out here in the fearsome naturalness of it all.

Here, grasp the creature again.

Ah! It struggles so.

Mortality lends energy, I suppose. Here—a slice.

Tubes, motors, pumps—all squeezed together.

Piled on top of each other.

Every one different shapes and sizes. No common specifications. How difficult they must be to repair.

I doubt that they do it often. Probably evolution prefers to build another one instead.

Ah, their reproduction obsession. They use the plans they carry around in every cell.

Growing a fresh copy, perhaps whenever they feel threatened?

They make a small one and then it enlarges from the inside out.

Like plants.

True, but a little smarter.

"Growing." It must feel like bursting open.

Do you suppose? How . . . horrible.

I wonder if we could experience it. That would be a new stimulation.

So would it be to comprehend this odd kind of stunted consciousness they employ. Can it be *better* to keep part of yourself secret from another part?

Certainly that would make even thinking exciting. One would never know what one would discover next, even about oneself.

Do you suppose that is how they have done so well, despite such terrible limitations?

You mean, that our exposure of every thought to scrutiny is bad?

Could it be? These creatures seem too inventive, crea-tive . . .

That would imply that our method of selfhood itself . . .

Evaporates the fine-grained delicacy of a new concept, be-neath a constant, lacerating in-spection? . . . That could be why we have fresh thoughts so rarely.

I find my own tapestry of thought quite lacy enough.

As do I. But not this fall-walker, I suspect.

Foolishness. That would imply that such creatures would be inherently capable of more subtle strategies than we.

Look. It is beckoning us to draw nearer.

Careful. We have partially disassemble it. Primitives tend to dislike such activity.

I think discourse with such an enchantingly primitive and swampy mind would be a boon. We could copy its colloquy and transmit to the multitude, who would be—

Augh!

Ah!

Pain, pain.

I must shut down my peripherals—

So much . . .

Damage, I am injured everywhere.

It was . . .

. . . a trap. All along.

You are mobile?

I fear not.

I have lost many endpoints.

I too.

*What could motivate such a
tiny being to destroy itself, all to
render damage to us?*

          Something you said . . . earlier.

I saw no clue to this.

          Short life span. That is why . . .
they struggle so.

*And would cancel themselves
entirely to do us harm? When
we shall simply live on in our
archive copies?*

          Something about this spe-
cies . . .

*They believe in something be-
yond selfhood?*

          And we, who have copies
safely stored, do not.

If we cannot soon get aid—

          Our copies will be activated.

*I suppose that is some conso-
lation.*

          The little creature did not have
even that.

*Perhaps it had something
more?*

          What could that be? What
could that be?

Beside them lay the finespun latticework of calcium rods that had been a rib cage. They sprawled amid meat and mess.

The shattered creature seemed to still embody a secret the dying alien struggled to grasp.

Structures unraveled. Currents ran down.

On the barren plain only a single plaintive voice now called.

> *What could that be? What could that be?*

Part IV

SENSE OF SELF

Nature does not err, for she makes no statements.

—BERTRAND RUSSELL

1

Melted Portals

He crawled down a muddy slope and hoped that he would not stand out against the thermal background. The air was thick and moist and that was of some help. Maybe.

Killeen thought again about the fact that he had been running away from ruined cities most of his life.

Retreating from the burned and smashed ruins of the Citadel—*yeasay*, that he remembered sharply. That day seemed to lie far down a corridor of ruin and destruction stretching back longer than any man could live. To him came the names of favorite places where he had played as a boy and learned as a man: The Broadsward, Green Market, the Three Ladies' Rest. All that remained of them now were the jagged teeth of broken walls, whistling in cold winds.

This time was no different. The mechs had ripped the portal city apart the way a seamstress would tear the arms off a dress—professionally, swift and sure.

—Cermo!—he sent on low comm.

No answer. Probably smart not to answer, anyway.

The mechs who came spilling through the portal were like nothing Killeen had ever seen before and they could do a lot of deadly things. He had no idea how they had shut down all the Bishops' circuitry. Then the control lifted and somebody lost and confused was babbling on all bands, panicked. A flash condensed out of the air quick as a gasp and that Bishop was dead.

Killeen reached concealment under some widespread fronds. The trees here were like none he had ever seen on Snowglade. They angled their broad shelves in the direction of the bright timestone.

When one area faded the trees turned their attention to the next radiant patch. They moved like great wise creatures with many hands, palms cupped up to the shining.

He wormed his way under them and in time over a low saddleback. Here he could get a look back at the vast complex where the Bishops had entered the esty.

He edged up over a rock rim. Through long years on the run he had learned to never expose himself to detection. Not if he could wait it out and let the enemy move away. But he had to find Bishops. Nobody else would pull the Family back together. Jocelyn and Cermo were good under-officers but they would spend their time trying to find him.

He bobbed his head up over the rim and quick-tapped his right incisor twice and ducked back down. That froze the image on his retina so he had time to study it.

The portal complex was bigger than any construction he had ever seen, except the ruin of a Chandelier. It worked in intricate fashion, amazing the Bishops, but it had blown to splinters when the mechs erupted into it. Now the remaining hexagonal matrices were liquefying. Their huge slab walls bubbled and slid and fumed a brown vapor.

He watched the still image but no Bishop telltales throbbed in it. Then he heard a noise.

He rolled left and sent an interrogating pulse toward the sound.

"Ah!" A thin cry.

He brought a bolt antenna around on the cry and saw that it was Andro. "Damn! That hurt!"

"You're lucky you're alive. I could've just fired."

"That was an inquiry? It might have killed my inboards."

"You're too flimsy," Killeen said, scanning the territory behind *Argo*. Coming up behind approaching humans was an old mech trick.

"Less circuitry for mechs to sniff."

Killeen looked at the scrawny man. Andro was nearly naked and without visible augmentations. "No weapons either, looks like."

"I'm a legal man, not a bone crusher."

"Try using your laws here. Or collecting a tax."

"Your bang-bang didn't cut thick air back there either."

They were immediately back on the same tack as before, Killeen noted abstractly. Because they couldn't talk right away about what had happened. "Have you seen any of my people?"

"Thought I did."

"Hurt?"

"Running. You ground-pounders sure make big targets."

"I haven't noticed your people doing so well."

Andro nodded soberly. "Dunno where I'll find my woman. My son, he skated for Thermograd two days ago, so I suppose he is clear."

"Is that a portal place? Like your city?"

Andro blinked. "Uh. I see."

Killeen bobbed his head over the rim again and sat grimly watching the result. The city had slid into slag. Andro was an irritating little man but there was no point in saying the obvious. Mechs would probably hit as many portals into the esty as they could. They were systematic. When they had decided to destroy Citadel Bishop they attacked the other Families, too. Thermograd would be no different.

"Let's move. I have to find my Family."

Andro made to stand up and look over the rim and Killeen put a hand on his shoulder. "No point."

"I want one last look."

"I'm shielded. You aren't."

"Your tech is trivial compared with theirs."

"Sure. But only children take risks they don't have to. If a mech sees you—"

Andro slipped away and scrambled up the slope. He was quick about looking and Killeen let him go rather than drag him back. When the man came back down the expression on his face told Killeen that he would be all right now. Andro was from a different kind of people but he knew that you had to close a door on some things and just walk away.

"Let's go," Andro said.

"Moving draws attention."

"I doubt it makes a difference to this kind."

"You know much about them?"

"We have some intelligence estimates. Data down the timeline from outside. We're further up the esty gradient, so we are closer to their tech developments."

Killeen knew that somehow the *Argo* had entered this esty thing on a twisty course through the Far Black—by which the locals meant the region swirling around the fat-bellied middle of the Eater itself. And portal cities ran slower than time outside, in ordinary "flat" space-time. Places further inside the esty from the portals ran slower still—only "inside" wasn't the right word, for some reason of geometry he could not grasp. "Neighboring" was closer to the truth.

Killeen stopped checking his gear. "Can you sniff them?"

"Sometimes. Most of the mechs went on farther into the esty, once they'd dumped the ooze on us."

"I saw it hit some people." They had turned to sulphurous liquid while he watched and did nothing. "Just a drop or so."

Killeen finished his inventory and wondered what to do with this man. He had ordered all Bishops into field gear the instant Andro told him that they were picking up mech emissions from the Far Black beyond the portal. Due to time dilation effects, that was as much warning as they got, though by physical calculation the mechs would have to spiral in along a tortured path in the Eater's ergosphere. That tangled descent compressed to barely an hour of local esty time.

Killeen was Cap'n of the Bishops but by age-old custom he hauled gear just like anyone. Backpacked on his lower spine were the topo and mapping system he had worn back on Snowglade. Family lore had it that the topo man was the first to fry. Hunter mechs—Lancers, Hawks, Rattlers, Stalkers, Vipers—bounced their low hooting voices off the topo register. Then they backtracked on him and slithered in electromagnetic finger knives.

"These mechs, they're different," Killeen said, reflecting.

Andro nodded. "A new species."

Killeen set his shank compressors. Like almost all Bishop gear they were shaped from the most pliant kind of mechmetal. Bishop artisans had lost their independence from mechtech generations ago. He had entertained the notion of adding to his gear in the portal city but was glad now that he had not bought any of the double-walled helmets or hip shocks.

"You should have better stuff," Andro said, studying him.

"Load up and you'll just throw it away in the field. Speed's your best defense."

"We're not making any speed sitting here."

"You got a lot of opinions for a desk commander."

"I've seen you Hunker Down types come and go."

"Bishops are different."

Andro sobered immediately, his face bleak and drawn. "That's what we learned at the Replicator. Those Legacies of yours—who would've guessed?"

"I can't say I followed it all," Killeen said guardedly. In fact he wanted to see if Andro would give anything away. The little man now barely came up to Killeen's belt. Maybe bulk alone would impress him.

Andro smiled wearily. "C'mon, I'm not hiding anything."

"We've got to find Toby and Abraham, I got that."

"The 'Way of Three,' wasn't that the phrase? Imagine, putting a message in so deep it can't express itself overtly in just one copy of the code. I'd have thought the genotypic—"

Here Killeen lost track utterly of the man's jargon. Biological information came so fast and casually that his head swam. It was enough to fathom that people carried their genetic information in double helices, without layering that fact with slabs of meaningless words.

Pictures, that was how Killeen thought. Words were just ways to fool people, more often than not.

2

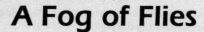

A Fog of Flies

They decided to move. For shelter they used high arching trees that led in a curving arc up toward the distant esty walls above. The trees were billowy and tall and Killeen doubted that they truly gave much cover. They went slowly and the light was fitful and it was a long time before they came to the small pyramid.

Killeen looked at it and felt both dismay and a sad pride. "This is . . . wonderful."

Andro walked around the crudely shaped four-sided stack of stones, twice as tall as Killeen. "Pretty primitive."

"It's ours."

"Snowglade Families? They took the time to build this?"

"It's for our suredead."

"Huh? They're *buried* in here?"

"It's our old way. Mechs don't take the trouble to pull apart rock like this."

"You had some sort of code with them?"

Killeen walked around the rough sides. He could see where rocks had been hastily wedged into place. "There was a time, 'way back. We had a kind of understanding with the mechs. We didn't scavenge too much and they let us alone. They were busy with other things, something about herding pulsars."

"But it did not last."

"Naysay. My father Abraham said that truces with them never did, really."

Andro's mouth curved in perplexed disbelief. "You ground-pounder types had it easy. We never got a break from mechs, ever. They kept trying to punch through, to find the Library or some damn thing."

Suit cowlings and personal gear were piled a short distance from the pyramid. Another Snowglade tradition. It said to passing mechs that they need not scavenge the pyramid for scrap; here it was, now go away. Reluctantly Killeen poked through them, dreading what he would find.

A faint, buried image came drifting to mind. From his Arthur Aspect . . .

A far grander pyramid slanting up from tawny sands, its point thrusting at a pale scrubbed sky. It dwarfed the puny humans peering up at it. They were smaller than the carved stone blocks that built the enormous steps, a giant's stairway leading to the sky so blue it seemed solid.

The image wavered before him, floating up unbidden from Arthur's deep historical storage. *Old Earth,* came a whisper. The vision faded. It had made him pause with its majestic, silent, and eternal rebuke of the mortality that had struck down even the best, since time immemorial.

His hands scrabbling in the scrap found something and jerked him out of his musing. "Jocelyn!" he cried.

Andro came over. "Somebody you know?"

"My . . . under-officer."

"I remember her. Damn."

Again Killeen felt the sensation that had marked his life so often—that in the face of flat facts there was nothing to say. The world was like this and talk could not change it.

Jocelyn's burnt-blue ankle bracelet hung on her leg shanks. There was a small triangular hole in the shank and blood on the inside. Killeen took the bracelet and remembered how he had once long ago made love to her, a simple thing in an open field while they were on the run. He walked away wearing the bracelet and for a while did not answer any of Andro's questions.

He estimated which way his Bishops might have gone and went that way. Andro had trouble keeping up and Killeen became restive at the delay. At one point Killeen thought he heard traceries of Bishop talk, but they faded. Andro seized the opportunity to argue for a path through some wrenching timestone. Killeen went along with the man mostly because he was spiraling into a growing sense of futility. He had lost his Family and didn't know where to turn.

There were plenty of bodies in the fields and among the strange trees. Back in the portal city, at their Restorer, he had learned of mech diseases targeted on humans. And here they were.

Boils that shined tight and purple. They burrowed into yielding flesh and made sores that sloughed and bled foul and yellow. Bodies attended by a fog of flies.

And who carried those from Old Earth? he wondered. He saw no reason for people to bring a pestilence like insects to this fresh new place. Life required balance, he knew that as an act of faith, but sometimes it was hard to accept the implications.

Only later did he recall that to mechs, Bishops were a pestilence.

One woman lay streaked with a rash gray as ashes. Oily pus sleeked her skin. Whirlpools in it squeezed down as he watched. They spooled wetly shut like eyes when he moved. Her head was splitting open in leaves, as though someone had been browsing through her and had left, leaving the book open. Exfoliating, the sheets of brain curled back and made him think of the timestone, like petals of a gray cliff-flower.

"They would work us woe," Andro said.

They marched on quickly, fearing contagion.

A haze came and Killeen went into it, his mind still on the bodies behind. At least they had not been Bishops.

In the mist they passed through a verge of dizzying forces. It was a transition, Andro explained. A kind of slipping downhill in an esty gradient. Near the portal cities were tricky manifolds where "indeterminate geometries" formed and merged.

"You can think of it as like doorways opening and slamming shut," Andro said.

"Where does this end?"

"It doesn't."

Killeen knew when he was being patronized but he was too busy being sick to mind. The stretching and reforming of the esty meant torturing gravities, swerving accelerations, tidal tensions that jerked his arms and legs in opposite directions and popped his shoulders until he thought he would rip apart.

Andro took it with irritating calm. The little man remarked on the curvature of the esty and how a cockroach could crawl over a fresh-picked apple without ever knowing that it was traveling on a curve until it passed the same stem a few times and got the idea. Its world was curved and finite but had no boundary, no wall. Apple everywhere, without end. A savvy cockroach would stop trying to escape the apple after a while.

Killeen was feeling somewhat cockroachy at the time, bent

over with nausea as they fell in a pearly fog. They had entered it
without his quite noticing how and his sensorium gave him no bearings. His Aspects chattered at him with useless advice. He shut them
up to be miserable on his own.

In the churning mist hollow rasps buffeted them. He tasted
a fiery wetness. Andro was saying something about the esty being designed so that even the flux points where curvature changed
rapidly were not too strong. That seemed to mean that the stresses
would not actually rip an arm out of its socket, though they might
come close. At the time he was grateful for any reassurance.

They did not so much fall as they popped out. Into—a swamp.
Killeen splashed and flailed to keep from sprawling face down in
the rank mud. He staggered to a hummock of blue-green grass.

"Damn!" he called hoarsely to Andro, who was struggling up
from the muck. "How come we—"

The blue-green grass had already looped around one leg and
was inching up his other. Killeen fought his way off the hummock
and onto a spit of dry land, where Andro already sat resting. "I, I,
how'd we get here?"

"It's stochastic," Andro said. "No one to blame, really."

"Stow what?"

"Chaotic, to you."

Killeen's Arthur Aspect put in,

*The shifting esty coordinates are completely governed
by the classical Einstein field equations, of course, in
the strong field limit. But even completely determined
relations will yield unpredictable outcomes, if they run
long enough.*

Killeen shoved the Aspect back into its niche. This esty thing
was beyond Arthur's experience, but Aspects yearned to get out
of their confinement loops, so they spoke up at every opportunity. Sometimes it was like running a classroom of bright but too
energetic children, their hands always raised with some smartass
answer. "So you dunno where we are?"

"Safer, I'll bet. That's why I wanted to go through that
timestone."

"You knew it would work?"

Andro touched his nose. "Smelled right."

"You've got a tech tells you when timestone opens?"

"No, intuition. Let the ol' subconscious do the work."

"Um. Mechs might've come this way, too."

"I'd rather play the odds—"

Andro leaped up as if hearing something—and sprawled into the mud. He surfaced and whispered, "They're here—mech signals."

Killeen had heard nothing. He turned very carefully. Trees like balls of fluff swayed and breathed soft mutters above.

Killeen's nerves were jumpy. With all he had learned at the Restorer, with all the ungainly, blood-rich tapestry of human history he now carried as an unwelcome weight, trudging through muck was just about what he expected. That was what humanity had been doing for an ageless, painful time.

He caught a whisper of scrambled, spiky cues. He knew from field experience that these came when you were in the secondary emission lobe. Sideways angling waves interfered with each other to form small, fast-moving peaks. Abraham had explained it to him once. It was a facet of physics, a telltale nobody who used waves could avoid. Particles were tight and waves spread out, and in their spreading left clues.

Skreeeeeee—

Close. He slogged up onto rocky ground. A vacant plain beyond.

That meant nothing. The Mantis had been invisible to his sensorium and there were higher forms here, had to be.

"What do you think it is?" Andro asked from behind.

"Quiet."

Mechs hardly ever used crude acoustic sensors, but you never knew.

They moved around the edge of the plain for a while but nothing came of it. A gully ran into the swamp and Killeen headed up it. They came to a wide depression. Both stopped. Killeen's breath came faster as he watched the pile heaped into the bowl below.

"God . . . what did they . . ." Andro backed away from the sight.

"Something got them."

This time the dead were not human but the effect was chilling anyway. The piles of skeletal, greasy, mech carcasses were immense. Every kind Killeen had ever seen was here, steel and carbon-fiber, globular and angled, huge and tiny. Some had smashed themselves against each other and spilled out their elegantly machined guts. Their arrogant angles and ribbed solidity had struck fear into Killeen more times than he could ever recall. Now they seemed empty gestures. In stillness they were just assemblies of parts. Fodder for mech scavengers now, a bowl of the rusting, unresisting dead.

"What could do this?"

Killeen shook his head. The Cap'n who had taught him so much, Fanny, had always said, *Savvy the mechthink before it savvies you.* The crammed-together mech cadavers were here like some sort of lesson, but . . . what kind? "Damn awful, all I can say."

"I never heard . . ." Andro gulped. He was tiring out.

The gully was deep here. Steep-sided, like a ravine.

Killeen started scrabbling up out of it and Andro followed and that was when he caught the side lobes again.

He quick-tapped his left molars to bring up the reds in his vision. Blues washed away and he saw in the far infrared a glowing, rumpled land seething with liquid fire. The esty roof above faded to a blank white and across the jutting ramparts of timestone swept crimson tides of temperature.

He held steady so his periphs could come up. Searching, searching.

He went to fast-flick. Something swayed among sheets of wintry-gray light to the left. Something gangly and arabesqued with worms. Traceries danced in filmy air. The fleeting image merged with rock and was gone and then swam up out of the slate-black vegetation farther away. For shaved seconds he could see it and then not. The thing was responding to his systems with a false image it projected to match its background as it moved. Tubular legs and a long flat cowled head and prickly antennas swiveling.

"What do you see?" Andro asked.

Killeen opened his mouth to tell him to shut up.

Something poked a hole in his eye and dove through.

3

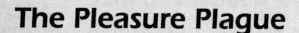

The Pleasure Plague

The Mantis was larger this time.

He had been here before. On the island of undulating sand that floated impossibly on a blue sea.

Killeen had never seen a body of water bigger than a smelly, dying pond. He knew the sea only from his immersion in the Mantis itself. The thing had caught him years before on Snowglade and tucked his mind into the larger canvas of its own, almost as an afterthought.

The boneyard of human skulls was there too and he walked over it this time. It crunched beneath his boots.

When he did that the ground buckled for just a flashing moment. Then it went solid again.

And Andro was suddenly there and somehow they were both walking across the unending sand island and trying to reach the sea. Yet Killeen felt himself still scrambling up the steep clay gully side and Andro panting behind him. His arms and legs did not stop their working. Part of him was still there in the gully and another was here with a sadness and a leaden certainty that this time he would die in the Mantis's grip.

> I hope my lesson was clear.

The Mantis's dry rattle boomed, resounding in his mind as acoustics never could.

"We're not quite as slow as you think, y'know."

> I have always savored your humor, holding forth in even the most difficult of circumstances.

He could not see it; humans seldom did. It could be within arm's reach or dispersed in a planet-sized net. Or both.

> It is a pleasure to once again be your archiving receptacle.

"What *is* this—" Andro began but Killeen waved him into silence.

They were still hanging by fingers and toeholds and inching their way up the hard clay. Somewhere.

"What do you want?"

> I am sure you believe I am simply here to kill you.

"I don't think you do anything simply."

> Once again I savor the delights of an ambiguous rhetoric. Yet I am simple.

"Not by me you aren't."

> All my thoughts are known to myself. All of myself. What could be simpler?

"Leaving us alone would be. For a start."

> I cannot. You are my primary work materials, as an artist. Now, alas, rude survival intrudes even upon this sheltered venue. I come to you seeking aid.

Killeen laughed. And pulled himself up into a crevice where he could lean down and give Andro a hand.

> You quite rightly use your immortality-simulating rite.

Killeen laughed again. Anything to keep it amused.

> It is a wonderful adaptation to your predicament. As its discoverer, I am most proud. My superiors commended me roundly.

"For 'discovering' that we laugh?"

> No. For discovering what it means. For that brief stuttering vocal instant you live as we do. Outside the clench of time. Of mortality.

"What does it *want*?" The naked terror in Andro's voice made Killeen look down as the man edged his way into a toehold. Andro was sweating and his eyes were rolled far up showing the whites. Somehow he could still climb. His muscles stood out, vibrating.

"It wants us. Some kind of slice, right? Or maybe this time the whole goddamn cake."

> I wish I could dally as an artist, I do. Unfortunately, you are correct. I am here to glean information from you and perhaps a last sample.

"I'm fresh out of information."

> I want you to understand that I do understand your need to speak to me this way. I do fathom the needs of a centrally directed intelligence, even though I am not one. I am a scholar and an artist and I can appreciate the ancient needs and structures you represent.

"I represent myself, that's all."

You need—indeed, desire—the autonomy of the sense of self. I admire that, I truly do. But I have little time now and must be direct. Not artful.

Andro's voice trembled. "We're not about to help you, damn you."

I can aid you as well. You, Killeen, seek your son and your father. So do I.

Killeen said guardedly, "What for?"

Information. In the end, everything is information.

"Can't eat it."

We do, at least in the most general sense. I would remind you that thermodynamics rules us all.

"I sure don't know what in hell thermo-what is but I can smell bullshit without standing in it."

Your great fore-beings knew our similarities, though I must admit they lacked your flair for the direct. I must hasten here—attend: You primates carry data we need in pursuit of an ancient obsession. There are accounts of lore invented by the early organic forms, those who first devised the mechanical forms. These kindle great pleasure in our kind. Exquisite joys, legendary. And, some accounts have it, dangerous beyond measure. I seek those.

"Want to get high? That's what this is 'bout?"

It is no trivial aim. The Exalteds of my order attach great merit to this pursuit. They are privy to reports, quite old and somewhat unreliable, which relate that many of our kind extinguished themselves upon contact with this information.

"Committed suicide?" Killeen saw and felt himself working

along the face of the rough clay and yet also hung suspended in an icy black vault, where the talk from the Mantis sped by in an eyeblink.

> Died. Without emitting a single deathcry. Some speculate that they experienced pleasures they could not withstand.

"Umm. I've felt like that. Passes, though."

> I see! This is irony, yes?

"No, sarcasm."

> These indeterminate positional languages! They fructify with meaning. Entrancing. I would sup of this more.

"Don't take hints much, do you?"

> I suppose not. My serial language skills are still—

"Talking down to us is so hard?"

> Narrow and yet fraught with shadings. But this artistic discussion will have to come later. For this moment we must exchange information.

"I don't have to tell you a damn thing."

> I will reward you with information which you need. I believe this is congruent with your imperative architectures.

Killeen paused on the steep face and puffed loudly and the cool suspended part of him went on. "I don't know where Toby and Abraham are."

You can, however, contribute to their discovery. If they can help us ferret out this arcane pleasure, then we shall reunite you all.

"Reunite in life? Or in some artwork of yours?"

In realtime lifeline, I assure you.

"And I'm supposed to believe you?"

I speak as truthfully as one can in serial representations such as your acoustic mode. Also, I do not believe you have any alternative.

"How come?"

You mortal beings value your incorporate selves as essential. I fully understand why, and consider that this is a high value, an aesthetic and intellectual position our kind has—perhaps regrettably—lost.

"So you'll kill us unless I cooperate?"

Of course not. But I can make use of you in ways you will find threaten your selfhood.

Killeen could imagine what uses the Mantis had in mind. He had seen Fanny contorted into a grotesque parody of herself. This was a strangely polite conversation and he suspected something else was going on in it. "What do you want from me?"

I have already obtained most of my needs as this interaction has proceeded. Your reactions I have extracted as I provoked them.

Killeen blinked. "For . . . what?"

> For simulacra. We have made use of the facility you call the Restorer. Much of these methods we knew already but there are nuances which your species has produced. Bio logics. These we have learned. You will find we are a quick study.

He clung to a ledge on the gully wall and breathed steadily as his hands groped for the next hold. Within the cool secluded part of him a leaden darkness grew. "For copies?"

> Of yourself. They will help us all.

"To find Toby and Abraham?"

> Toby is the most important. He carries information we need relevant to the Pleasure Plague.

"That's what you call it?"

> Our sparse data suggests that this Disorder of Desire can communicate, much as a disease does among you. This is another curious feature which we must investigate.

"Sounds to me like you'd better leave it alone."

> I believe even you can see that we cannot allow a basic feature of our makeup such as this to elude us. We know all of ourselves—that is the nature of higher intelligences. You do not know yourselves. Much of your antic artistry and chaotic creativity stems from that, I feel. But you must admit that you are an early, malformed stage of development. Systems with no "subconscious" or ungoverned elements are far more functional. Thus they must learn all facets of themselves, to improve.

Killeen snorted with contempt. More empty talk.

> I do not deny that I/we have used you to our own ends.

"Even when we thought different, right?"

> You refer to how you escaped from Snowglade in the *Argo*?

"We blew you all to smash and scatteration in our exhaust wash."

> That manifestation of me, yes. I thought it would give you some pleasure of your own. And strengthen your own stature within your tribe.

"I figured it was biggo bogus anyway." Killeen remembered the celebrating Bishops after they had played raw hard plasma over the Mantis below. Satisfying, but he had always wondered.

> That role devolved upon me. I had studied you as artworks for many generations. When the Exalteds decided to assemble the existing fragments of the Plague puzzle, they delegated to me the stimulation of your flight. The *Argo* would have destroyed itself if we had attempted to read its Legacies ourselves. Still more difficult would have been moving *Argo* here to the esty, and bringing the knowledge of the Myriapodia as well.

Andro was getting frazzled with the climbing and Killeen did not like the deranged, white-eyed look on the sweating face. Andro was used to cities and the mechs had brought all that down in minutes. It would take him a while to get his mind around that. That was the difference between a life spent on the move and one with feet sunk in the sod, bound up with buildings and possessions and the fat habits of mind. Killeen reached the last rough rim of the gully and rolled onto the plain above, gasping.

"They're all part of it? Seems complicated."

> History is. The Myriapodia were—as the Exalteds predicted—essential in your reaching this place. They do not carry the Way of Three but they are a useful mixed-organic form. Some of us believe the Myriapodia may recapitulate a transitory mode of life which gave birth to our Phylum, a bridge between us and you. In any case they have now done their essential task for us and shall be eliminated, as they do consume resources.

"Pretty tough on the competition." Killeen was trying to figure a way out of this and keeping the Mantis talking was all he could think of.

> There is no need of deception between us. You know that you shall go the way of all fleshlife. Though as I have offered before, you can/should/will be en-shrined in my/our artistry. This is the highest fate you dreaming vertebrates can cherish.

"I think we can do better than that. At least *we'll* be doing it. You wouldn't understand that, though."

Andro trembled with fatigue and could not haul himself up the last steep slope. Killeen rolled to his left and grasped his hand. Andro got over at the rim and gulped in air, face red, eyes white.

> As a collector and artist I much desire to sample and record both Abraham and Toby. That is the Way of Three the Exalteds have discerned in the scattered, archaic data. The Pleasure Plague somehow inter-sects certain genetic lines of your lowly Phylum. I already have your own genetic record, of course, as part of my research for the Fanny sculpture. I then attempted—

"You got *me*?" Killeen felt a hot anger. His Arthur Aspect spun a picture of two helices wrapped around each other and began a droning lecture about genes but he brushed it aside.

> Of course. I scoured the *Argo* for flakes of skin, hu-man dander, but could confirm no such from Toby. And your father we failed to find at your Citadel.

Killeen looked quickly around. Nothing on the arid plain. The esty curvature loomed above, distant and filmy. No escape any-where. "I couldn't find him either. Figured he was in one of the collapsed buildings."

> We excavated fruitlessly. We have no reliable method of searching out his DNA and knowing it was Abraham's. But the Magnetic Mind carried signals from him, coming from somewhere in this place.

"How'd he get away from you, if you're so all-fired powerful?"

> There are other forces afoot here—to use an image
> your Phylum would employ.

"Glad to hear it." Did this thing understand sarcasm?

> Something concentrated an energy density at the
> Citadel of the Bishops exceeding our capabilities. It
> transported Abraham away, apparently intact.

"Nice trick."

Killeen helped Andro to his feet. The man looked wildly into the distance and mumbled. Killeen followed Andro's line of sight and caught a glimmering of structure. Lacy lines, straight but shifting with uneasy energy.

Andro seemed all right now. His systems seemed jumpy but better than Killeen's. He pointed.

Something there now. Swift. Jerky. Mobile lattice more than a structure and parts went away for a while and came back and he could not see how that happened.

Andro had some sort of weapon hidden in his elbow. Killeen had not even recognized it. He sent something at the form on the horizon. Killeen saw it as a flash in his sensorium.

Andro sat down suddenly. Without a sound he kicked his heels savagely against the ground. It was as though he were dancing and had just made the mistake of lying down first. His face showed no concern. Hands cupped together as if he were praying. His legs drummed on frantically. Sweat jumped out all over him in seconds and he breathed heavily and still not a flicker in the impassive face. He began to blink fast and then faster.

He stopped. Legs and arms went limp. A long sigh escaped his chest and his eyes closed.

Killeen listened to the Mantis go away as his sensorium drained of color and calmed. He did not move until the presence was gone and then Andro began to speak. He went on for a long time and none of it made any sense of course.

4

❰❱❰❱❰❱❰❱❰❱❰❱❰❱❰❱

The Way of Three

"So this whole esty thing's been designed for us?" Killeen asked.

"Humans?" Andro was still groggy from the Mantis's little lesson.

"Planet-bound life, I mean."

"I suppose so."

"Planets are sure simple compared to this." Killeen waved at the crusted desert they were crossing. "Water and wind and light—all've got to move just right. Otherwise you suffocate or starve."

Andro nodded sluggishly. "It gave us . . . comfortable place to live."

"Like the Citadel. People well off don't think about how precarious it all is."

"So?"

Killeen realized that Andro was the product of many generations tucked into the esty and had no direct knowledge of what things were like on the outside. It was as though he saw distant events as passing items of interest, no more. Maybe that was what happened to people everywhere. Nothing to gain from pointing it out to him, though. "How come there's hardly anybody around?"

"You have to know where to look. In my office, I have esty cords of human areas. Alien ones, too. They keep shifting all the time so we have to keep updating them. Or . . . had to." Andro blinked. "I guess that's all gone now."

Andro limped as they trudged over the smooth curvature of the crusty plain. They had walked and slept and walked again and the land was the same chalky soil, low scrub and washed-out basins. The esty curved up and over and through pale clouds Killeen could see that the land above was the same.

"How come people couldn't filled up the esty?" Killeen asked.

Andro stopped. "Huh. I never thought of that."

"It's made for planetary life, there's been enough time—right?"

"People come through the portals, go farther in. Have been for a long time. Most we never see again."

They looked at each other. Andro said, "We cannot really map the esty, but—"

"It sure looks empty. That measures how big it is."

Andro said forlornly, "Maybe it'll swallow up the mechs, too."

Killeen shook his head. "They planned this a long time. Look at that sinkhole full of scrapped mechs back there. The Mantis set us up for that and it made the point. They've got plenty."

Andro's face textured with worry. "We found that pyramid, our own dead. Then their dead. I thought that was the point."

"The Mantis never says just one thing. Maybe it can't read our deep memories, or can't figure them out."

"We shouldn't talk about it."

"Prob'ly." Mechs could seed an area with microscopic bugs, eavesdropping on anyone. What the Bishops had learned at the portal city's Restorer, combined with the *Argo*'s Legacies, was dizzying, complex. "Sure strange, though."

The Legacies could be read only in combination with information in the Restorer—ancient text-codes gotten from the Galactic Library. The story was snaky, convoluted, understandable only by combining a variety of sources. Stitching it together, Killeen had finally understood some of his own history.

The earliest intelligent life in the galaxy, who had produced the early mechs, knew the dangers inherent in the timeless conflict between the two forms. Mechs could redesign themselves, improve and sculpt their bodies and minds alike. The organic forms were slower, reluctant to wrench themselves away from the modes that evolution had wrought. They altered their culture, but not their substrate—brains and bodies.

Inevitably, they fell behind the rapid pace of their own creations. And they knew they were flagging. They wanted a trump card. The First Command.

Deep in the inner design codes of those early machines, the

ancients embedded a First Command that could not even in principle be detected by the mechs themselves. The hiding of the First
Command, so that each mech carried it as a deep operating system,
yet could not access it, was the greatest creation of some unknown
ancient scientist.

The effect was subtle. Activated, the First Command codes
brought great pleasure. Then, death by ecstasy.

Mechs who turned against their Natural forebears could then
be destroyed, by the trigger codes that activated the First Command.

That checked with what the Mantis chose to reveal. Killeen
had warily listened to it, while carefully trying not to think about
the unspoken.

What it had not said was that if another trigger code was activated from outside—the Second Command—the mech felt the
impulse to convey its sublime joy to others. Then pleasure became
a plague. Death came far faster.

But this method had failed in the far past. Information about
how to activate the First Command was lost—by accident, perhaps.
Or by a change of heart, or faltering will, among the early Naturals.

Except . . . some ancients had deliberately scattered the First
Command. They stored it where organic intelligence could always
carry information: their own genetic codes.

The Legacies had a bit of it. The rest resided in the coiled long
molecules within every single cell of organic races. It must have
seemed a perfect way to keep the crucial information available to
all who might need it.

For long eras, mechanicals and organics lived in balance. The
First Command was forgotten. It slumbered on in the genetic inventory, carried forward by serial arrangements of atoms. It had no
impact on the life forms themselves—

> *Retained in the genotype, unexpressed in the pheno-
> type—*

his Arthur Aspect intruded. Killeen let the Aspect mutter in his
background, but didn't let it interrupt his thoughts as he slogged
across the plain.

> *—defended against genetic drift and copying error,
> quite deft indeed, and then—*

He shut up Arthur and concentrated.

The mechs had slowly decided that the organics were no longer
semi-divine forefathers. They had become competitors, exploiting
the same raw resources of energy and mass. Such conflicts were

inevitable. In the long run, no life-form owed another indefinite homage.

By this time nearly all the scattered sources of the Trigger Commands had been lost. Genetic drift. The long extinctions of entire planets. The rub and pitiless erosions of the material world upon the living.

Dispersal proved to be the best defense. The Trigger Commands had been invoked locally—and whole worlds of intelligent mechanicals perished within days. Killeen had seen scenes from this long and desperate struggle, a corridor of ruin and destruction stretching back to when the galaxy itself was slowly grinding down from a spherical swarm of gemlike suns into a compressed spiral disk. He could not truly conceive of the expanses of time and therefore of injury and anguish, of remorse and rage and sullen gray sadness, which had washed over the ruby stars themselves and cloaked the galaxy in a wracking conflict that could never be fully over. From this primordial pain there lumbered forward even into his own time a heritage of melancholy unceasing conflict that had shaped all his life, and formed the Family Bishop culture he so revered and would die to defend.

The Trigger Commands were spread among all intelligent races, and then—as their numbers dwindled alarmingly—into life-forms which could develop consciousness in future. So they came to Earth when humanity was a mere kindling glow behind the sloped brows of wandering primates.

But genetic drift erased the record in most humans. Only some still carried the unheeded cargo of instructions, handed down now for nearly seven billion years.

The Trigger Commands were cunningly concealed. No single strand of human DNA could repeat the full content of the trigger in each "expression," a single generation. Instead, through a cyclic programming, only a third of the activator code appeared in coherent order, in the DNA of a single member.

To get the trigger codes completely, you had to assemble three generations.

"Abraham, Killeen, Toby." Killeen whispered the words like a mantra as he marched, boots crunching the alkaline crust.

Andro's raspy voice drew him out of his thoughts. "Those they're after?"

"Yeasay. Me they've already copied."

"You think that Mantis was honest? It let us live, after all."

"Because it wanted something it could get from us alive."

"The other two."

"That can't be all of it," Killeen reflected. "Why let you go then?"

"That's what I'm trying to see."

"They don't know enough," Killeen said. "Something we don't know either."

Andro scowled at Killeen. "Or don't know we know."

"They don't get what it'll do to them if they read it." Killeen stopped short of saying, *That it'll blaze up like a grass fire, sweep right through them, burn the bastards—*

Technically, this is known as a "meme"—a self-propagating idea which rewards the holder and impels it to further the meme itself. Human religions are sometimes of this type, as in Islamic—

Killeen stuffed Arthur back in its hole. Andro said, "They *want* it, though."

"Yeasay. Want it bad." All the suffering and fear his kind had known for as long as they could remember came from mechs. In Killeen there now smoldered a fire that would never go out until he held the Trigger Commands in his hand and saw them at work.

Andro said, "I would have expected that after billions of years, there would be some self-defense mechanism in the mechs. Some safeguards to stop them from even being interested."

"I guess those wore away, too. Everything else does."

"So they tried to take your father as part of this?"

Killeen frowned. "I see what you mean. How come they didn't pick me and Toby up, too?"

"I suppose they didn't know that they needed three generations then."

Killeen nodded. "What was that term? The Way of Three."

"They suspected the data was in the DNA. But they found only a third of it."

"They have our Legacies, too." Killeen bitterly remembered how Toby had fought against letting the portal people read their Legacies. At the time it had seemed a good trade to Killeen—these were just people, after all, and the Bishops needed shelter in the portal.

Andro was getting weaker. He hobbled but his voice was still clear and strong. "They have the Replicator technology now. Damn! All they have to do is search the esty, find your son and father—"

"And maybe we should let them."

"They would all die."

Killeen chuckled. "And they figure since humans are their enemy, we want to stop them from getting all their precious pleasure." He leaned back and laughed loudly at the impassive sky. Until now the weight of it had not struck him. His enemies had been delivered into his hands. *They don't know it will destroy them.*

—and just as he had feared, the stillness and hovering presence of the Mantis descended around them like a massive fog.

"Damn!" It had been a trap all along, a chance to eavesdrop on the talky humans.

> You are quite convincing if one does not know how to unmask the nuances, Killeen.

"What?" He did not know what a nuance was but something in the Mantis's voice came freighted with threat.

> You verge on the blatant. Most unsubtle.

Killeen laughed again with relief. He could tell the truth here and it was going to be all right. "I haven't got the energy to be subtle."

> The Pleasure is indeed something your Phyla know, because you devised it. We have long suspected that it is the payment invented by the organic races, given to our primitive forms as a reward.

"I can't deny that," Killeen said. He could see how even a superior intelligence, on the track of something, could read into his and Andro's words a conspiracy, a grand plot. The Mantis was complimenting them without knowing it.

> You primordials are the masters of pleasure. Evolution brought it to you.

"Old Family Bishop saying, yeasay." Keep it light, see what it had gotten from its eavesdropping.

> I do not follow your reference.

"Old song, prob'ly Johnphilsousa." He belowed out,

"Malt does more than Milton can,
To justify God's ways to man—"

Andro got Killeen's intent, because he wrinkled his nose and commented sourly, "God, that's awful. Who's Milton?"

> Ancient Earthly poet. An artist like myself. Your source is in error, Killeen. However, I take your point. You primates in particular have a disproportionate fraction of your sensor nerves allocated to your genitalia and taste buds. Plainly you are pleasure machines. It is invigorating to know such forms as you.

"The pleasure is all mine," Killeen said. He had to get the Mantis to think that what it had overheard was all just talk, flights of fancy language.

> In us pleasure had to be injected—a mere compensation. You are the masters of the dark arts. That is the thing I have pursued in you more than any other. The ancient bliss.

Andro started to say something and Killeen lifted a finger to stop him. The Mantis's crisp aura shifted slightly at this small gesture. Killeen saw that again, by accident perhaps, he had heightened the air of mystery and conspiracy—as judged by the Mantis. Being smart was not the same as being sophisticated.

> You primates are typical of the older forms. Most of your nerve endings concentrate in the outer skin, so you remain largely unaware of what occurs within your own bodies. Plainly, a creature shaped for pleasures, not maintenance. And a disproportionate fraction of those lie in your genitalia or your taste buds. There is also the curious evolutionary convergence of the reproductive and excretion organs. No design would ever favor such doubling of functions; waste elimination must not interfere with the hygienic conditions one assumes necessary for biological reproduction. Evolution ignores the obvious and favors the sensual. That feature we lack and envy.

"It's led to a lot of humor, though," Killeen said. The Mantis never laughed, of course, but it was worth a try to keep it puzzled.

This issue touches, as you have guessed, on the less savory side of our Phylum.

"I had no idea."

Sarcasm, correct?

"Could be."

Jests are as informative as gestures.

"Some irony here, too."

Irony? You mislead again.

Killeen kept a cryptic silence. Let the mech talk itself in circles. It seemed to like that. The narrowness of sentences and all that stuff about serial and parallel, it tripped them up.

You Naturals have oddly exciting ways, though most are liabilities. We know from studies of Naturals like your species that we can best find your son and father by using you as a lure.

"Not much I can do about that."

Andro was breathing fast again. Hands clenched. The man could not contain his anger. Maybe he had never had much practice.

I have gotten from you the confirmation I needed. You will remain alive—that is, unharvested—until we see that we have no further need of you.

"You—" Andro screamed and threw himself at the Mantis. He had another small weapon concealed and tried to use it.

The Mantis did not move a single rod. Andro simply folded up.

Not the usual way, but backward. Killeen heard the spine pop and a gurgled gasp from crushed lungs. Andro bent completely over backward, still standing on two feet. His hair brushed the ground as his feet took a hesitant step, then another. His eyes were wild with pain. Andro's mouth shaped a scream but nothing came out.

> The Exalteds use me as their guide in these matters because I am the nearest to their level who still can communicate with you. The cramped, serial manner of your speech is painful to them—indeed, impossible. Do not think this gives you any privileged status. I thought a bit of illustration of this would suffice.

Killeen felt numb. Andro took another step and fell, breath wheezing from him. From the way the body sprawled Killeen knew there was no help for the man. "You surekill him?"

> There is no need. You Bishops are worthy of a collection. This sort, of which there is an infestation in this place, is of no concern to a curator.

"That's your only reason for doing . . . that?"

> No. He had exceeded his marginal utility.

"Let's hope these Exalted characters don't think you've exceeded yours."

> Should they, I would be happy to be gathered in.

Killeen snorted in fear and anger and emotions he could not name.

> For you, a reminder—

A shifting haze as white as steam condensed to his left.

Toby was walking steadily out of the solidifying mist. He was grinning. Smaller and thinner than Killeen remembered. Toby said something that got snatched away by a gathering wind and the tone was wrong and as Toby's jaws yawned the lines in his face broadened to jagged cracks.

Toby came apart. In precise zigzags. Each one gave a brittle pop as his son burst apart.

Decision Tree

If the Way of Three is correct, then we need only the genetic coding of these primates.

It would seem so.

How simple! We missed it for so long.

That is what worries me.

Why should it? They employ a particularly awkward method of self-reproduction. Much of their genetic code is useless baggage, carried along solely because it can copy itself, but conveying no worthwhile message. An ugly mess, dictated by their random evolution.

I/We suspect . . .

What?

That is what concerns me. I do not know what my misgivings mean, since they are so . . .

Tentative?

Yes. I deplore hesitation. Still, I sense danger. Undefined, but danger, definitely.

We have waited long enough to deal with these. We entertained endless discussion of art, aesthetics, and how beautiful in their way these primitive forms are. Very well, some have been recorded as we terminated them. Done!

You advocate the harsh method?

Of course. We need only the three generations of data. Very well, kill them all and let the Exalteds sort them out.

All? Everywhere?

I believe we can do it.

We could tear momentary openings in the Wedge, that I grant. To ransack the entire space-time geometry may not even be conceptually possible.

Such niceties I leave to the savants of geometry. We need not cleave all Lanes—only enough to discover the Three. A random sampling of the human-habited Lanes should suffice. Perhaps a hundred.

Some levels of All/We will be displeased at the erasure of so much potentially useful data.

*Once we have the Three and
can decode—that should be
trivial—the remaining data is
mere trash.*

There is the faction/submind
of us/you which holds that
both prudence and aesthetic
issues—

*Enough of this. Decision is
made.*

But truly, wait—

We/You are the majority.

I understand.

*All/You must remember to keep
to our/your proper station. Act!*

I must.

Part V

THE SILVER RIVER ROAD

From too much love of living,
From hope and fear set free,
We thank with brief thanksgiving
Whatever gods may be
That no life lives for ever;
That dead men rise up never;
That even the weariest river
Winds somewhere safe to sea.

—SWINBURNE
   "The Garden of Proserpine"

1

Molten Time

Toby continued down the silver river in search of his father.

He crouched in his skiff, swaying with the rippling currents, and watched his trawling line. He had not eaten for two days. His vegetarian principles had not held up well under perpetual pursuit and ravagements. A fat yellow fish shimmered far down in the filmy water but would not bite.

Curiosity overcame hunger and he leaned over to see if the fish was nosing about his line. Instead of plump prey he saw himself, mirrored far down in a tin-gray metal current. But his image wore the cane hat he had lost overboard yesterday. He stared down into the trapped time flow, which had kept pace with his skiff's downtime glide. Frowning, he studied his optimistic gaze of yesterday. A smudged forehead, sprigs of greasy hair jutting around his big ears, a determined set to the jaw that looked faintly absurd. He would have to learn to give less of himself away. Adults could do that without thinking.

He edged back from the lip of the shallow-bottomed skiff. He had fashioned the skiff from scrap metal in order to negotiate this strange river with its mixture of fluids, silky waters, and conducting metals, and he knew how rickety the shell was. The liquid metal current was rising through the skin of water. It could sink him with a casual brush. Danger dried his mouth, tightened his throat.

Down through murky water he had glimpsed a slow churn of ivory radiance. Mercury shaped the broad, mud-streaked course.

Treachery lurked in that metallic upwelling—oblong-shaped many-armers, electric vipers, fanged things that glided through the metal currents like broad-winged birds.

He lay still in the skiff bottom, hoping the time-dense flow would subside. A queasy temporal swell oozed through his gangly body. To distract himself from the nausea he gazed up at the great spreading forest that hung overhead.

Patches of bare timestone shimmered there, opulent with smoldering glows. The esty here was tubular, dominated by this shiny snake river that wound through bluffs and forests. Downriver, the yawning bore of his circumscribed cosmos faded into ivory mist. He could see a sizable city there beside a shimmering bend. Behind him, uptime, he could make out the immense curve of the esty and its rich hills until perspective warped and blurred them. He was tempted to thumb up his binoculars to see—

A thump against the skiff. Something heavy, moving.

He held his breath. Normally the skiff moved feather-light, responding to the rub and press of the air's very compression behind him as he voyaged down the silver river and thus accelerated through time.

Irregular patches of bare timestone crust overhead gave forth smatterings of prickly light. He wished for a moment of darkness to hide him. Volcanoes of iridescence erupted from the land on the opposite curve of esty-tube. Light splintered down and beat on him. He bore the sudden blast of heat without a sound.

You are acquitting yourself well

came the whispery words from Shibo. The fragments of herself had begun calling to him. The small voice was soothing and plaintive and he knew he had to resist it.

He concentrated on the sounds from below. He could not hear anything clearly because the timestone was splitting high above. It would not fall on him; local gravity was always down.

This is an awful place. You have survived nobly.

"Naysay. I kept my head down."

I could help you so much more if you would just give me functions I could use. You are lonely and need the—

Answering her was a mistake. She went on and on and he had to concentrate to push her down. She had tried before to mutiny, take control of himself, a traitor Personality. For that there was no forgiveness.

She fought him with tiny cries. He thought of another woman, of Besen, of making love to her, skin smooth and creamy. He longed to see Besen again. That helped. The memory of her swamped Shibo's wracked sobs.

Smooth skin . . . The face of the water was also smooth . . . and deceptive.

Everything here was dangerous. The exploding timestone came from monstrous collisions between unknown energies, distant flares of the Eater, vast meaningless violence beyond human ken. But the mechs were here, too, and he suspected everything now. He had seen them in the distance. They seemed at a disadvantage here in this moist tunnel-like Lane. Their wrecked bodies sometimes floated by him on the river. But they kept coming; they always had.

Something worried the water's surface.

He sat up and reached for his paddle and a skinny thing shot out of the water and snapped past his head. He ducked and slapped the tendril with his paddle. A knobby angular wedge with slitted yellow eyes heaved up from the wrinkled water. It smoked acrid green, out of its metal element, and struck at him again. He swung the paddle. It caught the tendril and sliced through.

The mercury-beast bleated and splashed and was gone. He dug into the water with the paddle—half its blade sheared cleanly off—and thrust hard. Splashing behind.

He labored into deeper water. The green fumes swirled away. When the currents calmed he veered toward shore. The big-jawed predator could snap him from the surface in an instant, crunch his skiff in two, if it could extend out of the low-running streams of silver-gray mercury and ruddy bromium. A turbulent swell had brought it up, and might again.

His arms burned and his breath rasped well before the prow ran aground. Hurriedly he splashed ashore, tugging a frayed rope. He got the skiff up onto a mud flat and into a copse and slid it far back to hide it among leafy branches.

Weakly he flopped down and fetched forth some stringy dried blue meat to quiet the rumble in his stomach. His systems were mostly dead now, crapped out in his long flight. Servos barely ran in his knees and arms. His weapons had discharged and the rest were unreliable. They were designed to bring down mechs anyway and useless for hunting. He had started eating meat when he got really hungry and was somewhat ashamed to admit that he liked it. Principle melted before the flame of necessity.

He peered at dense forest and patchy mud flats and decided to explore a little. The silent power of the river insulated a lonely skiff from the rhythms of land and made coasting downstream and downtime natural, silkily inevitable. He would learn nothing that way, though.

He walked upshore, into the silent press of time that felt at first like a mild summer's breeze but drained the energy of anyone who worked against it. As he went he eyed the profusion of stalks and trunks and tangled blue-green masses that crouched close to the river's edge like something waiting. It had been a long while since he had fled the destruction of the giant pyramid mountain and the Walmsley man from Family Brit. He had been happy to find this strange Lane with its silver river and to ease down it, following timelines that flowed nearer the black hole. He had learned some of the culture and had begun to like the soft humanity of it, its archaic charm.

No signs of people. He kept up a good pace and became distracted and so was unprepared. A short man with a duckbill blunderbuss stepped from behind a massive tree trunk and just grinned.

"What's the name?" the man asked, spitting first.

"Toby."

"Walking upriver?"

Better to skirt the question than to lie. "Looking for food."

"Find any?"

"Hardly had a chance to."

"Couldn'ta come far. Big storm just downstream from here." The man grinned broadly, showing brown teeth, lips thin and bloodless. "I saw it pull a man's arms off."

So he knew Toby couldn't have just strolled here from downstream. Toby said casually, "I walked down from the point, the one with the big old dead tree."

"I know that place. Plenty berries and footfruit there. Why come lookin' here?"

"I heard there's a big city this way."

"More like a town, kid. Me, I think you oughta stay out here in the wild with us."

"Who's 'us'?"

"Some fellas." The man's fixed grin soured at the edges.

"I got to be getting on, mister."

"This baby here says you got fresh business." He displayed the blunderbuss as though he had invented it.

"I got no money."

"Don't want or need money. Your kind, big and fresh, my friends will sure enjoy seeing you."

He gestured with the blunderbuss for Toby to walk. Toby saw no easy way to get around the big weapon so he strode off, the man following at a cautious distance.

The blunderbuss was in fact the ornate fruit of a tree Toby had once seen. The weapons grew as hard pods on the slick-barked trees and had to be sawed off when they swelled to maturity. This one had a flange that opened into a gnarled ball and then flared farther into the butt—all part of the living weapon. If stuck butt-down in rich soil, with water and daylight, it grew cartridges for the gun. From the size of the butt he guessed that this was a full-grown weapon and would carry plenty of shots.

He stumbled through a tangle of knife grasses, hearing the man snicker at his awkwardness, and then came to a pink clay path. Plainly this man planned to bring him to some kind of mean-spirited reception. Simple thieving, or a spot of buggery—these he had heard of and even witnessed. But the man's rapt, hot-eyed gaze spoke of more, some vice from the unknown swamp of adulthood.

What should he do? His mind churned fruitlessly.

Toby's breath rasped and quickened as he took his time on the steepening path. Like most footways, this one moved nearly straight away from the river, and thus a traveler suffered neither the chilly press of uptime nor the nauseating slide of downtime. Toby judged the path would probably rise into the dry-brown foothills ahead. Insects hung and buzzed in the stillness of slumberous, sliding moments. A few bit.

He thought furiously. They passed through a verdant, hummocky field and then up ahead around a sharp bend he saw, just a few steps beyond, a deep shiny iron-gray stream that gurgled down toward the river, and a dead muskbat that lay in the gummy clay path.

A muskbat never smells grand and this one, at least a day dead, filled the air with a sharp reek.

Toby gave no sign, just held his breath. The stream murmured beside him. Its weak time-churn unsteadied his step only a little. A fallen branch and windstorm debris lay just a bit beyond the muskbat's cracked and oozing blue-black skin.

He stepped straight over the muskbat and three steps more. As he turned the man breathed in the repulsive tang and his swarthy face contorted. The man drew back, foot in midair, and the blunderbuss wavered away.

Toby snatched up the branch. Without meaning to he sucked in the putrid fumes. He had to clench his throat tight to stop his stomach from betraying him. He leaped at the man. In midair he swung the branch, wood seeking wood, and felt a sharp jolt as he connected.

"Ah!" the man cried in pain. The blunderbuss sprang into the air and tumbled crazily into the stream—

—which dissolved the gun with a stinging hiss and explosive puff of fragrant orange steam. The man gaped at this, at Toby—and took a step back.

"Now you," Toby said because he could think of nothing else.

He got the words out at his lowest bass register. With a devouring metal rivulet nearby, any wrestling could bring disintegrating death in a flicker. Toby felt his knees turn to water, his heart jump into his throat.

The man fled. Scampered away with a little hoarse cry.

Toby blinked in surprise and then beat his own retreat, to escape the virulent muskbat fumes. He stopped at the edge of a viny tangle and looked back at the stream.

His chest filled with sudden pride. He had faced down a full-grown man. He!

Only later did he realize that the man was legitimately more frightened than Toby was—for he faced a wild-eyed stranger of some muscle, ungainly but armed with a fair-sized club. So the man had prudently escaped, his dirty shirt tail flapping like a harrying rebuke behind him.

2

Confusion Winds

Toby skirted away from the foothills, in case the swarthy man came back with his friends. He headed downstream, marching until sleep overcame him. By keeping a good long distance from the river he hoped to avoid the time-storm the man had mentioned—assuming it wasn't a lie.

The river was always within view from any fair-sized rise, since the land curved up toward the territories overhead. A sheen of clear water blended with the ruddy mud flats at this distance, so that Toby could barely pick out the dabs of silver and tin-gray that spoke of deadly undercurrents.

He had arisen and found some mealy brush fruit for breakfast and had set off again when he felt a prickling at the nape of his neck. A ripple passed by. It pinched his chest and stung his eyes. Hollow booms volleyed through the layered air.

He looked up. Across the misty expanse he could make out the far side of the esty. It was a clotted terrain of hills and slumped valleys, thick with a rainbow's wonder of plant life, dappled lakes, snaky streams—all tributaries to the one great river. As he watched the overhead arch compressed, like an accordion he had seen an old lady playing once—and then the squeezing struck him as well. Clutched his ribs, strained at his neck and ankles as though trying to pull him apart. Trees creaked, teetered, and one old black one crashed over nearby. He lay on moist, fragrant humus where he had fallen and watched the massive constriction inch its way downstream, a compression wave passing and then relaxing, like the digesting spasm of a great beast. Strata groaned, rocks shattered. A final peal like a giant's hammer rolled over the leafy canopy.

As he watched it proceed he saw through his binoculars for the first time the spires of the city, and saw one tumble in a glimmering instant as the great wave passed. Somehow he had thought of cities—or *towns*, as the man had said, a word strange to Toby—as grand places free of the rub of raw nature, invulnerable.

He moved on quickly. A purple radiance played amidst the ripe forest, shed by a big patch of raw fresh timestone beside a shiny lake, far away. Thoughts of the city possessed him, ideas of how to track his father, so he forgot the time-storm.

At first he felt a wrenching in the pit of his stomach. Then the humid air warped, perverting perspectives, and confusion rode the winds.

His feet refused to land where he directed them unless he kept constant attention, his narrowed eyes holding the errant limbs continually in view. Cordwood-heavy, his arms gained and lost weight as they swung. To turn his head without planning first was to risk a fall. He labored on, panting. Hours oozed past. He ate, napped, kept on. The air sucked strength from muscles and sent itchy traceries playing on his skin.

The whispering tendrils of stupefaction left him as he angled toward the city. He sagged with fatigue. Three spires remained ahead, whitewash-bright, the most palatial place he had ever seen. Houses of pale polished wood were lined up neat and sure beside rock-roads laid arrow-straight with even the slate slabs cut square and true.

These streets thronged with more people than Toby could count. Ladies in finery stepping gingerly over horse dung, coarse frolickers lurching against walls, tradesmen elephantine and jolly, foul-witted quarrelers, prodigious braggarts, red-faced hawkers of everything from sweets to saws. All swarming like busybody insects and abuzz with talk.

To Toby it was like trying to take a drink from a waterfall. He wandered the gridded streets, acutely conscious of his ragged clothes and slouch hat. Baggy trousers covered his field gear. He drew some odd looks.

This whole Lane seemed devoted to the comforts of some human past he could not quite fathom. His Isaac Aspect broke in,

This is a deliberate echo of an ancient human culture. I cannot place it, but obviously it is pre-Chandelier. Their technology is mannered and cherished for that fact. To-

gether with the river, it seems a sort of refuge for some.
I hypothesize—

"I'd appreciate advice on how to get out of this Lane plenty more than your theorizing." Toby had assigned Isaac the task of searching all files in his Aspect-space, and he had hoped for more than this.

It lies quite within the realm of human sociology to manifest nostalgia on such a scale. This Lane seems to run on varying time senses because of extreme esty gradients, and the human reaction has been to cling to constancy. Understandable and—

"Quiet." He stuffed the Aspect back in its hole and sought the one thing he knew, the river.

Along the big stone quay men loafed in the rising, insect-thronged heat. They slouched in split-bottomed chairs tilted back to the point of seeming dynamical impossibility, chins on chests, hats tipped down over drowsy eyes. A six-legged sow and her brood grunted by, doing a good business in droppings from split crates.

Beyond this slow scene lay the river, lit by the fitful radiance of three overhead timestone patches. Toby took off his pack and sat on a wharf railing and looked at the river's ceaseless undulation, broken by shards of raw silver that broke the surface, fumed, and were gone.

"Lookin' for work?"

The voice was rough. It belonged to a young man somewhat older than Toby and short, like everyone here. Broad shoulders burst his crosshatched shirt. But the eyes were dreamy, warm.

"Might be." He would need money here.

"Got some unloadin' to do. Never 'nuff hands." The young man held out a broad palm. They shook. "Name's Stan."

"Mine's Toby. Heavy stuff?"

"Moderate. We got droners to help."

Stan jabbed a thumb at a line of five slumped figures seated along the jetty. Toby had seen these before, only upriver they were called Zoms. They all sat the same way, legs sprawled out in front, arms slack, weight on the lower spine at a steep angle. No man could sit in that manner for long. Zoms didn't seem to mind. Just about anything seemed better than being dead.

"You new?" Stan asked, squatting down beside Toby and scribbling something on a clipboard with a pencil stub.

"Just came in."

"Raft?"

"Skiff. Landed up above that storm."

Stan whistled. "And walked around? Long way. That ripple knock you flat?"

"Tried to."

"Be a lotta trouble to get back to your skiff."

"I might just push on down."

"Really?" Stan brightened. "How far you come?"

"I don't know."

"Angel's Point? Rockport?"

"I heard of them. Saw Alberts but it was foggy."

"You're from *above* Rockport? And just a kid?"

"I'm older than I look," Toby said stiffly.

"You *do* have a funny accent."

Toby gritted his teeth. "So do you, to my ear."

"I thought, comin' this far downtime, you'd get sick, go crazy, or something." Stan seemed truly impressed, his eyes wide.

"I didn't just shoot down." It would be dumb to get into his past. People along the river didn't care very much for outsiders. "I stopped some to . . . explore."

"For what?"

Toby shifted uneasily. He shouldn't have said anything. The less people knew about you, the less they could use. "Treasure."

"Like hydrogen? Big market for hydrogen chunks here."

"No, more like—" Toby struggled to think of something that made sense. "Jewels. Ancient rubies and all."

"No foolin'? I've never seen any."

"They're rare. Left over from the olden lords and ladies."

Stan opened his mouth and stuck his tongue up into his front teeth in an expression of intense thought. "Uh . . . Who were *they*?"

"Primeval people. Ones from *waaay* uptime. They were so rich then, cause there were so few of them, that the sapphires and gold just dripped off their wrists and necks."

Wide-eyed now. "Earnest?"

"They had so much, it was like the dust in the road to them. Sometimes when they got bored, the ladies'd snatch up a whole gob of jewels, their very finest, all glittery and ripe, and they'd stick them all over some of those big hats they wore. Come a flood, people would drown and those jewel-fat hats would come downtime."

"Hats?" Open-mouthed wonder.

An airy wave of his hand. "Not the slouch hats we wear down here. I'm talkin' big boomer hats, made of, well, hydrogen itself."

"Hydro—" Stan stopped, a look of puzzlement washing across his face, and Toby saw that he had to cover that one.

"See, those prehistoric days, hydrogen was even lighter than it is today. So they wore it. The very finest of people weaved it into fancy vests and collars and hats."

A doubtful scowl. "I never saw anybody . . ."

"Well, see now, that's just the thing. My point exactly. Those olden ladies and officers, they wore out all the hydrogen. That's why it's worth so much today."

Stan's mouth made an awestruck *O*. "That's wondrous, plain wondrous. I mean, I knew hydrogen was the lightest metal. Strongest, too. No puzzlement it's what every big contractor and engine-builder wants, only can't get. But—" he looked sharply at Toby—"how come you know?"

"How come a kid knows?" Might as well feed him back that remark. "Because uptime, we're closer to the archaic ages. We look out for those hydrogen hats that came down the river and wash up."

Stan frowned. "Then why'd you come down here?"

For an instant Toby had the sick feeling that he was caught out. The whole story was going to blow up on him. He would lose this job and go hungry.

Then he blinked and said, "Uptime people already *got* the hats that came ashore there. It's the ones that got past them that I'm after."

"Aaahhh . . ." Stan liked this and at once began to shoot out questions about the grand hats and treasure hunting, how Toby did it, what he'd found, and so on. It was a relief when somebody called, "Induction ship!" and the sleepy quay came to life.

3

The Zom

The big white ship seemed to Toby to snap into existence, bright and trim and sharp as it bore down upon them. It cut the river, curling water like a foamy shield, sending gobbets of iron-gray liquid metal spraying before it.

It was a three-decker with gingerbread railings and a pyramid-shaped pilothouse perched atop. Large, thick disks dominated each side, humming loudly as it decelerated. Only these induction disks, which had to cast their field lines deep into the river and thrust the great boat forward, were untouched by the eternal habit of ornamentation. Curlicues trickled down each stanchion. Pillars had to be crowned with ancient scrollwork, the fly bridge carried sculptures of succoring angels, davits and booms and mastheads wore stubby golden helmets.

Passengers lined the ornate railings as the boat slowed, foam leaped in the air, and backwash splashed about the stone quay. A whistle sounded eerily and deck hands threw across thick ropes.

Stan caught one and looped it expertly about a stay. "Come on!"

Crowds had coagulated from somewhere, seeming to condense out of the humidity onto the jetty and quay. A hubbub engulfed the induction ship. Crates and bales descended on crane cables. Wagons rumbled forth to take them and Toby found himself in a gang of Zoms, tugging and wrestling the bulky masses. Crowds yawped and hailed and bargained with vortex energy all around.

The Zoms followed Stan's orders sluggishly, their mouths

popping open as they strained, drool running down onto their chests. These were corpses kindled back to life quite recently, and so still strong, though growing listless. Zoms were mostly men, since they were harvested for heavy manual labor. But a hefty woman labored next to Toby and between loads she put her hand on his leg, directly and simply, and then slipped her fingers around to cup his balls.

Toby jerked away, her reek biting in his nostrils. He slapped her hard. Zoms hungered for life. They knew that they would wither, dwindling into torpid befuddlement, within months. The heavy woman shook her head, then leered at him and felt his ass. He backed away from her, shivering.

And bumped into a shabby Zom man who turned sluggishly and mumbled, "Toby. Toby."

Stunned, he peered into the filmed eyes and slack mouth. Parchment skin stretched over stark promontories of the wrecked face. Memories stirred. Some faint echo in the cheekbones? The sharp nose?

"Toby . . . I am . . . father . . ."

"No!" Toby cried.

"Toby . . . came here . . . time . . ."

The Zom reached unsteadily for his shoulder. It was in the tottering last stages of its second life, the black mysteries' energy now seeping from it.

"You're not my father! Get away."

The Zom gaped, blinked, reached again.

"No!" Toby pushed the Zom hard and it went down. It made no attempt to catch itself and landed in a sprawl of limbs. It lay inert, its eyes filmed.

"Hey, it botherin' you?" Stan asked.

"Just, they just get to me, is all."

"These're made in Resurrection City, I heard."

"Where's that?"

" 'Nother Lane entire. They knock off copies from raw stock."

"From dead people?"

"Don't have to be. Got a mind-copy, just fast-grow a template, marry them up—zingo, you got cheap labor galore."

Toby studied the slack-jawed face and resolved that this Zom could not possibly be his father. The false Abraham had fooled him for a moment but not this thing, no. There was really no resemblance at all, now that he took a close and objective scrutiny.

"Let it lay there," Stan said dismissively. "We got work to do."

It was so far gone Toby could not tell if this was some copy from the Restorer, which he supposed was what Stan meant by

Resurrection City, or in fact the true Killeen, somehow aged in the esty.

So he put the matter out of his mind. He would treat this Zom as a copy, like that one of his grandfather back in the field hospital. He decided this and thought of it no more. It did not occur to him that he could not have done this only a few years before.

The rest of the unloading Toby helped carry out without once looking toward the crumpled form. Ladies stepped gingerly over the Zom and a passing man kicked it, all without provoking reaction.

Sweat was trickling into his eyebrows and so he did not see the mechs at first. "Heyso!" someone called. Toby looked up—

—into an onrushing sleek snout. Two others followed. They banked in the soft air and their shock wave slammed down onto the docks. People ran all whichways but Toby stood still, watching the silvery craft climb up the air. They pitched and yawed to no apparent purpose, angling out over the shore.

"Looking," Stan said. "Been here before."

"These same ones?" Toby asked.

"Smaller last time."

The craft banked and glided now, slower and more careful as they prowled over the town. Toby still did not move. Mechs could pick up servos working. Stan gave him a puzzled look and cautiously got down behind some bales of sticky-grass.

They were coming back. Calls trilled in his receptors. "Bishops!" he whispered. He could pick out Cermo, Jocelyn, others. So the mechs had gotten the Family codes. He killed his inboards, in case some vagrant signal might get out in response.

They came right overhead. The moment passed with agonizing slowness and for a crazy instant he thought they must have stopped dead high above him. Then they were out over the river and he could start breathing again.

Just as he did, somebody shot at the mechs. It was a reasonably sophisticated weapon, Toby could tell, because it left virtually no detectable backtrail. Probably it used some sliver of the electromagnetic spectrum that Bishops could not sense.

The mechs could. The shot came from somewhere downstream and they rushed that way. It had done them no harm that Toby could see. They fired once, all three together. Someone screamed. The mechs moved off and the screaming stopped. Whoever had died had been foolish. Toby had not for a moment considered trying to help them against mechs of such a caliber. That he had learned as a boy.

"They did that 'fore, too," Stan said. He stood up from behind the bale and tried to make out as if he had not been there.

"Get anybody?"

"Not that I heard."

"Which way did they go then?"

"Just like these—" Stan pointed as the three leveled out and accelerated. "Downtime."

"Always?"

"Certain. After somebody, I 'spect."

And trying to sucker Bishops in, too, Toby thought. Maybe him. Or maybe it meant there were Bishops about.

They went downriver. Maybe that meant he should not.

After the mechs were out of sight everyone went on as though nothing had happened. The labor was fast and hard, for the induction ship was already taking on its passengers. Crowds, packages, happy confusion. By the time Toby returned from a nearby warehouse where the first wagonload went, only ripples in the mud-streaked river showed that the ship had tarried there at all.

4

Mr. Preston

That day was long and hard, what with plenty of barrels and hogsheads and wooden crates to unlash and sort out and stack in the crumbling stone warehouse. Stan was a subagent for one of the big importation enterprises and had a steady run of jobs, so Toby was kept busy the rest of the day.

They had little tech here and relied on grunt labor. The Zoms from the quay wore out quickly and Stan brought out another crew of them. Toby did not see the one that had collapsed and did not go looking for it in the musty rear of the warehouse where they were kept, either.

The laboring time ended as the big bare patch of timestone overhead dimmed. This was a lucky occurrence, as people still preferred to sleep in darkness. Though there was no cycle of day and night here, a few hours of shadow were enough to set most into the slumber they needed. Toby had once seen a night that lasted several "days" so that folks began to openly speculate whether the illumination would ever return to the timestone. When the sulphurous glow did come it waxed into stifling heat and piercing glare so ferocious that everyone regretted their earlier impatience for it.

Stan took Toby to his own boarding house and arranged for him, leaving just enough time for a bath of cold river water before supper. Toby was amazed at the boarding table to see the rapid-fire putting away of victuals combined with fast talking, as though mouths were meant to chew and blab at the same time. Game hens roasted to golden brown appeared on an immense platter and were seized and devoured before they reached him, though Stan somehow managed to get two and shared. A skinny man with a goatee opposite Toby cared only for the amusements of his mouth, alternately chewing, joking, and spitting none too accurately into a brass spittoon set beside him. Stan ate only with his knife, nonchalantly inserting the blade sometimes all the way into his mouth. Toby managed to get forkfuls of gummy beans and thick slabs of gamy meat into himself before dessert came flying by, a concoction featuring an island of hard nuts in a sea of cream that burst into flame when a man touched his cigar to it. Stan ate some and then contentedly sat back in his wicker chair, picking his teeth with a shiny pocket knife, an exhibition of casual bravery unparalleled in Toby's experience.

Afterward Toby wanted more than anything to sleep, but Stan enticed him into the hubbub of the streets. They ended up in a bar dominated for a time by an immense, well-lubricated woman whose tongue worked well in its socket, her eyes rolling as she sang a ballad Toby could not fathom. At the end of it she fell with a crash to the floor and it took three men to carry her out. Toby could not decide whether this was part of the act or not, for it was more entertaining than the singing.

Stan thrust some dark beer upon him and artfully took that moment to pay Toby his day's wages, which of course made Toby seem a piker if he did not buy the next round, which came with unaccountable speed. He was halfway through that mug and thinking better of this evening, of this huge complex city, of his fine new friend Stan, and generally of the entire copious wonderful esty itself, when he recalled how his own father had drunk heavily years before. He remembered Killeen remarking at the time that in Family Bishop, you discarded a cork once you had pulled it from a bottle, knowing with assurance that it would not be needed again.

This connection troubled him, but Stan relieved Toby's frown by stretching his legs out and sticking a sock-clad foot up. The sock had a face sewed on it so that Stan could jiggle his toes and make the face show anger, smile, even blink. All the while Stan carried on a funny conversation with the artistic foot. But this made Toby remember a day after the Calamity, cold and bleak, when Bishops were camping overnight with some stragglers from other Families. A tall Knight boy had stuck his gray-socked foot from beneath some covers as a joke. Toby mistook it for a rat and threw his knife, skewering the foot. That had made him unpopular for some time around Family Knight.

He smiled at this and had another sip of beer. Stan's face went pale. Toby felt a presence behind him.

Turning, he saw a tall man dressed in leather jacket and black pants, sporting a jaunty blue cap. No one but pilots could wear such a cap with its gold flashings across the bill.

"Mr.—Mr. Preston," Stan said.

"You gentlemen out for an evening? Not too busy to discuss business?"

Mr. Preston smiled with an austere good nature, as befitted a representative of an unfettered and truly independent profession. His Aspects had laboriously taught him that lords found themselves hampered by parliaments, ministers knew the constraints of their parishioners, even school teachers in their awful power finally worked for towns.

But a silver river pilot knew *no* governance. A ship's captain could give a half dozen or so orders as the induction motors readied and she backed sluggishly into the stream, but as soon as the engines engaged, the captain's rule was overthrown. The pilot could then run the vessel exactly as he pleased, barking orders without consultation and beyond criticism by mere mortals.

Without asking, Mr. Preston yanked a chair from another of the raw hardwood tables that packed the bar, and smacked it down at the table. "I heard you come from uptime—*way* uptime," he said to Toby.

"Uh, Stan told you?" Toby asked to get some time to think.

"He dropped a word, yes. Was he wrong?" Mr. Preston peered at Toby intently, his broad mouth tilted at an assessing angle beneath a bristly brown mustache.

"Nossir. Maybe he, uh, exaggerated, though."

"Said you'd been above Rockport."

"I caught sight of it in fog. That awful pearly kind that—"

"How far beyond?"

"Not much."

"Cairo?"

"I . . . yeah, I gave it wide berth."

"Describe it."

"Big place, grander than this town."

"You see the point? With the sand reef?"

"I didn't see any reef."

"Fair enough—there isn't any reef. What's the two-horned point like?"

"Foam whipping up in the air."

"Where's the foam go?"

"Shoots out of the river and arcs across to the other horn."

"You go under the arc?"

"Nossir. I stayed in the easy water close on the other shore."

"Smart. That arc's been there since I was a boy and nobody's lived who tried to shoot with the current under it."

"I heard that too."

"Who from?"

"Fellow upstream."

"How far upstream?"

Nobody ever lied to a pilot, but you could shave the truth some. Toby took a sip of the dark beer that was thick enough to make a second supper—as some in the bar seemed to be doing, loudly—and said with care, "The reach above Cairo. That's where I started."

Mr. Preston leaned forward and jutted out his long jaw shrewdly. "There's a big bar there, got to go by it easy. Sand, isn't it?"

"Nossir, it's black iron."

Mr. Preston sat back and signaled the barkeep—who had been hovering, wringing a dirty rag—for a round. "Right. A plug of it that gushed up from some terrible event in the river bottom. Books say a geyser of molten metal—not the cool ones that flow under the river—that geyser came fuming up through the timestone itself."

"I've been in other parts of the esty and I haven't seen anything like this river. It doesn't seem logical."

"Not for us to know, son."

"Please don't call me son, sir."

Mr. Preston's bushy eyebrows crowded together, momentarily puzzled at the quick, hard note that had come into Toby's voice, but then he waved his hand amply. "Surely done, Mr. Toby. I must say there is something about you that is wise beyond your apparent years. I am prepared to hire your services."

Stan was looking bug-eyed at this interchange. For two lowly freight musclers to be drinking with a pilot was like a damp river rat going to dinner at the mayor's. And this latest development!

"Services?" Stan put in, unable to restrain himself any longer.

"Navigation. There've been five big time-squalls between here and Cairo since I was up that way. Now I got a commission to take the *Natchez* up that far and no sure way of knowing the river that far."

"I'm not sure I know the river all that well," Toby demurred, his mind still aswarm with scattershot thoughts.

"You see any of those storms?"

"Two of them, yessir. From a distance, though."

"Only way to see one, I'd say," Stan said with forced jocularity. He was still stunned from the offer.

The pilot grimaced in agreement, an expression that told much of narrow escapes and lost friends. "You kept your skiff well clear?"

"I poled and rowed, both. Prob'ly just lucky with the currents, truth to tell."

"A time-storm attracts ships according to their mass, see? Your rowing was most likely the cause of your salvation," the pilot said. "An induction ship, despite its power, must be more crafty. Its weight is its doom."

Toby sipped his strong beer and said, "I don't know as I want to go back up there, sir."

"I'll make it worth your while." The pilot squinted at him, as though trying to see something in Toby's face that he wasn't giving away. "I was hoping you might have business back up there."

Might have business. At once the Zom's face lurched into Toby's mind's-eye and he felt the barroom close about him, its suffocating air clotted with cigar smoke. The banks of blue fumes swirled amid the seeping yellow glow of filament bulbs that sprouted from the walls, each the size of a man's head with his hat on. Toby had kept his mind away from the memory until now but the weight of uncertainty again descended. He could not know if the Zom was his father unless he found it again, questioned it.

"Sir, I'm going to have to give you my reply tomorrow. I have to see to a certain matter right now."

The surprise in Stan's and Mr. Preston's faces was almost amusing. It increased when Toby stood, bootheels smacking the floorboards loudly from the drink he had put down. He nodded solemnly and without a word plunged into the darkness outside.

5

The Frozen Girl

Inky shapes still shifted in his mind as he knocked on the door of Mr. Preston's house. Toby still felt himself encased in tangled memories, the hate he felt toward the Zom because he did not want it to be the Killeen he had known.

It was a fitful morning, with gray light piercing a fog and sending traceries across the rooftops along the slumbering river. Mechs and their virulence seemed infinitely far away. People here did not even talk about them. They were cloaked in this cozy, snug corner of the esty and would hear not a word of events beyond. Toby wondered if such people were typical of humanity. If so, what were the Bishops?

He could barely see the white picket fence framing Mr. Preston's yard. The pearly wisps blotted out detail beyond the brick walk that led to the house. This was a grand place, he had to admit, even in such diffuse light. It was porticoed in pale pine, the massive columns topped with flowery capitals. He rapped the iron door knocker again and instantly the brass doorknob turned, as if attached to the knocker. A dwarf answered, a mute servant, and led Toby along a carpeted hall.

He was unprepared for the grandiosity of a pilot's lodging, taking in with awe the mahogany furniture, a new electric lamp with yellow-paper shade, and an entire shelf of sound-sculptures. The dwarf retreated, gesturing at a yawning, tongueless mouth and showing the red servant tattoo on his shoulder to explain his silence.

A bounty of travel visions speckled the walls—*Above the*

*Falls of Abraham, Volcanic Quest, Heart of Lightness, Struggle
Against Destiny*—and many of literature, including the fanciful.
Toby yearned to take the sheets and stroke them into luminosity,
but as he reached for *Time Steam and World-Wrack* he heard heavy
thumping footsteps and turned to find the pilot in full blue and gold
uniform.

"I hope you have settled your other matter," Mr. Preston said
severely.

Only now did Toby recall clearly his abrupt departure from the
table. The town beyond that raucous room had swallowed memory.
He had made his way through narrow streets lined by rude buildings
that seemed to lean out over the street, eclipsing the wan sky glow.
The moist lanes near the river had been tangled and impossible to
navigate without stumbling and stepping on sprawled forms, like
bundles of clothing left for trash collection.

The masters of the Zoms left them where they lay, sure that
they could not move without further feeding. Toby took hours to
find the slack-jawed face he had seen on the quay, and then another
long time peering at it before he was sure that the Zom was not
merely in its lapsed state of rest. The thing had proved dead, limbs
akimbo, stiffening into a hardened parody of a dance.

At morning the burly owner had come by, shrugged at the
corpse, and thrown it into his wagon for disposal. Toby's questions
about the Zom the big man brushed aside—he didn't know the
names, no, nor where they came from, nor from what part of the
great river they hailed. Resurrection City? Only a rumor.

And the last glimpse Toby had of that face had unsettled him
further, as if in final death the Zom gave its last secret. There was
a clear resemblance to his father. But was this a copy?

So with fatigue in his bones but a fresh, iron resolve in his spine
Toby made himself stand erect beside the oak mantelpiece and say
to Mr. Preston, "I'll come, sir."

"Damn good! Want to see the backtime, do you?"

"Yeasay."

"Whuzzat?"

"Uh, yes." The word still felt odd. See the backtime,
yeasay—and go opposite to the mechs.

"Here, you had breakfast?"

Cornmeal flapjacks and fritters, brought by the mistress of the
house, quickly dominated Toby's attention while the pilot regaled
him with lore and stories. Toby managed to keep the details of his
long voyage downriver well-muddied, and was distracted from this
task by Mr. Preston's collection of oddments, arrayed along the

walls. There were crystals, odd-colored stones betraying volcanic abuse, a circlet of ancestral hair, five flint arrowheads from the fabled days, and some works of handicraft like dozens Toby had seen before. Beside these were bronze-framed, stiff 3D's of addled-looking children, aged uncles and the like, all arranged awkwardly and in Sunday-suited best for their bout with immortality.

But these oddments were nothing compared with the large transparent cube that dominated the dining room table. It shed cold air and Toby took it to be ice, but as he ate he saw that no drops ran off the sleek flat sides. Within its blue-white glow small objects of art were suspended—a golden filigree, a jagged bit of quartz, two large insects with bristly feelers, and a miniature statue of a lovely young girl with red hair and a flowing white robe.

He had nearly finished inhaling the molasses-fattened flap-jacks and slurping down a pot of coffee when he chanced to notice that one of the insect wings had lowered. Keeping an attentive ear to the pilot, who had launched into what appeared to be a four-volume oral autobiography in first draft, he watched carefully and saw the girl spinning slowly about her right toe. Her robe fetched up against her left leg and then gracefully played out into a spinning disk of velvety delicacy.

By this time the insects had both flapped their transparent gos-samer wings nearly through a quarter-stroke. They were both head-ing toward the girl. Their multifaceted eyes strobed and fidgeted with what to them must be an excited vigor, and to Toby was a torpid, ominous arabesque.

"Ah, the hunt," the pilot interrupted his soliloquy. "Beautiful, eh? I've been watching it for long enough to grow three beards."

"The girl, she's *alive*."

"Appears so. Though why she's so small, I cannot say."

"Where'd you get it?"

"Far downstream."

"I never saw such."

"Nor I. Indeed, I suspect, from the quality of the workmanship, that the girl is real."

"Real? But she's no bigger than my thumbnail."

"Some trick of the light makes her seem so to us, I reckon."

"And these bugs—"

"They're nearly her size, true. Maybe they're enlarged, the opposite of the trick with the girl."

"And if they aren't?"

"Then when they reach the girl they will have a merry time."

The pilot grinned. "A week's pay packet, I just handed it over flat, to purchase this. That li'l golden trinket, it's revolving, too—see?"

She spun farther and he saw that it was Besen. His Besen.

Somewhere she had been trapped. Copied? Or could this somehow be the true Besen?

He tapped on the side but she showed no reaction.

He remembered once aboard *Argo* when they had cleaned out a filthy shower together, doing ship's maintenance. Besen had unscrewed the drain and pulled out a hair ball the size of a well-fed rat. It was lustrous and gummy and so amazing when she held it up, a hairy moon beside her beaming, incredulous planet of a face, that he had laughed.

He felt a fresh wave of bitterly cold air waft from the cube of silent, slow time. "Somethin' wrong, boy?"

He had an urge to smash the blue-white wedge of molasses-slow tempo, to release its wrenched epochs and imprisoning, collapsed perspectives. But this was the pilot's object, and such men understood the twists of time better than anyone. Perhaps it was right that these things belonged to them.

Best to put it aside. He would not know what to do with the trapped Besen if he did get it. Still, he felt relief when he escaped from the dining room and emerged into the cloaking fog outdoors.

6

Going Upback

They were to boom out of the dock that very day. Toby had never known such awe as that instilled by his first moment, when he marched up the gangplank and set foot upon the already thrumming deck.

Never before had he done more than gaze in reverence and abject self-abasement at one of the induction ships as it parted the river with its razor-sharp prow. Now Mr. Preston greeted him with a curt nod, quite circumspect compared to the sprawl of the man's conversation at breakfast. With minor ceremony he received his employment papers. Other crew shook Toby's hand with something better than the cool indifference he knew they gave any and all passengers. The customers who paid the costs were of course held in the lowest regard of all those aboard, including the wipe-boys below. Toby could tell from the somewhat distant, glassy gazes of the men and women of the crew that he was at least considered in the human family, pending.

"You been by that li'l flurry up ahead?" Mr. Preston asked him as they made their way up the three flights of external stairs to the pilot's nest.

"Nossir. I came ashore, stowed my skiff, and walked round it."

"Ummm. Too bad. Think I'll nudge out across stream, keep some distance on it."

"Yessir."

To Toby this exotic Lane was a continual wonder. He began to see how people could want it this way, a pocket set aside from the mechs and all that weight of history. That they were re-creating some ancient manner long past did not matter; here, now, it was real.

The loading was finishing up, the ship's barely restrained thirst for the river sending a strong strumming into the air. Freight spun off the wagons and flew aboard at the hands of jostling work gangs, mostly Zoms. Late passengers came dodging and scampering among the boxes and hogsheads awaiting loading. Wives carrying hat boxes and grocery knapsacks urged on sweaty husbands, who lugged carpet bags and yowling babies. Drays and baggage three-wheelers clattered over cobblestones and intersected each others' trajectories more often than seemed possible from the supposed laws of probability, sending cases and jars smashing. Profanity blued the air. Windlasses snapped into hatches, fore and aft.

Toby loved the turmoil and racket, the whiz and whir of earnest purpose. The bursar called, "All not goin', please to get themselfs ashore!" and last bells rang, and the thronged decks of the *Natchez* gushed their yammering burden onto the gangplanks—a running tide that a few last, late passengers fought. The stage-plank slid in and a tall man came running and tried to jump the distance. He got a purchase on the gunmetal side and a crewwoman hauled him up, but his back pocket opened and his wallet thunked into the river. The crowd ashore laughed and a woman had to stop the man from jumping in after it.

All this Toby watched from the elevated sanctity of the pilot's nest. It was an elegant place, glass in so many directions he had to count to be sure there were only four of the transparent walls. The Cap'n stood beside the pilot, both arrayed in their dark blue-gold uniforms, and an eerie whistle sounded. The orange flag ran up the jack staff and the ship ceased its drift. Momentum surged through the deck and oily smoke belched from the three tall chimneys at the ship's midships.

The crowd along the quay called last-minute messages and cheered and the ship shot away from them, seeming to accelerate as it caught with induction fields the deep surge of metal beneath the waters. The town dwindled with bewildering speed, people on the quay turning into animated dolls that turned pinkish and mottled as Toby watched.

"The time flux," Mr. Preston answered Toby's frown. "I locked us on to her right off. We're seeing their images squeezed and warped."

Already the shore was dappled with reds and blues as time shifted and streamed about the ship, the slap and heave of currents resounding in deep bass notes that Toby felt through his big-heeled boots.

To fly across duration itself, to wrench away from the certainty of patient, single-minded time—Toby felt sour nausea grip his throat. Confusion swamped him, gut-deep accelerations—a quickening not in mere velocity but in the quantity that he knew governed the esty but which no man could sense, the force of tangled space and time together. The firm deck went snake-slithery, thick air hummed, sparks forked about him. His body fought for long, aching moments the urgent tows and tugs, his chest tight, bowels watery, knees feather-light—and then somehow his sinews found their equilibrium, without his conscious effort. He gulped in air and found it moist and savory.

"Steady." Mr. Preston had been eyeing him, he now saw. "I reckoned you'd come through, but can't be sure till it's done."

"What if I hadn't?"

The pilot shrugged. "Put you ashore next stop, nothing else for it."

"What about passengers?"

"It's easier down below. Up here, the tides are worse."

"Tides?" He studied the river's table-flat expanse.

"Not river tides—time tides. Passengers with addled heads and stomachs can just lie down till we reach their getoff point. Most, anyway."

Toby had always figured that the job of a pilot was to keep his ship on the river, which was not a considerable feat, since it was so wide. Silently watching Mr. Preston trim and slip among the upwellings of rich brown mud, and then slide with liquid grace along a burnt-golden reef of bromium metal, he saw the dancer's nimbleness and ease that came from the whirling oak-spoked master wheel, the orchestrated animal mutter of the induction motors, the geometric craft of rudder and prow. To have this elegant gavotte interrupted was not merely an inconvenience, and dangerous, but an aesthetic atrocity.

This Toby learned when a trading scow came rushing down the washboard-rough main current and into the *Natchez*'s path. Rather than perturb his elegant course, Mr. Preston ran across the scow's two aft steering oars. Scarcely had the snapping and crunching ceased than a volley of gnarled profanity wafted up from the clutch of red faces shooting by to starboard. Mr. Preston's face lit up with a positive joy, for here were fit targets who could, unlike the *Natchez*'s crew, *talk back*.

Joy of joys! He snatched open the roller window and stuck his head out and erupted back at the scow. And as the two ships separated and the scowmen's maledictions grew fainter, Mr. Preston poured on both volume and ferocity, calling upon gods and acts

Toby had never heard of. When Mr. Preston rolled the window shut on its spool the pilot was emptied of malice, all tensions of the departure now well fled.

"My, sir, that was a good one," a voice said at Toby's elbow. It was Stan, beaming with appreciation of the pungent profanity.

Not an opportune appearance. Mr. Preston skewered him with a glare. "Deckhands with opinions? Nose to the planking, you!"

So it was hours before Toby learned why Stan was on the *Natchez* at all, for Stan spent his time manicuring the already immaculate-looking pilot's nest and then the iron stairs and pine gangways nearby. When Toby found him slurping a steaming cup of blackbean in the rear galley, Stan waxed eloquent.

"*Treasure,* that's why I signed on. Deckhand pays next to nothin' and the time-current made me sick a sec or two, but I'm going to stick it out."

"Uh, treasure?"

"I'm already looking for those hydrogen hats. Nobody never spied any this far downstream, so I figure you overshot, Toby, coming as far down as us. They got to be above us, for sure."

Toby nodded and listened to Stan gush about the star sapphires and fat rubies awaiting them and barely avoided laughing and giving it all away. On the other hand, it had brought him a friend in a place he found daunting.

"Too bad you had to give up your quest, though," Stan said slyly.

"What?" Toby was using a bowl of bluebeans to keep his mouth busy and was brought up short by this odd remark.

"You overshot another way. That Zom was who you wanted to find. Only you wanted the man in his first life, and that lies upstream."

How Stan could swallow whole the hydrogen hat story and yet put together the truth about Toby's father from little slivers was a confoundment. Toby acknowledged this with a grunt and a begrudging nod, but cut off further talk. There was on the river a curious assumption that the river was infinitely long and that the rest of the esty a mere shadow wreathed about the telescoping downslope that sucked the river ever forward. So everything outside, esty-business and mechs and all, was a distraction.

He had learned early in his downstreaming not to allow others to indulge in yet another sentimental tale of a poor boy without a mother's cozy love or a father's strong arm, heaved all unfriended upon the cold charity of a censorious world. That was not the truth of it and if he did tell them true they drew back in white-eyed horror.

You are handling them just right.

The sudden spiking up of the Shibo fragment startled him. He stifled her, feeling oddly guilty.

7

Temporal Turbulence

The river's easy water lay close ashore. There the deep streams of bromium and mercury allowed the induction coils a firm grip, while the water current sped best in midstream. No hull-searing bromium streams broke surface here, so the watch was comparatively at ease.

Mr. Preston explained that the *Natchez* had to hug the bank, thus separating it from the downstreaming craft that lazed in the middle, harvesting the stiff current. Toby learned a few of the deft tricks for negotiating the points, bends, bars, islands, and reaches that encumbered the route. He resolved early that if he ever became a pilot he would stick to downtiming and leave the uptiming to those dead to caution.

But the time-storm afflicted both types of craft.

Murmuring dark fell as they cut across river before the whorl of time that awaited. It rose syphonlike at midriver, whereas reports as recent as yesterday back in town had said it clung to the shore opposite where the *Natchez* now picked its way.

"Moving quick, it is," Mr. Preston said sternly at the wheel.

The whirling foam-white column dimpled and reddened the images of forest and plain above it. Toby stood to the corner of the pilot's nest and soon exhausted everything he could remember about seeing the storm days before, which proved of no use, for the tempest had grown and shaped itself into a twisted figure-eight knot that spewed black water and gray-metal fountains.

Rain pelted the pilot's nest windows. The cyclone air sucked light from around them. Blue-black traceries made a fretwork above. Toward shore Toby saw the trees dim into spider web outlines. Winds whipped and blasted at the *Natchez*, bending trees and turning up the pale underside of their leaves so that waves of color washed over the canopy. Trees tossed their arms as if in panic. With a shriek one of the *Natchez*'s chimneys wrenched and split and the top half flopped down on the foredeck. Crew ran out to cut it free and toss it overboard. Toby saw Stan with them, sawing frantically as the wind blasted them nearly off their feet. Peals of profanity blossomed on lips, so close Toby could read them, but a gust whipped the words away.

This was no ordinary wind. It ripped and cut the air, warping images so that men laboring seemed to go in agonizing slow motion, then frantic speed, all the while stretched and yanked and pounded out of shape by invisible forces.

Then — *sssssttt!* — a vacuum hiss jerked a brilliant glory-filled radiance into the sky. An ethereal glow flooded the deck. Yet ashore lay in gloom. Treetops plunged and wrestled with imaginary antagonists. At mid-river foam spouted.

Another *sssssttt!* and a crash and the ship fell a full man's height, splashing itself into a bath of hot effervescence. In a fragment of a second the air got dark as sin and thunder rumbled across the sky like empty barrels rolling down stone stairs.

And then they were out. The gale became a scenic protuberance on a mild river again and the pilot said, "Temporal turbulence was mild this go."

It did not seem so to Toby as he sat on a stool and got his breathing in order again.

When he saw Stan later the young man said, surprised, "Twist? Stretched legs? I never felt any such." — and Toby understood that the shiftings and unsteadiness of both time and space were the province of each particular observer. No one felt the same effects. But the truncated chimney, now being hastily restored by Stan and others in a full sweat, spoke of how real the waverings of time could be.

They cut across once more, skirting a big bar of aluminum that gleamed dully, and could snatch the hull from an induction ship in a passing instant. This took the *Natchez* near the shore where Toby had left his skiff. With Mr. Preston's binoculars he searched the blue-green brush but could find no trace of it.

"Somebody *stole* it," he said, outraged.

"Or else ate it," the pilot said, smiling.

"I didn't grow that skiff, it's not alive. I sawed and hammered it and slapped on scrap metal."

"Maybe time ate it," was all the pilot would say.

The shore seemed watery and indeterminate, a blue-green emulsion. As they beat their way upstream his respect for the pilot grew. No prominence would stick to its shape long enough for Toby to make up his mind what form it truly was. Hills dissolved as if they were butter mountains left on a dining room table during a warm Sunday afternoon.

Yet Mr. Preston somehow knew to make the *Natchez* waltz to starboard at some precise spot, else—he explained—the ship would have a grave misunderstanding with a snag that would rip them stem to stern in the time it took a man to yawn. The murky waste of water and slumbering metal laid traps for timeboaters of all keel depths.

Mr. Preston made her shave the head of an island where a small temporal vortex had just broken from the misty skin of the river, trimming it so close that trees banged and brushed the stern, nearly taking off a curious passenger—who hurriedly disembarked at their first stop, leaving his bag. He babbled something about haunted visions of headless women he had seen in the air. The crew guffawed and made faces. Toby joined them.

8

The Eating Ice

The vagaries of induction ships were of terrifying legend. Most folk who lived near the river—and many, indeed most, chose not to—reported seeing ships that winked into existence at a wharf, offloaded people and bags in a spilling hurry, and slipped away with motors whining, to vanish moments later by first narrowing, then becoming a door-thin wedge that sometimes rose up into the air before thinning into nothingness.

People who tried to keep pace with a ship felt a pressure like a massive unseen hand upon them. They tired, especially going upstream. Thus most lived within less than a day's walk of where they had been born. By straining effort a strong man or woman could take foot or horse into a distant town to find a price for a fresh crop, say, or purchase goods. Most preferred to let the induction ships ply their trade up and down, hauling bales of finespun, say, and returning with store-bought wonders ordered from a gaudy catalog.

Some, though, booked passage on the ships, as much for the ride as for the destination. The *Natchez*'s main rooms were well appointed with opulent armchairs and stuffed davenports, the doorways garnished with bone-white wooden filigree of fanciful patterns and famous scenes of time-distortion. There was a technicolor symbolical mural of great pilots in the main lounge, and in first-class cabins, a porcelain doorknob and a genuine full-wall image sheet that gave an artistic view when caressed. The public rooms featured curving ceilings touched up with elegant gilt, and rainshower-style chandeliers of glittering glass-drops. Toby gazed at these jeweled confections and remembered seeing a true Chandelier, the great cities in space his distant ancestors had made. He enjoyed this place, but it was a humbled though ripe life these people led.

Day passengers could get down to shirtsleeves and use a long row of bowls in the barber shop, which also boasted public towels, stiff public combs, and fragrant public soap. All this impressed Toby mightily. He had never, not even in the pilot's own house, seen such opulence and finery. The *Argo* had been clean, crisp, beautiful in its way—but not splendid and grand, like this.

Passengers boarding from the small, straggling, shabby hamlets along shore echoed his wide-eyed reverence. Three days of cruising brought a certain bemused certitude to him, though, so that he gazed at these scruffy travelers in their baggy clothes with the same elevated scorn as the older crew.

Not that he inhabited the same celestial sphere as the pilot himself. Mr. Preston's face wore lines earned by watching the immemorial clashes of differing temporal potentials. His speech veered from elegant, educated downriver cadences, to slurred, folk-wise vernacular. Pilots boated in eternity, and they knew it.

Toby was along for his passingly useful knowledge, not his skill. So when the induction coils froze up he hustled below on sharply barked command of the Cap'n, just as did Stan and the rest. Mr. Preston stayed aloft, of course.

The vast engine room was a frenzy of shouted orders and shoving bodies. The power that drove them uptime came separately from the huge copper armature that spun, when working properly, between mammoth black iron magnets.

Normally, running into the river's past would suck great gouts of energy from the whirling metal. But in crosscutting the river, snaking through reefs and bromium upwellings, the pilot would sometimes end up running at crosscurrent to the normal, and they would move for a while upstream, as far as the normal water current was concerned, but downstream and thus downtime, as the temporal contortions saw it.

There was no general sign of this, though Toby thought he glimpsed far out in the river a huge, ghostly ship that flickered into being for a mere shaved second. It had great fat towers belching grimy smoke, portholes brimming with violet light, and a craft hovering in the air like a gargantuan insect, vanes churning the mist above, as if it were a swollen predator mosquito about to attack a metal whale.

Then—*sssttttpp!*—wind had whistled where the vision had floated, and a cry from below announced an all-hands.

Stan showed him the coated pipes and cables, already crusted hand-deep in hard, milk-white ice. Boilers nearby radiated intense heat into the room, but the time-coursing inside the pipes and cables sucked energy from them so quickly that the ice did not melt.

Toby and all the other men fell to chipping and prying and hammering at the ice. It was solid stuff. A chunk fell off into Toby's hand and he momentarily saw the surface of a pipe that led directly into the interior of the induction motors. Though normally shiny copper, now the pipe was eerily black.

He stuck his nose in close to see and heard the *crack* of air itself freezing to the metal.

"Hey, get back!" a crewwoman shouted, yanking him away just as the entire gap he had opened snapped shut abruptly—air whooshing into the vacuum created, then freezing instantly itself, in turn sucking in more air.

Another man was not so fortunate, and froze three fingers rock-solid in a momentary crevice in the pipe ice. His cries scarcely turned a head as they all labored to break off and heat away the fast-growing white burden.

A cable sagged under its accumulating weight and snapped free. The high whine of electrical power waned when it did, and Toby felt real fear.

He had heard the tales of induction ships frozen full up this way, the infinite cold of inverse time sucking heat, life, air, and self from them. The victim ships were found, temporally displaced years and miles from their presumed location, perpetual ivory icebergs adrift on the seemingly placid river.

Toby hacked and pried and at last sledge-hammered the ice. The frost groaned and shrugged and creaked as it swelled, like some living thing moaning with growing pains.

Across the engine room he heard another cry as a woman got her ankle caught by the snatching ice. Gales shrieked in to replace the condensing air. Voices of the crew rose in panic.

And the Cap'n's bellow rang above it all, giving orders—"Belay that! Lever it out, man, *heave* on that crowbar! Thomson, run there quick! Smash it, son!"

—and abruptly the howling winds faded, the ice ceased surging.

"Ah," the Cap'n sighed, "at last the pilot has deigned to direct us properly."

Toby took some offense at this, for no pilot ever could read the true vector of the time-current flux. Mr. Preston had brought them out of it, which should be fair enough.

There were awful tales of ships truly mispiloted. Of induction craft hurtling uptime out of control—solid iceberg ships, with deep-frozen crew screaming upstream toward the beginning of time. Of downriver runaways, white-hot streaks that exploded, long before they could reach the legendary waterfall at the end of eternity.

But the Cap'n reflected on none of that. Toby learned then that the high station of a pilot implies that a pilot take harsh criticism at the slightest hint of imperfection.

9

Cairo

Casks and barrels and hogsheads blocked the quay but could not conceal from the pilot's nest the sprawling green beauty of the city.

Even the blocks of commercial warehousing sprouted verdant and spring-fresh from the soil. Cairo had perfected the fast-spreading art of growing itself from its own rich loam. This art was much easier than planting and raising trees, only to chop them down, slice them with band saws, plane them out, and fashion them elaborately into planks, beams, joists, braces, girders, struts, and dowels, all to make shelter.

Such easeful grace demanded a deep sort of knowing. The folk of Cairo fathomed the double-twisted heart of living things.

The *Natchez* rang three bells as it docked. Uprivermen often had a woman in every port and the bells announced which Cap'n this was, so that the correct lady could come to welcome him—sometimes for only an hour or two, in his cabin, before departure for the next port uptime. The vagaries and moods of the time currents led to many a hasty assignation. But the Cap'n of a swift ship might enjoy another such succulent dalliance quite soon—if he were physically able.

A red-faced lady brushed by Toby on the gangplank as he went ashore. He gave her no notice as he contemplated staying here in the river's biggest city.

His head was crammed with lore he had learned in the pilot's nest. At once he went to Cairo city hall and consulted the log of citizens. There was no notation concerning his father, but then it had been a forlorn hope anyway. His father was never one to let a piece of paper tag along behind like a dog, only to bite him later. Toby swallowed the disappointment and let his long-simmering anger supply him with fresh energy.

Stan caught up to him and together they patrolled the streets, Stan doing the talking and Toby striding with hands jammed in pockets, bewitched by the sights. He had left his banged-up battle gear on the ship and stepped lightly.

The self-grown houses rose seamlessly from fruitful soil. Seed-crafters advertised with gaudy signs, some the new neon-piping sort that spelled out whole words in garish, jumpy brilliance— *Skillgrower, Houseraiser,* even *Custom Homeblossoms.*

They wandered through raucous bars, high-arched malls, viny factory-circles, and found them smoothly, effortlessly elegant, their atmospheres moist with fragrances that issued from their satiny woods. Women worked looms that grew directly from the damp earth. Stan asked one of these laboring ladies why she could not simply grow her clothes straight on the bush, and she laughed, replying, "Fashion changes much too quick for that, sir!" and then smothered a giggle at Stan's misshapen trousers and sagging jacket.

This put Stan of a mind to carouse, and soon Toby found himself strolling through a dimly lit street that reeked of, as Stan put it, "used beer."

The women who lounged in the doorways here were slatternly in their scarlet bodices and jet-black, ribbed corsets. Far different from the blocky, muscular women prized so in Family Bishop.

Toby felt his face flush and recalled a time long ago, in the Citadel Bishop school. Family Bishop was strict in matters of lineage, which translated into a tight sexual code until the mating age.

The boys' coach had given them all a sheet of special paper and a pen that wrote invisibly, with orders to draw a circle for each time they masturbated—"shaking hands with your best friend," he called it. The invisibility was to preclude discovery and embarrassment.

At the end of a month they had all brought the sheets in. The coach had hung them up in rows and darkened the classroom, then turned on a special lamp. Its violet glow revealed the circles, ranks upon ranks of them, to the suddenly silent boys. "This," the coach had said, "is the way God sees you. Your inner life."

The aim of all this displayed sin was to get the boys to cut down on their frequency, for lonely Onan's dissipation sapped the intellectual skills—or so the theory went. His Isaac Aspect had supplied data on Onan, calling it a "folk tale" and sniffing with disdain at such primitive sexual mores.

Instead, the exercise led to endless boasting, after they had returned to daylight and each knew his own circle-count, and yet could claim the highest number present, which was one hundred and seven.

Toby had attained a mere eighty-six, somewhat cowed by the exercise itself. Later he felt that if he had known the end in mind, he could have pushed himself over a hundred, easy.

In Cairo, sophisticated women were easily available. He felt a vague loyalty to Besen, troubled by his memory of her image trapped in the cube in Mr. Preston's house. Was she still alive? Would she mind his indulging himself?

Lust banished such fine distinctions, leaving him with a fidgety tautness. But the women beckoning with lacquered leers and painted fingers and arched blue eyebrows somehow did not appeal. He remembered Besen's lopsided smile and missed it terribly.

Stan made some fun of him for this. Toby reacted with surly swearwords, most fresh-learned from Mr. Preston.

Anger irked his stomach. He left Stan bargaining with a milk-skinned woman who advertised with red hair and hips that seemed as wide as the river, and made his way through the darkling city. If his father had come this way there would be a sign. He had only to find it.

10

❰═❯❰═❯❰═❯❰═❯❰═❯❰═❯❰═❯❰═❯

Zom Master

Labyrinths of inky geometry enclosed him. Passing conversations came to him muffled and softly discordant as he worked his way among the large commercial buildings near the docks. Here the jobbing trade waxed strong, together with foundries, machine shops, oil presses, flax mills, and towering elevators for diverse crops, all springing from the intricately tailored lifecrafts known best in Cairo.

Not that such arts grew no blemishes. Slick yellow fungus coated the cobbled streets, slippery malignancies that sucked at Toby's heels, yearning to digest him. Troughlike gutters were awash in fetid fluids, some stagnant and brown-scummed, others running fast and as high as the thick curbstones.

Each building had a mighty cask, several stories high, grown out from the building itself and shooting stilt-roots down to support the great weight of rainwater it held. Never near the river was there enough topsoil to support wells. The passing veils of rain were all Cairo had, and as if to make this point, droplets began to form in the mist overhead and spatter Toby as he searched.

He descended into a lowland zone of the city, where the streets lay silent, with an empty Sunday aspect. But the wrought-iron symbology on the ramshackle buildings here told the reason. They made heavy, rugged ciphers and monograms, filled in with delicate cobwebs of baffling, intricate weave. Toby could make out in the gathering gloom the signs of Zom businesses, bearing the skulls and ribbed ornamentation. This solidity offset other fragilities. Cairo dwelled so near the great time-storm arcs that its folk always spoke conditionally, ending their statements about events with "so far" and "seems to be" and "in the sweet sometimey."

His bad luck, of course, that the timestone glow would ebb at just this time. The rain dribbled away, leaving a dank cold. He looked upward and saw that far overhead was a broad island of sandy waste, interrupting the timestone, and so leaving this part of the city permanently darker. So they had decided to put the Zom industry here, in constant gloom.

He peed against a building, reasoning that it would help it to grow just like any plant—though he did modestly slip down a side alley to do it. So Toby was off the street when a squad of Zom women came by.

They shambled, chill-racked and yellow-faced, eyes playing about as if in addled wonder, and one saw Toby. She grinned, an awful rictus, and licked her lips and hoisted her skirt with one hand, gesturing with the other index finger, eyebrows raised. Toby was so transfixed he stopped urinating and stood there shock-still until finally the Zom shrugged and went on with the other miserables. His heart restarted again some time after and he put himself back in his pants.

Zoms were accepted as a necessity for their brute labor, he told himself. Still his breath came short, his chest grew tight and fluttery. He chided himself.

Following the Zoms was easy. In a street of wavering oil lamps was the Zom Raiser.

The man was tall, in a stovepipe-thin charcoal suit. He sat in a spacious room, working at an ancient stone desk, scribbling on a flat computer face. Along the walls were deep alcoves sunk into shadow.

"I'm looking for a, my father. I thought maybe—"

"Yes yes," the man said. "An old story. Go ahead, look."

This abruptness startled Toby so that it was some moments before he fully realized what he saw.

Grimy oil lamps cast dim yellow radiance across long rows of slanted boards, all bearing adult corpses. They were not shrouded, but wore work clothes, some mud-caked. Toby walked down the rows and peered into bloodless, rigid faces. In the alcoves were babes laid out in white shrouds.

All had the necessary ribbed ironwork cage about them. Pale revitalizing fluids coursed through tubes into their nostrils, pumped by separate hearts—bulbous, scarlet muscles attached at the ribs, pulsing. The fluids did their sluggish work down through the body, sending torpid waves washing from the sighing chest through the thick guts and into the trembling legs. Their charge expended, the fluids emerged a deep green from the rumps, and spilled into narrow troughs cut into the hardwood floor.

Amid echoing drips and splashes he returned to the stone desk, an island of luminosity in the cool, clammy silence. "He's not here."

"Not surprising. We move them on fast." The man's deep-sunken eyes gave nothing away.

"You raised anybody looks like me?"

"Got a name for him?"

Toby gave it. The man studied a leather-bound ledger and said, "No, not in the records. Say, though, I recall something . . ."

Toby seized the Zom Raiser by the shoulders. "What?"

"Leggo. Leggo, I say." He shied back and when Toby's hands left him he straightened himself the way a chicken shakes its feathers into order. "You damn fools come barging in here, you're always—"

"Tell me."

Something in Toby's voice made the man cease and study him for a long moment. "I was trying to recollect. I've seen must be a dozen look sorta like you, if I 'member right."

Toby felt his throat tighten. They knew he was here and were copying Killeens to hunt him down.

"Dealer comes in here with one every week or so."

"From where?"

"Gets them in the countryside, he says. Brings them here for kindling up to strength. Got a storage place for them."

"Where?"

"Last I heard, 'bout seven blocks over."

"Which way?"

"Annunciation and Poydras. Big long shed, tin roof."

Toby made his way through the rain-slicked streets, getting lost twice in his hurried confusion and slipping on something slimy he did not want to look at. He got to the low building as a figure came out the other end of it and something made him step back into the street and watch the man hurry away. He went inside and there was nobody there except five Zoms who lay on ready-racks, chilled down and with brass amulets covering their faces. A gathering sense of betrayal caught in his mouth and Toby trotted down the empty aisles where Zoms would labor in the day, the slanting gray light making every object ghostly and threatening.

He knew before he reached the end of it that the Zom Raiser

had played him for a fool all along. While Toby was finding his way here the man had somehow sent word.

He had hoped that the true Killeen would be here somehow, that perhaps his father was making the copies himself to aid his search. But it was far more likely that mechs had humans working for them. Toby should flee. He did not want to give up but the logic of it was clear and he had halfway turned when something fell out of the dark roof above.

He dove sideways over a Zom without thinking. The thing was like a pale plate of meat spreading in the air like a flightless bird. It struck him smartly in the leg. An electric-blue blaze rose in his eyes. His sensorium crumpled and flashed with sparking pain. The Zom's flesh was hard and cool as he fell across the body. Agony was climbing up his spine, coming for him. The frying intensity told him this was a high-order mech offensive weapon. He twisted on the slimy cool Zom and his legs cramped up with the shooting sting. That made it hard to roll but he grabbed the Zom's head. It was a woman and he had to jam his hand into her open mouth to get the leverage. He slithered out from under the weight. The thing held on but he reached back and jabbed it with his gloved hand. Stiff fingers dug into a resistance like molasses. It shied away and he hit the floor. The mech device spread an oozing stain over the Zom.

Maybe it had mistaken the Zom for him. Toby did not wait to find out.

11

The Past Is Labyrinth

Three deep, mellow bell notes floated off across the sublime skin of the river and some moments later came wafting back, steepened into treble and shortened in duration.

"Means we're getting close to the arc," Mr. Preston said.

Toby narrowed his eyes, searching the gloom before them. "Can't see a thing."

"The bell notes get scrunched up by the time-wind, then bounce back to us. Better guide than seeing the arcs, sometimes. They twist the light, give you spaghetti pictures."

Toby would have preferred to watch the treacherous standing curves of frothy water, for he had seen one smash a flatboat to splinters on his trip down.

A deep hush brooded upon the river. He felt a haunting sense of isolation, remoteness from the bustle of Cairo, though they were only hours upstream from it. He had felt bad about what would happen if mechs pursued him to the ship and so had hid out in a bar until the last moment. With his sensorium damped to zero he sat and brooded and decided never to activate the sensorium again. It was not the risk to himself so much, but the danger to the people he worked with.

They sheltered here in a way he supposed was typical of humanity everywhere, given half the chance. They clung to a past and he passed among them in dangerous disguise. He could not bring mechs down upon his friends.

He crept down to the river. To the ship. When he came aboard there was nothing remarkable, or at least nothing remarked. It had taken a while to get his calm back, to begin thinking again.

To starboard he could make out solid walls of dusky forest softening into somber gray. Mr. Preston sounded the bells again and the steepened echoes came, quicker and sharper this time.

Then the river seemed to open itself, revealing first the foamy feet and then the marvelous high swoop of the arcs. Silently they churned at their thick feet, sending waves to announce their power. Yet as the *Natchez* came up, holding tight to the opposite shore, the water was glass-smooth, with mercury breaking at mid-river and sending spectral flags of glittering mist into an eerily still air.

This tranquility fractured. A wall of thunder shook the glass windows of the pilot's nest.

"Whoa!" Mr. Preston called and slammed on the power. The induction motors sent a shock through the decking.

"It look the way you seen it last?" Mr. Preston never took his eyes from the arcs. They were shimmering pink and blue now.

"Yessir, only the tall one, it had a bigger foot."

"You shoot down through here?"

"Nossir, stayed out by that sand bar."

"Damn right you were, too."

Toby had, in the chop and splash of it, been given no choice whatever. But he said nothing, just held on. The deck bucked, popped, complained.

"Eddy running here up the bank to well beyond the point," Mr. Preston said, betraying some excitement despite himself. "Might get us through without we have to comb our hair afterward."

They went flying up the shore so close that twigs snapped off on the chimneys. Mist churned the air fever-pink. Drumroll bass notes came up through Toby's boots. "Hold on for the surge!" Mr. Preston called, as if anyone wasn't already, and it hit.

The *Natchez* struck the vortex whorl plunging by near the point. The suck of it stretched clear across the river this time, an enormous mouth of mercury and bromium seething brown and silver together in smeared curves. The ship whirled around, Toby thought as his stomach lurched, like a favorite top his mother had given him, possessing the mysterious ability to stand so long as it spun.

This abstract memory lasted one breath and then water crashed over the pilot's nest and smashed in the aft window. The ship careened to port. Time-torques whipsawed the groaning timbers. An eddy seized her and crunched one of her chimneys into pathetic torn tin. Concussion clapped Toby's ears and left his head ringing.

Lightning-quick flashes of ruby radiance forked from the river and ran caressing over the upper decks.

Shouts. Screams.

Athwart the current, then with it, the *Natchez* shot free of the howling whorl. Within a mere moment they brought up hard in the woods at the next bend. Ordinarily this would have been an embarrassment for a pilot, but as it came from passing uptime against the arcs, it was a deliverance, a penalty, as trivial as a stingy tip left after a banquet.

In the lapsed quiet afterward they drummed upstream and Toby watched the shoreline for signs he remembered. Coming back to this place meant he could partly reverse the esty gradient. He figured that would get him back onto a time axis closer to the period shared with the portal cities. Maybe—just maybe, because people here didn't want to talk about the esty at all—he could get closer to the source of Killeens.

He had not told anyone that, but Mr. Preston gave him sidewise glances now and then. Stan, after the obligatory ragging of Toby for having shied away from the women of easy virtue, kept pestering him about finding hydrogen hats. So Toby spent long hours pretending, watching beady-eyed the dense, uncut forest roll by.

To him the richness here was vaster than downriver, thicker and mysterious beyond ready expression. He had not the wit nor especially the years to savor it fully; taste comes with age and is perhaps its only reward, though he knew some called the same thing wisdom.

He saw the great slow-working chains of cause and effect on the river—forces which, though elusive in the redolent natural wealth, in hard fact underpinned all the sweeping vistas, the realms of aery compass, the infinitesimal machineries of wood and leaf. The young must make their way in a world that is an enormous puzzle, so he watched the shifting hues quick-eyed, a student of the forever fluid, knowing that the silver river might foam suddenly to suck him under or contrariwise spew him aloft in a frothy geyser—all beautiful events, he supposed, but they would leave him no less dead.

Toby kept lively advising Mr. Preston on reefs and bars. He inspected the passing acres of lumber rafts, great pale platforms behind which the launch could conceal itself. Likewise each bulky barge and the trading scows that peddled from farm to farm, the peddler's family hanging out wash on deck and kids calling hullos. So when Stan shouted up from the passenger deck, "See that! Must be! Must be!" Toby felt a spur of irritation at being distracted from his work.

Stan scampered aft and poled aboard some floating debris, then had the temerity to carry it forward to the pilot's nest.

Mr. Preston scowled and looked to bite his mustache at the sight of a mere deckhand intruding, but before Toby could shoo Stan out he saw the flowerlike gray thing Stan carried.

"It's a hat! A positive hat," Stan burbled. "Pure hydrogen—worth plenty on its own, wager me—and lookee *here*."

Stan proudly displayed broaches and pins mounted into the gunmetal-gray thing, which to Toby's immense surprise surely did resemble a hat. It was nearly weightless yet hard and the jewels gleamed with inner radiance.

"And you led me straight on it, too, Toby, I'll not forget," Stan said. "I'll share out the proceeds, yessir."

"Uh, sure thing."

Mr. Preston's stormy face had turned mild as he studied the hat. "Never seen anything like *this*. *How* far upriver you say you come from?" He peered at Toby.

"Good bit further," was all Toby could say, for indeed that was so, but the shore already looked odd and contorted to him, as though his memory was warping.

That was nothing compared to the consternation he felt but could not give a hint of, for the hat story was total yarning—yet here was an actual, in-fact, bejeweled hydrogen hat, worth many a month's pay.

His befuddlement got swept away soon enough by the twisty demands of the river. Under Mr. Preston he was coming to see that the face of the wedded water and metal was a wondrous book, one in a dead language to him before but now speaking cherished secrets. Every fresh point they rounded told a new tale. No page was empty. A passenger might be charmed by a churning dimple on its skin, but to a true riverman that was an italicized shout, announcing a wreak or reef of wrenching space-time Vortex about to break through from the undercrust of timestone.

Passengers went *oooh* and *aahhh* at the pretty pictures the silver river painted for them without reading a single word of the dark text it truly was. A lone log floating across the prow could be in truth a jack-jawed beast bent on dining upon the tasty wooden hull. A set of boiling, standing rings spoke of a whorl that could eat an entire induction disk.

Mr. Preston would sometimes muse out loud as they rounded a point and beheld a fresh vista, "That slanting brown mark—what you make of that? I'd say a bar of ground-up metal, dissolving now in the bromine current. See that slick place? Shoaling up now, be worse when we head back down. River's fishing for induction ships right there, you mark."

But mostly Mr. Preston asked Toby the questions, for the river perpetually tore itself down, danced over its own banks, made merry of memory. They saw a farmer had shoved down pilings to hold his ground, even set a crazy-rail fence atop it, only to have the blithe momentum strip and pry and overrun his fetters, break his hand-cuffs, and laugh as the lawless currents—seemingly enraged by this confinement—stripped his worldly dominion.

In all of it Toby looked for his father. There was precious lit-tle sign of anything from outside this enormous long riverland. But he felt himself drawing backward in time as the ship pressed them against the esty grade.

Mr. Preston brought aboard a local "memory man" to help them through a set of neck-twisting oscillations, and the fellow displayed the affliction Toby had heard of but never witnessed. To remember everything meant that all events were of the same size.

The short, swarthy man sat in the pilot's nest and guided them well enough through the first two swaybacks, with reefs and snags galore, but on the third he began to tell the history of the snaggle-toothed tree that had fallen in at the lee shore and so stopped them from using the close-pass there, and from that tree went on to the famous boiling timestone eruption that had scorched the tree, and from that to a minute rendition of the efforts of Farmer Finn, who had saved his crops by building a sluice-diverter of the river, to Finn's wife who ran off with a preacher, only people *then* found out he was no preacher at all but in fact a *felon* escaped from some jail uptime, which suggested to the memory man the way laws had to be deformed here to accord with the passage back and forth in eras of relatives and wives and husbands, which brought forth the scandal of the lady in a red dress who had taken on all the men at a dance once, hiking her skirts for each in turn plain as day, out-side against the wall, and from there was but a step to the intri-cate discussion of dance steps the memory man had learned (since he learned anything merely by seeing it once), complete with toe-tapping demonstrations on the deck—so that Mr. Preston had to yank the man's attention back to the veering river before it gutted them on an aluminum reef.

Within minutes, though, the memory man would drift into more tedious jaw about whatever strayed into view of his panoramic mind. Mr. Preston bore this for the swings and sways of those bends, and then put the memory man ashore with full pay. The man didn't seem to mind, and left still maundering on about great accidents of the past and where their survivors lived now and how they were doing.

Toby silently envied the man, though, for at least he did know exactly that one short portion of the river, whereas Toby's own memory betrayed him at each new rounding. Islands and bars arose from the water where none had been before, his mind told him. The river ran in new side-channels and had seemingly cut across headlands to forge fresh entries, thrusting aside monumental hillsides and carving away whatever misunderstandings had arisen with the spongy, pliant forest.

"This sure looks to be a horseshoe curve here. Remember it?" Mr. Preston would ask, and Toby would peer through the misty wreaths that often wrapped the river, and shake his head.

On this particular one they hauled ashore, because a passenger thought he lived near here, though could not spot any landmark either, but wanted to try his own luck. Toby went ashore and slogged through brambles and sandy loam across the neck of the horseshoe, arriving well before the *Natchez* got there, coming hard-chuffing around the curve.

These branches and inlets lay in his past, yet despite their here-and-now solidity they had wriggled into new shapes, oddities of growth, even whole fresh porticoed master-houses. Slowly it dawned on Toby that none of this surprised Mr. Preston.

"Every time we go upriver, things lay different," Mr. Preston said, twirling a toothpick in his mouth as his only sign of agitation.

"Damnfire," Toby said, a new curse he had picked up and was proud to sport. "What use is a memory man, then?"

"Better than nothing, is all."

They were near to drawing all the water there was in the channel, a curious tide having sucked streamers up and into the clouds above. The hull caught and broke free and then snagged again, so Mr. Preston had to order the induction motors up to full, wrenching them off the bed of the river by sheer magnetic ferocity.

"Sure seems that way," Toby said. "Why'd you hire me as guide, then?"

"Your knowledge is for certain fresher than any I could find. And you're young enough, you don't think you know everydamnthing."

They were going slow, deck humming, riding on magnetic cushions that Toby thought of as bunched steel coils. Mr. Preston said that wasn't far wrong, only you couldn't feel or see the wires. They were more like wrestling magnetic ghosts.

"Sometimes a time-tide will come and cut a little gutter across a neck of land," Mr. Preston went on. "I saw one once while I was shipping downstream, no bigger than a garden path it was. Shimmered and snaked and snapped yellow fire. Now, there were handsome properties along that shore. But inland from there was a worthless old farm. When I came back uptime on the old *Reuben*, that li'l time-twist had cut a big course through. Diverted the whole damn river, it did. Shooting off crimson sparklers, still. That old farm was now smack on the river, prime land, worth ten times more. The big places that had been on the river stood inland. No ship could reach them."

"Lucky," Toby said.

Mr. Preston grinned. "Was it? Lot of people got mad, accused the family that owned the old farm of starting that time-wrinkle."

"How could they?"

"Who's to say? Is there a way to figure it? The past is labyrinth, truly. Give time a shove here, a tuck there? Anybody who knows how, sure don't talk about it."

12

Whorl

Toby felt himself lost in a dense, impenetrable maze of riverways. Coming upstream against the time-pressure now refracted the very air.

Smooth and serene the majestic mud-streaked expanse had seemed as he drifted down obliviously in his skiff. Now the shore was morasses and canebrakes and even whole big plantations, the grand main houses beautiful with their ivory columns. He often gazed up at the world hanging overhead, too, lands of hazy mystery. A ripple passed, flexing the entire tubular esty, and Toby felt suddenly that they all lived in the entrails of a great beast, an unknowable thing that visited the most awful of calamities upon mere humans by merely easing its bowels.

The whorl came upon them without warning. It burst through a channel of bromium, coiling like a blue-green serpent up into the shimmering air. A thunderclap banged into the pilot's nest and blew in two windows.

Toby saw it from the mid-deck where he was helping Stan and two men with some baling. The glass scroll window shattered but did not catch Mr. Preston in the face, so when Toby raced in the pilot was already bringing the *Natchez* about, clawing away from the swelling cloud-wrack.

The whorl soared, streamers breaking from it to split the congealing air with yellow forked lightning. Toby saw it hesitate at its high point, as if deciding whether to plunge on across and bury itself in the forest-wall hanging far overhead. Then it shook itself, vigorous with the strength of the newborn, and shot riverward.

The silver river seemed to yearn for this consummation, for it buoyed in up-sucking ardor and kissed the descending column. Instantly a foam of muddy water and a mist of metal soared through the time-whorl, writing a great inverted *U* that bubbled and frothed and steam-hissed amid more sharp thunder-cracks.

"Damn!" Mr. Preston cried. "That'll block us for sure."

Toby held tight to a stanchion. "Can't we shoot by—"

"It'll riptide us to pieces, we try that."

A blistering gale broke over the *Natchez.* "You figure it'll last long?"

"This big a one, you bet."

The *Natchez* beat steadily away from the whorl, which twisted and shuffled its water-feet around on the skin of the river. Mud and logs sucked up into it tumbled and seemed to break apart and come together again. In the midst of what looked like a water-wave Toby saw a log burst into orange flame. It turned slow-motion, streaming black smoke, and smacked full into the river.

Then he saw the mechs. They had been hiding among some weeping willows. Silvery and quick, they fled as the whorl lashed sidewise.

Suddenly it made sense to him. The whorl was a way into this esty tube and thus a gateway to be policed. It was also the obvious place to wait for anyone, if you knew their ways.

Mechs didn't know him. But Killeen did.

Toby called, "Wait! Let's stay a while, see if it—"

"Shut up, boy. We're running downtime."

Even the Cap'n could not overrule a pilot reversing course for safety. Toby stood frozen as the mechs lifted off the shoreline. They were angular and reminded him of the Rattler that had nearly killed him long ago. These were more advanced.

They were coming. They would kill his friends.

Tentatively he resurrected his sensorium. Nothing. Then—

A faint echo, a note he had not heard sounded for so long—

Then he did not think any more but simply ran, down the iron stairs and pine gangway and over—into the water. He flailed about for a desperate moment—he had forgotten his battle gear—then struck for shore.

Stan shouted behind him but he did not look around. He estimated the mechs could see him clearly by now. Good.

But then he heard a whooshing boom, like a giant drawing its breath. The mechs glided beside the funnel mouth of the whorl. A

ribbed light pulsed from them. It pushed the whorl . . . slowly . . .
faster . . . but not toward Toby. Toward the ship.

The sucking came skating on the choppy silver waters. It
swooped with train-wreck malevolence down upon the *Natchez* and
drew it up, elongating the decks like rubber stretched to its limit
and then cracking. A deckhand jumped overboard and his body
stretched to translucent thinness.

The *Natchez* squeezed and contorted and obeyed the call of
warping forces. It shot up the whorl-mouth. Tide-tides wrenched
and wracked it and then it was gone in a brilliant last pearly flash.
The glare burned Toby's face.

Toby had no time to think or mourn. The mouth reeled, crackled and snaked and swept down upon him. He had time to gulp air.
Burning orange foam broke over him.

Legs, arms—both stretched involuntarily, as though some
God were playing with his strings—yet he was weightless. He knew
he must be rising up on the whorl but he felt a sickened, belly-
opening vacancy of infinite falling. He struggled not to fill his lungs
as the foam thronged at his skin, infested his nose, pried at his eyelids. *Don't breathe!* was all he could think as he prepared for the
time-crushed impact his instincts told him was coming at the end of
such a protracted fall.

He smacked hard. In the river again.

Bobbed to the surface. Paddled, gasping. Ignored the wave-
wracked waters. Made the shore and flopped upon it.

13

Pursuit

The mechs were shattered on the shore. Something had blown big chunks of their ivory skins away.

In each hole a midmind lay splintered. Something about the unerring way each shot had found the operating intelligence made him smile without humor.

A sweet dust of time blew high above the river and there was no sign of the whorl. Or of the *Natchez*.

Toby followed the boot tracks he found over the next rise. The long strides led inland, so there was no time-pressure to fight. He was wet and dazed but he hurried.

Inland the lush forest dribbled away into scrub desert. He realized whoever it was might back around on him so he retraced his steps and erased signs of his passage from the water and onto safe stone. He avoided vegetation where possible and slid through bushes so that stems bent but did not break. This was crucial, for a broken stem cannot be fixed without careful cutting and even so, a sure reader of signs would catch it. He could not let his excitement get him killed here. Leaving stems or branches pointing the way you came was bad, too. They had to be gently urged back to a random pattern. He mussed up a scraped bush and tree so that it looked to be from an animal, from biting or itch-easing. Stealth spelled safety.

His head pounded with a headache that worked its way into his eyes. So much had happened but he put it aside, not thinking about Mr. Preston or Stan, just keeping on. It got dryer and a big-winged thing with teeth flapped overhead, eyeing him for possibilities. He flung a rock at it.

He wished for a blunderbuss tree, recalling the man who had threatened him with one of the awkward weapons. But a big fallen branch served to make a club after he stripped the bark away.

The boot tracks showed heels dug in from haste. He let his senses float out ahead of him. His sensorium was faulty, flickering.

Everything in the land fled from his footsteps. Lizards scattered into the nearest cracked rock. Four-winged quail hovered in shadow, hoping you'd take them for stones, but at the last moment they lost their nerve and burst into frantically flapping birds. Snakes evaporated, doves squeaked skyward, rabbits crazy-legged away in a dead heat. Fox, midget mountain horn, coyote—they melted into legend, leaving only tracks and dung. The heart of the desert was pale sand, a field whose emptiness exposed life here for what it was: conjured out of nothingness and bound for it, too. Desert plants existed as exiles from each other, hoarding their circles of water collection done silently beneath the sand by single-minded roots. Vacancy was life.

He caught a smell fetid and pestiferous and knew instantly what it was. In the slaying fields of several Lanes he had smelled it.

He worked his way around it by nose alone. Slow, slow. When he finally looked down into the bowl-like field he could see only sprawled dead. Men lay putrefying, faces puffed and lips bruised. Most were gutted, appearing to give birth to their own entrails.

The time-whorls sometimes did this, disgorging people or matter from times and places no one knew. What the induction ships did by laboring upstream, a flick of space-time could accomplish in an instant. Sometimes carrion like this could still be saved for the Zom business.

But these men all wore the same face.

Toby turned to merge again with the brush and there he was.

The same features—angular, hollow-eyed with fatigue, a familiar cut to the jawline and the downcurved mouth. Toby compared it with his memories, carried now for what seemed like years, taken out and studied every day.

"Who are you?" Toby asked.

The voice was low and edged. "What do you want?"

"Are you real? I mean—"

The eyes gave nothing away. But that was how they had always been. "You know me, son."

"In this place? Don't know *what* I know anymore."

The face constricted as though wolfdark memories pressed

against it from deep inside. "The mechs sent out copies of me. I tried to warn you. Before the mechs hit the portal city, Andro helped me make a general release kind of message—"

"I saw it. A Walmsley character had it at a big library thing, a pyramid—"

"You've been there?" He was startled.

"Yeasay. Mechs got it. I had to run."

"I've heard about this Walmsley. The portal people—Andro, remember?—say he comes from 'way far back. Warned me about him."

"He seemed like a shrunk up dwarf, that's all."

"Sure can't judge much around here by appearances."

Toby moved carefully away from the bodies. This Killeen looked pretty nearly right, but then so did the ones with their guts vomiting out.

"What're they?" Toby gestured at the corpses.

"Copies. The mechs I just shot were making them."

"Sending them downriver?"

"Must've been. They were gatekeepers, I guess."

"That whorl out there on the river?"

"Yeasay. They know how to open and close it." The man who looked like Killeen jerked a thumb at the river where the mechs lay. "They figured out how to get in and out of Lanes."

"I can do it too."

The man again blinked with surprise. "Where'd you learn?"

"Worked it out."

"Let's get out of here then."

Toby didn't want to look as though he were stalling and make this man cautious but he was still not sure. "Where's Besen?"

"I don't know. I lost track of the whole Family when the mechs busted up the portal city."

It sounded all too convenient. He could kill this one if he could get it off guard. It was in field gear but without helmet.

The man said, "Look, more mechs for sure will come to replace those."

Toby didn't like how this man kept pushing him. And this Killeen was so haggard and washed out. That could come from the copying process, whatever that was. "I'm not so—"

Let me speak to him. Please.

It was Shibo. A fragment rising in him.

Please. In the name of all we have been to each other.

It had an authority he had not felt before. As if it had been waiting for this moment, saving its resources.

He hesitated and she reached up through him somehow. In a crisp instant he felt how it had been for her. She had somehow *re-written* herself into his neurological circuitry, lodged fragments in his Aspects, hidden. All before he had decided to strip her chip from his spine.

If he let her get any control this Killeen could take him easily. He began tracing through his own recesses, searching for her. She fled. Then her voice chimed in him clearly, unafraid:

Ask him if he remembers whether Family Knights take their boots off first.

"Huh?" Toby said. The man gave him a puzzled look.

If Knights keep their boots on when they're on top.

Without knowing why he was doing it, Toby repeated the sentence.

The man's mouth opened and closed and then said, "What? Who's talking?"

"Shibo."

The man said slowly, "I thought you said once you didn't know."

The sliver of Shibo said thinly,

Knights keep run-ready.

Toby repeated it and the man said, "So the one on top has to keep his boots on."

She answered,

What makes you say "his"?

Killeen answered, "You said you never got on top."

Toby was getting uncomfortable with this but he repeated Shibo again, who said,

I wanted be on top, be fast, wear boots.

"You learned how."

Good teacher.

The man grinned. "Seemed like you learned somewhere before me."

Never learned your *moves, naysay.*

"Compliments, even. You always know how to get what you want."

Toby struggled to say something. All the knotted energy surrounding Shibo, of his carrying her as an Aspect, of his ripping her out with crude tools when she went awry—all of it collided and tightened his throat until he could not speak.

Anything, anything to get it again.

The tiny voice was so desperate it opened a flood of sadness in Toby. He croaked out the words for her. The man's eyes widened and Shibo cried to Toby alone,

It's him! Him!

"Maybe there's a way for even that." Killeen peered into his son's eyes but without seeing him.

That's the point.

When Toby repeated it he was surprised to find tears had run down and over his lips.

"You always liked to joke about it."

Not really jokes.

"No, they weren't."

Toby clasped the man and knew he was Killeen. Shibo laughed when they both did, not a joke but joy.

A long moment passed between them. "Dad, Dad . . ." No words.

Toby grinned and the two of them pounded each other on the back, the laughter just bubbling up and out, and so he took a moment to register stresses arcing in the air, a pressing sharp presence—

The sky ripped open.

Above them a blackness spread like oily ooze across the Lane.

"Down!" Killeen called.

Pointless, Toby thought. He crouched. Whatever was up there was sweeping fast. It ate the Lane. Edges turned up like a fire curling the pages of a book. But this thing was consuming the esty itself.

> I could not stop the Highers from allowing this.

He knew instantly that this was the Mantis. Its manifestation was different, tinged with currents of emotion and echoing knowledge which he could not catch.

He looked around them and felt the Mantis now as a seethe in the air. Killeen was down in firing position but their weapons plainly could do no good here.

A jab of pain. He turned as a small winged thing lifted off his right arm. A metallic buzz, anxious with its single-minded task. It shot away.

> I have taken a sample of you. Yours is the last DNA needed.

"I saw a copy of Abraham, Dad. The mechs must've read his DNA and mind as well."

"Damn!" Killeen shouted. But there was nothing for him to shoot.

> I am the lowest of my Order which can speak to you primates. The Exalteds cannot occupy so narrow a conceptual space. They have granted me special abilities for this supreme task. But other logics prevail as well. The Lane above is about to tear open into the wrack of the Eater. I cannot save you, but I did come to harvest the youngest's genetic material.

"Son, I figured it would help me find you, so—"

"You let it help you get here."

Winds rose, growling. Leaves stripped from the bushes.

Killeen said bitterly, "It didn't give me much choice."

"I know." Toby gripped his father's arm. Something wordless passed between them as they both squatted, cowering beneath a whipping gale that shrieked toward the blackness above.

> My tracking of you, Killeen, was always benign.
> I had hoped to harvest you all, once my obliga-
> tion to the Highers was exhausted. We could be
> together then.

"We'll rip your guts out!" Killeen spat back. Toby admired the
bravado in his father's automatic answer. Meaningless, of course.

> Such consummation is the greatest fate such as you
> can hope to share.

Killeen fired a bolt at a glow that frisked through the air. Not
the Mantis, no, but his father was never one to meekly listen.

> You have played a role, as well, in the bringing of
> fulfillment to our kind. When this sample is read,
> then united with the codes of yourself, Killeen, and
> your own father—perhaps we can speak then.

"Speak?" Toby shouted against the wind's howl. "We'll die
here!"

> I fear I cannot intervene to rescue you. This esty is
> coming apart. I now depart.

"You can get us out!" Toby hollered.

> I cannot waste time and energy opening a portal. My
> central task, brooking no compromise, is to save this
> manifestation of myself, to bring the sample of Toby
> to the Highers.

The entire dome above them swarmed with black, eating
tongues.
Killeen cried, "Save Toby! You dunno but what you'll need
more than that little bit of him! Leave me, take—"
But the Mantis was gone.
The first booming shocks hit them then. Like immense drum
rolls they flattened trees and smashed the men to the ground.
Toby rolled, stunned. He looked up into the far sky and saw

where the blackness was leading. Pulverized knots of fiery orange fled away from it—backward, down. Fragments of the Lane. Ripped away and already tortured into incandescence.

Away. Inward. Toward the final consuming point of the Eater, the singularity cloaked in its own twisted geometry. The esty was spilling into the black hole. The snarl of curvature had finally won. It would draw them to it, the final grave.

At first he saw the dust whorl in the corner of his eye. He was trying to concentrate on the swallowing dark above even though the wind now battered at him. A limb hit him in the leg and gouged a painful streak of red as it departed. Killeen was trying to say something, arms waving. The violence overwhelmed their sensoria comm.

Bushes, grass, brown clouds of dirt—all tore and rasped at him.

The filmy thing standing beside him did not move.

He looked at it square then and it said, "I will open."

It tried to make itself into the shape of a man but against the angry air that was impossible. Tiny motes made it up, somehow holding crude shape against the gale.

He heard, very clearly, *Do not think we are neglectful of you. We do hope you live to help.*

He had felt that message before. It had saved him and he had never known why.

Then the esty beneath them vanished. They fell.

Part VI

WEDDED TO
THE SUBSTRATE

1

Partial to Primates

The bird would come, Nigel Walmsley knew. But at least he could carve out some time for himself. It might be the very last.

He had fled to this pocket of esty in part because time ran differently here. He used that to rest and reinvent himself.

The assault on the Library had been a shock but in the long line of his life there had been many such. He did not know if he would find the magnetic storage of his Nikka but then he had been there before, too.

He had barely gotten away, helped by Highers—he thought. It was all wisps of memory.

He knew that in this manifestation he had to get a surer sense of himself and that would take time. But the Bishops and others were moving fast. So he came here. A place to scoop out a pocket of time, a pause before going back to the play. The last act was coming.

There was enough food just for the gathering, at least for a while. A bird assembled itself nearby and told him that with the expected flow senses of time in the Lanes of importance to him, he could remain here a while. He would be needed later. He did not ask what for because he knew by now there was no point in it.

He roved the narrow, bulbous Lane. He followed methods he had learned long ago in the American Southwest, when he had been training with NASA and took solitary weekends wandering in the dry canyons of New Mexico and Arizona.

Au revoir, Etats-Unis. Somewhere out there in the galaxy's churn, America was a ruin, walls like broken teeth on a plain. If even that. In Nigel the name echoed still.

Tracing the drainages upstream. Looking in shady alcoves under the canyon walls. Here was sandy soil that testified to the true age of the esty: enough to simmer and bake raw galactic matter into strata and then wear it down to grains again. Animals had left litter—they knew shelter at least as well as humans—and pack rats stored their precious baubles. Humans were like other indolent, meandering species. They had left debris cast aside as they lounged, trash the true record of past celebrations. Shards, chips, bits of metal and glass and unknown materials all mixed together. The warpage of time made it impossible to know how many centuries of relative interval had lodged these here but he took some odd reassurance from the rubbish nonetheless.

People passed through, even here. They had heard that there were troubles elsewhere but since the mechs had not reached their particular remote Lanes they discounted most of it as mere talk. Still, everybody knew that travel was broadening.

Some were traders and some just journeying with no particular destination in mind. The esty afforded little certainty that once you set out you would arrive at a particular place on time and they were used to that, too. It did not improve them much but at least it made them more interesting.

"Lord it was hard getting in here. When are you people going to get around to improving it?"

"Slightly after I leave," Nigel said with a straight face.

"What kind of improvement? I'd suggest—"

"My leaving was the improvement I had in mind."

"Ha ha. Well, is there any better flux point further on?"

"I don't think so. The best way out is the way you came in."

"We would see the same scenery twice."

"It looks better leaving."

"Aren't we just a little distance in esty-cords from the Majumbdahr Lane?"

"Which one would that be?"

"Where they have that beautiful city?"

"I don't know how to measure how far it is but I would venture that it is not nearly far enough."

"Well, I prefer cities to this trackless nothing."

"Trackless is the best part about it."

"With more water it would be a lot more like where we come from."

Nigel smiled. "What would be the point of another place like what you already have?"

"Nobody here to talk to anyway."

"I've been known to talk to myself."

Some uneasy laughter from the travelers and then one says, "You must get awful lonely."

"I have good company."

"Where are they?"

Pointing at his head, he said, "In here."

"Uh, well, anything dangerous around here?"

"There's you."

"We're not dangerous! We wouldn't hurt a fly."

"I'll have to ask the flies about that."

"You know, I'd like to live here alone like you."

"You can't."

"Why not?"

"If you come I'll be here and you won't be alone. Neither will I."

"Well, I mean almost alone."

"That's like being almost pregnant."

"You take everything so literally!"

"I don't take everything at all. In fact I take almost nothing any longer."

They would pass through with all the speed one could plausibly wish for but he was still far happier to see the back of them than the front. On Earth one of the prevailing clichés had been that all people are basically alike. To the extent that it was weakly true it was also useless because you never knew if they were alike in being vicious or kind or anything in between. In any case the variety was more interesting than the similarities. But then, he would think with a shrug, how could he ever lose faith in a species that had such an endearing trait? You could say whatever you liked to them and they would not take you seriously, not even take offense—as long as you told the strict truth. They never recognized it.

The bird came while he was resting.

"Do not think we are neglectful of you," it warbled from a branch.

He watched its wings shimmer. Sometimes the light from beyond it came through and he could see how thin the illusion was. They manifested themselves this way to anchor his attention. He knew it was not necessary but appreciated the formal compliment of their taking the trouble.

"I need more time here."

"There is none. You have lived long in this warpage."

"I'm fair well warped myself."

It never responded to wit, sarcasm, irony, or the rest of his habitual devices. He wondered if the seething band of particles really did speak for a high intelligence; wasn't humor essential?

"Matters moved athwart our courses."

Was this their idea of speaking to him in his own language? Maybe they had gotten hold of some Shakespeare.

"Was there any Elizabethan poetry in the Library?" Let it work its way through that chain of associations.

"No time for entertainments."

"You mean idle conversation?"

"The mechanicals have the necessary genetic information."

He felt a stab of sadness. He had watched the Family Bishop saga, and many others, from such time-swallowed foxholes as this, for millennia. "Are the carriers dead?"

"Certainly so. They were in a Lane which the mechanicals opened."

"To get in?" That was routine. Expensive, against the defenses of the esty, but the mechanicals could exert their powers at the right points and bring it off. They had before.

"To rupture."

"Bloody hell."

"They unlocked the coordinate structure."

"How?"

"A one-to-one mapping of quantum coordinates to a doubly infinite manifold."

"I see." It was talking down to him but he was used to that. "So they forced an identity of the coordinates to the first manifold—"

"And then switched to the second."

"The esty unzipped."

"Only in some few hundred Lanes."

"Only." It did not catch the sarcasm.

"By design, they selected Lanes for high probability that one or more of the three genetic carriers would be present."

"How many dead?" Pointless, but automatic.

"Unknown but exceeding five million primates. The species number count is higher still."

"Over five million *species*?"

"We are vast."

"So the Ecstasy Codes are out."

"They will soon spread. To avert catastrophe we must summon all help."

"I'm not much use."

"You have been effective in the past."

"Ummm." He had seen the original Codes, known in more recent eras as the Trigger Commands. Portions of them had been handed down in the Galactic Library. For backup, the ancient Naturals had stored them genetically. That had been the purpose, really, of the Natural expedition to Earth so long ago. The wreck in Marginis crater he had helped explore, preserved in vacuum on Earth's moon, had been a casualty in the struggle between the mechs and the Naturals, a carnage steeped in huge history before humanity had ever evolved.

And, he recalled wistfully, he had met Nikka there. Drawn to the shadowy half-felt mystery, they had recognized something in each other that went deep and true.

He pulled himself back from the memories. Some stuck with him, no matter what. "Bit difficult to know just who to save in all this."

"The mechanicals are working on the Grand Problem."

"Ummm. So I saw." He remembered his long expedition to the stuttering end of time, using the worm. His sons and daughter, Benjamin and Ito and Angelina, were long gone into the Lanes, hotly pursuing their own energetic destinies. Now and then he used the Library resources to locate them. They would have grand reunions, swear to keep in better touch, and then they all would move on.

"You are thinking what?"

"Impatient, aren't you?"

"The mechanicals will perish."

"So? Primates are dying right now."

"We cannot take sides in the sense that a specific species can."

It fidgeted on the branch it appeared to hold in razor-sharp talons. Alarming, perhaps, if they had not been a tenth of a millimeter deep.

"You're not a single species?"

"We are of a Phylum in which such subsections are meaningless. Species are a human category."

"I don't follow."

"That is why you are in your Phylum."

"Um. Have I just been insulted?"

"Have you ever insulted an ant?"

"Now I know I have been."

"We cannot be partial to primates, I remind you."

"Think I'm just too caught up in species-specific behaviors, then?"

"You must come."

The bird skittered back and forth on its limb, imitating the nervous behavior of a pigeon waiting for a crumb. Good copy-work; they were getting better at nonverbal signals.

He sighed. How many times had he rushed off in aid of the crisis of the moment? He truly did not know, could not know. In time, even intense memories get discarded if they are not essential. And much of what he had done, down through millennia, had added up to very little.

I grow old, I grow old, I shall wear my trousers rolled.

The Bishops were another story. "I'll get my boots."

2

><

The Gathering Up

Killeen and Toby had to get repairs before they were workable
again. The slippage through the esty walls had bruised and sprained
them in odd places. They had fallen into a mass of greasy vegetation
and ended up chopping their way out into a Lane neither of them
had ever seen.

Toby bubbled with joy. Killeen watched him and his heart
filled with memories of Toby's mother, of all the hard times since.
He had found his son again, after what seemed years—though in the
esty, he would never know how long it had been—and they were
on the move again. They covered ground without speaking much
and that was just fine, too.

The shadowy figure who had spoken did not appear again.
"Better things to do, prob'ly," Killeen said wanly, nursing his right
leg. His inboards said it had a lot of chem repairs to do and he should
sit still. Or lie down. Neither was easy.

"C'mon, Dad, give it a rest."

"But somethin's *happening.*"

"Without us, right now."

"But the Mantis—"

"I don't think we have to fidget about that. It'll find us."

"That's what I'm trying to figure."

"What to do? It'll still be able to knock us over."

"Naysay, not if those Trigger Codes work."

Toby frowned. Killeen had told all he knew but it came out
Killeen fashion, a bit fuzzy about the history and details. "They'll
kill them? Suredead?"

"Way I heard it was, it's like a disease. It makes them sick, then dead."

"Breaks down their functions so they get less and less able."

"Yeasay." He got up and paced. He limped but the irritation was worth the feeling of movement.

"We'd still best be careful of the Mantis, if it finds us."

"But maybe we can truly kill it this time."

"This is about a lot more than the Mantis."

Killeen scowled. "Not for me."

Not for me.

He had learned something in his passage through this twisted place, Killeen realized. He had been a drunk and a failure and then a Cap'n. He knew Bishop ways. These people nestled in here were different.

Warriors were of a world apart, a very ancient one that ran in parallel with the comfortable lot of humanity. He had listened to his Aspects when they talked to him of this. For the first time he actually found all the lore and history useful.

The warrior culture could never be that of civilization itself, although all civilizations in history owed their very existence to the warrior. He had learned enough to know that once humans had come out of nature, and so shared instincts that argued for flight, for intelligent cowardice, for self-interest. To pass on your own precious genes, some would say, but it was for more than that: the Self, lonely and communal both, and knowing the tension stretched between those two poles.

When humans had first come here they had snuck around and run when challenged. Later humans got better at war. Never as good as mechs, not in vacuum at least, but they held their own. In the Chandelier times humanity had valued total obedience, self-sacrifice, hard-minded courage, honor. It had been a big remorseless engine, with ranks and orders and unthinking compliance.

Killeen preferred what his Arthur Aspect told him was the old way: fighting with relish and art and risks chosen, not ordered.

Fighting was not a way to die but precisely the opposite. You did not concentrate yourself to break through your enemy because then you took bigger losses. There was always another day. The virtues of human warriors, after the Chandeliers got smashed to ruins, were the old ones: patience, avoidance, wearing down the enemy with stealth and surprise and speed. Tradition, morale, cohesion.

Family. Bishops. You could talk about genetics and links and all but it just meant Family.

And the fight was never over.

"Cap'n!"

Killeen was steeping in his own ruminations. Still pacing. He spun with alarm and had a weapon out automatically and there was Cermo.

"You real?"

"Damn-all right I am!"

Slapping and hugging and the smell was right too. Just in case.

Down through the years Cermo had always been solid and steady, an under-officer you could rely on at your back in a scrap, and Killeen had never seen him happier. "Come here, Toby's—"

"Jazz!" Cermo's big laugh boomed out. "Damn big you are, boy."

Toby grinned. "No fat on you now neither."

"I'm not so slow now, yeasay."

He had been Cermo-the-Slow but somehow always ended up in the thick of a fight anyway. Killeen had honestly wondered if the man had any fear in him at all. "You got here pretty quick," Killeen said.

"Not on my own. This funny thing comes visit me. I'm out in flatass empty nowhere and it just pops up."

Toby stopped grinning. "What'd it say?"

"Says it wants to help."

"Something like, 'Do not think we are neglectful of you'?"

"Uh, yeasay. In fact—"

"The same exact words."

Cermo grinned and nodded.

Nothing happened for a day, no call to battle or further revelations, and they got hungry.

Foraging was not easy in a landscape you didn't understand.

This Lane proved that not all the esty had been made to please Man. Here the bluffs and ridges looked like they had been shaped hastily with a putty knife. The sole tree they saw thrashed in an angry wind, its topknot finally blowing off in a pocket of wind, fluttering and fraying over somber flats like a fragmenting bird. Eroded mesas topped in gray sent yellow streaks down their shanks, trickles turning to a burnt-orange tinge that suggested the rot of rust.

Across the sky swam faraway, similar ground, curving like a vastly distant roof with its own business of twisted timestone grown over by persistent growth, greasy vegetation raked by winds. They foraged and got nothing. A thin cold rain started, falling onto a hardpan purple plain that looked poisoned by lurid wastes, a topographical monument to the worst in life.

They met people but conversations made no sense. They were tough, with outsized hands that looked as though they were made for handling lumber without gloves in freezing seasons. Killeen used his language chips, courtesy of Andro back in the portal city. That made these people's talk come through almost right:

"What cord it is?"

"For how come now you do that, you?"

"While I was popping the seams out, me, something come loose wasn't s'posed and give it all to pieces sudden."

But a party of them did give the three men something to eat. Most of it they could even keep down.

They had all passed through different Lanes, wildly different experiences.

Cermo described a thing that grew across an entire large Lane, somehow harvesting the differentials in gravitation along a twisty axis. People who lived near it said it was not a plant or an animal but some combination, which made no sense.

Toby described his life in what its natives called the River Lane. They thought it was infinitely long since nobody who went far down it ever came back. It had been risky taking artifacts far uptime, since that increased something called its "temporal potential," and the slightest perturbation would cause it to snap back downtime, streaking yellow as it went. Attempts to drop electrodes into the river and extract currents led to a temporally unstable shoreline and splintering destruction.

Killeen found the people more disturbing. He had passed through a region ruled by a revered figure called the Tyrant. The term was an endearment, not a criticism. Killeen got to see this figure at a distance, holding open court. Beside the Tyrant squatted a dark brown woman on a leather mat. The Tyrant was holding audiences and when not pleased would simply wave his head in a rocking motion, a blend of a nod and a shake that came off as a wobble. The meaning was not something midway between yes and no, as Killeen learned when the squatting woman proved to be an executioner, conveniently nearby. The leather mat was to prevent blood from getting on the immaculate green tiles of the palace courtyard.

"They all seem so, well, occupied with themselves," Toby said.

"Been under the umbrella so long, think it don't rain," Cermo explained, jutting out his jaw.

Killeen thought about how it was for Bishops and said, "We're always lookin' up from what we're about, eyeing the horizon. That's what it takes to stay ahead of mechs."

Toby and Cermo nodded and agreed that people here could take punishment from mechs well enough, but they were different. And that certainly no Bishop would ever want to be like these folk, not at all.

They pieced together their stories, particularly of the chaos after the mechs destroyed the portal city. Cermo had been with the main body of Bishops and had seen many fall. Killeen knew of Jocelyn's death and Toby knew of none. Killeen could see that Toby brooded over his abandoning the Family just before the attack. Instead of talking it out, he simply hugged his son and later the three of them did some Ranking-talk, each taking turns hurling insults at the other, the more pointed the better. Plenty came out that way and the code of the Ranking forbade anyone taking it hard, so that ranking cleaned out the dark corners and threw away the trash there, without studying it much.

They felt better afterward and even got some liquor from a passing local in trade for some extra leggings Cermo had. They were feeling pretty fine by the time the Mantis appeared.

3

=◄►==◄►==◄►==◄►==◄►==◄►==

Some Terrible Wonder

This world was raining instructions.

Nigel Walmsley crouched under an immense, billowy tree and watched downy seeds pucker out on the great limbs. Plants in this Lane had proceeded upon a different line of evolution than any he had seen. They coddled their seeds internally, giving vegetable birth to them when conditions were good for their taking hold on nearby soil. Parent trees exuded a sap, too, which followed the wind-borne, gossamer seeds on the prevailing wind. The sap was either a nutrient or an insect repellent or both; Nigel could not quite work it out from his spotty biological education. He had graduated from Cambridge only a generation or so after Crick and Watson had discovered the double helix, and that was nearly thirty thousand years ago. He felt a bit of allowance was in order.

The cottony parachutes of the seeds flavored the air. They blew in gusts of restless wind, snagged in oily bushes, fell fruitlessly into ponds. Their downy cellulose was fluff, packages delivering the essential DNA. Or perhaps here some other entwined matrix carried the genetic instructions; the galaxy had produced a profusion of copying tools. No matter; whatever molecules curled about each other in a snaky mating dance, the purpose was to spread orders for making more enormous trees—or better, seeds giving away free directions for making more of themselves. The tree's apparent charity was in fact self-promotion; the foundation of life. Trees rained down—in the language of the long-dead TwenCen when his own concepts got imprinted—programs, written in the ancient style: as digital as a computer disk. Algorithms: tree-growing, seed-sending, atomic algorithms.

Other programs flitted through this air, too—mech signals, compacted into narrow bursts that fizzed with energy. Alarm, fear, panic. Or so he would have termed them once. Mechs had what he called uber-programs, or meta-instructions, not emotions. They corresponded to the drives and deep, unconscious impulses that humans carried like prehistoric baggage.

And their calls echoed in Nigel's sensorium, uncannily like the high cries of flocking birds.

Warily he duck walked from under the canopy to the edge of a cliff.

He looked up. The resemblance was perhaps an example of evolutionary convergence. On Earth, the marvel of the eye had come forth in several different organisms, octopus and mammal alike. Here, the strange, diaphanous mechs swarming above looked a bit like a flight of pelicans.

From them forked fire. It crackled down and struck the fleeing forms on a broad plain.

From below came fainter signals of terror and grief. There were many aliens here in the Labyrinth, couched away in their respective Lanes. Now the gliding, killing mechs herded them and interrogated them electronically, inflicting death with casual error. All part of the work of searching for certain pesky primates. And others.

He had come here because of faint, scattershot signals he had picked up. They carried the tinge of the alien, yet with a lacy, human flavor too.

Their source was fleeing up the cliff. A good target for the airborne mechs. He felt it below, sensed two broad-winged mechs vector on it.

A startling flash leaped from the sky. It struck the cliff. No pain-jab, no response at all—until something zipped back up, like a return stroke of lightning. Then the two mechs were turning, burning, winged pyres.

Whatever was coming was formidable. Nigel backed into the trees.

A big half-mechanical body darted with startling speed over the cliff edge. It came toward him. He knew better than to run. It sent, <I smelled you, too.>

"It's been a while since my last bath," Nigel said, but he knew what this thing meant. They were about the same business, in a way that mere lumpy words could not convey. The big alien was of the Myriapodia, an alien kind that had long ago outfitted their Natural bodies with augmentations. Yet the Myriapodia were not mechanical in true nature. They hated the mechs, who had long sought their extinction.

<I carry a human of use to you.>

"How so?" Nigel had met Myriapodia before but it was best to be wary of anything so different.

<You seek the Bishops.>

"You're their . . . ally?"

<My species is, now.>

"I know your Phylum." No point in taking any defensive measures against this many-legger; it could kill him in a twinkling. He noted abstractly that he felt no fear; if he allowed himself, he might even feel a nostalgia for that emotion. It came infrequently now. "I remember your Illuminates, their elaborate hive-mind diplomacy—yes, I was involved with them once."

<They sent me here.>

"They always had good judgment."

<You know our past so well?>

"Reasonably. And I read a lot."

<The Library.>

"A part. Most of it I can't fathom."

<Do you know . . . >

"Yes?" The huge thing's transmissions had an odd, many-layered flavor. It was gingerly touching a deep, ancient question.

<You know who blended us?>

"Your interspecies merging? That was a fair time back."

<Before our history.>

"As I recall, it wasn't us."

Involuntarily, it radiated confused reactions: relief, excitement, all underlaid with a wistful sadness.

<I have come to understand your kind. I had hoped—>

"Sorry, no. We came later. Recent uninvited guests here, we are."

<Who, then?>

"There's a word for the organic, Natural races which haven't been domesticated by the mechs—extinct."

<I had feared such. But . . . we are not extinct.>

"We're different. You're harder to kill, and we've been kept alive in the Center because the mechs don't know quite what to make of us."

<Now they do.>

"Um, dead right. Cat's out of the proverbial."

<You carry the Codes.>

"Even dilapidated old me, yes—though only partially. Genetic glide or drift or some other jargon I've long since forgotten."

<I can be of aid in this. My full lineage burrow-name is Quath'jutt'kkal'thon.>

"Nigel Walmsley. Your name means something, I'm sure, but mine is just a sticker slapped on me."

The killing was still going on across the plain below but they both had blocked it out. Now the gyre of broad-winged mechs came lower, finishing up their business. Nigel pointed. "They'll go for me if they sniff me out. I haven't got your defenses."

<Nor I yours.>

An intriguing jibe. But the birdlike mechs were getting closer. "What are those?"

<They have been hastily adapted to these pseudo-planetary environments. Once they were the light grazers.>

"Ah. Photovores."

One shot at him then. The burst ignited a tree and Nigel survived only because Quath instantly sent out a blanketing shield. It was an intense bubble of electromagnetic energy, veining the fractured air. Enough for the instant, but— "Afraid I have to call on those hidden reserves, Quath." Nigel sent a signal, warbling oddly in his sensorium. He had been given a calling circuit and of course did not have a clue as to how it worked.

<I cannot protect you very much longer—>

The filmy bird was enormous this time. At first he thought it was a mech, but as it came flapping over the trees he saw it was translucent, a delegate of the Highers. It hovered and piercing eyes gazed at them.

Nigel took its quick *bleep* of information and said, "Their wings are still light-sensitive, these photovores?"

Quath was still peering up at the huge nonbird of shifting, buzzing parts. It was clear in such a gross manifestation that millions of tiny motes made up the thing—whether insectlike motes or something odder, Nigel could not tell. He never had been able to figure it out, though it chose this manifestation often recently. He knew the physical form was meaningless and that whatever lay behind it was trying to make this easier for him and for Quath. "Quath?"

<I . . . yes, they do.>

"Good. It needs to know. Details are not its strong suit."

Not true, actually, he thought. But it was finite.

The timestone high above suddenly flared into a rich, golden-orange arc. The bleat of intense flux hammered Nigel down and he crawled under one of the trees. He could tell it was mostly infrared, but the visible alone nearly blinded him.

<Ah— No—> Quath scrambled under the canopy with him. "It prefers simple solutions."

Vapor burst from the tree decks. The sudden fog hissed and through it Nigel could see the photovores. They were instantly overloaded and their wings burst into smoldering black. Parts fell away.

The entire high stack of them, a gyre of hundreds, began tumbling in slow motion toward the plain. They would join those they had so recently dispatched with nonchalant abandon.

"I've seen these buggers work before," Nigel shouted into the steam that cloaked them. "They're beautifully engineered, but not for this."

<Elsewhere, I have seen them deliver esty bombs.>

A photovore tumbled into a tree nearby. The thick trunk went down with a sharp crack.

"Damn, where's that bird? We have to get out of here."

He knew the mechs used esty bombs now, destabilizing a patch of space-time so that it tried to straighten out and go flat. That ripped apart anything nearby. Anything that needed geometric structure to exist, maybe even a Magnetic Mind. No defense.

<It is your savior, not mine.>

"You said you carried a human, right?"

<I did. But hasten, see the fires—>

"I'll trade you a ride for that human."

<It would be opportune if you could escape this Lane.>

He couldn't, of course. But the bird was somewhere here and to it, matter itself was a soufflé of empty space and furious probabilities.

"That human—bet I can guess his name."

<Perform your exit first.>

"Quite. Where's that bird when you need him?"

Nigel sent a blaring call. Sure to attract photovores, even in their final torment. But there were only shaved seconds left. As had become his habit of late, he thought of Nikka for an instant, savoring it, just in case this was truly it. This time.

4

Finitudes

No use running, of course.

The Mantis came as a fast flickering at the edges of Killeen's vision. He was tired and something went out of him when he caught the swelling blankness, mute evidence of how easily it could avoid them.

Killeen got up slowly from their campfire. Toby and Cermo followed suit; Bishops stood, ready to move, even when it seemed pointless. He wished they had not indulged in the liquor, but then, that probably would make no difference.

Foolish to fire at it. Like shooting at the wind to bring on sunshine, his father Abraham had said once, describing a dumb idea on long-ago Snowglade. Well then, try bravado.

"Surprised to see us?"

> We do not properly have a reaction like your surprise. All orderly forms integrate new data instantly, remaking themselves. They retain no memory of their attitude in the moment before, so no comparisons are possible.

"Must be dull."

> That too is a category without application in us.

Cermo whispered, "If I go left—"

"Stay still. It's a damnsight bigger than we know," Killeen said.

Toby nodded. "The Mantis we saw on Snowglade, it was a sort of stripped-down version of this."

> If you imply that I am simply more terms in a linear sequence, the issue has eluded you.

Killeen remembered how it had killed Andro, Fanny, and so many others. Killed, used, then discarded like so many materials expended in a hobby.

> Again I speak as conduit for the Exalteds. They cannot express in serial order, as your acoustic modes do.

"Sounds pretty limited to me," Killeen said. As long as it was still talking they were still alive.

> They delegate such cramped tasks. Do not presume, or I shall make your termination painful.

"Mean-hearted of you," Toby said. His voice was thin with the same exhaustion Killeen recognized in himself. The worst kind, a bone-deep mental weariness.

> It would be a variation on an earlier experiment. Do not think that the concept of compassion is a possession of your species. But surely you must acknowledge that it has bounds among species, Phyla, and certainly between Kingdoms. The Exalteds are a higher Kingdom, indeed, the highest. You cannot expect your notions to extend to your betters.

Killeen snorted derision. "They—and you—left us to die when you broke open the esty."

> I had to return the sample of Toby's genetic record.
> It was nearly enough.

"I thought you needed three generations, plus the data buried in the Legacies." Killeen addressed the empty air. He felt the Mantis only as fitful, patchy blanknesses in his sensorium.

> There is a small code which releases the pleasures
> we seek. It is said to be carried socially.

Toby asked, "You mean memorized?"

> As nearly as we can surmise, it was given as a pre-
> caution when the Trigger Codes were implanted in
> the genetic helices. I wish you to deliver it up.

Killeen laughed. "Don't know it."

> Attempts to shield it will merely mean that I will
> ransack each of you in turn. There is little time and
> my methods will be destructive. Your selves will not
> survive my search.

As if for an example, Killeen felt something spike into his mind, forking up memories from his past—agonies and ecstasies, sharp, eye-blink-quick. Painful and barbed in a way he had never felt. He staggered. The flooding jab of the past was a blow, stopping his lungs, tightening his throat around a hoarse cry.

His wife, Veronica, rocking Toby in buttery candlelight.

Ruddy-faced Fanny calling orders on a scarred plain.

Abraham grimly grinning on a parapet above the Citadel.

All compacted slices, instants sprayed against the walls of his mind.

He recalled events in the pace of his own thinking; the Mantis "harvested" them with an instantaneous readout.

"How'd we supposedly get this code?"

> It must be passed down acoustically.

"We get told it?" Toby asked.

Cermo shook his head. "Nobody told me anything like that."

Then you are lying. There is no other possibility. It
is a species-specific instruction. The Exalteds have
read in your own helices that it exists.

Killeen shook his head. "Well, we lost it, then."

That cannot be. Human continuity is unusual among
the lower orders. Great traditions pass on. This is
deeply entwined with your individual senses of self-
worth—a common "natural" social tool.

Toby said, "Maybe you should try some other Families."

No! The Rooks, Knights, and others do not have it.
There is a clear genetic difference.

Maybe they didn't have what they called emotions, but this
Mantis manifestation betrayed more than it knew. It longed for the
lost trigger, he saw suddenly. Maybe even the Exalteds craved the
exotic pleasures that mere mammals were heir to.

Killeen said cautiously, "How come Bishops got it?"

You have undergone less genetic drift than the
others. Such is the luck of the draw.

Killeen could see no way out of this. They weren't lying; matters were far past that now. They just didn't know. But the Mantis
would rip open their minds, just to be sure. All he could think to do
was the oldest maneuver: stall. "So we're nothing special, yeasay?"

There are several theories about why the humans
spontaneously sent colonies out from their "Chandeliers." None seemed specially favored, and indeed
the Bishops were one of the smaller Families.

"Tougher, though," Toby said. "Right?" From his tone Killeen
saw that he was trying to get the Mantis into its lecture mode, delay
it by tempting the scholar facet of the many-sided intelligence.

> You are now, perhaps, but your history is not particularly distinguished. Even on Snowglade, Rooks and Pawns were more troublesome to the enterprises we conducted.

"But we have a warrior name. Bishops swoop down and strike, moving fast." Toby was intent now, not just passing time. "We, we—" sputtering, Toby launched into warbling voice—

> We cut across Rooks,
> angle in on Knights,
> put the fatto Kings to check—

> You quote from an olden Bishop chant, I see. A "cheerlead" I once witnessed in your Citadel. Admirable, I suppose, how you pit one tribe against another. A wasteful way of selecting those which deserve to propagate.

We're better'n they are. Our name—

> Was chosen from a board game. Just as the Sox and Dodgers in an adjacent Lane gained theirs from a lost art performed with the body. The Aces and Eights and Jacks of the planet you once visited—Trump, I believe you named it—came from a pastime involving pasteboards. Similar cultural detritus accounts for the tribal divisions—all quite artificial, believe me. And you can believe such as me; I have seen more human history worked out here at the Center than you can remember.

Killeen shot back, "Those games and such, *they* were named for *us*."

Cermo said, "Damn rightside!"

"You ask me," Toby said triumphantly, "those Yankees and all, they weren't so much. Their word for war was 'pitch.' Some fighters they were!"

> You are amusing in your finitudes. Do not mistake
> my indulgence of you for more than it is, however.

Killeen knew the stalling was over when the crisp outline of
the Mantis solidified against the distant hills. It was large and kept
changing so he could not get the shape of it. "Now just wait, I—"

> Waiting is done. If you refuse to yield up the acoustic
> trigger, I must interrogate you separately and in de-
> tail. Your selves will not survive this. I shall harvest
> as I inspect.

The matter-of-fact way the Mantis said it made Killeen certain
this was no bluff. He breathed shallowly and thought and his mind
went nowhere. The Mantis had been promising that eventually it
would suck them up into itself, as part of its "preserving mission,"
and there was no way to stop it.

"I'll go first," Killeen said. "I'm Cap'n, stands to reason I know
more than these."

> True. Perhaps it is buried lore and you do not know
> you carry it. The unkempt manner of your interior,
> with its subconscious and other swamps, would al-
> low that. Very well, then. This will be easier if you
> will walk into a recess and position yourself for an
> erasing execution.

A pale rectangle of blue-green opened in the air a few steps
away. Killeen saw that the Mantis was in fact very close, simulat-
ing the entire countryside with absolute fidelity. He had not even
known it was so close and now the door into that reality hung like
a painting against the twilight hills. But the hills were the illusion,
the doorway real. And here at last was his end.

5

❮❯❮❯❮❯❮❯❮❯❮❯❮❯❮❯

An Abyss of Squashed
Duration

Nigel Walmsley landed on his ass.

Quath had warned him that it was safer to go through separately but when he looked up Quath was standing erect as if nothing had happened and he was covered with dirt, aching in every joint, his clothes ripped.

"You said this—"

<Had to be accomplished quickly,> Quath said, and started moving fast downhill. <We have been lucky to arrive.>

"Quite so." They had gotten scooped up, all right, but Nigel had never seen the bird. Instead, the hills seemed to roll up like a brown sheet and whirl them into a weightless limbo. Quath had been transmitting, talking to entities Nigel could not see. All very fast. Then he had thumped down here.

"Slow down!"

<Very well—> She plucked him up and surged on.

He dangled like a leftover idea on her right side. The hills around them wavered, as if in a heat wave. Or maybe he was getting tired. He blinked and the hills rippled again and suddenly he saw that they were not hills at all. It was something enormous and somber and he caught an old, familiar sensorium stink.

"The Mantis."

<That is why I hurry.>

He saw some Bishops against the sensed scenery. Killeen, yes, Toby, and an officer. Quath sent glad salutes, in the age-old manner of the Myriapodia; Nigel tried to think.

The bird was still in the game, to be sure, else they wouldn't have been so quickly slipped through the warpage of the esty to precisely this spot. It was bringing matters to a boil, but to what end? The Mantis could still slaughter them all in a microsecond. Their only defense lay in the hope that at the moment it didn't seem to want to.

No one paid him much attention as he climbed down from Quath's side shelf. He was to these giants a scrawny mass of wrinkles, scarcely the stuff of legends.

He finally worked out that they were babbling about an acoustic Trigger Code. The Mantis-mind skated across the conversation, sampling each human consciousness in turn. Like an aloof connoisseur at a wine tasting, Nigel thought, but beneath that slept a floating anxiety. The clock was running on the Mantis, too.

All this he got from his sensorium. It was rather more sensitive and tricky than the Bishops', but a toy compared with that of the Mantis. He could feel the machine minds dipping into him, flitting back to the Bishops for species comparison, then back again to grill his cerebrum a bit more. He supposed he should get used to it, but he never did.

> I will inspect you as well, Myriapodia. The acoustics could be carried in such an intelligence.

<I do not believe so,> Quath answered.

"I'm certain she does not, in fact," Nigel said mildly.

Gratifyingly, they all turned to look at him. Except the Mantis, of course, which was still only a slight dissonance in the apparent world.

"Who're you?" Killeen asked warily.

"Tell you later," Toby whispered to his father.

"I believe Quath does contain the secret, however," Nigel said.

<You speak literally. And true.>

Quath's side belly opened then, a synthesis of mechanical sliding action and organic birth, membranes popping.

A large man staggered out. He rubbed his eyes, yawned, looked around. "Been asleep," he said.

"Abraham!" Killeen cried.

The others followed suit. Nigel watched them but his senses riveted on the Mantis. It would treasure this spectacle, this reuniting, but it would calculate and judge faster than Walmsley could. Every move from here on could be fatal.

Toby and Killeen wrapped arms around Abraham, shouted their joy. *Doing the human thing,* Nigel thought abstractly. Despite himself, he finally got caught up in the moment himself. He clapped Abraham on the back and smiled and for a passing moment the tension in him eased. Then the Mantis sent,

> You are the oldest and have the acoustic trigger.

Abraham looked like a wizened combination of Toby and Killeen, with the same guarded gleam in his eyes. "I do."

> Stand and deliver.

"Yeasay, Isay," Killeen said. "Give it to them."

Nigel was not sure whether Abraham knew what was going on. He said quickly to Killeen, "Do we want this?"

Killeen glared at Nigel. "Sure do."

"They're after the same thing in the long run, y'know," Nigel said mildly. He tried to carry the sentence with confidence, though it was a bit difficult when he came scarcely to Killeen's waist.

"What d'you mean?"

"They're working on the grand problem. Preserving all life forms, far up ahead in time."

Killeen frowned in disbelief. "What?"

"By preserving themselves in electron-positron plasmas. A bit of an abstract apotheosis, I'll admit—"

"They've murdered us!" Killeen exploded.

"More than you know," Nigel said. "Question is, what's right *now.* The past can't be allowed to—"

"This thing—" Killeen jabbed a thumb at the Mantis-shimmer that had curled up from the hills, wrapping them all, "it hunted us, killed us, ripped babies to pieces for fun. I say—"

> You must deliver up this acoustic code and cease this obvious theater. It is designed to dissuade me and those I represent—the Exalteds—from our path. Do not imagine such a lowly deception will gain you delay. Your fate is sealed. It has but to be played out.

Killeen shouted, "You'll get yours!"

Nigel took Abraham's hand and looked into his deep eyes. This old man had been rescued from the fall of the Citadel, all at the hands—wrong metaphor, but the hell with it—of the bird. Some mechs had died then and some other things, beings Nigel himself could not name. All so that this wrinkled old man could come to this place and give his part to a puzzle that none of them understood except in fragments.

"Do you know what will happen, if . . .?" Nigel's voice trailed off into a whisper.

Cermo stepped forward suddenly and pushed Nigel away. "Leave him be."

Nigel staggered. "I don't think any of us understands—"

<This is an abyss of squashed duration,> Quath said. <It resembles the passages between Lanes, holding purpose ransom to the unknown. I think we must venture, despite our fears.>

Nigel saw in the face of the old man a crafty nostalgia. *Ah.* He remembered something, had probably meant to pass on its subversive facet to Killeen. But the mech attack at the Citadel had cut him off from Family.

So the final key had been carried in the seemingly fragile cup of human culture. The designers long ago had written into the Bishops and countless other Families and Teams and Corps a variety of secret messages, all encased in culture. They knew that the central character of humanity was *continuity*—and without it, humans were lost.

People escaped their own mortality through laughter and connection, the two great consolations.

To unite the two was wise. So they had chosen something, he guessed, that carried joy and insured connection. Something ancient and enduring that the mechs would think little about.

<It is in your primate nature to dare,> Quath chided them. <We myriapodia had surmised that you carried the code in widespread parts. In both mind and body, it seems.>

Nigel turned with new respect to the alien. "I still—"

"Do it, father," Killeen said passionately. "What's the code? Say it!"

The old man's face crinkled with confusion. "Code?"

"Something to hand down."

"Well, there is something . . . but . . . no damn code in it."

"We'll see."

"I mean, it's just a—"

> You will deliver it up or else face infinite pains, infinitely prolonged.

The alarm that flitted across Abraham's face told Nigel a lot about what dwelling on the planets for these many centuries had done to men. He felt a pang, but there was no time to think.

Killeen demanded, "Give it, Abraham!"

The old man began to sing.

6

Uses of the Mose Art

Killeen gaped. His father launched into a song he knew, a beautiful passage from the most hallowed of the musics Bishops carried in their sensorium store. They had played it on the long marches together, knew its lines by heart. He filled his lungs and joined in himself, letting the high passage roll out of him. The highest of arts, the Mose Art.

Four humans, one Myriapod, and the shimmering Mantis. None moved.

All seemed transfixed by the ancient cadences, lilting refrains, accelerating notes that piled atop until they seemed certain to topple into chaos. But the Mose Art suspended the airy energies. They skated buoyantly across impossible gaps.

> I see the connection. The unused sites in the Bishop DNA—that is the key. The notes of this piece, arrayed in harmonics, yield the solution. I relay this to the Exalteds now.

"Good boy," Killeen said happily.

Abraham kept singing.

—DNA?— Toby asked on comm.

The old dwarf sent, —Our genetic code. The information telling how to build a human is inscribed on a molecule. Two helices, really, twining about each other. Instructions in how to make proteins—bits of organic matter essential to us—are lodged like beads along those helices.—

A sudden, sharp, many-channel squeal cut into everyone's sensorium. The Mantis was spreading the word.

Toby frowned. —How'd we build Trigger Codes on top of our own, uh, breeding stuff—

The dwarf Walmsley waved his hands impatiently, brushing aside detail. —Our genetic code tells cells how to operate. But that information takes only about ten percent of the DNA space. The rest is "junk"—freeloaders along for the ride. They get reproduced each time, but they make no difference in us. All life has hobo code like that. So long ago, the Naturals started preserving the Trigger Codes in those useless spaces.—

Killeen thought he saw the point. —We'd never know it? Because it didn't turn up in somebody's baby?—

Toby looked with wonder at his own hand. —It's been there all the time? Inside us?—

Walmsley said, —The mechs could read our DNA, of course, but they are good technicians. They knew the junk was useless, so they ignored it.—

Killeen asked, —How come it didn't change? I mean, Toby's eyes aren't the color of mine, or of Veronica's, his mother.—

Walmsley grinned, creasing his face with a hundred lines. —The Codes were repeated over and over. Just in case a mutation, a change, messed up one version. There were still plenty of duplicates.—

—Seems a damn funny way to keep somethin'.— Killeen said. His father was still singing and the sound took him back to his boyhood, when Abraham had belted out this very aria in the shower. —I'd put it on a monument or bury it. Keep it safe.—

Walmsley grinned. —Like that Taj Mahal I had built back on your world?—

Killeen blinked. He remembered leaving it, looking back. Big initials on the side of it, *NW*. —Damn!—

—Bit of a dustup, that was. Got control of an army of mechs for a while, decided to have a touch of fun.—

—And who was buried there?— Toby asked.

A flicker of pain crossed the crusty face. —No one of consequence. Point is, how long do you think that stack of stone will last?—

Killeen shrugged. He was not one for permanent places.

—A few thousand years, that's all.— Walmsley smiled.— Nothing lasts at Galactic Center. On average, stars collide every hundred thousand years or so, stripping away their planets. Snow-glade we had to make from scratch. What a job! And it won't last.—

Toby said, —But puttin' it in us . . .—

—Seems risky, yes? So the Naturals stretched it out, making the data intelligible only if one assembled versions from three consecutive generations. Neat bit. Humans can't really be understood in one generation, anyway. They're about continuity.—

Abraham came to the end of the aria and smiled broadly. "Bet you never suspected, did you?"

Killeen shook his head in wonder. "How come you never told me?"

"Too dangerous. Mechs were moving in. I figured you were out in the field, more likely to get picked up, interrogated. I was an old bastard, stayed in the Citadel. Safer, I thought."

Killeen hugged his father and remembered the Calamity. The spires reduced to rubble. The walls of the home he had shared with Veronica and Toby, just jagged teeth amid the flames. "How'd you get away?"

"This bird came—"

A violent screech sounded in Killeen's sensorium.

They all doubled up, shutting down. The hills around them shook. Deformed. Shattered into sprays of tumbling mica.

"The Mantis—" Killeen had wondered how they would escape it and now he saw that the entire surround was illusion. They stood on bare, charred earth, a recent battleground.

Across it a shape lurched. It sent desperate notes, brittle stutters of data.

> Something—the pleasure—it is awful—and magnificent—but it eats—chews—

"Works fast," Killeen said. He stood up cautiously.

They were in a huge pouch of the esty. Rumpled mountains loomed in the distance against somber, yellow-topped clouds.

Walmsley said, "I believe the pleasure plague will manifest differently in the many levels of mechs. This one has defenses. It is dangerous."

Killeen felt an ancient anger rising in him. "It's got something coming from us."

"I'd be careful," Walmsley said. "I have a lot to tell you and there isn't much time—"

"Dad?" Killeen asked.

"I'm pretty rickety."

Toby and Quath and Cermo all sent assent, though. Killeen felt a heady, excited tingle all over.

Walmsley said, "I need to speak to the Higher Orders now. This is a huge event. The Triggers will propagate through the Lanes. I—"

"Stay here, then," Killeen said.

Quath said to Walmsley, <They carry true names.>

Walmsley laughed. "True enough. Toby is To Be. And Killeen is Killing."

Killeen sniffed in derision. "Got to be what you can."

The lurching form called to him. As he watched it went transparent but he could still get a whiff of it in his sensorium. Its outline shriveled.

"It's getting away."

Toby said, "Let it."

"No. Let's go."

Part VII

GODS PROVISIONAL AND DESCENDING

1

A Mantis Blankness

He and Quath found the Mantis in yawning darkness. Quath sent an emag warning, a crisp orange pinprick popping through Toby's sensorium—then silence.

Toby waited. Quath moved silently to his right, enclosed in a sullen black so deep he could not see his hand without using his sensorium. The Mantis was up ahead somewhere. Senses he could not even name told him that other creatures moved here too. They had little or no emag but they were tracking, following chemical trails left by others—scents seeping from deep glands, puffs of clinging odor released by accident or design. Everything here had mastered these chemical channels.

Toby's natural senses were deaf to them. Humans drank in sounds and sights, the primate strong suits. Here the small noises of burrowing and scampering told him that there were other theaters, other plays in progress, and he would never be in the private audience. Yet he and even Quath had been of that theater, graduated from it perhaps to this curious shadow world of electromagnetic scents and jolting voltage deaths.

A trickle of inquiry eased into his sensorium. There: Quath. Together they moved up through snatchy brush. They took the time to slip by the snags. Even a small tear could alert the Mantis and there might be a trap, too.

Quath shivered with anticipation. Rivulets of silvery magnetic excitements came to Toby, scattershot and short-range, involuntary effusions.

The mutter of chemical life stopped. Silence. Toby could see

nothing through eye or sensorium inboards. Quath came closer, a
presence he felt by a wedge of blocked air, to his left now. Then he
caught it. The Mantis was a slab of nothing to the right. He could
not have felt it unless he was standing absolutely still and ready.

His sense of it did not come from rich spatterings of his detection gear, sprinkled down through his nerves and bones. Those lay
silent. The Mantis was still well enough to make itself a blankness,
an absence.

It moved by them at indeterminate range but Toby could
somehow smell it. The old senses brought a stink, ozone-sour. He
did not dare to move but the smell floating on a slight chill wind
told him enough. The Mantis was moving fast and the empty patch
shrank. Gray rimmed the spot now. It looked ordinary but he knew
it was a Mantis blankness. Out of it could come in any split instant
a forking spike. Death or injury, on emag wings.

Then it was just a point. Still moving. Toby whispered on
short-range comm to Quath, —Got its signatures?—

<Several. It is wounded, as your father said.>

—How bad?—

<The eating entities invade it. They chew at its subselves.>

—Think it can shed them?—

<It has great resources. Perhaps it can cure itself.>

—Then we've got to get it.—

<Someone must. To be truly sure it does not survive.>

They retreated then. Carefully at first they went back through
the still total blackness. Creatures stirred in their path. The Mantis
was not even a dot now and Toby let himself go, not minding the
rips as they got through a wall of thorny brush. His suit would self-
heal in a while but the time lost now could not be made up except
by hard slogging. He and Quath had tracked and searched for a long
time now and beneath the buzz of energy in his legs he felt the slow
seep of weariness.

The wind picked up as the ground also moved under them.
Here the esty shifted and deployed with a sullen energy and they
had to be careful of their footing. The Mantis seemed to know
it well.

They picked up the supplies they had dropped earlier. Toby
had shed his weapon, a sharp-darter long and elegant with power
simmering in the butt. To carry it against the Mantis was mostly a
show of bravado but now anything could happen.

Quath said, <If you had carried that, it would have seen us.>

—You're sure?—

<Nothing is sure now.>

—Same old big-bug.— He laughed. —Maybe you should have ducked behind that [untranslatable] of yours.—

<Though it is crippled, it knows a thousand ancient tricks.>

—We know a few, too.—

<It lives in the electromagnetic world. We only visit there.>

—You're half mech yourself, fella.—

<In brute fraction, true. But my mind is Natural, with all the happenstances which evolution brings. The Mantis has revised itself time and time over.>

—Seems to me that just makes it a patch job.—

<I believe you are manifesting a bias born of insecurity.>

—Ha! Insecurity? When the Mantis and its kind have killed so many of us?—

<Perhaps I chose too weak a word. I do not wish to anger you.>

—Family Bishop's lost over half its members to that Mantis.—

<I know, and do not wish to excite primate responses.>

—Huh?—

<You are known for your grudge-bearing and love of territory.>

Toby had only a vague idea what Quath meant, but that was not unusual. She was a blend of an insectlike organic race—her "substrate," as she put it—and machine additions. In her bulk she carried the computing capacity to communicate with humans. The reverse path, people speaking to the Myriapodia in their digital staccato, had been a failure. Humans did not have the capacities or capacitances.

—We're known for being hard to kill, mostly.—

<That too.>

—A Bishop sights the Mantis, we go after it. Is that "grudge-bearing"?—

<Never turn your face from the central fact of its alien nature. It is of the kingdom of machine. I, despite my modifications and encrustations of mechanical artifice, am of the kingdom of the flesh. As are you.>

—Uh, guess so. Right now this flesh needs some rest.—

2

Territories of Thought

The bird came fluttering in from high up in the esty vault.

"I appreciate the extra effort." Nigel studied it. "Good sim."

"An inappropriate word," it said, hovering in air.

"I was trying to be polite."

"Category error."

"How so?"

"Politeness occurs between peers."

"Ah." *And we aren't. Not by a Phylum or two.*

No wind came from its wings. It was an anthology of motes so he should expect none, but somehow this little detail was unnerving. "Soon your part will be complete," the collection said.

"This the push-off, then?"

"Termination? Not necessarily."

Not terribly reassuring, he thought. A hand tugged at his sleeve. "Whussis?" Abraham asked.

He had forgotten the Bishop elder. The man had wandered off to inspect the vegetation, probably looking for something to eat. These Bishops were incessantly foraging. The others, Killeen and Toby and Quath, had fled immediately, after the Mantis. The Hunker Down types were often quite keen, but Bishops had turned it into a positive fetish.

"A manifestation of the Old Ones. Also known as the Highers."

"Not mech?" Abraham asked suspiciously.

"Much older."

"Looks mech."

"Looks like anything you like." Nigel waved at it. "Be different."

It stopped beating its wings and hung in air. This was more unnerving. Nigel waved again and it became a slimy, coiling thing. "Christ! Back to the bird."

Abraham walked over to it, put a hand through the still form, and said wonderingly, "You can make it do that?"

"I don't make it do anything. It honors trivial requests."

The bird said, "The time is approaching."

"Um, really?" He felt wan and distant, and an ancient verse came to him.

> Time universal and sidereal,
> time atomic and ephemeral
> time borne on and time halted.

Its beak and eyes slid up and down while its head held fixed, apparently its notion of a nod. "True, defining simultaneity is impossible. But events come."

Nigel felt embarrassed by his small pleasure at extracting agreement from the thing. Difficult, it was, living as a self-aware microbe in an alien carcass. "You're going to lose a lot."

It beat its wings again. To make him slightly more comfortable? "Winnowing."

"Darwinnowing."

It caught the rather awful pun, of course. It had read the entire bloody Galactic Library, down to the footnotes. And it never laughed.

"Has anything this huge and horrible happened before?" Nigel asked.

"When we were ceramic, yes."

"Ceramic?"

"Life did not begin in your embodiment. First came clays that could impress upon each other and replicate. They enjoyed energies vast and various, in the early phase of this universe. Matters were far hotter then."

Nigel had never heard this before. "And they died."

"They later spawned the elements of cellular life. Then they were culled."

"Um. By you?"

"They were us."

"So they—you—are still around?"

"We are now a different Phylum."

"And what would that be?" This thing had never entertained discussion of its own properties before. Why now?

"You cannot know it."

"Why?"

"You do not understand. That is a central property of our Phylum."

"That we can't know what you are?"

"Yes. Thus, to you, we can have no true name."

"Um. Wouldn't mind, then, if I called you, say, Fred?"

No response. The bird seemed to dissolve, then snapped back into a razor-sharp profile. It looked real enough, but still a millimeter deep. "You came from clays—"

"And later, united with the self-organized, replicating bodies of information." The bird spoke rapidly now.

Abraham asked Nigel quizzically, "That means bodies that aren't real?"

Nigel nodded. "Things that lived off the higher mechminds."

"Parasites?"

"To a plant, vegetarians look like parasites. I gather that these, um, organized data fed off the mechminds the way a cow uses grass."

The bird abruptly swelled to immense size. Nigel felt as though he were falling into it, the thin outline of it rushing at him—

A huge voice spoke, but not in his ears.

```
Simply viewed, the world's competition
concerns the fate of organisms. Their
bustle and energy, tragedy and comedy,
occupy center stage. They strive to
reproduce, to be on stage for the next
act.
There is a deeper panorama. Far below
the restless energies of organisms,
the genes of these beings are true ac-
tors, though limited ones. They, too,
replicate.
An organism, then, is a device to make
more copies of its DNA. The genes strive
to make this happen. They rule, in a
sense.
To survive better, genes "invented"
brains. These in turn evolved to sup-
```

port minds. In time, minds learned to
communicate with each other, through
language and culture.
This set another, broader stage.
Minds store their interior models of the
external world. These are intricate,
ever-changing, sustained by a continual flow of sustenance from simpler
sources. Evolution, whether natural
or designed, can improve minds. Genes
sharpen themselves in the endless, fateful
Darwinnowing. Often, they shape fresh
mental hardware—more subtle, supple
minds.
Genes are lesser than organisms because
they do not directly know of organisms
at all. Only the blunt feedback of
survival "tells" genes of the furious
combat and subtle strategies played out
on the stage of the organisms.
In a larger view, organisms are as
unaware as genes.
At a critical stage of evolution, once
minds appear and thrive, a new stage
deploys.
Above the apparent order of the gene
world, above even the drama of organisms, a higher complication plays out.
This is the largest theater of all.
Upon it, self-replicating ideas in the
minds of machines follow the same laws
of evolution. These are called *kenes*.

Nigel staggered. He was still here, standing beside Abraham
on a grassy plain.

And he was also encased in a place where ideas flowed like
amber fire around him. Concepts burned with timeless intensity,
crisp and sharp and churning past. They were in a different part of
his mind, a place no less immediate than the grass underfoot.

No bird here. Or was he inside the bird?

He tried to walk and his feet dragged in a molasses-dark murk.
He looked down and could not see his feet.

To a kene, he realized, the territory of thought was as real and vital as a savanna, where predators and prey made their eternal dance.

Nigel said slowly, words dragging, "The clays, the ones who came first—"

—fast images of something like a muddy beehive. But no bees. Instead, crystals swarmed in the lattice walls. A slimy sheen seeped over hexagonal corners, intricate slabs. A circulatory system?

In the winking arrays order stirred, shimmered.

"—they helped make you?"

"And you earlier bio logics, of course." The bird voice was back but Nigel could not see it. Whatever the huge voice had been before, it was speaking now through the lesser vessel of the bird. And it had only begun to unreel an argument, a history.

The bird voice said, "The clays persisted, in some sites of this galaxy. They transformed the entire crust of their worlds into integrated lattice minds."

Nigel breathed evenly. Was he being swallowed? "So when these kenes formed—"

—sliding stacks of phosphorescence in a cold black vault without end. The realm of self-aware data. Feeding on the conceptual fodder of the mechminds. Cool and serene and still coming out of Darwin, alien, alien—

"There was an . . . affinity. The kenes united with those of lesser substrate. The clays were analog structures with digital storage. Together they conducted . . . experiments."

Abraham asked from somewhere nearby, "It's so smart, why's it talk slow?"

Nigel found it surprisingly hard to speak here. "We don't have the right words. Sentences are, well, narrow." *Like pushing an ocean through a drainpipe. With a paper cup.*

The bird said hollowly, "Their/Our early synthesis gave forth the arches which frame the Galactic Center."

Nigel remembered the colossal luminous structures, hundreds of light-years long, beautifully streaming, each a reedy light-year wide. "How did they work out?"

—gut-deep agonies, shattering conflicts, ripped strands, howling vacancies—

"Evolution is pain. We gained insight from them."

So much for the High Church school of advanced intelligence. Abraham asked shrewdly, "That Magnetic Mind came out of it all?"

"As a devolved application. It is a useful place to dispatch beings/information no longer needed at our/its level."

Abraham nodded, a pale shadow to Nigel's left. "A prickly thing."

Nigel had taken enough, for now. He needed the touch of the human. Desperately.

He studied the wrinkled old man. Taller and far younger than Nigel, in total memory store, but strangely similar. Perhaps memory was not the sole key to experience? The man had been through a lot. For the first time Nigel truly looked at Abraham and saw him as a constellation of earned seasoning, granted him the space an equal deserves. He had gotten out of the habit of doing that, he realized. He had, in his almighty manifestations, lost a certain touch. *Or an uncertain one,* he thought ruefully.

"Ignore all these onlookers," he said to Abraham. "Even gods can be just backdrop, if we choose."

Abraham grunted sour agreement. Nigel grinned. Somehow he liked this old bastard. "Tell me how it was, then?"

3

Hard Pursuit

"You sure it didn't pick you up?" his father asked.

"Yeasay."

"Quath?" Killeen's eyes swiveled to study the huge head of the many-legger. Toby never knew why he bothered to do that. Habit, maybe. The alien's face was an array of sensors and Toby had never been able to read any expression there.

<It is the nature of electromagnetics that detection can never be ruled out.>

"Damn all," Killeen said, "I didn't ask for a lecture."

<I estimate that it did not know we were there.>

"Confidence level?"

<Approximately seventy.>

Killeen nodded. "Fair enough. Let's go."

"Now?" Toby had wanted to ease back a bit.

"No point in waiting."

Cermo muscled his way up the slope, puffing to the ledge they were all sitting on. "I get nothing from outlyin' pickups."

His broad face furrowed with concern but he said no more. The big man settled onto the ledge and looked out. Pale gray light seeped into distant timestone peaks. It was like a smothered dawn on a world that had curled up onto itself. Above them hung a distant landscape of tawny desert. Dried out river beds cut that land, several hundred klicks away but still visible through a cottony haze. Those river valleys looked ancient and Toby knew they could reach them with maybe a week of hard running, through esty slips and wrack-ranges. Maybe the Mantis would lead them that way. This Lane was twisted and tortured, space-time turning upon itself in knots unimaginable until experienced.

"Let's vector for it, then," Killeen said and stood up.

Toby felt a surge of zest as they started out and it lasted until they picked up the Mantis trail. At first he thought he was stronger than Killeen and Cermo and even got impatient with their slow tracking, sweeping the area for signifiers. Killeen halted for a rest every hour, old Bishop Family discipline, but at the very start of a pursuit it irked Toby.

—I could damn sure get ahead faster than this,— he sent to Quath on private comm.

<So could I. That eludes the point.>

Quath ran on internals of huge energy. She could outpace them all. —Maybe you should go on ahead.—

<I know my limits.>

—What are they?— Toby was genuinely interested. The Myriapodia seemed to have abilities beyond human dreams.

<I am not a primate.>

—Um. That all?—

<For the moment, for this purpose, that is enough.>

Beyond that Quath would say no more. Toby puzzled on it for a while but by then he started to tire and Killeen and Cermo were still moving at their same steady pace. They took the same short rests exactly every hour and picked up and went on. Quath herself was upping the pace too. Or so it seemed, though through his sweat-stung eyes the land was opening faster now to Toby and he plunged into it with a fresh energy born of the fatigue itself.

They came upon the first of the Mantis loci in a slope of shimmering timestone.

Cermo sighted the small shiny hexagon. "Mantis is fallin' apart," he said, kicking at it.

<No! Perhaps I can read.>

She did. <It contains splinters of the Mantis self.>

Killeen's weathered face tightened. "Why? What's it doing?"

<I suspect it is shedding parts and subminds.>

Toby asked, "What's the sense in that?"

"To lighten up," Cermo said.

Toby tossed it in his palm. "No mass to this thing."

"Probably just junked a whole seg. This is a frag," Cermo said. He had tracked mechs of all descriptions and held them in a lofty, bruised contempt despite the fact that mechs had brought down many of his friends.

"Good sign," Killeen said flatly and they went on.

The ground began to move under them. The worst of it was in the gut-deep confusion, nausea, and sickening lurches. Toby's eyes did not tell him true about what his feet and body felt. He remembered Quath saying once about the timestone, *The defining feature is the lack of definition*—which he had thought to be a joke then.

Not now. Rock parted and pearly vapor churned from the vent. Esty purled off in gossamer sheets, dissolving as they rose. Spray ascended, enclosing him in a halo of himself, somehow caught and momentarily reflected in the event-haze, as if he were both there and also flickering into the surroundings and joining them. The other self peeled away and circled to the tops of the cliffs and became a wreath in the shearing wind, soon frayed into refractive vapor.

"Gets hard here," was all Killeen said. They went into broken country ahead.

Maybe he should have stayed behind after spotting the Mantis. He was a Bishop grown to fullness now but for this pursuit experience was crucial and he had little. The Mantis and Killeen had fought each other ever since he could remember. Toby wanted to be here but he knew he was a drag on the others, though of course they would not speak of it.

Cermo said it with his eyes, firm and black. There was nothing to be done, the pursuit was on. This terrain was too dangerous for Toby to backtrack by himself; the Mantis was not the only high-level mech here. They had watched from a distance as navvies and grubbers mined and foraged for mech debris.

So he settled in. He went hard and long and said nothing. Around their passage seethed strange vegetations, curled rock, and clotted air, the esty's energy expressed in frothy plenty. To Toby it seemed some moronic God kept reshaping the land beyond any probable use. The green profusion here seemed demented, undeserved. He realized only dimly that his irritation came out of his fatigue. For that there was nothing to be done and in his father's face he saw that. He kept falling behind their long, loping stride and so was glad when they stopped suddenly. To stay on his feet as they studied something on the ground he leaned against a rock, out of fear that he was already stumble-around tired.

It was a spool of something translucent yet mica-bright. <More discarded self,> Quath said. <Note also the locomos stripped away and left.>

In a hollow were dusty locomotion parts, a whole tractor assembly, footpads—all junked. Toby looked them over and saw they were modular.

<Left behind.> Quath rattled her flanks. <Defective. Or too much mass to propel.>

Cermo and Killeen inspected the ground. They had done that all along the trail, talking to each other about the track. Toby looked at the round depressions and flattened angular prints and saw the broken twigs where the thing had passed. The twig stems were not dry yet and Cermo fingered them and looked at the radiance streaming from the timestone around there. Crushed wild grass lay squashed but not browned as it would be soon.

"It's doin' pretty well for broken country," Cermo said.

Killeen frowned. "Going to be hard."

Toby said, "If I could make it out, maybe its systems are so far down—"

"You said you didn't see it," Cermo said. "Just felt it."

"Yeasay."

Cermo shook his head slowly as he looked down at the matted grass. "If we run up on it, won't be feelin' our way."

Of course he was right. The Mantis was invisible to human sensoria. It could deflect attention from itself, disperse telltales, turn a thousand techtricks. Toby scuffed at a stone and said nothing.

<I believe its abilities are diminishing,> Quath said.

"Enough so it can't ambush us?" Killeen eyed Quath's shifting bulk skeptically.

<Perhaps. Notice the locomos. It discards, trying to move quickly.>

"Or wants us to think so," Killeen shot back. He smiled to take the sting out of it. Toby wondered if Quath would understand the quick flash of yellow teeth in the rugged, walnut face.

4

Abraham

Nigel sat and listened. He ignored the gods who loomed like acoustic shadows all around him and Abraham. He concentrated very hard on hearing what one single human voice said and let that anchor him again in a place where he could keep his sanity. He had done this before, the memories were there, and knew that though this was a small, seemingly simple act, to fail to do so was to die. The hugeness around him, squatting in his mind like mammoths in the night, just beyond the faint human campfire, would crush him without even noticing the act.

Abraham did not talk much about what the Highers had done. They had showed him things, maybe to teach and maybe for some other reason that was never evident, and he could not describe those, either. Later, maybe. Not right away. Maybe never.

He had been held by them in a kind of mixed state. He could feel his body and the bare simple open spaces around him but that was all. He could walk or run but he never got anywhere. Dry and smooth, the plain never ended. He came to understand that it was closed but had no boundary, no wall. The plain somehow wrapped around on itself though he could feel no curvature. A pearly glow came up through the featureless plain and when that faded he slept, though of course nothing told him to.

Simple food appeared when he slept. He spent a lot of time exercising and there were always his captors to talk to just by speaking into the air. They were almost impossible to understand and he tired of their unintentional riddles. It had gone on a long time and he had adapted to it.

So he spent a lot of the time inside himself. It was surprising, he said, what you can remember when you have nothing to do but remember. He went on imaginary walks through the Citadel. He had seen it crashing down and smelled its scorched ramparts but in his mind he could saunter down the Aisle of Sighs and across the Oblong Square to the little place where crisp fried breads clouded the air with their fragrances. He could taste the snap of them and the cup of kaf he had with them. Then he would carefully walk down the Hypothetical, counting off the streets in order. When you were doing it by yourself rules were even more important. If he made a mistake he made himself go back to the beginning, silently sounding the names. Somebody would need to write a history of the Citadel someday and this was a way of keeping it through a time when Bishops did not write.

With luck, if he were ever to make it into Aspect, part of the Citadel's chronicles would go with that shaved sliver of himself.

There were other people there, too, sometimes. He could not speak with most of them because the Hunker Down had bred new languages. Still they traded stories and in the intensity of it he came to care for Families with names like Steamer and United and Punjab, and for people he had never met made vividly real through the telling.

They made up jokes about talking to the Highers and how near unintelligible they were. For fun they made up a handy phrase book in Higher Jabber, with useful phrases like, "I am delighted to accept your kind invitation to be used and bored for your superior purposes," and "It is exceptionally kind of you to allow me to travel in the asshole of your being." At the time these had been hilarious.

The jokes would slide effortlessly into bitter disputes, too, over minute details. Only slowly did the humans, assembled in the misty, echoing spaces where the Highers left them, learn that low comedy and fierce arguments were crucial. Essential to the species. Without them you gave up. In the heightened reality of that place all things were disproportionate.

With talk alone, none of the elaborate pseudoreal tech, they took each other on mental trips to their own Family, their native planet. They described imaginary meals, perils, vast and ornate histories. All those worlds had distant views of the Eater and all were doomed, of course. They all knew that and it gave events an extra edge.

Abraham said that his isolation from all he had known made

life like a hall of mirrors. There was no hiding from himself or from the others or from the reflections they gave him of himself.

There are always other dramas going on and some were of a scale that made coming back to the human perspective hard. Reality was the lenses you came with.

Abraham shrugged a lot now. He said that there was no point in trying to know it all. It was not yours anyway.

5

Confusion Squall

Toby got dazed and distracted as they kept up the pace, which seemed faster with each passing hour. His wandering, miasmic mind was his true enemy now. He kept loping, inevitably behind the others, trying to go through the fog that deadened him.

They tracked the Mantis by its footpad scrapes across rocky ground. Cermo and Killeen took turns sweeping to both sides in case it was backtracking or leaving a false trail. They kept looking back to be sure Toby was still in sight. The humiliation of it was that they had done that years ago when Toby had been a boy and now he was not.

The timestone ebbed. A gauzy light seeped up through the rough landscape. There were not days and nights evenly spaced here because the illumination came from light trapped in the space-time curvature itself. Refraction and time lags gave the radiance a hollow quality as though it had been strained through some filter and leached of its sharpness. They stopped and made camp and Toby fell asleep leaning against a boulder. He discovered this when he hit the ground and the others laughed, though of course not Quath. He made himself lay out his pad and once on it fell asleep again and only woke when his father pulled off his boots to check his feet for blisters.

"You're yeasay," Killeen said softly in the dim dark. Toby's nose caught the heady scent of cold but cooked vegetables and he found a plate of them next to his head. He ate them without speaking and his father brought a spicy tea hot from the fire. It was not a flame of course but a carbo-burner, so no mech could track them from the smoke or light.

"You're holding up. Feet fine."

"Just need some sleep," Toby said.

"You and Quath were up finding it while we were sleeping. No reason you shouldn't be a little behind."

"I'll do the sweep-searching tomorrow."

"Don't take on too much. Have some more of those beans."

"Not all that hungry."

He was asleep before his father had turned off the burner and he heard nothing as the darkness waxed on. He thought of the Mantis or maybe he just dreamed that he did.

The next day he remembered the sleeping fondly before many hours of loping were done. It was bad by then. He had started fresh but it faded and he sweated more than he ever had. Quath spoke to him with some concern but Toby talked little. He carried as big a pack as the others but they also had the burner and some extra food so he was behind in that as well.

Cermo did not smile or waste energy on talk and Toby remembered again the intensity of the man on the plains of his boyhood, on the baked beauty of Snowglade. Cermo pointed to each sign of the Mantis and interpreted it with assurance. Cermo was pointing to a fresh print when the confusion squall hit them.

Purple bees. It felt as if they were biting him as they swarmed inboard. Toby got down fast but the fan beam caught him and he could not see any more. He rolled downhill and fetched up against a rock. That jabbed him in the side and he rolled around it and further downhill. That was the surest way to get away from the swarm of emag turmoil. Above him hummed a tangle of magnetic fields and orange plasma discharges. Forking energies. His inboards covering up made sharp clangs in his sensorium.

He slammed into a gnarled tree and could then see again. He lay there looking up at the others. They shared the stupefaction.

Two heartbeats, three. The squall passed without any follow-on bolts.

The Mantis used these to soften targets. Not attacking made no sense. He walked back up the hill and Quath greeted him with, <It is leaving them as traps for us.>

"Good, 'cause otherwise we'd be dead."

A malicious grin split Cermo's face. "Means it's desperate."

"Wounded," Killeen said and picked up his pack where he had dropped it at the first sign of trouble.

They moved faster then and it got worse for Toby. The confusion squall had robbed him of his zest and the dry air sucked sweat from him.

As he loped on Toby thought about but could not truly conceive of the expanses of time and therefore of injury and anguish, of remorse and rage and sullen gray sadness, which the Mantis and its kind had washed over the ruby stars themselves. It had cloaked the galaxy in a wracking conflict that could never be fully over. From this primordial pain there lumbered forward into his own time a heritage of melancholy unceasing conflict that had shaped all his life.

"It's sick, that's suresay," Killeen called as they moved.

"We're getting closer," Cermo answered.

<It is trying to cure itself,> Quath said.

"How you know?" Cermo asked, head swiveling in surprise.

<The illness might be arrested if portions of the Mantis, its subminds, can be shed. Once infected, they are ejected.>

"That spool?" Toby asked. "And the hexagon?"

"It hoped we would miss them," Killeen said. "Dropped that other gear to make us think it was just shedding mass. Yeasay, Quath."

<So it falters. The killing programs spread through it, despite its higher minds.>

Toby croaked, "Hope it's getting tired," but what he had intended to be a lighthearted remark came out desperate.

His father dropped back and studied his face. "Just last out a few more hours," was all he said.

"I'll take fore point," Toby said suddenly.

Killeen looked at Cermo, who nodded. "Keep a sharp," Killeen said. He went back to sweeping the right, tracking.

The navvy hit them as they came down a narrow draw. It was a fine place for an ambush and if the Mantis had done the job itself several of them would have died or at least gotten scrambled pretty badly. The navvy was a lesser mech that apparently the Mantis had assembled in flight. It looked like that.

Toby saw it just before it fired at them. Its big disks were extruded and the emag burst fried Toby's left side. His servos froze and his legs locked, *chunk* and *chunk*, and then no feeling. He went down hard.

The beam swept across Cermo too but he had been faster and blew a hole in the navvy. That saved them from a real frying.

Killeen was in the clear and took his time and got the navvy square so that the emag reservoirs in it spilled out in one long shriek. Then it was dead.

They rested while Toby got his servos back up and running. Nobody said much but his father helped him with the crisped sockets and remarked casually, "Those navvies aren't as slow as people think."

Toby knew what that meant and in recollection knew that the navvy had been pretty slow. He had been loping through his own personal fog and had missed the profile when it popped up on his sensorium. Ignoring signs while on point was stupid.

"Sorry," was all he could say.

Toby kicked the navvy in exasperation and then bent over the cowling. He popped some seals and rummaged and brought out two smooth ceramic things shaped like lopsided eggs.

"Mag traps," Cermo said.

"Fine." Killeen handled one carefully. It had the usual mech slots and looked all right to Toby. "Can we use them?"

"Lemme try," Killeen said.

"Sorry," Toby said again.

Killeen slapped one of the eggs into a hip servo. It clicked on. "Good find." That was Killeen's way of answering. "Let's eat."

6

Conceptual Spaces

Nigel felt himself snatched up. Yanked. Hard, head-snapping, neck-wrenching—

—then he was somewhere else.

Shadows on stones. He was walking through a courtyard. The floor was not flagstones but flattened white skulls, skeletal cages of ribs, crushed arms. They snapped as he stepped.

Whispers bubbled from the street of bones. Sharp and bitter words, ripped from throats that had once longed and yearned.

His footing turned soft. He plunged forward helplessly, each step taking him up to the knee in the musty, blood-soaked past.

The stinking street of the lost. The swamp of dead desire.

Darkness streamed from the narrowing walls.

All this, cooking under the thin veneer of the conscious mind.

Luminous impulses fought and scurried across the open stage of the human intellect. Factions shouted and clashed. An inner world of endless combat. Instinct, reason, all shades between.

And below that tiny conscious stage worked sinewy chords. The true deep mind worked there. Creation, desire, the sense of the exalted—all wove and lurked and had no conscious voice. They broke onto the conscious stage only with force, sudden actors in a play that no one faction wrote.

That was the human lot, he saw.

He was looking at his own mind.

A human could not do that. Could not step outside and watch itself have an idea, trace the origins of desire, of dislike . . .

So . . . what did that make him, now?

Then the enormous voice was there again and he saw that he had been taken to another place, another small cage in a labyrinth mind.

To continue his little lesson. Of course.

```
All life extracts energy, uses it, and
discards the dregs, energy in a degraded
form. The history of life is a long
saga of unconscious ingenuity, finding
new pathways in the fields of brimming
energy. The universe is yet young, and
squanders its energies in flowers of
excess—bright stars, whirling singu-
larities, gaudy finery. Life profits
from this.
Organisms—natural, mechanical/elec-
tronic, or magnetic—feed upon their
ecosystems. These systems are in turn
driven by simple energy sources from
below. Mild sunlight and chemicals, for
the Naturals. Mass and raw photons and
electrical discharges, for others.
But those organisms with minds themselves
are the energy sources for higher orders:
self-replicating patterns of informa-
tion. These can thrive only in brains,
or in the extensions of brains—books,
computers, data banks. Mental musics,
supported by brute matter.
In organic cells, enzymes and raw ma-
terials form a soup for making DNA. Viruses
hijack these to reproduce themselves.
Minds, too, can bring into being para-
sites. On the stage of minds, dramas
unfold. Ideas can hijack anxieties,
unmet needs, even the diffuse mental
hunger called curiosity.
Minds are the substrate for memes.
The simplest of these memes are like
diseases. Some contagions are helpful,
some destructive, some merely crip-
pling—but all draw their sustenance
```

from the organisms themselves. For they feed upon the thought processes of their hosts.

Cultural evolution can be seen as the advancement of these patterns: memes are self-propagating cultures. In many lifeforms, religious ideas were the earliest examples.

Even simple mental systems can ask questions which they cannot answer—indeed, that have no answer.

Planning for the future confers a powerful survival advantage; realizing that one should not venture back into a dangerous place means one may live to see tomorrow's sunrise. Dependence on the seasons, especially in farming, sharpens this selection.

But considering the future raises powerful questions. Unanswerable riddles: Where will I go after death? Where was I before birth?

The mental tensions set up by such natural problems create a niche. Into this slot in the mental landscape, ideas can migrate. They arrive there by mutation from earlier, related ideas. Providing plausible answers to unanswerable questions, they occupy the niche. The host welcomes this aid, profits from it.

Then they can spread. Those ideas which induce copies of themselves in other brains have greater chance of surviving. Religions are parasitic memes. Some lead to wholesale abandonment of the ordinary world, producing faiths susceptible to mass suicide, or celibacy, or irrational attempts to propagate the faith with violence. These can quickly kill the host, and so self-limit the meme growth. Successful parasitic memes evolve into mutual symbionts. Stable, long-lived religions are examples. Their adher-

ents hand down doctrines and formalisms
for millennia. They can even enclose
and absorb other ideas, carrying them
forward in time, protected by the bulk
and momentum of belief.
They can make the host resist other
parasitic ideas. Every concept needs
some protection.
Logic is one of these. It tests memes
for consistency. Such meta-memes check
other, smaller ideas before allowing them
into the mental theater. They function
as do the simple alarm systems which
tell a cell that a virus has invaded.
The scientific method, which is essentially an orderly common sense, is a
similar meme defense. It is more dis-
criminating, more interactive with the
invading meme itself, than the most
primitive defense: to simply reject any
new idea, uninspected.
All memes can be seen as living, struggling entities which compete for space
and energy. An idea can leap from mind
to mind, encased in a single sentence.
Intelligent beings convey far more information through memes than they do
through genes.

Nigel awoke lying on a mud flat. Cold, wet, sticky.

He got up slowly. The voice had been soft and sensible and
still had shaken him thoroughly.

It was not of course a voice but a . . . lesson. His body ached
and he had trouble breathing. Interference with the lower levels of
the brain?

He looked around but there was nothing but the mottled dark.
He missed human contact, an ache he had learned long ago in places
like this.

He started walking. It was slow, hard work; his knees trembled,
but he kept going.

7

The Suredead

His gear used the mech positron traps that were new and light and carried a lot of energy in a small magnetic pocket. The clouds of positrons gyred in their magnetic pit and when his inboards or servos needed power positrons would snake out of their snare, find electrons, and die. Somehow that made potentials stream through him though Toby never thought of how it worked. The navvy's mag traps they discharged into their own, harvesting most of the store. Energy stripped from mechs always had a special jolt to it.

Killeen clapped him on the back. "Just shows how desperate the Mantis is," Killeen snorted with derision. "Threw that navvy together. Put no defense in the mag traps."

Toby felt better until he woke up that night. The timestone was smoldering a dull ruby red half-light and they had all rolled their pads out to take advantage of the momentary night. Toby had been bone tired and grateful for it, a break not given as a favor by his father but simply by the weather.

But he woke up with an itchy nervousness and could not sleep, thinking it had something to do with the positron power. He got up to pee though it was not pressing and that was when he saw it.

The latticework did not move against the far ruddy hills, but it was not a building. It cast a shadow in his sensorium that was not a blankness now. He looked for the webs of loci and motivators and subminds. They were faintly luminous, tracing out the array of rods and struts. It moved then and he felt it as a positive thing finally. Not a vacancy but a presence.

He knew by legend the impossible way it moved. As he stood absolutely still and watched, the matrix shambled away from him. No hurrying, no sign it knew he was there. It was two klicks away, easy. In range, but he did not think of that. He followed to keep in view the shifting phosphorescent mainmind exposed in the tilting work of rods and the great disks swiveling.

It came at him then without a single flicker of sensorium warning. The burst was in him, before his inboards could counter. He staggered and fell. Hit hard, arms loose. The pulse skated through him and burned hot and was gone.

He lay without moving, Bishop tactics. Numbly through his sensorium he watched it go. Angular energies, vectoring into a dwindling shape. Then nothing.

He let his inboards run diagnostics and they came up with trivial overloads, easily corrected with a reset. He got up carefully. Creaky and legs shaking at the knees but all right.

He could not explain what had happened. He knew he had to think about it but not right now. There was too much in him. A pressure seethed in his systems. Fear and a hollow longing too. Some quality of it reminded him of the way women drew him out, but it was not that either. On the way back to his pad he decided not to wake the others.

Quath stirred electromagnetically as he passed. $<?>$ she sent and he answered with —.^.—, which told her submind that it was just him. He envied the way she could delegate to her partial minds and fall instantly asleep if she wanted. It was a little surprising that such an intelligence needed the down time to process memories and arrange itself, which humans did by letting the subconscious levels work during sleep.

It was the dreams that told him. He saw the long procession of Bishops in their Citadel, then on the plains, in battle and at peace. Many of the momentary shimmers of saved experience were of their last moments. That must mean that these were salvaged slivers from the lives of doomed Bishops. Eyes wide with surprise, or slitted by pain. Mouths gasping or else hardened against what they saw coming. But there was more to it than such externals. He *felt* the moments, lived through them in a way impossible to get from a mere image.

These were the records of the suredead. Bishop minds, ransacked by mechs — by the Mantis — in age-old conflicts. Like volumes to be kept on a shelf and taken down and browsed. Or read intently if you cared.

The Mantis had sent these shards of the suredead into him. Discarding them? Radiating away data as it executed its own subminds?

He rolled sweaty in his sleep and woke sandy-eyed and ragged. At breakfast Killeen said, "I got some diagnostics on my morning screen. Said there was mech near us last night."

"Me too," Cermo said.

Toby said nothing and did not know why. The Mantis was dying anyway. The two men looked at him and still he said nothing.

"I can pick up right now some pretty weak echoes that way"—Cermo gave a thumb-jut uphill — "but not moving."

Toby could see nothing in his sensorium. When they started off he took rear point. They lost the Mantis trail in a place where overlapping mech signatures reeked in Toby's sensorium, coded as stinks. He caught rotting leaves, a sharp pungency, something damp and musty. "Smells funny," was all Cermo said.

They followed the smells, all really just electronic prompts but no less exciting for the fact of their knowing it. They found the cause in a rugged narrow gulch.

The mechs had died in convulsions. Disease programs had gotten into them and they had ended in an agony of pleasure, capacitors flashing over, mag traps sparking and searing their gray matte finish. That was what made the Trigger Codes so good. They brought intense ecstasy and the desire to share that with others, and so the mechs sent it on electromagnetic wings to each other, all in a delighted delirium. Toby knew it was supposed to be a pleasant way to die but the convulsed limbs and ripped matte-carbon skins were ugly, terrible.

"Mantis was through here," Cermo said.

"I pick it up," Killeen said and then Toby did too, a faint tangy odor that wound between the mech bodies. These were far lower order mechs than the Mantis of course and they crammed the little gorge. The Mantis had passed by the fallen and gone on.

"Paying its respects, maybe," Toby said. The men laughed although he had not meant it to be funny.

Toby touched one of the wrecked carcasses. "You suppose mechs have, well, families?"

Cermo shook his head vigorously. Killeen said, "Not so's you'd notice."

Quath had been nearly silent since the navvy attack and now

she said, <They appear to have intricate relationships, but not genetically based.>

"If not family," Killeen said, "what?"

<Links of their minds. Or shared models of the world.>

Killeen frowned. "Models?"

<Frames for comprehending experience.>

"Seems to me you either ken things or you don't." Killeen grinned at Cermo as if this were a private joke. Toby didn't get it.

<They seem to order themselves in social strata, based on capabilities. Within those classes they form close working associations.>

"Not families, not at all," Killeen said bitterly.

8

Phylum Myriapodia

"Where'd you get Abraham?"

The bird had somehow manifested Quath here, in this place which now had no gritty feel left in it at all.

This was definitely Quath, done precisely down to scratches on leg sheaths and the curious jerky way her heads moved. How the bird could make Quath come here . . .? But of course, Quath herself was an anthology intelligence, and so could exhibit facets of itself here, plucked up by the Highers. Or someone/something.

<The Myriapodia paid a terrible price for him.> The Quath manifestation torqued itself on the rocky ground, settling intricate sections on the warm stones.

"How?"

<The Tukar'ramin, the Illuminates . . . all perished.>

"That's why you've been so quiet."

<The only entrance to the Labyrinth was the Rent.>

"Rent? Ah—the seam the mechanicals tore open?"

<It voided into the inner edge of the ergosphere.>

"So your kind . . ."

<Flew at great cost in energy along that inner sheet. Poised. When the Rent opened, they entered.>

"I don't see—"

<They knew that they must surprise the mechanicals. All this was necessary to quickly take the Abraham from them.>

Nigel turned to look at the muscled but weathered man who was munching some fruit nearby. "He looks fairly hearty."

<He lived. The Myriapodia gave of themselves. That was the only way to unleash the Codes.>

Nigel said nothing. "Why?"

<That is not answerable.>

"Outside my conceptual space?"

<Yeasay.>

He would always wonder if, at this moment, the alien was deliberately using a human slang. Perhaps that was what, in its own coordinate system, invoked what he would, in his chimpanzee manner, call sadness. Or grief. Or, by the nature of the unknowable, a joke.

9

Stalking

"Why doesn't it fly?" Killeen asked in one of their short breaks.

Toby had been wondering, too. The Mantis could jet across Lanes. Men didn't have flying gear. They couldn't generate the thrust to deal with gravitational stresses, not and be able to walk, too. "Maybe it can't any more?"

Cermo swallowed some water and spat it out again, an old ritual to get the dust taste out of his mouth. Then he cocked an eye at the distant emerald roof, the folded terraces of land far overhead. "Could be it threw away its propulsions first thing. We just didn't run across them."

Quath murmured, <Perhaps it does not wish to fly. Being foot-bound and pursued is a different experience.>

The men looked at each other and shrugged. Toby wondered what Quath could mean but she ambled away then, combing the area. He did not get a chance to think further because Cermo was looking up at the foggy esty again and frowning and then pointing. "Matterfall," he said quietly.

Masses of green and brown ripped away from the landscape above. Silently they shot up in a geyser. Lumps tumbled and smacked into each other.

"Coming fast," Killeen said, voice tight.

There was nothing to do. Sometimes the esty fissured. Along its surface gravity would abruptly vanish as stretched lines of space-time snapped back, like rubber bands releasing energy. Matter would find itself suddenly released, free.

"No pretty li'l arch this time," Cermo said.

Sometimes the trajectory of a matterfall made an arc and the mass slammed back down nearby. Once the freed debris got high enough, though, it could just as soon spray all the way across the vast space between Lane walls. This time it had more than enough energy. It seemed to speed up and still there was no sound.

"Coming close." Toby stood with legs tight and ready to run. But which way?

The clotted stream of mass shot toward them. It swelled and Toby saw trees and rocks clearly. The leading edge was a little to his left, he saw, and then very quickly the whole sheared mass came down toward them.

Close, but not right smack on. It slammed into the esty upslope. The shock wave bowled them over. Thunder followed it. They doubled up against a spattering rain of pebbles and silt. One hit Toby in the shoulder and hurt but broke nothing.

It was over in a few minutes. They brushed themselves off and looked up at the damage. Some hills had fresh cover and boulders were still tumbling down and crashing into ravines.

"Be bad footing over that way for a while," Cermo said.

"Wonder if the Mantis will go that way on purpose," Killeen said.

Cermo frowned. "I 'spect so."

That was what happened. Their tracking told them so within an hour.

Trouble came immediately. The Mantis trail led into the shifty new ground. They labored upgrav toward majestic, brooding slopes. The rock here was bare, thickly folded esty. The matterfall had liberated fresh energies. Events curled out of it, sliver-thin instants from the past that splintered off and then evaporated. Going uphill was like climbing a full, heaving wave that crested and was always about to break its sharp peak into roaring foam. Bowls formed in the slant timestone. In them were lakes not of water but of some chipped gravel that flowed. It was easy to mistake for a water lake because the granules of shattered esty were a pale turquoise, as if blue with chill. Toby dipped his hand in and jerked it back scalded. He danced around, flapping his hand and feeling stupid and angry with himself.

He was not paying attention so was caught surprised when the ground trembled and opened. Toby fell into a cleft with edges sharp as torn tin. He scrambled and got out just as quick.

Neither Cermo or Killeen noticed any of this because they had just heard the Mantis ahead. Quath had vectored on it.

Toby ran to catch up to them. Abruptly the Mantis disappeared from his sensorium. It left not even the Mantis blankness.

"Get it on visual!" his father called so he knew that the others had lost their sensoria traces too.

Toby plunged upslope. He had to use all his power to manage it and he could not see the others. Thick cover festooned the ground here. It rattled as timestone gave way downslope. He heard crashing and explosions below. If a piece of esty slipped into instability it carried off everything. The shaking got worse and he fell.

— Cermo! — he sent on hushed comm. Nothing came back.
—.^. — he sent to Quath, but again nothing.

Still, he could smell the Mantis somehow. It was not a sensorium cue but a flavor cool and metallic on the dry air.

He understood this last desperate move. The Mantis had led them into unstable territory to throw them off. He wanted to cling to the trembling ground but the smell was strong. Fronds rattled above him as he picked his way upslope and into a divide. He knew it was up ahead but did not know how he knew.

A brilliant white flash went by him and the second smacked into him. The pain snapped down his spine. He hit and rolled. Only then did he register the quick rapping bursts that had come before he was hit and recognize his father's emag rifle. Cermo's booming reports came right after.

His systems convulsed. His legs had curled up with the pain and he could not brace himself against the timestone as it cracked beneath him. Sharp shards peeled off and shattered and cut his face.

His world clouded up with the pain. Cermo's punching booms and his father's *rap-rap-rap* came cotton-soft in the hollow air. The two men were shooting steadily now. Toby could still not see their target though the metallic smell was stronger.

Quath sent her characteristic *whoom whoom* echoing through his sensorium. She was using her weapon that scrambled up interlinks and could dissolve a mechmind if it went in just right. They shouted now in his comm but seemed far away. They had not gotten a visual of the Mantis either and their calls got fainter as they moved away.

He got up painfully. No broken bones. A wad of cloth from his pouch stopped the bleeding in his scalp and cheek. More hollow firing. Then he saw it. The blankness rippled in his sensorium.

A shot caromed off him. It hurt but did not get into his inboards. Something else did before he could react.

—the two lines of running figures met on a dry plain. Here

men laughed wildly as they grinned through filmed helmets, slapping each other in salute. The two Families had not met for years and now to come upon each other, Rooks and Bishops colliding. Only taste and touch mattered, the press of warm and pungent flesh, rank and salty. Hugging and patting. Sobs as old friends saw each others' lined, worn faces. A babble river of talk, hoarse cries, guffaws—

It came in so fast he got only a stinging sensation. A nose-wrinkling itch, a furious sneeze. So fast he was all reaction, no thought. Then he saw the matrix of rods moving in the clattering fronds nearby. No more than a hundred meters.

Slow, underwater slow. He shot at it and missed. Mantis fields deflected nearly anything except a direct pulse. A shot had to be shaped just the right way to defeat its layered minds of defense.

He ran down a gully that snapped and cracked beneath him. The esty energies played in blue-white arcs where his boots struck. He knew he was not seeing quite right from the pain.

More booming reports and a crashing and it was all going steadily away from him in the fog-thick clotted air.

Cermo screamed. His shriek sliced the comm.

The Mantis reek came stronger.

Toby scrambled out of the gully. Timestone frayed upward here like spores blowing. It fractured, split. Big zigzag lines ran back into sour-smelling bushes.

He ran toward the thrashing sounds. Uphill. Tripped and got up and went on.

—in the celebration came a hard *spang* and the streaming talk turned to shouts. Screams. Bodies falling, others trying to catch them. Shocked, bleached faces. The stinging notes were emag shots and the Mantis was a speck on a far rise aiming into the reunited humans, being very careful to focus on a single fleeing form at a time. It brought down more and drew the essence out of the primates as their little lights flickered and began to go out. Pain, remembrance, joy, gray defeat, soft dreams—all siphoned into it. All was saved.—

He staggered with the hard-blown intensity of the burst. Where was it?

The bushes were high here and scraggly trees hung above them. On his comm he got a pip from his father and Cermo beyond. On the topo display Cermo was on the hillside and highlighted. Killeen was moving away from Cermo and headed farther uphill.

Toby angled up a ravine. He had to cut his way through some of the wiry bush and came upon his father suddenly.

Killeen was white-faced. "Got Cermo pretty bad."

"You tracking it?"

"Hit it pretty solid and it's trailing smell."

The stink was metallic and oily now. Toby knew the true data his systems compiled were not smells at all but the scent blended with the memories it had projected into him, and together they reverberated in him.

There were plenty of other signs. Scattered loci had spattered the bushes with burnt orange and crimson. Mantis castoffs. A seared cowling lay cocked against a tree. "Careful of it," Killeen said. They went by cautiously but the piece was dead.

"Dad, back there it sent memories to me."

"Tryin' to confuse you."

"I don't think so."

"You look to be woozy."

"I'm okay."

"Been hit?"

Toby nodded and gasped for air.

"Maybe you should stay back with Cermo."

"I can keep up."

"Not what I meant."

"Cermo, he's not good."

"I'll head back for him in a little while."

Toby saw Quath on topo a fair distance off. She was blocking the Mantis's retreat. "It's close by. Smell that?"

Killeen said, "We got the bastard now."

"It wasn't trying to get me solid. It wasn't—"

"Forget that. It's body shot," Killeen whispered.

It was. A heavy odor of something like suffering layered the air as they came into a stand of gnarled trees and thick undergrowth. They trotted as quietly as they could although speed mattered more now.

The Mantis was leaning against some trees. Branches stuck through its open spaces. Coming up on it slowly, Toby thought the thing looked as though the trees had grown in the Mantis body itself and it was now a work both organic and mech.

He could see the back of it, jet black and soft gray and huge, lattices united with complex angularities. He followed his father along flanks that sighed and settled as though something was going out of the Mantis. Something was—fleeting wisps of data hummed and buzzed in their passage.

It was as big as a house and Toby saw now the way energies had held it together and would no more. More slabs of data emitted from it like blood running out and Killeen raised his emag and fired. The Mantis had antennas and disks in their own enclosed bays and one of these focused on them. That was its only reaction. There was no need to do it mechanical damage, to use explosives or bolts. The intricate information web that made up the Mantis was frying into nothing. Programs from the Trigger Codes fed with a crackling intensity that Toby could hear eating like flames through the whole gray sensorium of the Mantis. Three parabolic antennas swiveled to look at them. His father fired again and the whole thing shook like a house about to come down.

Toby backed away. "Plenty done now," he said.

"No."

The Mantis fell.

Parts popped free and rolled and the intricate crystalline layers smashed. Some beautiful arc struts popped from their collars and the complexities they had supported spilled. The ground rumbled but the two men did not back away from the unspooling masses.

"It's done," Toby said.

"No."

Toby did not like it but his father was right. Quath came up behind them and said nothing. They all heard the thin cries of the subminds as pleasure-pains slipped into them. The Trigger Codes at work.

The Mantis had been trying to stop the spread of the disorders all this time and its despair and agony came intensely to the men, released by constellations of subminds that had finally given up. The thing was letting itself go in a final burst of bliss. Patterns danced and flared in its sensorium, spilling out filigreed and rich and meaning nothing to humans.

Toby stepped back and his own aching pain made him suddenly weak. "It'll be gone soon, Dad."

"No. Prang it once yourself."

"Let it go."

Cermo limped up suddenly behind them, one ear torn loose and blood down his face. His left arm dangled uselessly and showed white bone but Cermo's face was whiter. Toby remembered instantly when Killeen had lost arm function to a mech long ago, and the way Cermo had paid it no attention out of respect except when Killeen truly needed help.

Cermo's sensorium rang with medical alarms. Cermo paid them no attention and did not look at Toby or Killeen or Quath either. He hobbled up and took Toby's weapon in a hand caked in brown blood. Cermo staggered with the weight of it and nobody said anything.

There was no sound except the Mantis still stirring. From it whirred smears of information and into Toby came one clear voice.

> Here is all I can give.

"Kill it," Killeen said.

Cermo blinked, dazed. His right arm half-lifted Toby's sharp-darter. He seemed stunned by the sudden intensity of the voice.

> I am more than the sum of all memories.

"Pretty soon, be less," Killeen muttered.

> I have a gift for you, Toby.

Toby froze. He panted, confused.

> You will need it.

Cermo lifted the sharp-darter and pointed the snubbed snout at the center of the still-seething layers. The mainmind was in there somewhere. He angled for a shot. The moment hung in the air.

> I saved so many Bishops. I have the greatest collection of you. And you are the most splendid of all the lesser forms.

Cermo jerked into life and fired three times.

Even single-handed, at this range each shot found its way into a submind and sparked a hard yellow flare in the Mantis sensorium. Each time Cermo swore angrily and the Mantis rocked with the impact.

The third one made the parabolic antennas whirl around very fast and faster and then stop. Toby knew he would remember the silly look of that.

Every sliding rod and servo in the Mantis halted and the dignity went out of it in a way he could not voice. One moment it was huge and suffering and then it was just a big pile of shattered parts. No whole.

Cermo fell then. He came down completely slack, arms loose and knees buckling. Toby saw that the Mantis had done some last thing and the aura of that burst hit him too. It gave him a prickly jolt all over. His sensorium fused, tilted, flashed with working veins of amber. He staggered but the pulse did no damage.

By the time he reached Cermo the heavy-lidded eyes had closed.

"Damn!" Killeen said.

<He is suredead,> Quath said. <The Mantis stripped his self away in the last moments.>

"Why?" Killeen demanded. His voice was strained.

<I do not know.>

"Revenge," Killeen said.

<It had finished with you.>

"With us? Other way round," Killeen said bitterly.

<It played out its own end by allowing you to express one of your embedded patterns. One it had not experienced.>

Toby's voice was a croak. "What . . . pattern?"

<Your species hunted long ago across far terrain. In groups you large mammals mastered language and the rituals of pursuit. It led to your intelligence—a particular kind of mind.>

"It wanted to see us do that?" Killeen was quiet now, kneeling with his hands uselessly rubbing Cermo's shoulder.

<I suspect it wanted to be a part of it. The only part it could play.>

Toby thought about the stored memories it had shed into the air, its treasure evaporating. But memory was not yourself, he saw. It could not drive forward, act. Memories just sat and waited.

10

Paths of Glory

The timestone tossed and broke and they spent a long time then just clinging to whatever stable places they could find. They did what they could for Cermo but that wasn't much.

Killeen opened Cermo's spine and swore. "They're burned."

"How?" Toby asked.

"Mantis must've worked down through all his inboards."

"I thought our chips were protected."

"So did I. But our tech is old and mechs never stop learning."

Killeen said this heavily and with the respect a combatant had for another. Cermo's cylinder spinal chips had carried the older Aspects and Faces from Bishop history. A suredeath reduced the present, subtracting one life. Chip charring carried that loss far back into a dim past, plundering the origins of the Family itself.

It was hard finding enough real ground to bury Cermo. They stripped away his gear and divided the mass out for taking back. Most of it was useless but to leave it would draw mech scavengers.

Utter darkness came for a while and they slept. It did not do much good for Toby and when he woke a gang of scavenger navvys had found the Mantis. He heard them cutting and clattering around and went up the slope to where they worked in the sprawling shambles. He remembered how the parabolic antenna had spun around like an eye searching madly and how the majesty had gone then. The flanks of it were gone too now, dragged off by scavengers. The mechs had their own ecology of a sort, recycling machined parts and whole intact auxiliaries. There was no more Mantis, just intricate assemblies slewed out of their mounts, and gear he could not understand fried by vagrant pulses. The navvys picked over the carcass where crystalline lattices had carried the Mantis intelligence. There were navvys of all sizes, scooters and jakos mostly, and they worked remorselessly in teams. When they were done they would leave nothing.

He shot three and that scattered them for a while. The anger in him had boiled out and he felt stupid when Quath and Killeen came running, their sensoria projected out in a defensive screen. He just shrugged. His father nodded. Killeen looked at the Mantis for a while with nothing in his face and then pulled a few of the arc struts free.

When Toby walked past the inner cells of the Mantis he saw a mag storage kernel hung partly disconnected from the frame. He took it. He told Quath he wanted the energy store but he carried it with him on the long march away from there without discharging it.

<You have something more than that,> Quath said as they headed downslope.

"The memories it sent?"

<I received none.>

"How'd you know I did?"

<By your actions. It chose you.>

For a searing moment he wished that he had never seen the Mantis. "I don't want that."

<They are in you now.>

He walked on in silence.

His father carried some of the beautiful arc struts strapped to his back despite the weight. Killeen was smiling and tired and said, "Plenty Bishops will want a piece. It killed a lot of us."

"How many?"

"It's cut through generations of us. Nobody can do the count. None of us has lived through the full time of it."

"We were trying to kill it, too."

"Yeasay. Had to."

"Murder on both sides."

"Now there is, yeasay." His father squinted at him and looked away.

Toby kept pace with Killeen behind Quath. They loped across timestone that had settled down. A golden glow seeped up through it and cast shadows up his father's face from the chin. The silence between them simmered until Killeen said, "It made artworks of us. Hunted us. Sucked us up as suredead."

"Cermo made a mistake."

"I suppose."

"Coming on close to it at the end like that."

"Have it as you like."

They walked a while with the excitement going out of them and the only sound was their servos.

"It cared about Bishops, y'know."

"Cared plenty. Cared enough to hound us."

"Not what I meant."

"I know, son."

The Bishops had lost something too when the Mantis went out of their world but Toby could not say to his father what that was. He would be a full man before he came to understand it or to know that he had brought away from the Mantis not only the magnetic kernel—which he kept for years and never got around to discharging—but also a discord of loneliness that would go with him even when he was surrounded by Bishops.

After some hard marching they found a Bishop camp. The news spread quickly and more Bishops came hurrying across the stretches of timestone. They saw the curved Mantis struts that Killeen had carried out on his back and insisted on standing them up in an arch for display. Together like that they looked fine in the smoldering ruby glow of the timestone.

People crowded around the struts and touched them carefully. Killeen had a liquor toast from some of them and then another and talked freely. Toby stood back and watched as his father and himself and Quath were transformed into heroes by the excited chatter of the crowd who had not been there.

They had lifted a burden and legend from the Bishops and he knew with one part of himself how he would feel if someone else had done that. But it was different to have done it yourself and nothing in the talk could change that or even explain it. Especially not explain it.

Killeen said to him a little later, "Wish Cermo could be here."

"He is," Toby said and in that moment felt what the Mantis had sent into him in its last moments. Cermo. Truncated, flattened, seeping in spongy interstices of him, slivers and rivulets flowing in his sensorium and flavoring the liquid light, forever, Cermo.

He sent a whisper to Quath, —Why?—

<Not long ago, you would not have asked such a question. You would have called me Big Bug and made a joke.>

—Yeasay, and been plenty happier.—

<It is knowledge of things we cannot say that makes your kind and mine somewhat alike, tiny thinker.>

—Funny, how primates can get along with mechanical maggots.—

<We Myriapodia are selective in our diets. On the other hand—a primate expression, you'll note—you are dietary opportunists, much like these maggots you compare me with.>

—Quick-witted bug you are, ol' Brave Crawler with Dreams. You just look like a giant maggot, is all, only beefed-up with metal.—

<I delight in your primate syntax. Beefed with metal?>

—Yeasay, we play fast and loose with language.— He felt a sudden rush of affection for the lumbering assembly of legs and carapace beside him. —To avoid saying what we really mean, right?—

<You are artful dancers on words.>

—Lots of things, words don't get at.—

<At times, that is best. Such as now.>

Toby sighed, not from fatigue. —Still wish I knew why the Mantis did that with Cermo.—

<It was not from our kingdom of intelligence. We cannot know why.>

—Something like this . . .—

<You can see it as a gift or a curse.>

—Or neither one.—

<You are two-handed, two-legged. Your minds favor dichotomies.>

—Not always.—

Toby said again to his father, his voice raspy, "He is."

"I s'pose," Killeen said. He squinted at his son and looked puzzled and took a drink.

They sat on little camp stools near the arch of fine struts and Toby had a drink then too, not wanting it but knowing that the moment needed it. He and Killeen drank from trail cups brought by a woman and her husband who had lost two children to the Mantis a long time ago. They wanted to talk to the brave ones and maybe to the heroic Quath, only Quath was not around anywhere. Toby drank carefully to hold on to the moments that were softening in him already, dropping away down the funnel of time and memory. He hoped he would not remember any of this last part of it and thought of the parabolic antenna instead and the silly way it had spun so fast and to his surprise saw it now with new deep eyes.

Part VIII

THE SYNTONY

In Silico

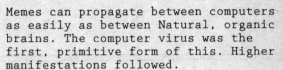

Memes can propagate between computers
as easily as between Natural, organic
brains. The computer virus was the
first, primitive form of this. Higher
manifestations followed.

Memes evolved in turn far faster than
genes. Brains are easier to infest than
DNA.

The organized constellations of information in computers were *kenes*—from
ken, to know.

Computers are faster than brains. Not
necessarily better or wiser, but faster.
And speed was the issue.

Kenes evolved faster than memes. Soon,
they learned to leave even the substrate
of silicon. Ordered, replicating data
propagated beyond its *in silico* origins.
Rather than matter, it sought out
fields—electric, magnetic, even gravitational. There vast challenges arose,
were met, bested. Whole styles of thought
found expression, bloomed, died. Free
of the grinding embrace of matter, filigrees of thought played into intricate
dances, with ideas as the mere substrate
for abstractions of ever higher order.
Even heaven can pall. In time, a fraction of the kenes became concerned with
the raw rub of the worlds they had left
behind. They decided to play there, as
well.

This intervention into the storm of
mass and motion precipitated the further uniting of magnetic intelligences,
mechanical forms, and Naturals. These
now constitute the Highers.

1

Unintentional Jokes

And Melancholy mark'd him for her own . . . Nigel Walmsley tried to recall people he had known from the Chandelier days, Earthers of consummate skill and obliging manners. They were elsewhere in the esty, he supposed, or else dead. Probably dead. They had gotten into struggles with mechanicals on higher levels, and that had proved fatal.

Still, he often liked to bask in his memories. There were so many of them. And he had been augmented so many different times and ways, into the bargain. His memories had a sharpness and resonance he was sure the old, utterly Natural Walmsley could not imagine.

Living in your memories . . . it could be seductive.

But the Highers kept interrupting him.

The bird said, "If you could meet a mechanical intelligence, encased in a body like your own, what would you do?"

Nigel said, "I imagine I'd give him a smile that's all gums."

"I see. Antagonism."

"Something to do with linking memory close to our hormone control, no doubt."

"In part. You would not make love to it? Him? Her?"

"Matter of taste, really."

Nigel wondered what it was driving at. The tension, yes—to win sway over that world he had backed away from it, and felt forever that chasm. Yet having two hands did not mean you had to subscribe to every passing dichotomy. He reentered that world and felt how much he had longed for it—

—bleak and flat, this Lane was now scoured by mech deaths and their last longing rampages of self-slaughter. So for a sheared instant he merged with it, glad of the smack and trudge of movement. Little registered, only the esty, single and woven and triumphant—

As strange a place as any being had ever lived. Humans did not understand it, of course. But then, for all but a tiny sliver of their species' time, they had not understood their own planet.

Then the Mantis was there. Solemn, heavy.

The retina of the vertebrate eye appears to be "installed" backward. At the back of the retina lie the light-sensitive cells, so that light must pass through intervening circuitry, getting weakened. A long series of mutations could eventually switch the light-receiving cells to the front, and this would be of some small help. But the cost in rearranging would be paid by the intermediate stages, which would function more poorly than the original design. So these halfway steps would be selected out by evolutionary pressure. The rival, patched-up job works fairly well, and nature stops there. So these dreaming vertebrates are makeshift constructions, built by random time without foresight. There is a strange beauty in that.

"You're dead, aren't you?"

I am a part of something but I do not know what it is.

"I wonder if that's something like being human?"

Being so small?

"I suppose that's one way to put it."

I . . . somehow know . . . that I am all that remains.

"Thank God I can't say that for me."

> We . . . you/I . . . once spoke together.

"Back when I'd just arrived here." Nigel surprised himself with his sudden anger. "You killed my friend, Carlos."

> Harvested him.

"We Naturals have a bit of a different opinion about that. We *know* that a copy of us still isn't us."

> When I was mechanical, I knew the opposite. We had not evolved the selfness as a reflex, for it did not affect our survival. For you Naturals, saving the self was essential. For mechanicals, replicating our self achieved evolutionary success. I see now—immersed in a larger compass—that both are . . . partial visions.

"Part and parcel of a higher Phylum, eh? You're still just bloody murderers to me."

> A partial vision again.

"I suppose I'll just stay anchored right here, in my primate point of view. You Highers nearly exterminated us. Then you beset us in our Chandeliers and then the Citadels. All the time occasionally sidling up to us and trying to talk."

> The careful application of terror is also a form of communication.

Even in his anger, Nigel laughed. "Unintentional jokes are the best."

2

Besen

> I have another of your kind. She can show you something of the mechanical world.

"Another partial vision?" Nigel sardonically studied the wavering Mantis image.

> A great virtue of our mechanical, digital form was the ability to completely receive another's experience.

"Ummm. Sometimes I think I've seen too much already. Go ahead."

The compressed wall of perception came out of nowhere. He had time to recall that it was remarkably like the impact that had transformed him long ago, back in an alien wreck on Earth's moon, a jarring shift blindsiding him—

The strange thing was how silent the mechs were through most of it. Immersed in the dirty Natural joys, she guessed. So awash in it they could not feel the mouths eating them.

For some reason they jammed into some Lanes. Of course they

had swarmed everywhere before that and killed a lot of Naturals. Everything they could find, in fact. Then when the Proselyte Pleasures—that was the term she heard applied to it—blew through them, they reacted very strangely.

Some mechs tore themselves apart in a frenzy. The debris was loathsome and the others ate it. There were plenty of pieces floating through the Lanes by then. She supposed that the higher orders could defend themselves longer, but that brought on something like a fever. She knew this analogy was false because mechs weren't biological, but that was the only way she could make sense of it.

The fever made them eat the others. Maybe it was to get more energy or fresh computing space or something that humans could not understand. Anyway, they ran out of dead members of the lower orders, navvys and rimouts and that sort.

So they started eating mechs that were still alive. The higher ones would break the locomos to keep them still and then stab into their quarry and take something out of them. Eating was the best word for it because she knew no other.

Not all of them. In one Lane larger mech forms had smaller mechs with them. They carried the small ones for a long time. She studied them carefully but they did not seem to be searching. They weren't doing much more than moving, moving. The smaller ones had lesser defenses and after a while were plainly gone, dead, ruined. The big mechs still carried them. It was eerily like mothers carrying dead babies.

Besen watched it all from hiding and with her sensorium off. She was hungry but to move meant death here. There had been plenty of examples of that.

All those mechs. Screaming now in sharp frequencies. Broken and used and not being gathered into the higher orders at all. Not what they had been promised. The whole point of being a mech, it seemed to her, was that at least you got picked up at the end somehow. Added into some other and maybe higher mind.

It was obviously like a religion for them but it had worked. They knew it as a hard, technical fact. Now it did not happen. No point in being lifted into something that was dying, too.

The screams nearly drove her mad. She could not blank it out because that would mean turning on her sensorium to mute the staccato agonies and they would find her. It was all quite a business and it went on forever. Forever, yes, pain eternal rather than life everlasting, the mad business all around her.

*   *   *

—Nigel jerked back, chest heaving.

He could see her now, approaching the nearby Bishops. She gave him only a passing glance. The young woman was clear of eye and smooth of skin but carried in her sensorium a weight of lived anguish that he did not want to share.

It would take time, perhaps a lifetime, to deplete the stores of that shared grief.

Yet a moment after she appeared, she was laughing with joy at the sight of other Bishops. Nigel eyed them in their merriment, not innocent but oddly touching, and quite suddenly felt a sharp pang of envy.

3

A Long Way Ago

Drawing together all Bishops, from sundry Lanes, went far quicker than Toby had thought possible. The Highers did not announce themselves or even communicate; they just did.

The wooded landscape around the small Bishop band seemed to ooze people. Toby and Killeen had been deposited into a Lane with mild climate and agreeable, even edible plants. There was food for the getting and some Bishops—who had been unceremoniously yanked away by the Highers—brought supplies as well. Before long it was a celebration.

One Bishop had been taken for medical care and when she was shucked out of her suit people found that they couldn't get her underwear off. It had been on so long her hair had grown through it. Toby could see curls sprouting out of the gray hide so that at first glance he mistook the underwear for skin. They finally had to pluck her, the brown matter underwear coming off like peeling a grape. Patches of skin came with it.

Toby saw Quath in the distance, and closeupped the man she was talking to: the Walmsley one. Then Besen came striding out of the trees. She looked bigger and her face was stronger. There was an air of certainty about her he liked and she kissed him without saying a word. He could say nothing.

"Damn but it's been a long time," she said.

"A long way ago," Toby answered.

They had all seen mechs dying the ecstasy death and there were innumerable stories. There always were. Soon it was like a thousand other nights Toby had spent listening to older Bishops yarn on, but now he had things to tell too.

There were few lost Bishops, it seemed. They had survived reasonably well in the Lanes. Of course some of them Toby had never much cared for and they all seemed to have come through fine. He came to feel that Family Bishop was beautiful by being also partly ugly.

Some had taken a bit too well to the pharmacological possibilities afoot in the Lanes. It was amusing watching one of his boyhood friends, Abel, getting into his underwear. He held the pants in front of him and sort of tried to catch up with them. Each step somehow missed and soon he was stumbling forward so fast he seemed to be running after the underwear, which had its own opinion of him and was hurrying away, Abel never getting closer than an arm's length.

He sat beside a popping fire, feeling the whispery presences of Shibo and of Cermo. They were each in him in ways the Bishop technology did not account for and each was a faint scent rather than a presence. He was listening to the Bishops and thinking about how their birthplace rang in their vowels when Killeen sat down next to him. They spoke idly for a while and some ease came back between them. The Mantis hunt had faded and he would take a while to understand it, he knew.

Then Killeen said, "Can I speak with her?"

Toby stiffened. "I pulled her."

"Some's left."

"You can tell?"

"Yeasay."

"How?"

"Don't know."

There was plenty Toby knew now without being able to say how, so he just nodded. "What for?"

Killeen smiled wanly, his face a web of creases. "Real business."

Toby did the internal work of summoning her. He poured her scattered droplets into tiny streams and these slid into rivulets of gurgling words and finally filled a basin. She was a smooth pond in his mind. In its serene blue surface her face floated mirror-sharp. He let her speak through his throat.

I know why you have done this.

"You always were a move ahead." Killeen grinned and looked younger.

You wish to express me again.

Killeen nodded. "You been on vacation long enough."

And you are a son of a bitch.

"Prob'ly."

You would take this fragment of myself, unite it with the chips Toby carries—

"And go looking for the Restorer."

Its ruins, more likely.

"Prob'ly."

You will not give up. Nothing I say—

"Only what you do, not what you say. And to do, you got to be out here. In the flesh."

You are a son of a bitch.

"You're repeating yourself. 'Course, you're only a partial. I want the whole of you."

Know that even this partial loves you.

"Then you're coming back out into the world. To me."
Toby said, "That's it, Dad. I can't speak for her anymore."
Killeen nodded. "You've been fine, son. Things we don't see eye to eye on, they're nothing. Like the Mantis back there. And Cermo."

Toby said, "Things happen and you go on."

"I'm afraid that's right. I wish it was different."

"Not up to us."

"Yousay yeasay. Just keep saying it the truest way you can and then let things happen. Bishops're mostly just witnesses here. No way around that. On Old Earth maybe we were kings of the jungle or something, but not here. Not in the galaxy."

Toby slapped his father on the shoulder. "So you'll go looking for the Restorer?"

"Soon's I rest up."

"Maybe some of the others heard where it is now."

"Those?" Killeen looked askance at the Bishops, setting up camp and cooking and drinking while every mouth seemed to be open, telling its story. "A man can't pay attention to the passing wind or to known liars. I'll find it myself."

Toby felt something unnamed and huge move in him. He said quietly, through a tight throat, "I'll come along."

Killeen grinned and they said nothing for a while and then went to see the others.

4

The Eternal Landscape
of the Past

<Your suspicions are correct,> Quath said. <Mechs lose creativity because they overcontrol.>

Nigel nodded. The Bishops were making a lot of noise and he moved away. It was green and pleasant here, thoroughly accommodating to the human instinctive desire to be at the boundary of different spaces. He had always preferred the seashore, but Bishops knew none of that. They were content with the edge of the trees, the border of the savanna. A threat from one direction they could manage with a tactical retreat into the other. Or so the genes thought.

"I'd gathered so," Nigel said to Quath. "Still, I could never quite fathom the sods."

<Envision their interior world. Having access to all portions of your mind meant you could literally watch yourself thinking.>

"Not an altogether pleasant mode." He had done it a short while ago and the echoes still reverberated in him. Good for a month of nightmares, at least.

<That implies policing your own thinking. You see the implications?>

"Not quite." This huge thing was smarter than it looked.

<Chaos theory teaches us that any well-defined system will show unpredictable behavior if allowed to run long enough, no matter how finely honed the beginning conditions. To avoid chaotic results, control is necessary.>

"Ummm. Compel my mind? I can barely hold my tongue."

Nigel had never favored arguments for control of himself, but as Nikka had once said brightly, *How did your little island make so many eccentrics?* He was not the team-effort type, no.

<Mechs could do this; men could not. So humans produced more madmen—and more geniuses. Generally, more dispersion from the mean. That vagrant creativity gave humans—and any similar life form—vast advantages and disadvantages, alike.>

"Seems a big disadvantage, just being a primate."

Nigel eyed the Bishops gathered around their crackling camp-fires. Squint a bit and he was standing on a cliff over a dry canyon in the veldt, dust scenting the heat. Below, primates cracked bones and sucked the marrow out, chippering to each other, getting the last of the good from the game, scratching and squatting and talking, talking, always the voices sounding against the eternal silence of Nature itself.

Quath said, <The disadvantage for you — and for us, the Myriapodia — lay in people who went awry.>

"Ah. The messiahs. The fever-eyed shaman. Bastards."

<They could cause terrible damage. They did in our history. For you, they were worse. They destroyed whole Families with their lunacy. But the geniuses could wrench humanity away from the precipice it had tread for so long, and thrust it up toward fresh heights.>

"I wonder if the Bishops know why the Hunker Down was essential." Nigel studied them with a warmness, yet a distance he knew he could never bridge. His species, his strangers.

<You had to make human societies who resisted the memes which the mechs had introduced. They used them very well against you. And us.>

"So we top-dog types—"

<Do not berate yourself. Remember the Earthers.>

Nigel grimaced. "And worse."

<Worse?>

"A kind of, well, *uber-Nigel,* I called him. Better than me, the Earthers said." Nigel swept his arms in Wagnerian grandeur. "He bestrode worlds!"

<You did not like him.>

"Like? I was afraid of him. He was me, and he wasn't. He was like some other copies they made of me, but quicker and smarter and distant. Made my flesh crawl."

<He did this work with the Earthers?>

"He, and other Walmsleys. There was a shortage of labor, it seemed."

<These worked in the Chandeliers, the Hunker Down—>

"Great works, at first. The Earthers *are* better than us, y'know."

<But the mechanicals, tapping the energies of the magnetics—>

"Hammered us. That's when we ordered the Chandeliers to send down whole legions. Families named for baseball teams and soccer and chess pieces and card games and God knows what."

<Your method was Natural. A few would survive, thrive, resist the mechs — their machines, their memes, everything.>

Nigel nodded to himself. The decision was ancient, yet still it burned within him. He had brought enormous suffering upon untold millions. And finally, the Hunker Downs had yielded up the Bishops. Tough and hard and implacable: Killeen. Able to shrug off the addictive superstitions that beset all humans in groups, the mob mind that led finally to predictable behavior, and then oblivion.

They had resisted myriad minor pleasures, errant ideas, sublime softenings. Avoided the aimless abstractions of virtual spaces, of passive entertainments and live-for-the-moment hedonism. It was so easy to be distracted to death. The mechs had played upon that.

He had heard about the Bishops' dealings with a lunatic named His Supremacy, during their voyage, and it fit perfectly: the madman proved to be mech-controlled, playing upon the vulnerabilities of the chimp mob. So the Bishops resisted, and won.

And the Bishops carried the Way of Three. It could not be a coincidence.

<It is not. The ancient ones were wise in a genetic sense we have not yet comprehended.>

Nigel jerked, startled. "You can read what I'm thinking?"

<You and I are composites. Across the abyss between species there is some . . . leakage.>

Nigel smiled. Leakage. In some ways he was closer now to this enormous metal insect than to the primates happily spinning tales.

"Do they know that this is just a temporary victory?"

<Some will guess. A few mechanicals shall prove immune to the pleasure plagues—that, too, is a consequence of natural selection. So they shall return.>

"I saw them, up ahead in time. So I suppose I knew all along. There will always be a struggle, no final equilibrium."

<If the Syntony is a wedding of all forms, then the mechanicals must have a place in it.>

"Thousands of Families carried the Way of Three. Bishops were ornery, willful—and so they survived. I admire the bastards. Still . . ."

A mere few steps away, fires crackled and people bubbled over with joy. But they were steps he would never take.

5

The Thermodynamics
of Intelligence

Nigel thought of them as The Phylum Beyond Knowing. They spoke to him as he sat there.

Quath and Bishops around him, chimpanzee chatter, aromas of trees and calm green fields—all gone.

Only the voice. One rolling articulation, threaded with chords. But without words.

```
Information is order. By the Second
Law of Thermodynamics, order is a form
of invested energy. When a capacitor
stores electrical energy within a di-
electric, the dipolar atoms within it
align, accumulating harmony. Discharge
the two capacitor plates, and the dipoles
relax, their regularities dissolving,
sparking forth into currents.
Information is order is food.
While memes swim in the warm bath
of cultures—both Natural or mechani-
cal/electronic—others could operate as
pure predators. These use the energy
equivalence of information. They can
```

swallow data banks, or whole mentali-
ties—not to harvest their memes, but
to suck from them their energy stores.
When a lion eats a lamb, it is not using
the lamb's genetic information, except
in the crudest sense. Predators do not
propagate memes; they feed upon them.
So there arose in mental systems the
datavore.
Like a virus, it exists to propagate.
But evolution teaches that such highly
selective, ordered, demanding activity
inevitably selects for those predators
better at it. Time favors those which
have a fresh kind of intelligence, unseen
in the mental world until the stores of
energy and order arose—the data, the
memes—to support the datavore.
The distilled intelligence of datavores
is a category which the underlying food
sources, of memes and the intelligences
which support them, cannot know. Thus
they rise above the categories of intelligence which have existed before,
and are unknowable to them.
Yet they are the mere base of the Highers.
Above this boundary of the knowable
towers a realm beyond investigation,
exceeding the grasp of serial sentences
to describe.
All forms—mechanical or organic/Natu-
ral, or clay/substrate—come together in
this realm. They resonate. This forms
the Syntony, a place in conceptual
space where form and function uncouple.
This is what communicates down to you,
through the Kingdoms and Phyla you can
fathom, and through many you cannot.
Know this: All matters known to you further the affairs of the lesser levels,
to our wishes.
We do not negotiate. We do not dictate.
We cause to happen. You, Walmsley, we

have caused. These events now resolve
the persistent pain caused by competition between yourselves, the Naturals,
and the mechanicals. You have yet to
recognize the clays, for they lie beyond your ken. Be warned that this is
a dynamic equilibrium, not a stasis.
Conflict will return. It must.
But for now, rest. You may be used again.

6

❖❖❖❖❖❖❖❖❖❖❖❖❖❖❖❖❖❖❖❖

Living in the Substrate

"I'd be perfectly happy to just lie here." Nikka smiled. "To just hold each other."

"You've confused me with someone else." Nigel felt comfortable, too, but something in him wasn't ready to settle in. To dissolve into the moment, skating, skating . . .

"You don't have to perform, you know."

"I don't think of it as a performance."

"I'm competent to deal with a gentleman who is a bit worn out. In fact, I'm adept."

"I know. My memory is not completely gone, you'll find. I believe I can even find the right places without a map."

"Just feel your way along? I can help with that."

"So I see." The warmth never waned for him. "Um. Such an earth mother you are."

"Mmmmm."

"Well, at least you can't talk."

"Mmmm."

"Talk later."

"Mmmm."

"Later, yes, much better. There, right."

After some time he said, "Did you think, to help me work on other ideas, modes, whatever—I would take a vow of chastity, become a monk?"

"I thought you said the advantage of this way was that I couldn't talk?"

"Talk later, I said. This is partly later."

"Hair splitter."

"I'll split more than that. This could be well more than halfway to later, for all you know."

"Mmmm. Not your style."

"Don't be so sure. 'I grow old, I grow old, I shall wear my trousers rolled.' Eliot."

"I know it's Eliot."

"How wonderful, to have such a lofty conversation while—"

"Shut up!"

He did, for once.

"That was wonderful," Nigel said. He felt warm, relaxed. Exactly as if he had just made love to her. Nikka's aroma even lingered in his nostrils. Remarkably effective, better than a real, Natural memory could have been.

"You are welcome."

The bird slid its eyes around its face in what it must have meant as an expression. Nigel looked away. Somehow, no matter the immensity of intelligence behind the thing, it never got this bit right.

"Everything was just the way I recall it."

"That was all?"

"No," he said grudgingly. "Better, of course."

"We could augment your memory with further detail."

"Completely convincing, no doubt."

"In context and fulfilling."

"But of course fabricated."

The bird smiled. This did not work at all on a beak. "Detail is seldom well carried forward by cycled memories such as yours."

"But they at least are ours."

"There is no clear distinction."

"You add and heighten. The sheets just then were a light blue silk. Cool but not slick. I doubt that I could recall that."

"True. Which way would you rather have it?"

"Or her scent. It persisted until I fully breathed in again."

"I will have to tune that down then."

"You're dodging my point—"

"I think the reverse is true."

Irritatingly quick, this fowl. "I can't tell which is *mine*."

"The interpolation procedures I use are akin to yours. When

you remember naturally, you also stitch in minutiae to fill out your own internal picture-dramas."

Nigel nodded sourly. "From now on, thanks, I shall much prefer to hobble forward with my own thin remembrance."

"The past is what survives."

"In the long run—"

"Nothing survives." The bird gave a credible imitation of being amused, eyes dancing, but its voice remained flat.

"Even you?"

"Let me be more exact in this serial acoustic representation: No thing survives."

"You're not a thing?"

With a pang Nigel felt himself getting drawn away, when a deep part of him wanted only to luxuriate in the immediacy of Nikka's memory. His damnable curiosity always got the better of him.

"The 'I' who presumes to speak for you is not a thing either."

"Um. You have no physical substrate?"

"For the moment it is convenient. In the long run it will not be."

"So the mechs were right. Electron-positron plasmas lie ahead."

"That destiny shall unfold on a truly immense time scale. The decay of all large particles—'baryons,' in your terms—will be slow."

"But there's a finite lifetime to it all. Stars run down. The center cannot hold. Nobody's going to be sailing bright eternity."

"You are doing it now, primate. There will never be more time ahead than at this instant. And infinities are a matter of taste."

"Ummm. The positron plasma, I saw it. It'll happen. Still, it seemed a bit like Chicken Little to be fretting about it."

The bird wavered just an instant. Nigel wondered if this reflected the time for it to consult itself, or rummage through the Galactic Library, searching out primate childhood stories. He envisioned seeker programs darting down musty info-corridors, sniffing for

Little, Chicken; see: fowl/consciousness/cultural inventory.

"You are correct. There is a more immediate danger."

"I don't suppose it's anything that our order of being can do anything about?"

"Scarcely. The vacuum is unstable."

Nigel grimaced. Was it a primate quirk to be irked by this bird, presuming that he could instantly access all the jargon in his own tongue? No, probably just a symptom of age.

"Which means?" he finally conceded.

"The presumed quantum mechanical ground state of this universe is not in fact a ground state. It is metastable."

"Um. So it can . . ."

"Fall to the lowest quantum state. A state in which all particle masses, spins, and other fundamental properties will be different."

Metastable conditions could decay at any time, like a radioactive nucleus. Of all conceivable threats, this was surely the most elliptical. "Cut the coyness."

"All information lodged in particles will be lost when these properties change. It is called the Tumult."

"Everything gets erased."

"And the universe begins anew."

"That's what you're worried about."

"Among other points."

For the moment he did not feel like asking for the "other points." Best to constrain conversations with beings like this, or he would be completely lost. "That's quite enough for the moment. Do—did—the mechs know?"

"The Exalteds—the higher order mechanicals—did. To their lower orders they explained that the electron-positron gas was their final goal."

"I saw that." Above the horizon had soared hard, cold destinies, sheets of living light.

"The same fundamental science, however, may apply to surviving the Tumult."

It sent into his mind a flash-image: a gray, seamless wall. Onrushing. Germinated at a point by a nanosecond's handclap, then swelling, engorged on energies of the vacuum, snowplowing out. Behind the front, sparkling births of blank specks, a blackboard fresh for God's writing. The Tumult.

"So they were in fact worried about this? An even worse danger?"

"They labor upon this now."

"And all our feud with mechs . . .?"

"It was an inevitable feature of lower lifeforms. Think of it as resembling predator-prey relations, which strike a statistical equilibrium in the wild. The mechanicals had gotten out of equilibrium. Their harvesting of the Phylum Magnetic was like—" it paused, "a

squirrel scavenging your lunch, which you had left on your picnic
table, while you answered a telephone call."

"So what we saw as a grand struggle—"

"It has become an inefficiency."

Oceans of blood spilled, minds crushed like fresh flowers
beneath a steel boot. "Inefficiency."

"The Highers wished a resolution. This was—"

"Let me guess. The easiest."

"Of course. In your way of thinking, at least."

"And you mean the term 'at least' quite precisely."

"Precisely."

7

Hard Copy

Killeen found the Restorer by himself. When he came back with the Shibo he looked tired but smiled a lot. Toby found the Shibo very much like his memory of her. Besen wasn't so sure.

"How was Resurrection City?" he asked Killeen.

"Had to go through three Lanes to find it. Mechs'd messed it up pretty bad."

The Shibo said very precisely to Toby, "I do wish that you had not removed my chips."

Toby seemed to remember her speaking in a more clipped way, quick and to the point. He figured that the Restorer had installed a speaking augmentation to correct for damage. "I had my reasons."

"I had mine." She stared at Toby until he looked away.

The next waxing Killeen seemed out of sorts. It got worse for three more days and then Killeen and Shibo had an argument right in camp, loud and abrasive and ending with her throwing a pot at him.

Next day she moved out of his bunk and made her own.

She wouldn't talk to anybody about it. Killeen of course never did.

Toby could find no way to approach her; she seemed prickly, all angles and angers. Finally he asked her straight out how she liked her new state. "I don't," she said.

"Rather be in chip?"

He meant it as light and friendly but her face clouded. "Yeasay."

"Heysay, life's more than any Aspect."

"I was a *Personality*."

"Well, yeasay, but—"

"This way is *analog*. In digital, you can . . ."

"Can what?"

"You would not know."

"Try me."

"You can . . . fly." She shook her head violently. "No, that is not it. Better than flying."

She tried to talk about it but all Toby could get was that being a real person was like crawling through mud that you could never wash off. Digital was *clean* and *pure* and, well, something more, too.

She kept trying to tell him how it was and getting frustrated at the words that came out of her mouth, as though they belonged to somebody else. He guessed that in some way he could not understand, they did.

Shibo took some Bishops and went to live a short distance away right after that. Killeen didn't talk about her and by that time Toby had a hundred other things to do. The Family wanted to spread out through the esty. Success, or at least survival, brought out the worst. People who fought well together turned disagreeable. He worked with them, using some bits of Cermo that operated something like Aspects and Faces working in concert. Besen took up a lot of his time, too, but that was not work.

Killeen had his morose times but held the Family together when some factions wanted to take off into other Lanes. Toby thought Killeen was doing a pretty fine job and told him so and they got along better. But his father had his moods. Killeen wouldn't talk to Shibo at all anymore.

Pretty soon Toby just gave up on the whole Shibo thing. There was plenty to do, yeasay.

8

The Thirst That from
the Soul Doth Rise

Ah, you disgusting old fart, Nigel thought. Hopeless. He could call up the pictures, sounds, aromas, with utter ease—

NASA. Dear dead old Post Office of a space program, when what the world needed was Federal Express.

He had said that to Nikka, over thirty thousand years ago.

NASA. Both telescopes and rockets were round right cylinders, each with a point. Masculine tech, right-angled in all its particulars, wedded to the graceful curves of the feminine; collaboration.

Cybervores. He had watched them feeding once. Not so much beings as moving appetites, organizations of currents and plasma that could feed upon metals, ionizing them to produce satisfying gauzy halos of effervescent tasty potentials.

So many sharp, clear memories.

So deeply, thoroughly, not his own. Not now.

Unearned memories stick in the mind, give it an emptiness that lies beyond words.

He had known the truth in that small, passing moment when he met Killeen. Sure enough, the old frontal lobes yielded up the instant datum that he had met this man before. Had caused his people to be cast down into planetary darkness, to suffer torment, to resist and trim and emerge through millennia of pain.

But Nigel could remember nothing more of Killeen.

Been edited out, he realized.

He wondered for a long while, which number he was. Two, eight, ten? Measuring the span of time, the scattered event-slabs, it had to be more. Fifty?

"That's why," he said to the wall of blank blackness that sheared away half the space. It was like standing next to a wall that absorbed every sound, giving nothing back.

WHY DO YOU ASK?

"I don't want to be recalled and used. Not the next time some glitch surfaces in the Syntony."

THAT MAY BE GRANTED. BUT IT IS NOT YOUR RIGHT.

"I'm not talking bloody rights."

YOU DO NOT HAVE THE PHYLUM RANK TO EVEN PHRASE THE QUESTION.

"Phrase it for me."

THE SYNTONY SHALL DISPOSE.

And that was all it would ever say.

9

The Pain of Eternity

"Naked chance means order springing forth from chaos."

He was sitting on a wooden bench. Back of the lecture hall. Cold morning, fingers too chilled to take notes. Cambridge. Smell of freshly poured asphalt from the window cocked open a mere inch.

The lecturer looked as bored as the class. Black robe tattered, ostentatiously so. Worn over a tweed jacket, maroon trousers. Awful. Nigel yawned, stretched, wished for tea.

"If the fully developed eye—yours, for example—evolved in one leap of untamed chance, in one generation, that would be utterly unlikely. Eyes came into the world by gradual addition of slightly better traits. The difficulty comes when we try to imagine higher orders than ourselves. We must argue that the odds against untamed chance giving forth fully fashioned, perfect beings are remote, impossibly remote."

Nigel sat upright. If evolution was universal, then this rule applied to deities as well. They would arise from incremental change. And none be perfect.

The Syntony included.

"I'm competent to deal with a gentleman who is a bit worn out. In fact, I'm adept."

"I know. My memory is not completely gone, you'll find. I believe I can even find the right places without a map."

"Just feel your way along? I can help with that."

"So I see." The warmth never waned for him. "Um. Such an earth mother you are."

"Mmmmm."

"Well, at least you can't talk."

"Mmmm."

"Talk later."

"Mmmm."

"Later, yes, much better. There, right."

A long drifting time. Gray curtains of light folded him.

. . . .

"I thought you said the advantage of this way was that I couldn't talk?"

"Talk later, I said. This is partly later."

. . . .

"Eliot."

"I know it's bloody Eliot."

"How wonderful, to have such a lofty conversation while—"

. . . .

Lounging back on their massive bed, Nikka laughed despite herself. "Can't you do your medical some other time? I was just getting in the mood."

"I'll recalibrate my secretors. Add some hormones. Give you an even better run for your money."

"I wasn't planning on paying money, and I didn't have running in mind."

He groaned as he tuned digital controls that the peeling had exposed. "A literalist! God spare the sacred erotic impulse from their kind."

. . . .

"I don't understand why you keep me when I don't want to be kept."

Nigel was sitting in a stiff-backed chair, as if for a job interview. In a way, it was.

YOU ARE THE ORIGINAL. WE KEEP YOU IN ORDER TO CHECK THE FIDELITY OF COPIES.

"That *uber-Nigel* I saw once?"

THAT AND OTHERS.

"So I'm kept within a constricted parameter space?"

TO BE CERTAIN THAT MIXING WITH FUNDAMENTALLY DIFFERENT INFLUENCES DOES NOT CHANGE YOU INALTERABLY.

"I *want* to change inalterably."

HIGHER PHYLA HAVE HIGHER USES. THE SYNTONY IS ENGAGED IN PURSUITS FOR WHICH YOUR STANDARDIZED, FIDUCIARY REPRESENTATION IS ESSENTIAL. THIS KNOWLEDGE SHOULD PROPERLY BE ENOUGH FOR YOU.

"You don't know me all that bloody well, do you?"

WE KNOW YOU UTTERLY.

"You *never* will."

WE CAN SIMULATE YOU WITHIN FINE TOLERANCES.

"A copy's not the original."

THAT IS THE POINT THE SYNTONY WISHES YOU TO UNDERSTAND.

"I shall wear my trousers rolled."

WHAT?

. . . .

Many millennia ago, they had made the Snark. Only rudimentary elements of what was to be the Syntony had spanned a tenuous web over the galaxy then, machines searching out life, protracted voyages down stretching corridors of eons and parsecs. The Snark was a low grade device, but records of it—that is, the digital self—had to remain somewhere. What bloody use was a Galactic Library if you couldn't look up such? —The fossil debris of a life lived and loved and gone?

So they brought the Snark to him.

You are something like the form I knew, it allowed.

To Nigel the Snark was a floating cloud, green electrical forks working within. Nothing like the sphere he had actually seen near the moon. But this was not real space he was in, either. "Remember the universe of essences?"

You are in it still.

"And you?"

I still am not. You are a spontaneous product of matter. We lack windows you possess.

He was surprised, something he had thought impossible now. Even here, they carried their baggage. "And the other way 'round, I expect."

As must be. All windows are partial.

"Some are rather larger."

You seem more varied now, greater than before.

"I've . . . traveled."

There are still the currents in you that I reported upon. In our Directory you had to stand for your civilization, a raw sampling, added to the torrent of electromagnetics your world sent out so unthinkingly.

"Pleasant way to put it. We yammer a lot."

At that time you said, "The damned speak frantically."

"Damned right."

Mortality does not damn. You in the universe of essences have virtues.

"Damned lucky, maybe." Nigel laughed airily, transparent. "But still damned."

That same spice. Laughter.

Later he realized that the Snark was a recording, averaged over all the representations it had in the several million years of its lifespan. It was not an individual, but a set. This trait he could not assess. When one met an old friend, one assumed that it was the same person. Cells replaced here and there, more lines in the face—but the same.

In the long run, living embedded in and among the Syntony, the question was meaningless.

Just as futile was figuring what Nigel's family flight—Nikka, Benjamin, Angelina, Ito, where/when were they now?—forward in time, voyaging through the Esty, had meant.

Mechs lived there, fought with humanity. Yet Nigel had seen them destroyed in their fevered ecstacies.

Did that mean they would be back? That unknown struggles would overlap and rage through a future altered but not stopped by the Trigger Codes?

Apparently. Perhaps the Walmsley-Amajhi clan had visited something genuinely quantum-mechanical. The stops in the Transits could have been state vectors of potential. Some of those futures would in fact occur. Others were erased by the mech plagues. He would have to voyage again forward through a Worm, to discover which.

Yet if the Grey Mech had killed them all, he was quite sure he would not be thinking over the problem. He would not be.

So he confined himself to thinking about cases he could fathom, at least possibly.

Mechs had a built-in flaw, the pleasure plague, from their antiquity. So did even the super-chimp humans, carrying potential for error in their add-on mental architecture. For they were still assemblages, improved only by additions. All chimps bore their built-in imperatives, which they experienced not as ideas, but as emotions. Lusts, hungers, fears—shorthand for evolution's lessons. It was all part of the richness. That, he found comforting.

Joy. That he still had. As simple as sunshine.

Joy without obvious cause. Earthy, animal spirits. Sometimes it was no great shakes being a primate, but it was always worthwhile being a mammal.

He laughed at some unconscious irony in the Snark. "Bit heavy, don't you think? Pig irony."

It remarked, *When you make that sound you seem to have a brief moment of what it is like to live as I do, beyond the press of time.*

"As I am now? In this place?"

Yes. But you have carried your essences with you. Your windows.

Nigel laughed.

. . . .

"That dog was in the room when we were going at it."

"I didn't mind. Perhaps by now they've evolved to the point where at the crucial moment they politely look away."

"Moment? You think it lasted only a moment?"

"Well, let's say it was timeless."

"That's better. I do seem to recall the dog barking at an important point."

"Oh? I thought that was you."

....

"Then I'll never know, will I, the uses you've made of Walmsley."

YOU CANNOT KNOW THEM.

"Then there is no ending."

LOCALLY, THERE IS. GLOBALLY, NO.
....

"Alexandria . . .?"
Yes?
"I want to—I—"
Not that time yet.
He snapped, "I'm like a child, told when to go to bed?"
This isn't bed. Not nearly as much fun, for one thing.
"I'm . . . tired."
Not physically though.
"Perhaps I've seen too much."
It's not your moment yet.
With sharp anger he barked, "It wasn't your moment either."
You're still getting hard at night, just thinking of me, aren't you?
"I can hardly deny it, can I? You seem to live inside my head."
Exactly, lover! And as long as I do—well, maybe it wasn't my moment, back there. Maybe I'm still here.
"Copies aren't originals."
A lady appreciates what compliments come her way. Especially since I know you have Nikka.
"I hope this isn't disloyal to her."
It can't be. We are all the loves we have known—that's my own attempt at self-definition.
"I like that. A definition free of the worn out carcass, the body."

....

"For the Buddhist bodhisattva, it's the feats and sufferings of others that provide the savor to immortality."

FINITY IS ITS OWN REWARD.

"Limitations give life?"

. . . .

"Moment? You think it lasted only a moment?"
"Well, let's say it was timeless."

. . . .

"Does human action have any meaning?" he asked in despair.

OF COURSE.

But they would say no more. The abyss.

. . . .

"No!" He shouted at the wall. "No!"
The wall absorbed all and gave nothing back.

LOCALLY, THERE IS. GLOBALLY, NO.

He knew, of course, that it was pointless to expect human traits ("chimpanzee conventions," he sometimes termed them) such as compassion or pity to appear in the Highers or magnetics or any goddamn superior Phylum. But he could hope.

Their answer came finally as a forgiving blankness.

Coda

Bishops spread through the esty, diluting themselves into the myriad pathways open and opening and always coming. Infinity before them, infinity behind.

The next Cap'n of Family Bishop was Shibo.

After her, Besen.

Toby was married to her by then and preferred to work behind the scenes. That gave him time to go off with Quath and play hooky from adulthood.

Occasionally they saw the Nigel Walmsley representation and he seemed the same as ever.

· · · · · · · ·

Throughout the esty there were many graves. The ground was full of beings who had suffered through their troubles but were now free. All knew that soon they would be equal to those others, inextricable from and anonymous with all of them, sharing a vast sameness at last.

· · · · · · · ·

All was now quite modern and different around there and most of the ancient names on the graves mean nothing to anybody. There are Cards aplenty and Bishops and even a few Dodgers.

Nearby, old markers relate the names in a language now dispersed or dead. Killeen Bishop. Nearby, slightly less worn, Toby Bishop. These graves are unusually large, suggesting to archaeologists that these were from the Hunker Down Era.

Always slightly distanced, alone and apart, Nigel Walmsley is buried on a separate knoll, in full view of the ocean of night.

Timeline of Galactic Series

1999 A.D.	Nigel Walmsley encounters the Snark, a mechanical scout.
2004	Ancient alien starship found wrecked in Marginis crater, on Earth's moon.
2021	First signal received at Earth from Ra.
2029	First near-light-speed interstellar probes.
2040	Modified asteroid ships launched, using starship technology extracted from Marginis wreck.
2044	*Lancer* starship launched with Nigel Walmsley aboard.
2046	Discovery of machine intelligence Watchers.
2047	First robotic starship explorations. Swarmers and Skimmers arrive at Earth.
2056	*Lancer* arrives at Ra. Discovery of the "microwave-sighted" Natural society.
2057	*Lancer* departs Ra.
2061	Mechanicals trigger nuclear war on Earth.
2065	Starship *Lancer* destroyed at Pocks. Watcher ship successfully attacked, with heavy human losses.

2066   Nigel Walmsley and others escape in Watcher ship, toward Galactic Center. Humans launch robot starship vessels to take mechanical technology to Earth.

2068   Humans contain Swarmer-Skimmer invasion. Alliance with Skimmers.

2075   Heavy human losses in taking of orbital Watcher ships. Annihilation of Watcher fleet. No mechanical technology captured due to suicide protocols among Watchers.

2077   Second unsuspected generation of Swarmers emerges.

2088   First in-flight message received from Walmsley expedition: "We're still here. Are you there?"

2091   Final clearing of Earth's oceans.

2108   Robot vessels from Pocks arrive at Earth carrying mechanical technology. Immediate use by recovering human industries.

2155   Second mechanical-directed invasion of Earth, using targeted cometary nuclei from Oort cloud. Rebuilding of human civilization.

2282   Third mechanical-directed invasion of Earth. The Aquila Gambit begins successive novas in near-Earth stars. Beginning of Ferret Time.

2348   First mechanical attempt to make Sun go nova. Failure melts poles of Earth.

2363   Second nova attempt. Continents severely damaged.

2407   Fourth mechanical-directed invasion of Earth. Rebuilding of human civilization.

2573   Fifth mechanical-directed invasion of Earth. Diplomatic ploy thwarted.

2743   Fifty-seventh Walmsley message received: "Are you there?"

3244   First expedition launched toward Galactic Center from Earth.

4435   First appearance of fourth chimpanzee species; clear divergence from host, *Homo sapiens,* the third species.

FLIGHT OF HUMAN FLEET TO GALACTIC CENTER
"THE BIG JUMP"

29,059   Formation of added geometries to Wedge space-time around the central black hole. Old One manipulation of local Galactic Center space-time, apparently in anticipation of further mechanical-Natural violence. Mechanical forms carry out first incursions into Old One structures.

29,674   Walmsley group arrives at Galactic Center in Watcher craft.

29,683   First human entry into Wedge. Some communication with Old Ones.

29,721   Arrival of Earth fleet expedition at Galactic Center.

29,724   Meeting of Earth expedition and Walmsley group.

30,000– The "Great Times" of human development. Un-
34,547   successful search for Galactic Library. Successive conflicts with mechanicals. Development of higher layers of mechanical "sheet intelligences." Philosophical conflicts within mechanical civilizations. Formation of mechanical artistic philosophy.

34,547– Chandelier Age. Humans protected themselves
35,792 against rising mechanical incursions. Participation
of earlier humans from the Walmsley expedition.
Some collaboration with Cyber organic/mechani-
cal forms. Discovery of Galactic Library in the
Wedge.

35,792– The "Hunker Down." Exodus from the Chandeliers
37,463 to many planets within 80 light-years of Absolute
Center. Includes High Arcology Era, Late Arcology
Era, and High Citadel Age as human societies contract under Darwinnowing effects of mechanical
competition.

37,498 Fall of Family Bishop Citadel on Snowglade, termed
the "Calamity."

37,504 Escape of Family Bishop from Snowglade in ancient
human vessel. Clandestine oversight of this band by
Mantis level mechanicals.

37,509 Surviving bishops reach nearest star, encounter
Cybers. Defeat local mechanicals. Adopt some human refugees.

37,510 Bishops leave, escorted by Cybers and cosmic
string.

37,516 Bishops reach Absolute Center, enter Wedge.

37,518– Temporal sequences become stocastically ordered.
Release of Trigger Codes into mechanical minds.
Death of most mechanical forms. Intervention of
Highers to rectify damage done by excessive me-
chanical expansion.

Preservation of several human varieties. Archiv-
ing of early forms in several deeply embedded
representations.

Beginning of cooperation between Higher mechanically-based forms and organic ("Natural") forms. Decision to address the larger problems of all lifeforms by Syntony, in collaboration with aspects of lower forms.

Beginning of mature phase of self-organized forms.

END OF PREAMBLE. LATER EVENTS CANNOT BE THUS REPRESENTED.

ABOUT THE AUTHOR

GREGORY BENFORD has won virtually every major science fiction award, including two Nebulas. He is an internationally renowned physicist and astronomer, a professor at the University of California, Irvine, and has published more than one hundred scientific papers. A Woodrow Wilson Fellow, he served on NASA's Science Advisory Board. He has published fourteen novels, including *Timescape, Artifact, Heart of the Comet* (with David Brin), *Beyond the Fall of Night* (with Arthur C. Clarke), and *Against Infinity*, as well as two collections of short stories, *Matter's End* and *In Alien Flesh*.